Thornton Wilder

and the Puritan Narrative Tradition

Thornton Wilder

and the Puritan Narrative Tradition

Lincoln Konkle

University of Missouri Press

Columbia and London

Library of Congress Cataloging-in-Publication Data

Konkle, Lincoln.
    Thornton Wilder and the Puritan narrative tradition / Lincoln Konkle.
        p. cm.
    Includes bibliographical references and index.
    Summary: "Fresh examination of the works of Thornton Wilder emphasizing
continuities in American literature from the seventeenth through twentieth
centuries. Sees Wilder as a literary descendant of Edward Taylor who drew from the
Puritan worldview and tradition. Includes indepth readings of Shadow of a Doubt, The
Trumpet Shall Sound, and others"—Provided by publisher.
    ISBN-13: 978-0-8262-1624-3 (alk. paper)
    ISBN-10: 0-8262-1624-2 (alk. paper)
    1. Wilder, Thornton, 1897–1975—Criticism and interpretation. 2. Narration
(Rhetoric)—History—20th century. 3. English language—United States—Rhetoric.
4. Puritans—New England—Intellectual life. 5. Christianity and literature—United
States. 6. Wilder, Thornton, 1897–1975—Technique. 7. Wilder, Thornton,
1897–1975—Religion. 8. Taylor, Edward, 1642–1729—Influence. 9. Influence
(Literary, artistic, etc.) 10. Puritan movements in literature. I. Title.
    PS3545.I345Z73 2006
    812'.52—dc22

                                                                    2005026382

♾ ™ This paper meets the requirements of the
American National Standard for Permanence of Paper
for Printed Library Materials, Z39.48, 1984.

Designer: Jennifer Cropp
Typesetter: Crane Composition, Inc.
Printer and binder: The Maple-Vail Book Manufacturing Group
Typefaces: Baskerville and Demian

This book is dedicated to
those most important people

Bridget, Matt, Brooke

Contents

Preface

The aim of this book is twofold. The first objective is to return attention to a great American writer who was accomplished both as a playwright and as a novelist. In fact, he is still the only writer to win Pulitzer Prizes in both drama (for *Our Town* and *The Skin of Our Teeth*) and fiction (for *The Bridge of San Luis Rey);* he also won the National Book Award for *The Eighth Day.* Despite this unique achievement in American letters, Wilder's works were relatively neglected by academia in the last quarter of the twentieth century. Theater artists—whether amateur or professional—have continued to appreciate the extraordinary dramaturgy of Thornton Wilder's plays, but scholars, anthology editors, and college instructors apparently find his plays and novels passé. That is a shame, because Wilder has much to offer audiences and readers in our disturbing times. In fourteen years of teaching Wilder at the college level, I have seen my students respond enthusiastically to both his drama and his fiction; they appreciate his humor, warmth, and affirmation of life while acknowledging the universality of suffering to which his works respond with deeply moving empathy. Wilder's works also inspire them to think about universal questions: Is there a God? If so, how involved is God in human affairs? Are we, as a race, making progress over time, staying the same, or getting worse? What are the best attributes of American culture (or any culture) and how are they manifested in daily life? What is the nature of love and why does it cause so much suffering? What meaning does an individual's life have in the context of the billions of lives of the past, present, and future? These issues are, of course, timeless, which is why Wilder's works are performed, read, and studied in other countries (e.g., Germany and Russia).

The second objective is to correct the misapplication of the term "Puritan" and concepts associated with it to Wilder's life, plays, and novels. He did indeed inherit a Puritan legacy from his family, American literature, and the broad American culture, but the way previous studies have defined that legacy is historically inaccurate, which has led them to a misreading of Wilder's texts. Indeed, this misreading may partly account for the academic neglect of Wilder's works. Demonstrating the pervasiveness of Puritan vestiges in Wilder's life and works will establish just how American of a writer Wilder was. This is not to suggest that the Puritan literary tradition and the American literary tradition are one and the same. Many other religious and ethnic influences make up what we now think of as the American literary tradition and American culture: Native American; African American; Enlightenment deism; Irish, Italian, Polish, and other Catholicism; Judaism; Russian and other eastern European Orthodoxy; Islam; Hinduism, Buddhism, and other Eastern religious and cultural influences. However, New England Puritanism preceded all but Native American culture.

Each of the following chapters emphasizes different aspects of Puritan theology, ideology, or aesthetics that have been suppressed or repressed into America's cultural unconscious but are manifested in Wilder's texts. The analysis of his works is arranged chronologically because the Puritan themes, structures, and styles do not all appear at the same time; rather, they are variously expressed over the course of his career, sometimes in response to world events and sometimes to events in his life.

After demonstrating the need for such a study of Wilder's works, the Introduction surveys previous scholarship on Wilder, reviews the biographical background of his family to bring to light Puritan influences, and examines his own American literature scholarship in *American Characteristics and Other Essays* and *The Journals of Thornton Wilder, 1939–1961* to demonstrate the similarity between his description of American literature and New England Puritan writing. Chapter One, "The First City: The Continuity of Puritanism in American Culture and Literature from Taylor to Wilder," first summarizes the argument that Puritan writings in the seventeenth and early eighteenth centuries constitute the beginning of American literature, and that vestiges of that writing and culture are present in classic American literature. It then delineates the salient features of New England Puritan theology, ideology, and aesthetics and illustrates the dramatic expression of these features in Edward Taylor's seventeenth-century work *God's Determinations Touching His Elect.* Chapter Two, "Judgment Day in the Jazz Age: Eschatology and Providence in Wilder's Early Plays and Novels," demonstrates the presence of Calvinist doctrine and the belief that Judgment Day was imminent in Wilder's plays written in school, *The Angel That Troubled the Waters and Other Plays* (1915–28) and *The Trumpet Shall Sound* (1919–20), and in his first two novels, *The Cabala* (1926) and *The Bridge of San Luis Rey* (1927)—the latter winning him his first Pulitzer Prize.

Chapter Three, "The Puritan's Progress: Typology and Plain Style in Wilder's 1930s Drama and Fiction," compares the Puritans' providential and typological interpretation of history to Wilder's avowal of progress on the macrocosmic and microcosmic levels in three one-act plays published in 1931—*The Long Christmas Dinner, The Happy Journey to Trenton and Camden,* and *Pullman Car Hiawatha*—and in his novel set during the Great Depression, *Heaven's My Destination* (1935), which reads as an American *Pilgrim's Progress.* Chapter Four, "Dramatic Jeremiads: Wilder's Revival of the Puritan Rhetoric of Crisis," applies Sacvan Bercovitch's study of the legacy of New England Puritans' sermons in American history and literature, *The American Jeremiad* (1978), to Wilder's most famous plays, *Our Town* (1938), *The Merchant of Yonkers* (1938; rewritten as *The Matchmaker,* 1954), and *The Skin of Our Teeth* (1942)—the first and last winning Pulitzer Prizes—and to the Alfred Hitchcock film for which Wilder wrote the screenplay, *Shadow of a Doubt* (1943). All of these works were written during the global crisis of World War Two.

Chapter Five, "Cold War Wilderness: The Dark Night of Wilder's Puritan Soul," examines Wilder's postwar malaise that manifested itself in several little-known one-act plays: *Our Century* (1947) and two unfinished play cycles, *The Seven Deadly Sins* and *The Seven Ages of Man* (1957–62). Chapter Six, "Covenant Reborn: Wilder's Reaffirmation of the American Errand," primarily analyzes his penultimate novel, *The Eighth Day* (1967), as a last grand expression of the Puritan vision of America, but it also briefly discusses his last novel, *Theophilus North* (1973), as a return, after much progress, to the beginning. Finally, the Conclusion, "Passing the Torch: Thornton Wilder and His Influence on American Drama," summarizes the influence of Wilder upon other American dramatists, especially Tennessee Williams and Edward Albee.

This study of Thornton Wilder's life, drama, fiction, and other writings was written to appeal to a wide range of readers: scholars of Wilder, Puritanism, American literature and drama, modern drama, and religion and literature; drama critics, dramaturgs, stage actors, and directors; and, finally, members of the general reading public who are fans of Wilder's plays and novels. It is my hope that you will enjoy reading about Wilder as much as I have enjoyed writing about him.

Acknowledgments

They say it takes a village to raise a child. While writing a scholarly book is nowhere near as difficult and complex a task as that, it does take more than an Olympian effort by a single scholar. In terms of the analogy, then, researching, writing, and revising a book-length study of literature takes a neighborhood, or at the very least a block. It is great fun to mock actors and actresses who in their acceptance speeches for Tonys, Oscars, and Emmys attempt to thank everyone they have ever known, but I now understand that impulse. It has taken many people over many years to help me write this book, and since—like the actor—this may be my only appearance in the limelight, I would like to acknowledge their contributions.

To begin at the beginning, my mother, Colleen Brooks Konkle, who despite being prevented by illness and premature death from nurturing me, somehow taught me to read and to love reading; my father, Merwin K. Konkle, who in his own way taught me to dream big; my fellow survivor of being reared by our father, my brother, Chris Konkle, with whom I am able to commiserate over the lingering effects; my cousin Bill Rogers, who turned me on to science fiction (Robert A. Heinlein, mainly) when I was nine years old, thus providing an escape from unhappy reality; Pastor Don DeBoer, who bore the good news of the One who stands at the door and knocks, and who inspired me at twelve years old to read that most challenging of all texts, the Holy Bible (the King James Version, no less) on a daily basis, a ritual to which I still mostly adhere.

As with the hero of Wilder's novel *Heaven's My Destination,* education has been a way up and out for me; that is, it has given me my shot at living the American dream, and so I want to acknowledge my high school mentor, Mr. Robert Mulligan, who first introduced me to the genius of Thornton Wilder and helped me find my niche; at Indiana University, Professor Georges Edelen, whose high estimation of my literary analysis further inspired me to pursue a career in teaching and scholarship; at Kansas State University, Professor Don Hedrick, who refused to fill his classes on Shakespeare with lecture, thus allowing and even requiring graduate students to voice their interpretative ideas, which he was genuinely interested in hearing; also at Kansas State, Professor Ben Nyberg, who provided a role model of a professor with a sense of humor and for whom teaching was fun; at the University of Wisconsin–Madison, Professor Michael Hinden, who provided gentle and supportive directing of my dissertation; Professor Sargent Bush Jr., who first taught me about the Puritans and mentored me on my first scholarly publication; Professor Joseph Wiesenfarth, who came to my defense (and to my Defense); Professor Robert Skloot, who helped me to contact the greatest living American playwright, Edward Albee; and my thanks to Mr. Albee for being patient with a precocious graduate student and a couple of years later with a bewildered assistant professor.

At the College of New Jersey (formerly Trenton State College), I want to thank colleagues Alex Liddie, Jean Graham, and especially Michael Robertson for reading the rough draft of this book and making helpful suggestions; in the Department of English Office, Angie Velez, Paulette LaBar, Jo Carney, and especially Francine Roche, without whom I could not have coped with the trauma of converting the manuscript from MLA to Chicago style; and Susan Albertine, Dean of the School of Culture and Society, for a mini-grant to offset the cost of indexing.

Beyond my academic home I want to acknowledge the many excellent suggestions from Albee scholar and the editor of *American Drama,* Norma Jenckes; early American literature scholar Emory Elliott; and especially fellow Wilder scholars and editors of my work on Wilder—Martin Blank, Chris Wheatley, Tappan Wilder, Jackson Bryer, Dalma Hunyadi Brunauer, and especially David Garrett Izzo, my publishing Jedi master and friend. I would like to add an additional thanks to Tappy for providing encouragement, facts, and overall support; and the Thornton Wilder Society for allowing me to spread the Gospel of Wilder around the world, one question and answer at a time. At the University of Missouri Press, my thanks go to Beverly Jarrett, Jane Lago, the editorial board, and especially to Gary Kass for presenting my manuscript to the board and, along with copy editor Tim Fox, offering many good suggestions for how to revise it.

Finally, and most importantly, in my home of homes, my wife, Bridget Palmer Konkle, without whom none of it—M.A., Ph.D., tenure, promotion, the book—would have been possible; and especially to God Above, who saved a messed up kid from Indiana in every way a person can be saved; may He keep saving me, Bridget, Matt, and Brooke, and all those who call upon Him, and, if He be willing, even those who don't.

Abbreviations

AC	*American Characteristics and Other Essays*
BSLR	*The Bridge of San Luis Rey*
C	*The Cabala*
CSPTW I	*The Collected Short Plays of Thornton Wilder Volume I*
CSPTW II	*The Collected Short Plays of Thornton Wilder Volume II*
DD	*The Day of Doom*
ED	*The Eighth Day*
GD	*God's Determinations Touching His Elect*
HJTC	*The Happy Journey to Trenton and Camden*
HMD	*Heaven's My Destination*
JTW	*The Journals of Thornton Wilder 1939–1961*
KJV	*Holy Bible, King James Version*
LCD	*The Long Christmas Dinner*
M	*The Matchmaker (The Merchant of Yonkers)*
OC	*Our Century*
OT	*Our Town*
PCH	*Pullman Car Hiawatha*
PD	*Proserpina and the Devil*
SD	*Shadow of a Doubt*
SOT	*The Skin of Our Teeth*
SSGUD	*And the Sea Shall Give Up Its Dead*
TN	*Theophilus North*
TP	*Three Plays*
TSS	*The Trumpet Shall Sound*
WWP	*Wonder-working Providence of Sion's Savior*

Chronology

The Life, Works, and World of Thornton Wilder

1897   Born April 17 in Madison, Wisconsin, to Amos and Isabella Wilder; his twin brother, Theophilus, is stillborn. Christened Thornton Niven Wilder, after Isabella's father, the Reverend Thornton Niven, in the First Congregational Church. Brother Amos Niven Wilder is two years old.

1898   Charlotte Elizabeth Wilder born. *Spanish American War.*

1900   Isabel Wilder born.

1901   *President McKinley assassinated; Theodore Roosevelt assumes office. U.S. signs Panama Canal Treaty.*

1902   *William James publishes* The Varieties of Religious Experience; *publishes* Pragmatism, *1907.*

1903   *American film* The Great Train Robbery. *The Wright Brothers make the first successful powered flight at Kitty Hawk, North Carolina.*

1904   *Max Weber publishes* The Protestant Ethic and the Birth of Capitalism. *Broadway subway opens in New York City.*

1906   In May Wilder family moves to Hong Kong after father appointed as Consul General by the Roosevelt administration. In October Isabella and children move to Berkeley, California.

1908   *Henry Ford's company produces first Model "T"; pioneers assembly line manufacturing, 1913. Gertrude Stein publishes her first book,* Three Lives.

1910   Janet Frances Wilder born. Wilder family returns to China; Thornton attends a mission school where he rooms with Henry Luce, future founder of *Time* magazine.

1912   Returns to Berkeley; graduates from high school, 1915. *Woodrow Wilson elected president.*

1914   *World War I begins.*

1915   Matriculates at Oberlin College in Ohio; meets Robert Maynard Hutchins, future president of the University of Chicago; contributes short pieces to the *Oberlin Literary Magazine. D. W. Griffith's controversial film* Birth of a Nation. *Ford invents farm tractor.*

1917   Transfers to Yale University in New Haven, Connecticut. Meets future writers Stephen Vincent Benét, Philip Barry, and possibly future director of *Our Town,* Jed Harris. *U.S. enters the war.*

1918   Enlists in the Coast Guard Artillery Corps (other service branches won't accept him because of his weak vision). *Excavations on site of ancient Babylon. Hundred-inch reflector telescope built at Mount Wilson, Calif. U.S. population tops one hundred million.*

1919   *World War I ends; President Wilson presides at first League of Nations meeting. Wins Nobel Peace Prize. H. L. Mencken publishes* The American Language.

1920   Graduates from Yale. First full-length play, *The Trumpet Shall Sound,* published serially in *Yale Literary Magazine* and wins Bradford Brinton Award. Spends a year's study at the American Academy in Rome, which inspires his first novel. *Eighteenth Amendment begins Prohibition. Nineteenth Amendment gives women the vote. Tercentenary of the Pilgrims' landing at Plymouth. Eugene O'Neill wins Pulitzer Prize for Drama for* Beyond the Horizon, *his first of three during the 1920s.*

1921   Hired to teach French at a private boys' preparatory school in Lawrenceville, New Jersey; over the next seven years spends many hours in the Firestone Library of neighboring Princeton University.

1923   Philip Barry, a Yale acquaintance of Wilder, has his first play produced on Broadway, *You and I;* subsequently has at least one play per year produced through 1928's *Holiday.*

1925   Takes leave from The Lawrenceville School to attend graduate school at Princeton University and to work on his novel. *Scopes "Monkey" trial.*

1926   Publishes first novel, *The Cabala.* Earns an M.A. in French language and literature from Princeton University. *The Trumpet Shall Sound* produced in New York at the American Laboratory Theatre under the direction of Richard Boleslavsky. Attends party given by F. Scott Fitzgerald in Delaware and meets critic Edmund Wilson; meets Ernest Hemingway in Paris.

1927   Returns to teach at Lawrenceville. Publishes second novel, *The Bridge of San Luis Rey.* Meets boxer Gene Tunney through Hemingway.

1928   Awarded the Pulitzer Prize for fiction for *The Bridge of San Luis Rey.* Resigns from teaching post. Takes much-publicized walking tour in Europe with Gene Tunney, who will marry his fiancée at the tour's conclusion. Meets George Bernard Shaw through Tunney. A selection of his three-minute plays is published as *The Angel That Troubled the Waters and Other Plays.* Signs contract for a five-year lecture tour.

1929   With royalties from his international bestseller, *The Bridge of San Luis Rey,* has a house built near Yale in Hamden, Conn., which will be the Wilder family home and his base of operations when not teaching. *U.S. stock market crash.*

1930   Accepts offer from President Robert Maynard Hutchins to teach classic literature and creative writing at the University of Chicago. Publishes third novel, *The Woman of Andros.* *Sinclair Lewis first American winner of the Nobel Prize for Literature.*

1931   Publishes *The Long Christmas Dinner and Other Plays in One Act.*

1932   Translates André Obey's *Le Viol de Lucrèce,* which is produced on Broadway starring Katharine Cornell and published in 1934 as *Lucrèce.*

1934   Meets Gertrude Stein who guest-lectures at the University of Chicago; Stein, Alice B. Toklas, and Wilder become close friends, as evidenced by the many letters written to each other over the next ten years (see Burns and Dydo's *The Letters of Gertrude Stein and Thornton Wilder*).

1935   Publishes fourth novel, *Heaven's My Destination.* Meets Sigmund Freud in Vienna.

1936   Wilder's father dies; Wilder resigns from University of Chicago post to write full time. *Eugene O'Neill wins Nobel Prize.*

1937   Adapts *A Doll's House* by Henrik Ibsen for a Broadway production directed by Jed Harris and starring Ruth Gordon; runs for 144 performances, a Broadway record for the play until 1997.

1938   *Our Town* produced on Broadway, starring Frank Craven, produced and directed by Jed Harris; runs for 336 performances; wins the Pulitzer Prize for drama. *The Merchant of Yonkers* (later revived as *The Matchmaker*) staged by German director Max Reinhardt; runs for 39 performances.

1939   Unhappy with the Lillian Hellman–penned script for producer Sol Lesser's film of *Our Town,* Wilder makes extensive suggestions for adaptation. Performs the role of the Stage Manager in various productions of *Our Town.* *World War II begins.*

1941   Serves, along with John Dos Passos, as U.S. Representative at PEN writers conference in London and for State Department on South American goodwill tour. *U.S. enters war.*

1942   Accepts Alfred Hitchcock's offer to write the screenplay for the film *Shadow of a Doubt.* Enlists in Army Air Force as intelligence officer (captain). *The Skin of Our Teeth,* directed by Elia Kazan, produced on Broadway; runs for 359 performances.

1943   *The Skin of Our Teeth* awarded Pulitzer Prize for drama (Wilder's third); stationed in north Africa and Italy during war.

1945   *V.E. Day, May 8. U.S. drops atomic bomb on Hiroshima, August 6, and Nagasaki, August 9.* Discharged from Air Force with rank of lieutenant colonel.

1946   Wilder's mother and Gertrude Stein both die.

1948   Publishes fifth novel, *The Ides of March.* Wilder's translation of Jean-Paul Sartre's *Morts sans sépulture* is produced off-Broadway as *The Victors.* Plays George Antrobus in summer stock productions of *Skin.*

1949   *Under Mao Tse-tung, Communists seize power and establish People's Republic of China.*

1950   Appointed the Charles Eliot Norton Professor of Poetry at Harvard; lectures on American Characteristics in Classic American Literature. *Korean war begins.*

1952   Receives the Gold Medal for Fiction from the American Academy of Arts and Letters. Serves as a member of the American delegation to UNESCO conference in Venice. *First hydrogen bomb exploded by the U.S.*

1953   *Arthur Miller's play* The Crucible *paints the Puritan origins and legacy in a deadly portrait of the seventeenth-century Salem witch trials as an allegory of McCarthyism.*

1955   *The Matchmaker* (a rewrite of *The Merchant of Yonkers*), starring Ruth Gordon and directed by Tyrone Guthrie, produced on Broadway; runs for 486 performances. *The Alcestiad* (with title *A Life in the Sun*) produced at the Edinburgh Festival.

1957   *Bernice* and *The Wreck on the Five-Twenty-Five* produced in Berlin; Wilder awarded the German Booksellers' Peace Prize.

1961   The opera *The Long Christmas Dinner,* libretto by Wilder and music by Paul Hindemith, premieres in Manheim, Germany. *Alan Shephard first American in space.*

1962   *Infancy, Childhood,* and *Someone from Assisi,* under the title *Plays for Bleeker Street,* produced off-Broadway, directed by José Quintero. The opera *The Alcestiad,* libretto by Wilder and music by Louise Talma, premieres in Frankfurt, Germany.

1963   Awarded the Presidential Medal of Freedom. *Martin Luther King de-*

livers "I Have a Dream" speech in Washington, D.C. President Kennedy assassinated. U.S. commits more troops to Vietnam.

1964   *Hello, Dolly!,* an adaptation of *The Matchmaker,* is produced on Broadway.

1965   Awarded the National Book Committee's Medal for Literature at the White House.

1967   Publishes his sixth novel, *The Eighth Day;* wins the National Book Award for Fiction; remains on the bestseller list for twenty-six weeks.

1973   Publishes his seventh novel, *Theophilus North;* remains on the bestseller list for twenty-one weeks.

1975   Dies December 7 in his sleep at home in Hamden, Conn.

1977   *The Alcestiad: or, A Life in the Sun: A Play in Three Acts, with a Satyr Play, The Drunken Sisters* published.

1979   *American Characteristics and Other Essays* published.

1985   *The Journals of Thornton Wilder: 1939–1961* published.

1992   *Conversations with Thornton Wilder* published.

1996   *The Letters of Gertrude Stein and Thornton Wilder* published.

1997   *The Collected Short Plays of Thornton Wilder Volume I* published.

1998   *The Collected Short Plays of Thornton Wilder Volume II* published.

2001   *Tour of the Darkling Plain: The Finnegans Wake Letters of Thornton Wilder and Adaline Glasheen* published.

Thornton Wilder

and the Puritan Narrative Tradition

Introduction

America furnishes the landscape for the story of the pilgrim's progress. Like the prairie of Cooper, the woods of Thoreau, or the whale of Melville, America presents an untouched sheet of wilderness upon which to record the trials and spiritual conversion of a saint.

—John O. King III, *The Iron of Melancholy: Structures of Spiritual Conversion in America from the Puritan Conscience to Victorian Neurosis*

In retrospect, what may well deserve attention in the cultural history of our period will be Wilder as a distinctive type and product of our American society.

—Amos Niven Wilder, *Thornton Wilder and His Public*

Thornton Wilder (1897–1975) is but one of many nineteenth- and twentieth-century British and American writers who have been said to bear the imprint of the cultural movement known as Puritanism. Unfortunately, by the middle of the twentieth century the word "Puritan" had become one of the most notorious labels in Anglo-American culture. The term calls to mind images of witches being put to death, a woman bearing an embroidered scarlet "A" for adultery, and drably dressed families sitting rigidly in church pews as they listen to a dour preacher threaten them with hellfire. In fact, the *Puritans* have been displaced, in the psychoanalytic sense, in our cultural psyche as the *Pilgrims*—that is, when referring to the 1620 immigrants to Plymouth, Massachusetts; however, when referring to those involved in the Salem witch trials or to the founders of an American prudishness, Puritan is the term of choice.

Puritanism began in the sixteenth century as part of the Protestant Reformation and had run its course in both England and America by the eighteenth century, but it has left its mark on nineteenth- and twentieth-century culture as well. As E. Digby Baltzell notes, "Man is a product of his history, where nothing is entirely lost and little is entirely new." Though Puritanism has sunk deeper and deeper into the American cultural unconscious with the passage of time, one can find within the literary works of American authors traces of Puritan thought and form that have persisted close to the surface of cultural consciousness or have become manifest in response to various cultural stimuli. Not surprisingly then, a point commonly made in American literature scholarship is that so-called Puritan themes of transgression, guilt, and repressed sexuality can be found in both nineteenth- and twentieth-century literary works. The problem with such observations is that they are based on a stereotypical, superficial, and inaccurate understanding of the Puritan colonists of the seventeenth and eighteenth centuries. As Kenneth Murdock explains, "The very words 'Puritan' and 'Puritanism' have been given so many different interpretations that they have almost lost meaning. Some critics have operated on the simple principle of calling Puritan any idea or mode of behavior of which they disapprove."[1]

Only in the last three decades have scholars specializing in early American literature begun to examine Puritan texts in depth for their own sake as well as for their influence on later American writing. Employing an interdisciplinary cultural criticism approach, Sacvan Bercovitch, Emory Elliott, Mason Lowance Jr., Larzer Ziff, Karl Keller, and others have convincingly argued that the American literary tradition began in the seventeenth rather than the nineteenth century; they have also demonstrated that the continuity between these periods of American literature is much greater than had previously been thought. That is, within the broad American literary tradition overall there exists a narrower Puritan tradition with specific attributes of form and content that cut across genres, now as in New England during the seventeenth and eighteenth centuries. In addition to poetry, allegory, epic, and closet drama, New England Puritans wrote biography, autobiography, hagiography, history, and sermons—genres that have been subjected to

---

1. Baltzell, *Puritan Boston and Quaker Philadelphia: Two Protestant Ethics and the Spirit of Class Authority and Leadership,* 7; Murdock, *Literature and Theology in Colonial New England,* 174.

the kinds of literary analysis that was once practiced on fictional narrative only. The Puritan writers, who were usually ministers, did not write formal literary criticism, and their brief comments about the appropriate use of poetry and other modes of literary expression are not sufficient to establish a poetics of Puritan narrative for the kind of critical analysis to be performed here on the works of playwright and novelist Thornton Wilder. However, the thematic and formalistic similarities between Puritan narratives suggest that Puritan writers did work from an aesthetic derived from their theology and biblical hermeneutics, typology in particular, and that this aesthetic, along with aspects of their ideology and theology, has persisted within American literature and culture.[2]

The thematic and formal characteristics the Puritans bequeathed to American literature can be found in any one of several seventeenth- or eighteenth-century narrative works, but they are perhaps best illustrated by Edward Taylor's seventeenth-century morality play *God's Determinations Touching His Elect,* as I have argued elsewhere.[3] Taylor's dramatic work is essentially a Puritan version of *Everyman,* as it illustrates such New England Puritan beliefs as Calvinistic predestination of the elect and reprobate, Covenant theology, and a typological and eschatological interpretation of history. The Puritan aesthetic that produced *God's Determinations Touching His Elect* is comprised of didacticism, abstract mimesis, allegorical action and characterization, progressive and episodic plots, a microcosmic foreground against a macrocosmic background, and plain style. The strength of this study's argument lies in the similarity between the gestalts of *God's Determinations Touching His Elect* and, for example, Thornton Wilder's two major plays, *Our Town* and *The Skin of Our Teeth,* and his two best novels, *The Bridge of San Luis Rey* and *The Eighth Day.* Holding up Taylor's and Wilder's works side by side, an innocent observer might well deduce that an unbroken line of literary tradition exists between the two writers, that there is perhaps even a direct influence of Taylor on Wilder. That *God's Determinations Touching His Elect* was not published until 1939, when Wilder had already published four novels and had three full-length plays produced, is beside the point; Taylor's work is the quintessence in both content and form of the beginnings of one significant vein of the American literary tradition, the salient features of

2. Much of what the Puritans practiced in their literary writing was a manifestation of their religious beliefs: "The strength, the homeliness, and the 'life' come from the organic relation of Puritan style to Puritan concepts" (Murdock, *Literature and Theology,* 185), or an imitation of the techniques found in the one unconditionally sanctioned work of literature, the Bible.

3. See my "Puritan Epic Theatre: A Brechtian Reading of Edward Taylor's *Gods Determinations.*"

which have found their way even into the "profane" space of the American theater.

Beginning with the fiftieth-anniversary production of *Our Town* in 1988, there has been renewed interest in the works of Thornton Wilder, as evidenced by a centennial symposium at Yale, a theater festival in Louisville, a conference at Wake Forest University, two Wilder sessions at the 1998 Modern Language Association convention, a session on Wilder's novels at the Association of Literary Scholars and Critics Conference in 2002, and sessions the last few years at the American Literature Association convention, as well as by the publication of a selection of his interviews, his letters to Gertrude Stein, one book-length study of his drama, one collection of previously published articles and reviews of both his fiction and his drama, a collection of new essays, and a volume of Wilder's translations and adaptations forthcoming from Theatre Communications Group. Furthermore, during the 1990s Wilder's short plays that had been long out of print reappeared in a two-volume collection along with several one-act plays that had never been performed or published; finally, all seven of his novels are being reprinted.[4] Projects in the works include a new biography, a collection of his letters, and operas of *Our Town* and *The Bridge of San Luis Rey*.

Although Wilder is still the only writer to win the Pulitzer Prize in both drama and fiction, he has received little or no attention in recent critical studies of twentieth-century American drama and fiction, and his works do not appear in recently published anthologies of American literature and drama. Two aspects of Wilder's writing might explain this omission: first, the perception that the body of his work is small; second, its affirmative tone stemming from his spiritual interpretation of daily life and history, which stands in stark contrast to the skeptical, cynical, even nihilistic tone of most modern American literature and drama admired by scholars and critics.[5] However, to briefly address the first claim, when one examines everything from his first attempts at drama written and published while he was in college during the 1910s and 1920s to his last novel published in the seventies,

---

4. These are, respectively, *Conversations with Thornton Wilder* (1992), ed. Jackson R. Bryer; *The Letters of Gertrude Stein and Thornton Wilder* (1996), ed. Edward Burns and Ulla E. Dydo, with William Rice; *Vast Encyclopedia: The Theatre of Thornton Wilder* (1995), by Paul Lifton; *Critical Essays on Thornton Wilder* (1996), ed. Martin Blank; *Thornton Wilder: New Essays* (1999), ed. Martin Blank, Dalma Hunyadi Brunauer, and David Garrett Izzo; and *The Collected Short Plays of Thornton Wilder, Volumes I and II* (1997). HarperCollins is publishing the novels in new editions with forewords by renowned fiction writers and critical afterwords by Wilder's nephew and literary executor, Tappan Wilder.

5. In "Life Viewed as a Totality versus Gobblydegarble," Henry Mitchell sarcastically explains even more specifically why, perhaps, Wilder has been dropped from the canon: "Critics have generally praised his plays, with occasional digressions to wonder if Wilder's work is not a bit, well, optimistic (one of the filthiest words in the critical vocabulary) or, ah, somewhat Christian (which is pretty awful, too, to say of a writer)" (H2).

the size of Wilder's oeuvre compares to that of F. Scott Fitzgerald, Clifford Odets, Arthur Miller, and other modern American dramatists and novelists. Wilder wrote five full-length plays that have been published and had at least one production; eighteen one-act plays that have been published, most of which have been produced at least once; sixteen "three-minute plays" published and staged at least once; seven novels; a collection of essays; and two screenplays that were filmed and released. As to the second point, if read attentively, these works reveal a dark side of individual characters, society, and human nature that Wilder's affirmative vision transcends through a compassionate response to suffering on the personal and global levels. Much of the book that follows explores in detail this important aspect of Wilder's work.

Previous studies of Thornton Wilder have one point in common: they all presume that the aesthetic of this American author was derived from non-American movements, authors, or works. Undeniably, modern European movements and figures influenced Wilder, and those influences have been well documented in previous studies of his drama and fiction. What has not been considered is that the European writers and styles Wilder admits to reading and admiring may have simply struck a chord in a native tradition already inculcated during childhood through family, education, and his reading of classic American literature. After all, it isn't as though Wilder was a tabula rasa when he read books or attended productions of plays by European authors. In his 1980 monograph *Thornton Wilder and His Public,* Amos Niven Wilder, Thornton's older scholar-poet-minister brother, lamented the paucity of criticism on his brother's works:

> A number of critics like Malcolm Cowley have remarked upon the lack of thoroughgoing and substantive studies in this country of my brother's novels and plays. This situation, again, raises a number of interesting questions about the focus and scale of much contemporary criticism. There appear to be moral ingredients and universal motifs in Wilder's work which elude their tools and canons. Preoccupation not simply with the *zeitgeist* but with the dominant movement of emancipation in our epoch leaves out of account works that reflect deeper continuities. . . . The fact is they do not know what to do with him. But of course these issues should be and can be spelled out in terms of a more adequate and sophisticated attention to Wilder's fabulation and dramaturgy. And it is just this which is so far lacking.[6]

Even more pertinent for the purposes of this study, Amos writes of Richard Goldstone's 1975 biography, *Thornton Wilder: An Intimate Portrait,* which superficially applies the term "Puritan" to Wilder, "My own chief issue with

6. A. N. Wilder, *Thornton Wilder and His Public,* 16.

the book, however, arises in connection with the author's view of the 'Puritan' influence on my brother and its handicaps. . . . Such a main study of my brother should be in the hands of someone more congenial to his humanism and to his own kind of Americanism."[7]

Thus, this study fills a long-standing gap in Wilder scholarship: a reading of Wilder's life, drama, and fiction as a product of the oldest branch of the American literary tradition. My contention is that Wilder is, in effect, a direct literary descendant of seventeenth-century New England Puritan writers such as Edward Taylor in that his aesthetic is not just generically allegorical but typically American, and his religious sensibility is not just generally Christian but specifically Calvinist. In his plays and novels, even in his own American literature scholarship, there exists a continuity with seventeenth- and eighteenth-century New England Puritan beliefs and literary forms. Wilder may not have read any of the major American Puritan authors like William Bradford, Anne Bradstreet, Michael Wigglesworth, Edward Taylor, or Cotton Mather, but he did read John Bunyan's *The Pilgrim's Progress*,[8] as well as works by American authors who had read or whose parents or grandparents had read the American Puritans: Nathaniel Hawthorne, Herman Melville, Ralph Waldo Emerson, Henry David Thoreau, and Emily Dickinson, all of whose works have been examined in studies by early American literature scholars demonstrating the continuity of Puritan ideas and forms.

It is likely that many of the theological concepts and aesthetic forms and styles traceable to seventeenth-century Puritan writers this study detects in his works were employed unconsciously by Wilder as part of his American aesthetic heritage. However, given that he was consciously aware of the role the Puritans played in the evolution of American culture, as well as his own family's ties to the Puritans, it is also possible that some of the resemblance between the texts of Wilder and the Puritans was intentional. For example, in *The Cabala,* his first novel, Wilder has a European character say to the American narrator, "Now in America you are all descended from your Puritans, are you not, and your ideas are very different" (36). Even so, conscious awareness and deliberate use of seventeenth-century concepts and styles represent merely the tip of the iceberg of New England Puritanism in

7. Ibid.

8. In *The Enthusiast: A Life of Thornton Wilder,* 1, 6, Gilbert A. Harrison quotes letters written by Wilder's father from China that instruct the Wilder children to read *The Pilgrim's Progress.* Although an English work, it was popular in colonial America and continued to be widely read through the nineteenth century, even serving as the literary model for popular culture writing, including temperance movement literature; see David E. Smith, *John Bunyan in America.*

the American psyche of Thornton Wilder. This study undertakes to trace and analyze those conscious and unconscious Puritan paradigms and codes as they progressed through the writing of this eminently American writer.

Review of Wilder Scholarship

In previous attempts to classify the philosophical point of view in his works, scholars have affixed such labels to Wilder as Christian, humanist, Christian humanist, New Humanist, optimist, yea-sayer, Unitarian, transcendentalist, and Platonist.[9] As a dramatist, Wilder is said to have derived his aesthetic from German expressionism, though some scholars have denied that his techniques are expressionistic; the disagreement is due in part to imprecise definitions of terms like "expressionism" and to disputes over which individual or school originated or most purely practiced such modes. Louis Broussard deduced that since Wilder lived in China he must have borrowed from the Chinese theater, but Jean Gould and Ethan Mordden have noted that this is an unsupported assumption. Wilder's dramatic mode has also been described as theatricalist, surrealistic, romantic, and didactic.[10]

Whatever the precise term, Wilder's plays clearly belong to the period of nonrealistic experimentation in dramatic form and production techniques that occurred during the first half of the twentieth century as a reaction against late nineteenth-century realism. Since modern nonrealistic theater was initially a European movement, scholars have assumed that the formal characteristics of Wilder's plays (and novels) are European in origin; thus the contemporary figures Wilder is said to have been influenced by or directly

9. For the classification of Wilder's philosophical point of view, see, respectively, Helmut Papajewski, *Thornton Wilder;* Joseph Firebaugh, "The Humanism of Thornton Wilder"; Edward K. Brown, "A Christian Humanist: Thornton Wilder"; Rex Burbank, *Thornton Wilder;* Gerald Weales, "Unfashionable Optimist"; Bernard Hewitt, "Thornton Wilder Says 'Yes,'"; Francis Fergusson, "Three Allegorists: Brecht, Wilder, and Eliot"; Malcolm Cowley, "Introduction" to *A Thornton Wilder Trio;* and Robert Corrigan, "Thornton Wilder and the Tragic Sense of Life."

10. See A. R. Fulton, "Expressionism—Twenty Years After"; Douglas C. Wixson Jr., "The Dramatic Techniques of Thornton Wilder and Bertolt Brecht: A Study in Comparison"; and Donald Haberman, *The Plays of Thornton Wilder* for discussions of Wilder's plays as expressionistic. See Firebaugh, "Humanism"; Louis Broussard, *American Drama: Contemporary Allegory from Eugene O'Neill to Tennessee Williams;* and Oscar G. Brockett and Robert R. Findlay, *Century of Innovation: A History of European and American Theatre and Drama since 1870* for exclusion of Wilder from that aesthetic. For the other descriptions of Wilder's dramatic mode, see, respectively, John Gassner, *Form and Idea in Modern Theatre;* Burbank, *Thornton Wilder;* Joseph Wood Krutch, *The American Drama since 1918: An Informal History;* George D. Stephens, "*Our Town*—Great American Tragedy?" and Firebaugh, "Humanism."

borrowed from are European: Pirandello, Obey, Jarry, Proust, and Joyce.[11] It is not the intent of this study to deny the significance of these European contemporaries as inspiration and sources for Wilder's drama and fiction, since he acknowledged reading and/or seeing many of their works. But we know from Wilder's own statements and the findings of his biographers that it is no exaggeration to say that he read everything—every writer, every work then considered significant to the western canon of literature; he even read many of them in their original languages.

What has not been sufficiently considered is the role of the "American melting pot" of Wilder's imagination. To attribute his narrative practice to European influences is to imply that his Americanness is irrelevant to understanding the nature of his literary production. That is impossible from a cultural criticism approach, which investigates how a particular culture "writes" the writer who writes the text. Therefore, previous studies of Wilder have treated the phenomenon of literary influence too simplistically and selectively. I suggest that the European intellectual and aesthetic elements that sparked Wilder's enthusiasm were, like tuning forks, vibrating in harmony with similar concepts and narrative forms within American culture at large and the American literary tradition in particular. As John F. Lynen notes, "Though it is natural to suppose that the characteristics of twentieth-century literature reflect a broadly cosmopolitan sensibility . . . , the techniques which seem to relate Eliot to Yeats and Faulkner to Proust have a very long history in America, and can be seen emerging in the early Puritan writers."[12] Thus one intention of this study is to reclaim Thornton Wilder as an *American* author whose place in one branch of the American literary tradition has not been fully understood.

The following quotation from the last book-length study of Wilder's entire oeuvre indicates the need for an analysis of his works and life in the context of American culture:

> [H]e had no reservations about adapting, absorbing, and accepting the European tradition—so long as it suited his purposes. . . . The anxieties of European influences were with him throughout his career, enriching his work and life, haunting him, sometimes distracting him, and frequently casting shadows on his reputation. . . . The author of *Our Town*—a play that has unfortunately entered our consciousness as if it were a protracted dramatization of the Pledge of Allegiance—had a mind that was distinctly *un-American* in its ap-

11. See, for example, Richard H. Goldstone, *Thornton Wilder: An Intimate Portrait;* Haberman, *Plays of Thornton Wilder;* David Castronovo, *Thornton Wilder;* and Burbank, *Thornton Wilder* for discussions of the respective authors.

12. Lynen, *The Design of the Present: Essays on Time and Form in American Literature,* 33.

proach to the writer's craft and vocation. That mind endured in the midst of the threats of American literary and social life. Wilder's career was pursued against the resisting currents of twentieth-century American sensibility and taste.[13]

More specifically, Bernard F. Dukore comments, "The religious conviction that shapes it [the tradition Wilder's drama stems from] is non-doctrinal, non-sectarian, anti-puritanical and above all non-didactic."[14] This study will demonstrate that the tradition Wilder's drama and fiction stem from is heavily doctrinal, Puritan, and didactic.

This is not to say that there has been no mention of American literary influences on Wilder in studies of his life and literature, but only two American authors have been argued as direct influences: Theodore Dreiser and Gertrude Stein.[15] However, not only would expatriate writers like Dreiser and Stein not be accurately described by the terms for Wilder's philosophical bent listed earlier, but neither do the particular occurrences of abstract representation and other nonrealistic traits in works by Stein or Dreiser account for the aesthetic pervasively employed by Wilder in both his plays and novels throughout his career. Granted, Wilder himself cited Stein as a major influence; however, the plays and novels he had written *before* his "apprenticeship" with Gertrude Stein already demonstrate the philosophical themes or formal characteristics shared by Wilder and a representative seventeenth-century Puritan writer like Edward Taylor.

Every study of Wilder's drama notes that in the collection *The Long Christmas Dinner and Other Plays in One Act* (1931) Wilder had expressed the same themes and employed the same techniques that he was to develop in the full-length plays for which he is best known, *Our Town* and *The Skin of Our Teeth,*

13. Castronovo, *Thornton Wilder,* 3. In *"Our Town": An American Play,* Donald Haberman almost certainly was attempting to refute Castronovo; however, he does not discuss the ways in which Wilder's best-known play is an outgrowth of the very roots of the American literary tradition. For other descriptions of Wilder's influences as European, see Burbank, *Thornton Wilder,* 35; Malcolm Goldstein, *The Art of Thornton Wilder,* 6; Haberman, *Plays of Thornton Wilder,* 121–22; Goldstone, *Intimate Portrait,* 257; Martin Blank, "Thornton Wilder's Early Work in the Theatre," 20, 28–29, 33–34; and Lifton, *Vast Encyclopedia,* 11, 69.

14. Dukore, *American Dramatists, 1918–1945,* 122.

15. Haberman's (*Plays of Thornton Wilder*) consideration of Dreiser's and Stein's influence on Wilder's dramatic form is more in-depth, but see also Goldstone, *Intimate Portrait,* and Burbank, *Thornton Wilder.* Apart from the occasional brief comment made in passing that Wilder's plays are imbued with an Emersonian transcendentalism or a Whitmanesque affirmation of America (see, for example, Thomas P. Adler, *Mirror on the Stage: The Pulitzer Plays as an Approach to American Drama,* 125), scholars have not linked Wilder to classic American authors.

first performed in 1938 and 1942, respectively; yet these same studies assert that it is from Stein that any American influence contributes to Wilder's vision and aesthetic. Only Mildred Kuner has acknowledged that Stein's influence came after Wilder's shift to American subjects: "In the end he might have come to it alone. As it happened, Gertrude Stein encouraged, if she did not initiate his quiet revolution." However, Kuner also suggests that it was Stein who showed Wilder how to express what he wanted to say: "Thanks to her, he learned how to recast his philosophical concepts in a more appealing manner."[16] This study's contention is that Wilder reached maturity as a fabulist in the novel with *The Bridge of San Luis Rey* (1927) and in drama four years later with *The Long Christmas Dinner and Other Plays in One Act,* both of which he wrote *before* meeting Gertrude Stein in 1935.[17] The consistency of worldview and aesthetic throughout his works, whether drama or fiction, attests to an underlying influence greater than the intersections with individual figures such as Dreiser and Stein. They were American writers who chose to be expatriates in order to live in the ambiance of an aesthetic they believed to have been antecedent to their American influences, thinking that this aura would enhance their art directly. Wilder's visits to Europe were not for the purpose of shoring up any sense that he was lacking a full aesthetic for his work; rather, he saw the equation as one of a clear *distinction* between the European and American influences. His first novel, *The Cabala,* has this contrast as a major theme. The influence uncovered in this study is the more diffuse absorption of *osmosis,* as it were, of American culture, including American literature, and the traces of Puritan thought and form within it.

The term "Puritan" does appear in Wilder scholarship, but it is almost always used in the reductive, stereotypical sense of "puritanical." Such uses of Puritan or Calvinist in reference to Wilder or to his works are found primarily in discussions of the characters Samuele in *The Cabala,* who is identified as a Puritan in the text of the novel itself, and George Brush in *Heaven's My Destination,* and in biographical readings of Wilder's inherited cultural "baggage" critics think he had to outgrow in order to achieve any artistic success. As Amos Niven Wilder notes, "Cosmopolitan and artistic circles in our cities and intellectuals in our academies are often not well fitted or disposed to understand the so-called Puritan tradition in our culture. It is associated for them with authoritarianism, with special sex attitudes, with the Puritan

---

16. Kuner, *Thornton Wilder: The Bright and the Dark,* 111.

17. Lifton also writes that Wilder's theatrical aesthetics "were fixed at an early stage of his career," citing the "three-minute plays" published in *The Angel That Troubled the Waters and Other Plays* and *The Long Christmas Dinner and Other Plays in One Act* (*Vast Encyclopedia,* 208).

ethic of work, thrift, and success, with antiaesthetic bias and with law-and-order mentality."[18]

In the most egregious example of scholarly misuse of the term "Puritan," Richard Goldstone in *Thornton Wilder: An Intimate Portrait* refers to Wilder as "The Last American Puritan" and calls Wilder's last novel, *Theophilus North,* "A Puritan Swan Song." Goldstone's definition of Puritanism makes clear why the present study is not a repetition of his: "Puritanism, the denial of nature in general and the appetites of human nature in particular, opposes the consummation of sexual drives that do not have procreation as their aim; it detests sloth, vanity, gluttony, and outward shows of affection. Puritanism embodied in a work of literature generally appears unpleasant." To illustrate the extremity of the negative connotations Goldstone associates with Puritanism, he writes that after World War I all the repressive values of Puritanism "gave way as the Roosevelt grin ushered in the New Deal and as the ascetic Puritan Hitler emerged the most deadly fallen angel of them all." Ironically, Goldstone later uses the term to describe Wilder's attackers: Wilder "had written the early novels and had been derided by the left wing Puritans (for who were more puritanical than the Jewish intellectual Marxists of the 1930s?)." Wilder himself was so displeased with Goldstone's biography that, according to Gilbert A. Harrison's biography *The Enthusiast: A Life of Thornton Wilder,* he dissuaded Harper and Row from publishing it as a matter of loyalty to him, though Dutton subsequently published it. As noted above, Wilder's brother, Amos, wrote his monograph *Thornton Wilder and His Public* to answer Goldstone and to call for the kind of study of his brother's works attempted here. Amos even speculated, "In reading the book one sometimes wonders whether Goldstone really enjoys Thornton's work."[19]

Thus, although Wilder scholars have not denied the affinities his works have with the vestiges of Puritanism in American culture, clearly their understanding of those characteristics has little to do with what seventeenth-century

18. A. N. Wilder, *Wilder and His Public,* 47. For examples of scholars using "Puritan" in this stereotypical sense or "Calvinist" as a label for conservative Protestant faith, see Papajewski, *Thornton Wilder,* 13; Goldstein, *Art of Thornton Wilder,* 22; Burbank, *Thornton Wilder,* 18; Kuner, *Bright and Dark,* 117; Castronovo, *Thornton Wilder,* 42; Firebaugh, "Farce and the Heavenly Destination," 16; and Hermione Popper, "The Universe of Thornton Wilder," 77.

19. Goldstone, *Intimate Portrait,* 252, 261, 6, 253, 257; Harrison, *Enthusiast,* 375–77; A. N. Wilder, *Wilder and His Public,* 16. Not to pick on Goldstone but to demonstrate that others who were not part of the Wilder family objected to his reading of Wilder and his works, in the Wilder collection at the Beinecke Library at Yale is a file containing letters to Wilder from Malcolm Cowley; in one letter Cowley writes, "I just had the rather unpleasant task of reviewing *Thornton Wilder: An Intimate Portrait* for *The Times Book Review*" (October 21, 1975). In another letter to Wilder about the book Cowley writes, "That Goldstone book is so dreadful I don't like to think about it" (November 4, 1975).

New England Puritans believed in their daily lives or what they wrote in their literary works. Of course, Wilder was not literally a Puritan—Protestant Christians in America have not identified themselves by that name since the eighteenth century. My claim is that Wilder inherited the best of the Puritans' worldview and drew upon those features of the Puritan narrative aesthetic within the American literary tradition that would strike a fundamental chord in his American audience.

Following the publication of Amos Niven Wilder's monograph, several books and articles on Wilder have been published, but these also missed the significance of the influence of American culture and the American literary tradition on Wilder and his drama and fiction. For example, in the most recent book-length study of Wilder as dramatist, Paul Lifton compares Wilder's dramaturgy to "symbolism, naturalism, expressionism, futurism, and existentialism" and also to "classical Greek, Medieval, Elizabethan, Renaissance, Spanish, Chinese, and Japanese theater, as well as American popular folk entertainment."[20] Clearly, then, there is a need for a study that considers Wilder in the narrower context of American literature and that examines not only his plays but also his novels, essays, journal notes, family background, and the milieu in which he grew up and wrote his works.

It is not so difficult to accept that a twentieth-century writer's life and works manifest vestiges of seventeenth-century culture when the background of Wilder's family and upbringing are analyzed. In fact, several studies have made that very observation, but none has done so with accurate and in-depth knowledge of Puritanism, Puritan writing, or the Puritan legacy in American culture.

Wilder's Puritan Heritage

Thornton Wilder's parents were born and raised in Maine and New York of Congregationalist and Presbyterian denominational descent; both denominations were, like Puritanism, mostly Calvinistic in doctrine. According to Linda Simon, his father belonged to a family that had immigrated to Massachusetts in the mid-seventeenth century and ultimately settled in Augusta, Maine. As Burbank notes, "Amos P. Wilder was a devout Congregationalist who inherited his Puritan conscience and dedication to duty from his New England Calvinist ancestors." Wilder's own description of his father's heritage concurs with Burbank's: "I don't think there's any doubt that the New England tradition is the highest point to which civilization culture ever at-

20. Lifton, *Vast Encyclopedia*, 10.

tained. . . . My father, for all his faults, was the personification of the tradition."[21]

Most biographical sketches of Thornton and Amos Parker Wilder's relationship characterize it as the sensitive son domineered by the tyrannical father, but both Wilder himself and his brother, Amos Niven Wilder, objected to the description of the relationship as Oedipal. In his biography of Wilder, Harrison shows that although there were differences between Thornton and his father, they still had much in common, as suggested in a letter to Thornton's brother from their father: "On Thornton, too, was the Puritan mark, 'less affirmative than in you or me . . . but let each singer choose his own tune.'" Thornton wrote to his father, "Your religious self-examination I cannot duplicate," which does indicate that even as a young man Wilder was in conflict with the Puritan heritage in his family. However, Wilder later admits, "Your queer 'aesthetic,' over-cerebral son may yet turn out to be your most fundamental New Englander."[22] What is interesting about these excerpts from family letters is that Amos Parker Wilder, a member of the twentieth-century Congregationalist church, conceived of himself and his sons as inheriting a legacy from the Puritans; and Thornton himself used "New Englander" to describe the potential development of his beliefs and his character in much the same sense as Perry Miller's *The New England Mind: The Seventeenth Century* (in other words, as the religious, political, and social values and lifestyle characterizing the majority of the people who reside in the region originally settled by the Puritans). Thus the relationship between Thornton Wilder and his father was not an incitement to rebellion; as Cowley notes, "He had worshipped in his father's church and followed the profession his father picked out for him. In a way he represented continuity and tradition, so far as they existed in American society."[23]

The fact that Wilder himself was not raised in New England does not preclude the inculcation of regional vestiges of Puritanism in him as a child; as Popper writes, Wilder "was born in Madison, Wisconsin, a geographical

21. Simon, *Thornton Wilder, His World,* 3; Burbank, *Thornton Wilder,* 18; Wilder's journal entry is from a file labeled "Aphorisms" at the Beinecke Library at Yale University, where most of Wilder's archival materials is located.

22. Harrison, *Enthusiast,* 59–60, 8, 68. Although the young Wilder was almost certainly not using the word "queer" as the contemporary epithet for "homosexual," biographies do mention, at least briefly, the issue of his sexuality. See Goldstone, *Intimate Portrait,* 262–65; Simon, *Thornton Wilder, His World,* 64; and Harrison, 165–76. While it is irrelevant to this study (unless one subscribes to the formula "Puritanism = repressed sexuality → homosexuality," which is an outdated view of both homosexuality and Puritanism, at least among early American literature scholars), being gay with a father as religiously conservative as Wilder's, and at a time in America when homosexuality was still literally a crime, would undoubtedly have been the source of intense conflict, guilt, and suffering.

23. Cowley, "Introduction," 7.

accident that cannot disguise the dominance of New England in his heritage."[24] However, Wilder's Wisconsin years need not be factored out of the equation of his Puritan heritage; a review of the history of the Congregational Church in the United States overall and in Wisconsin in particular lends further support to the claim that the cultural and literary legacy of Puritanism was infused into Wilder at several points in the years prior to the formal beginning of his writing career.

The Congregational Church

In the early nineteenth century the members of many churches of congregational polity were divided between those who wanted to become Unitarian and those who wanted to adhere to Calvinist principles; the result of this conflict was the birth of a denomination out of what had been a system of church organization. Marion L. Starkey explains the result of this division: "The near disaster of the separation forced the orthodox for the first time to consider themselves as a denomination. While the secessionists organized themselves under a title they had at first indignantly denied, the faithful of the Calvinist old guard became the Congregational Churches."[25]

The Congregational Church of the nineteenth century was not identical in its beliefs and devotional practices to seventeenth-century Puritans, but Congregationalists themselves, while acknowledging differences, thought of the Puritans as their forebears. Writing in 1893, Williston Walker writes in his introduction to *The Creeds and Platforms of Congregationalism,* "The ecclesiastical genealogist has no difficulty tracing back American Congregationalism to the churches of the Plymouth, Massachusetts Bay, Connecticut, and New Haven colonies." As Walker is one such genealogist, he concludes his work thus:

> The fathers of the sixteenth and seventeenth centuries, applying the reformation principle of the authority of the Word of God to polity as well as to doctrine, sketched out the essential features of a Congregational church as they believed it to be divinely appointed. In common with their Puritan brethren they formulated the doctrinal system of the Gospel as they read it in the same divine record. On the basis of their two-fold work Congregationalism still stands. The essential features of the church as it appeared to them are the distinctive characteristics of a Congregational church today. The great truths

24. Popper, "Universe," 73.
25. Starkey, *The Congregational Way: The Role of the Pilgrims and Their Heirs in Shaping America,* 182.

which they maintained constitute, in their broad outline, the doctrinal basis of modern Congregationalism.[26]

Walker's view of the Congregational Church as an outgrowth of congregational churches founded by the Puritans is corroborated by the history of Congregationalism in the then-called "western" territories. According to Harry R. Butman, the rapid settling of what today are the midwestern states was in part an effect of "a renaissance of Congregationalism" in the mid-nineteenth century. Butman elaborates, "The missionary call to the western states reawakened Congregational consciousness. After two hundred years of ebbing force there was a powerful burst of life in Congregationalism. The Puritan faith, which had stopped at the Berkshires, suddenly stretched out into the middle west."[27]

Starkey notes that the Plan of Union in 1801 for sending missionaries to the western territories resulted in a predominance of Presbyterian churches over Congregational, but "No doctrinal dispute was involved, for both sects were firmly Calvinist." In Wisconsin, however, this national trend was reversed:

> Congregationalism in Wisconsin had a relationship different from that in any of the regions in which the Plan of Union operated. Here there was no amalgamation of the two bodies. The individual churches remained either Presbyterian or Congregational, while the convention for the Presbyterians was a presbytery and that for the congregationalists was an association. Nor in Wisconsin did the Presbyterians tend to dominate the situation as in most other places where the two bodies work together. This was due to the fact that not only was denominational consciousness among the Congregationalists on the increase during the years of early Wisconsin settlement but that also immigration from New England and New York prevailed over that from other regions.[28]

Traces of the Puritan legacy in Wisconsin are found in statements made by Wisconsin Congregational historians and in frontier documents included in those histories. For example, in the following letter written in 1845 to the American Home Missionary Board by O. P. Clinton, a Congregational missionary during the initial settlement of Wisconsin, it is evident that these missionaries saw themselves as reenacting if not continuing the Puritan errand into the wilderness:

26. Walker, *The Creeds and Platforms of Congregationalism*, x, 583.
27. Harry R. Butman, *The Lord's Free People*, 52, 70.
28. Starkey, *Congregational Way*, 183; Richard Day Leonard, "The Presbyterian and Congregation Convention in Wisconsin," University of Chicago thesis, 1938, quoted in William Warren Sweet, *Religion on the American Frontier, 1783–1850*, vol. 3 of *The Congregationalists*, 368.

I came to this country with such fears of the tendency of things, as have kept me on the lookout for these chisms [sic], these dangerous breakers, upon wh our Zion has been so often wrecked for the last few years—I think you are not entirely ignorant of the high esteem in wh [sic] I formerly held the old Puritan landmarks, the value and importance of wh have not in the least degree lessened while labouring to contribute something towards setting them up in this great valley. . . . We have from time to time thanked God and took courage when you have been sending us men furnished for their work, and ready to sustain the great principles which have made *New England an example to the world.*

Sweet also includes in his history of the frontier church a letter from another missionary, Stephen Peet, who expressed his concern that the Old School Presbyterians and ultra-Congregationalists were making greater advances in the territory than the moderates such as himself (as he saw himself, at least). He claims that the situation, from his point of view, was critical in Madison, where as a child Thornton Wilder would attend the First Congregational Church with his family. Peet even refers to this activity as the "interference of the Puritan."[29]

The Puritan providential hermeneutic was still operative in Wisconsin early in the twentieth century, as indicated by the preface to *A Hundred Years of Congregational History in Wisconsin* by Frank N. Dexter, which expresses a providential interpretation of frontier history written with an epic tone similar to Puritan historians':

It is part of the purpose of this book to make it clear that not by accident were the wilds of Wisconsin subdued, houses built, churches and schools established, revivals of religion promoted and the Kingdom of God advanced by men and women who counted not their lives dear unto them in the pursuit of their vision. With the eye of faith they saw beautiful Wisconsin ready to be taken and set as a polished gem in the crown of the Lord. . . . Forward! It is a happy task committed to us to relate the thrilling story of Congregational work in Wisconsin, and to recall the heroic service of the men and women who directed the flow of the river of blessing whose course is described in this volume.

Dexter also quotes a bold statement made by a Beloit College alumnus in the 1870s: "Beloit College is as truly the child of New England Puritanism as though its walls were standing on Plymouth Rock."[30] Whatever concrete realities such an assertion might represent, it is clear that Congregationalists in Wisconsin believed in the cultural myth of an American Promised Land

29. Sweet, *Religion on the American Frontier,* 392–94 (emphasis added), 396–97, 398.
30. Dexter, *A Hundred Years of Congregational History in Wisconsin,* x, xi, 146.

and regarded themselves as direct descendants of the Puritan founders of that myth. Thus Wilder need not have been born and raised in New England to have been inculcated with the Puritan habit of mind.

After leaving Wisconsin Wilder continued to encounter sources of influence that reinforced his Puritan heritage. His sister Isabel notes that the family attended a Congregational church in Berkeley (*JTW,* xiv). The middle school Wilder attended in California was advertised as having "the moral and intellectual atmosphere of a New England community." Even when he left home, his father's choice of college for him provided a consistency of environment, as noted by two Wilder scholars: Oberlin College was "a congregationalist plain-living-and-high-thinking college" with "compulsory chapel, fine humanistic curriculum, and social progressivism"; "His twenty-three year-old hero [of the 1935 novel *Heaven's My Destination*] George Brush, resembles himself as a young man in his hardheaded Calvinism and, what is more, attended a college in which that severe mode of belief prevailed among the student body, as it did at Oberlin." Finally, Wilder's first teaching job was also colored by a peculiar trace of the Puritan past: "The Lawrenceville School, a boys' preparatory school in Lawrenceville, New Jersey, was then headed by Mather Abbott . . . , a descendent of Cotton Mather; [he] brought to the school a proud Puritan morality."[31]

Ultimately Wilder would become a cosmopolitan world traveler, but he built a house to use as a base of operations in Connecticut near Yale University; there he lived for the remainder of his life, except for his tenure at the University of Chicago from 1930 to 1936. Although Goldstone's sense of what "Puritan" means is erroneous, the following statement by him is nonetheless an accurate summary of the matter of Wilder's ties to New England Puritanism: "Neither China nor California nor Rome and neither sojourns in the capitals of Europe nor association with the intellectually gifted men and women of the world's great cities could wean him away from his American Puritan heritage."[32]

And it was in his American Puritan heritage that Wilder was out of step with the writers and intellectuals of the early and later modernist period. Anti-Puritanism was prevalent in the works of such intellectuals and writers as George Santayana, H. L. Mencken, and Eugene O'Neill. Santayana, a philosopher and writer in various literary and scholarly genres, wrote the satirical novel *The Last Puritan* (1935). Mencken, a newspaper and magazine writer and editor, was famous for his verbal attacks on Puritans; in one he

31. Simon, *Thornton Wilder, His World,* 19; Castronovo, *Thornton Wilder,* 6; Goldstein, *Art of Thornton Wilder,* 63; Simon, *Thornton Wilder, His World,* 34.
32. Goldstone, *Intimate Portrait,* 120.

claimed, "The great artists of the world are never Puritans, and seldom even ordinarily respectable." He cast his more famous satirical jab as a definition: "Puritanism—The haunting fear that someone, somewhere, may be happy."[33] An anti-Puritan motif runs in several of O'Neill's plays, but the best-known examples are *Desire under the Elms* (1925) and *Mourning Becomes Electra* (1931).

However, in mainstream American culture during the late teens through 1920, when Thornton Wilder was coming of age, there were many references to the approaching tercentenary of the Pilgrims' landing at Plymouth Rock, and the tone of these was affirmative, even patriotic. According to articles in the *New York Times,* celebrations were being planned as early as 1916, and they were to be widespread, not limited to New England: "It is expected that the events marking the tercentenary will be distributed throughout all parts of the United States, and will touch upon all sections and classes of people, from highest officialdom down to little private groups of people, social clubs, embracing in this downward sweep institutions, schools, organizations and societies." Indeed the highest of American officialdom, President Warren G. Harding, had this to say in a speech a year after the tercentenary:

> It is a difficult task to single out and measure the factors in political and social progress. The germ of progress is doubtless universal, but requires favorable conditions for its development. Conditions were favorable in the New World, and the Plymouth Colony was destined to begin the surpassing story of three centuries of ardent, eager pursuit of human justice. . . . The pageant which we have just seen shows in vivid, spectacular form how much we of today owe to that sturdy Pilgrim spirit which the first founders of our nation brought with them from across the seas. I believe most firmly that that stern, indomitable spirit, with which the Pilgrims faced the perils of an unknown land for sake of conscience, represents that which is truest and best in the America of today.[34]

During this time Wilder was either at Yale, completing his undergraduate degree, or Rhode Island, serving in the Coast Guard; he undoubtedly was aware of some of the public events marking the anniversary as he finished up his senior year at Yale in New Haven, Connecticut, which was originally colonized by Puritans. What his reaction was to this epochal moment we cannot know, but it is certain that a portion of popular American culture ran contrary to the anti-Puritan sentiments of modernist writers.

In addition to the narrower path within Wilder's family and education,

---

33. Mencken quoted in John Bartlett, *Bartlett's Familiar Quotations,* 16th ed. (Boston: Little, Brown, and Co., 1992), 642.

34. "Plymouth Plans Celebration of the Landing of the Early New England Settlers," *New York Times,* June 25, 1916, sec. 2, 8; "Soon to Celebrate Pilgrims' Landing," *New York Times,* March 7, 1920, sec. 2, 4; "New Pilgrim Spirit to Lead World, Declares Harding," *New York Times,* August 2, 1921, 1, 2.

the continuity of the Puritan ethos and aesthetic followed a broader avenue within the American literary tradition. Although *The Pilgrim's Progress* is the only seventeenth-century Puritan narrative work it is certain that he read, some of the formal characteristics of Puritan writing that occur in Wilder's plays and novels are undoubtedly the result of indirect transmission through classic American literature. That is, Wilder may not have read New England Puritan histories or other narrative works, but he did read the literary works of nineteenth-century American authors who read the New England Puritans' histories and biographies, or who—by virtue of their closer proximity to the seventeenth and eighteenth centuries—inherited cultural aspects of Puritanism more directly than would a twentieth-century author. Therefore, an examination of Wilder's own scholarly view of American culture as exemplified by classic American authors and their works will further indicate how the Puritan ethos and aesthetic influenced him as an American playwright and novelist.[35]

Wilder's Reading of Classic American Literature

Choosing Wilder to be the Charles Eliot Norton Lecturer on American Literature at Harvard University during the 1950–51 academic year may have appeared curious to some, given that his most recent novel, *The Ides of March,* was set in ancient Rome, and his first three novels were seen as not concerned with American themes. However, his qualification for making pronouncements on American literature was earlier attested to by Archibald MacLeish, who wrote in a 1941 letter to the PEN congress, "No one can speak for American writers with more authority and understanding than Thornton Wilder."[36] During the year of the lectureship, if not before, he would undoubtedly have become aware of Harvard scholar Perry Miller's excavation of Puritanism in American intellectual and literary history; one could even imagine Wilder making the following continuity statement in deference to Professor Miller, who may well have been seated in the audience:

> The Americans who removed to this country, then, during its first century and a half had these characteristics in common. The conditions under which they lived and the institutions which they created engraved these characteristics still more deeply into their natures. . . . Those basic characteristics have had to suffer violent opposition. It is still a question whether many of them

35. Other studies of Wilder have made use of *American Characteristics and Other Essays* to support their interpretation of individual plays and novels and to illustrate his aesthetic (see, for example, Haberman, *Plays of Thornton Wilder,* and Kuner, *Bright and Dark*).
36. Burns et al., eds., *Letters of Stein and Wilder,* 296 n. 1.

may survive. The force and prestige of the original traits remained, however. One has the feeling that their expression—personal, social, and literary—has been driven underground. Perhaps they are so powerful that they will yet be able to furnish a framework—a religion, a social thought, and an art—within which an entire continent can understand itself as unity and as growth. (*AC,* 11–12)

In "Toward an American Language," the published version of one of his Harvard lectures, Wilder writes that those Europeans who settled in America during the seventeenth century all had one thing in common: "Their sense of identity did not derive from their relation to their environment" (*AC,* 10). He further notes, "This unrelatedness to place goes so deep that, in an Old-World sense, America can have no shrines. . . . Americans are abstract. They are disconnected. They have a relation, but it is to everywhere, to everybody, and to always" (*AC,* 15). This essential abstractness in the American psyche, according to Wilder, is related to other definitive American features:

Americans can find in environment no confirmation of their identity. . . . There is only one way in which an American can feel himself to be in relation to other Americans—when he is united with them in a project, caught up in an idea and propelled with them toward the future. There is no limit to the degree with which an American is imbued with the *doctrine of progress*. Place and environment are but decor to his journey. He lives not on the treasure that lies about him but on the promises of the imagination. "I am I," he says, "because my plans characterize me." Abstract! Abstract! (*AC,* 16–17, emphasis added)

Furthermore, because of the disconnectedness of time and place in the American psyche, "The only thing that can arrest the attention is the archetypical. . . . The central figure of the superior works of our literature is Everyman, and that for some time that will probably remain the literary objective" (*JTW,* 217).[37] As we will see in Chapter One, the New England Puritan aesthetic also focuses on the archetypal in both allegorical and typological representation. Seeking a unity of idea and form, Wilder conceived of an allegorical narrative to illustrate his points on American characteristics that would be inserted as interludes between the chapters of the published book

37. In *Contemporary Allegory,* Broussard argues that allegory is the definitive feature of modern American drama, and he discusses Wilder's work in support of his thesis; however, Broussard attributes American dramatists' use of allegory to the influence of European drama, rather than considering that American literature as a whole depends heavily on allegory, as F. O. Mathiesson, Richard Chase, Charles Feidelson, and Daniel G. Hoffman, among others, have observed in their studies of the American literary tradition.

of his Norton lectures; he called it, "The Life of Tom Everage, American." In the second episode, "He Aspires to Be a Reasoning Being," Wilder describes Tom's reflection on the cause of his suffering:

> When he fell down the front steps and was laid up for two weeks with water on the knee, he found the experience "trying," a real trial, and he did not contradict his wife when she said it was a "judgment on him." When he burned himself trying to repair the oven, it was a real "blow" to him. He consoled himself with the thought that no one "escapes" hard knocks and that these are "sent" to teach us patience and that it was a "mercy" that he had been "spared" a broken leg. This confusion was diffused throughout all his thinking. He ringingly told the Rotary Club that America had been blessed with three years of unprecedented prosperity (prolonged applause), though a few years later from the same banquet-table he deplored with his fellow members that our country had been the "victim" of unprecedented reverses. (*JTW*, 252–53)

In a 1931 interview Wilder seemed to uphold the beliefs he would later mock in "The Life of Tom Everage, American," claiming that every American has a

> sense of identity with destiny that has been born of Protestantism. I believe that the real Americanism which will be important in the future is belief in the significance and even in the concealed implications of every event. It is precisely the same thing as the much abused doctrines of predestination and inward asceticism. In daily life this belief sometimes takes well-known, grotesque forms, such as when the money that one has earned is looked upon as proof of God's mercy or justice. But that is only the ridiculous reverse side of a very deep and very fruitful life feeling. Just think what it means to every American to believe himself permanently, directly, and responsibly bound to world destiny.[38]

His irony notwithstanding, Wilder's parable—the purpose of which was to illustrate his thesis about the essential Americanness of Poe, Thoreau, Hawthorne, Melville, Whitman, and Dickinson—depicts the American Everyman's sensibility as strikingly similar to the way Puritans interpreted history and daily events as exhibiting God's "wonder-working providence." Wilder even incorporates the Puritan aversion to the theater in this American allegory:

38. Bryer, ed., *Conversations with Thornton Wilder*, 10. Lynen makes a similar comment about Taylor's perspective and American literature: "Edward Taylor seems to have understood, as Wigglesworth did not, that the predestination faith bore directly upon the nature of narrative. In *God's Determinations* he provides the first example in poetry of the rather special ways of manipulating time which would become characteristic of American narrative literature" (*Design of the Present*, 61–62).

Tom Everage "had also his peculiar detestations. He could not be persuaded to go to matinees at the theatre—they were filled with silly women (who should be at home where they belonged)" (*JTW*, 254). Wilder characterized his lectures as "Lay Sermons," acknowledging the American propensity for the production and consumption of didactic writing; his own literary works have been described by many scholars as, in effect, sermons.[39]

Another American characteristic identified by Wilder-the-scholar and practiced by Wilder-the-writer is "the postulated 'American' way of keeping one's eye, at the same moment, on the Most General and on the Particular" (*JTW*, 248). That is, Wilder sees American literary works simultaneously representing the macrocosmic and microcosmic levels or perspectives, as is the case with Taylor's *God's Determinations Touching His Elect*. Discovering the general or macrocosmic in the particular or microcosmic is a prevalent theme in Wilder's plays and novels, such as *Our Town* and *The Bridge of San Luis Rey*, as we shall see. In his scholarly writing it is also a method of support for his thesis on American characteristics. Performing a close reading of one page from *Moby-Dick*, Wilder demonstrates all the defining features of the American mind expressing itself, which he put forth in his first Norton lecture. For example, one of the American traits Wilder finds on that page of *Moby-Dick* resembles what the Puritans called plain style: "It is directed to a classless society—to Everybody. . . . There are not two doors for words in America, no tradesman's entrance: all can go in the front door. . . . The United States is a middle-class nation and has widened and broadened and deepened the concepts of the wide and broad and deep without diminishing the concept of the high" (*AC*, 26, 32). In other words, the objective of literary style is not to set itself off from common usage but to communicate clearly to all readers.

To review the American characteristics that Wilder derived from studying classic American literature, he cites the following features: abstractness, interest in the archetypal, allegory, a providential hermeneutic, faith in progress, didacticism, simultaneous focus on the general and the particular scales (macrocosm/microcosm), and "egalitarian" or middle-class language (plain style). The only aspect missing from how seventeenth-century New England Puritan narrative practice will be characterized in Chapter One is typology, which has only been identified and studied by scholars of early American literature in the past three decades. However, when Wilder notes that the colonists identified with biblical characters to the point of naming their children—and he might have said, their literary characters—after them, he comes close to recognizing typology as an American characteristic as well (*AC*, 18). Wilder also commented elsewhere on this naming practice within

39. See, for example, Haberman, *Plays of Thornton Wilder*, 28, and Ethan Mordden, *The American Theatre*, 200.

his own family: "We Calvinists from New England (the thirteen original colonies) have always been strongly influenced by the Old Testament. . . . We take names from the Old Testament: my father's name is Amos; and my brother, who is studying theology, also is named after that old prophet."[40]

Of course none of these traits is exclusive to either Puritan or American narrative works, but the combination of these characteristics existing typically in New England Puritan works and in Wilder's works does suggest a continuation of an aesthetic based on Puritanism within the larger American literary tradition. As stated earlier, this is not to say that all American literature fits this description or that the American literary tradition is synonymous with the Puritan tradition. One could not make the continuity argument with narrative works by more pessimistic nineteenth-century writers working from an aesthetic of realism or naturalism (for example, Mark Twain or Stephen Crane). Furthermore, the characteristics listed can be found individually in other twentieth-century writers of narrative, whether in drama or fiction, but with no other American author do they exist coextensively and in so pure a form as they do in Wilder's oeuvre.

Again, it is probable that most of the features of Puritan narrative that we will find in Wilder's plays and novels are there unintentionally; that is to say, he made use of them unconsciously as he wrote. However, because there is strong evidence that Wilder thought of the Puritans as the first chapter in the American story, it is not impossible that he consciously appropriated some aspects of Puritan theology, ideology, and aesthetics. Some of the most explicit evidence for Wilder's thinking about America in Puritan terms will be examined in Chapter Two, but one document in his unpublished papers at the Beinecke Library will suffice as support here. In a typed manuscript of a screenplay titled "The Melting Pot," the opening shot description reads, "View of New England Coast, as seen from the air. A wilderness." The camera shows the audience Indians, then crosses the Atlantic and shows "Thames Valley 1620," one character asking another, "Brother Wilkins, will ye remove with us?" Another shot description reads, "The following scenes are to remind the viewers pictorially of the locations and groupings shown earlier of the Puritan fathers in the Thames Valley sequence." Later in a montage to show American history passing, one shot shows a cradle with "Thomas Weston, Plymouth 1640" on it; another shot shows a gravestone that reads "Maria Weston born 1642 Plymouth died 1651 Boston." That Wilder thought of the Puritan migration not only as the genesis of American culture but as continuing to be the paradigm of what it means to be American (at least in his time) is evident in this attempt to formulate the quintessence of America for his book based on the Norton lectures:

40. Bryer, ed., *Conversations with Thornton Wilder,* 57.

[Americans] are very busy doing something of great importance. . . . It is not easy to be an American because the rules aren't made yet; the exemplars are not clear. It is like leaving the Known and Comforting and *crossing an ocean* into a trackless *wilderness* in which one must gradually set up a form of government and one must decide what should be taught in the schools and one must *build a church*. And one can't rely very much on those one knew before—over there, because, for us, those weren't quite right.[41]

What is important about Wilder's American literature scholarship for the purposes of this study is that his description of the distinguishing characteristics of American literary expression are almost identical to the description of the Puritan narrative aesthetic in Chapter One; furthermore, these descriptions apply equally well to Wilder's own plays and novels. It is reasonable to conclude, then, that Wilder absorbed from his reading of classic American literature concepts and structures stemming from seventeenth- and eighteenth-century Puritan writing that he would later express as a twentieth-century American author and scholar. This is too indirect an influence to argue that Wilder borrowed from the Puritans, but in combination with the infusion of a residual Puritan ethos and aesthetic in American culture, and his own family heritage, it is not at all surprising that certain characteristics of Wilder's plays and novels so strongly resemble those of works by New England Puritan writers like Edward Taylor, Michael Wigglesworth, and Joseph Morgan. We will see that throughout his writing career, beginning in the 1920s and lasting till just before his death in 1975, Thornton Wilder's drama and fiction manifest remarkably specific traces of New England Puritan theology, ideology, and aesthetics. This will not only further our understanding of the literary potential of Puritanism, but it will also contribute to the ongoing reexamination of American literature and how much Puritanism has contributed to it. Furthermore, that the Puritan tradition has had a significant influence on the way a twentieth-century dramatist wrote his plays indicates that a closer relation exists between American drama and the American literary tradition than is generally perceived.

Chapter One's review of the major studies of Puritanism and its literary legacy by early American literature scholars, as well as an analysis of Taylor's *God's Determinations Touching His Elect* for its manifestation of Puritan theology and ideology and its representativeness of the Puritan aesthetic, will provide the necessary background for examining Wilder's drama and fiction as products of latent Puritan content and forms in American literature and culture.

41. Harrison, *Enthusiast,* 280 (emphasis added).

One

The First City

The Continuity of Puritanism in American Culture and Literature from Taylor to Wilder

The American Revolution may be seen as a political Great Awakening in which the people were reconverted to their national mission, expressed in an amalgam of religious and political terms. In so recasting the Puritan vision, the leaders of the Revolution played an important part in the process of transmission in which we may discover the continuity of American Puritanism and nineteenth-century American thought and writing. They preserved the Puritan vision of the city on the hill and the garden in the wilderness and refined the Puritan idiom for use by later orators and politicians. It is to this recognizable transmission of Puritan habits of thought and psychological response that such writers as Hawthorne, Melville, Twain, and James reacted and which continues to fascinate American writers in our own century.

—Emory Elliott, *Puritan Influences in American Literature*

Near the beginning of his last novel, *Theophilus North,* Thornton Wilder's alter ego and narrator expresses a peculiar way of conceptualizing his surroundings:

One of my discarded ambitions had been to be an archaeologist; I had even spent the large part of a year in Rome, studying its methods and progress there. But long before, like many other boys, I had been enthralled by the great Schliemann's discovery of the site of ancient Troy—those nine cities one on top of the other. In the four and a half months that I am about to describe

I found—or thought I found—that Newport, Rhode Island, presented nine cities, some superimposed, some having very little relation with the others— variously beautiful, impressive, absurd, commonplace, and one very nearly squalid. (14)

In Theophilus's subsequent explanation, three of the cities are identified with historical periods: the first city with the seventeenth century, the second city with the eighteenth century, and the fifth city with the nineteenth century. The other six cities are defined by class or occupation (rich, middle class, military base, seaport, servants, parasites), which have existed from earlier times up to the twentieth century (14–16). In the course of the novel, North has adventures in all nine of Newport's cities.

The trip to Rome Theophilus refers to was straightforward autobiography on Wilder's part. Before beginning his career as a teacher and a writer, Wilder participated in an archaeological dig in Rome and was transformed by the experience: "Once you have swung a pickax that will reveal the curve of a street for thousand years covered over which was once an active, much-traveled highway, you are never quite the same again."[1] This now-famous anecdote has been cited in virtually every book-length study of Wilder's plays and novels as an illustration of the dominant theme of his works: the time-lessness of the essential human condition. However, an archaeological dig serves equally well as a metaphor for this study's attempt to uncover the legacy of seventeenth-century New England Puritan narrative in a twentieth-century writer's plays and novels. Given the impression that the early archaeological experience had on him, it seems that Wilder would almost certainly have approved of a study that seeks to "unearth" in his works the remains of an earlier culture's beliefs and the characteristic forms with which those beliefs were expressed. This is the first study to excavate the American "First City" in the Wilder canon.

From Winthrop to Wilder:
The Continuity between the Seventeenth and Twentieth Centuries

In naming the collection of his earlier studies of Puritanism *Errand into the Wilderness* (1956), Perry Miller was not only observing but also contributing to the continuity of a Puritan ethos in American culture. His work spawned three decades of further studies of the seventeenth- and eighteenth-century

1. The version quoted here appears in Richard Goldstone's interview of Wilder in *Writers at Work: The "Paris Review" Interviews,* ed. Malcolm Cowley (New York: Viking, 1958), 113.

New England Puritan antecedents of nineteenth-century American literature.[2] In his essay "From Edwards to Emerson," Miller suggested that the errand or mission the Puritan immigrants enacted was not only into a
geographical unknown; it was also into a temporal unknown: the future. The
colony they built did not survive as the Puritan utopia their leaders, at least,
had intended it to be, but their efforts have had far-reaching and long-lasting
effects on the development of American culture and especially American literature. A cursory examination of contemporary American culture reveals a
variety of signs that attest to the Puritans' commitment to the errand and
the effectiveness with which they established their ideology on a societal
level. Vestiges of Puritan beliefs, lifestyles, institutions, and writing include
Thanksgiving Day pageantry; the "Pilgrims"; an automobile named the
"Plymouth Voyager"; a moving company called "Mayflower"; stark white
church buildings; churches called the Congregational Church; cities and
towns named "Providence," "Newark" (i.e., New Ark of the Covenant), and
"New Canaan"; the phrase "city on a hill"; Marilynne Robinson's novels
and her jeremiad-like collection of essays *The Death of Adam,* and so forth.

The advent of interdisciplinary approaches to the study of literature has
helped scholars make an even stronger case for the existence of a cultural
continuum between the seventeenth-century Puritan writers and nineteenth-
even twentieth-century American writers. Borrowing terminology and ana-
lytical methods from such fields as linguistics, anthropology, political theory,
psychology, and sociology, contemporary scholars regard literary works primarily as cultural artifacts that reflect the prevailing paradigms and structures of the time in which they were written. In the past three decades, major
studies of the American literary tradition by such scholars as Sacvan Bercovitch, Emory Elliott, Mason Lowance Jr., Larzer Ziff, Karl Keller, Perry
Westbrook, Patricia Caldwell, William H. Shurr, John Lynen, Andrew Del-
banco, and others have established that a line of literary influence runs from
the Puritan texts written in the seventeenth and early eighteenth centuries
through the political rhetoric of the revolutionary period to nineteenth-century
romanticism and transcendentalism, extending even into the twentieth century. As Sacvan Bercovitch, the preeminent scholar of New England Puritan
literature since Perry Miller, has said, "The fact is that the Puritan vision
survived the demise of the church-state . . . from Puritan colony to Yankee
province . . . from ante-bellum America to the Gilded Age of reconstruction,
industrialization, incorporation, and the Dynamo. . . . New England retained

2. New England Puritanism was examined in depth, virtually for the first time, by
Perry Miller in his seminal works *Orthodoxy in Massachusetts* (1933), *The New England Mind:
The Seventeenth Century* (1939), and *The New England Mind: From Colony to Province* (1953).

its mythic status as the origin of American identity (long after the region had lost its national importance)."[3] These scholars have successfully argued that the traditional view of American literature—that it began in the early nineteenth century when Charles Brockden Brown, Washington Irving, and James Fenimore Cooper were self-consciously attempting to give birth to a new literature for a new nation—is inaccurate.

Bercovitch and other authors of studies of the Puritan legacy in American culture and literature do not limit their findings to expressions of the Puritan ethos; they also demonstrate that the shapes those expressions take are inherited from the Puritans. That is, if every force evolves a form, it is primarily the forms of Puritan belief that have been transmitted through three centuries of American cultural history, as John F. Lynen explains:

> The Puritan quality that has persisted in American literature, even to our time . . . had best be called a habit of mind. . . . So conceived, the habit of mind is not the content of experience but its form and condition. . . . No doubt the habit of mind and the theology grew up together, each fostering the other, but it is the habit of mind that has proved more fundamental, since it has persisted long after the doctrines of Puritanism have lost their authority. Because it is less than a religion, is merely a *form* of consciousness, it has been able to accommodate itself to altered subject matter.[4]

According to Bercovitch, the survival of Puritan elements in American culture is no accident: "The point was not just to arouse the sons to emulate the fathers, but to assert progress through continuity." One of the major institutional means of maintaining that continuity was higher education, as Baltzell has noted: "The cultural hegemony of the natives of Massachusetts and their descendants in Connecticut, New York, and Ohio can be traced to the original Puritan attitude toward education." Many writers, ministers, teachers, and professors have gone to Harvard, the first American college established by the Puritans. A number of major theater and literary critics attended Harvard—Norman Hapgood, Walter Prichard Eaton, John Corbin, John Mason Brown, Robert Benchley, and Brooks Atkinson. But Harvard was not the only institution of higher education founded or influenced by the Puritans: "In addition to Harvard and Yale, Dartmouth (1769), Williams (1785), Bowdoin (1794), Middlebury (1800), and Amherst (1821) all stemmed from Congregationalist groups (the successors of the Puritans)."[5]

---

3. Bercovitch, "The Modernity of American Puritan Rhetoric," 62.

4. I owe the connection of this American proverb to thinking about aesthetics to Guy Davenport's essay of that title; see Guy Davenport, *Every Force Evolves a Form: Twenty Essays* (San Francisco: North Point Press, 1987). Lynen, *Design of the Present: Essays on Time and Form in American Literature,* 29–30.

5. Bercovitch, *The American Jeremiad,* 71; E. Digby Baltzell, *Puritan Boston and Quaker*

As Emory Elliott explains, education, religion, and literature were parallel avenues along which traces of Puritanism traveled:

> In Connecticut, religious disputes and a reluctance to depend upon Harvard for their ministers led a conservative group who shared many of the positions of the Mathers to found Yale College, from which Jonathan Edwards (1703–58) graduated in 1720. Most scholars agree that, with many qualifications over finer points of theology, a line of theological tradition can be traced from Leverett's liberal Harvard through the Universalism of Chauncy to the Unitarianism of William Ellery Channing and the Transcendentalism of Ralph Waldo Emerson. On the other side, from Edwards's Yale, an opposing evangelical, and eventually fundamentalist, tradition evolved, which can be traced down to Timothy Dwight and Lyman Beecher in the nineteenth century and to many kinds of religious enthusiasts in the twentieth.[6]

Elsewhere Elliott writes, "Even though the theology had become diluted in the eighteenth century, these ideas and images were transmitted throughout the colonies by the itinerant preachers who struck out from Princeton and the other Presbyterian colleges to carry this vision to the back country of the South and the West."[7]

The use of Puritan aesthetics by later American writers can be accounted for in a number of ways. As in any national or other tradition, the next generation of authors will mine the previous generation's literary works for useful materials and techniques: "For the rhetoric survived, finally, not by chance but by merit, because it was compelling enough in content and flexible enough in form to invite adaptation." Or, impelled by an "anxiety of influence," as Harold Bloom calls it, to break with the literary past, authors may reproduce the style of predecessors even in the act of parodying or arguing against the old school. However, much of the continuity between the literary styles of intelligent, educated writers of different generations is not a matter of self-conscious borrowing, as Kenneth B. Murdock explains:

> The point is not that the later American artist has consciously chosen the New England colonists as literary masters, but that at times certain of their stylistic habits fixed in New England books and speech have served him well when moral or religious issues have stirred him to an ardor comparable to theirs. Any reader who turns from [*The Education of Henry Adams*] or to the journals of

---

Philadelphia: Two Protestant Ethics and the Spirit of Class Authority and Leadership, 35n; Denise Lardner Carmody and John Tully Carmody, *The Republic of Many Mansions: Foundations of American Religious Thought,* 42.

6. Elliott, "New England Puritan Literature," 282.
7. Elliott, "The Puritan Roots of America Whig Rhetoric," 108.

Emerson or Thoreau or Hawthorne recognizes that there is a link between nineteenth century New England and the New England of the Puritans.[8]

While scholars have demonstrated the contribution of the Puritan jeremiad to the political writings of the eighteenth century,[9] most studies of the legacy of New England Puritanism in the American literary tradition have focused their attention on the classical American authors of the nineteenth century: "If the origins of American poetry are involved in the life and death of the Puritan imagination, then its first great period, in the nineteenth century, is truly an American Renaissance." Nathaniel Hawthorne is the obvious example of a nineteenth-century writer directly influenced by and consciously appropriating seventeenth-century Puritan culture, and Emerson and Thoreau—and the transcendentalist movement overall—are sometimes described as the heirs of New England Puritans' providential reading of history, the New World, and daily events. Melville, Dickinson, Whitman, James, and even Poe have been placed within a Puritan literary tradition operative in nineteenth-century culture and literature. As Karl Keller succinctly puts it, "Whatever a writer like Emily Dickinson was thinking in the middle of the nineteenth century, there was a metastructure that was thinking her." Keller and the other early American literature scholars cited here have successfully argued that the nineteenth-century metastructure "thinking" major American authors was imbued with New England Puritanism (along with other influences, e.g., Enlightenment thinking and rhetoric).[10]

Once traces of Puritan themes and forms have been detected in works of American literature in the nineteenth century, "finding evidence of these in-

8. Bercovitch, *The Puritan Origins of the American Self,* 153. A common enough example of "patricidal" parody is Mark Twain's pervasive use of romantic elements in his satire against a cultural and literary romanticism in *Huckleberry Finn;* see Richard Chase, *The American Novel and Its Tradition* (Garden City, N.Y.: Doubleday & Co., 1957). Murdock, *Literature and Theology in Colonial New England,* 185.

9. As Bercovitch explains in *American Jeremiad,*

> By all accounts, the jeremiad played a central role in the war of independence, and the war in turn confirmed the jeremiad as a *national ritual.* The Whig sermons and tracts express a rite of passage into nationhood, an official coming-of-age ceremony, which had long been in rehearsal. . . . As the Whig Jeremiads explained it, independence was not the spoils of violence, but the harvest of Puritanism. It was not some sudden turbulent challenge to the system, but the consummation of a process of uprising that began aboard the *Mayflower* and *Arabella* and matured in the struggles of 1776. (132)

See also David Minter, "The Puritan Jeremiad as Literary Form," 45–55.

10. Roy Harvey Pearce, *The Continuity of American Poetry,* 19; Keller, *The Only Kangaroo among the Beauty: Emily Dickinson and America,* 49. For in-depth studies of the Puritan structures underlying classic American literature, see, especially, Mason Lowance, Jr., *The Language of Canaan: Metaphor and Symbol in New England from the Puritans to the Transcendentalists,* and Bercovitch, *Puritan Origins.*

fluences in later American writing, even in mid-twentieth century literature, is not difficult"; however, Lowance, Bercovitch, and others have not presented such evidence, apart from brief discussions in the introductions or conclusions of their studies. Faulkner and Frost are cited as examples of twentieth-century writers influenced by Puritanism by Lowance; Wallace Stevens by Lynen; F. Scott Fitzgerald, Ernest Hemingway, Norman Mailer, and James Baldwin by Elliott. That these scholars do not go beyond merely asserting that some features of Puritan writing reach into the twentieth century is perhaps explained by the fact that all of them specialize in early American literature, not twentieth-century literature. A defense of the continuity argument requires knowledge of the specific features of texts on both ends of the continuum. Where it can be proven that a twentieth-century writer read the works of Hawthorne, Melville, Dickinson, and other nineteenth-century figures, the historical chain has been established. In other words, classic American literature of the nineteenth century functions as the link between the seventeenth century when Puritanism flourished in New England and the twentieth century in which the Puritan legacy has diminished in its constitution of the American character due to the infusion of other influences, including those from non-European and nonwestern cultures. Thus, as Perry Miller writes in support of his thesis in "From Edwards to Emerson," "We do not need to posit some magical transmission of Puritanism from the seventeenth to the nineteenth century"—or, in the case of Thornton Wilder, from the seventeenth to the twentieth century.[11]

The Force that Evolved the Form:
New England Puritan Theology and Ideology

Space does not permit a delineation of all the complexities of Puritan doctrine, social organization, and literature or other writing meticulously analyzed in Perry Miller's exhaustive studies or in the works of scholars who have followed in his footsteps; but a summary of the major tenets of New England Puritanism and a demonstration of their literary expression in Edward Taylor's *God's Determinations Touching His Elect*[12] will serve as a touchstone for the subsequent analysis of Wilder's drama and fiction.

11. Lowance, *Language of Canaan*, 8–9; Lynen, *Design of the Present*, 15–17; Elliott, *Puritan Influence*, xii–xiii; Miller, *Errand into the Wilderness*, 200.

12. The full title is *God's Determinations Touching His Elect: AND The Elects Combat In Their Conversion, AND Coming Up to God In Christ: TOGETHER WITH The Comfortable Effects Thereof*. My practice in quoting seventeenth- and eighteenth-century texts will be to leave spelling and grammar as they appear in the published editions. The only correction made according to modern convention is the insertion of the possessive apostrophe in *Gods* of Taylor's title. Edward Taylor, *The Poetical Works of Edward Taylor*.

The most fundamental thing to understand about the Puritans is that they were Calvinists; as the Carmodys succinctly note, "John Calvin was the theological father of the Puritans." But it wasn't just the Puritans who followed the teachings of Calvin; Perry D. Westbrook explains that "American theology, for the first 250 years at least, was constituted overwhelmingly of Reformation theology. Hence, American concepts of the will were those of the Reformers, especially John Calvin, whose doctrines are basic to the Puritan, the Presbyterian, the Dutch Reformed, and even the Anglican sects—in other words, the denominations adhered to by the vast majority of early colonists in British America."[13]

According to Randall Stewart, Calvinism may be summarized by five essential points of doctrine: 1) election or predestination, 2) limited atonement, 3) total depravity, 4) irresistibility of grace, and 5) perseverance of the saints. The potential for a tragic vision of life is inherent in any philosophical system in which large forces determine the fate of individuals, groups, classes, or species, but in the case of Puritanism, predestination was a pessimistic doctrine only for those who were "reprobate" rather than "elect"—that is, those predestined by God for damnation in hell rather than salvation in heaven. The Puritans believed that as a group they were part of providential history controlled by a benevolent but sovereign God who had chosen them for "an errand into the wilderness." Thus, as Miller says, "Cosmic optimism [was] the indispensable premise of all Puritan belief." That is, while they saw damnation for the majority of the human race as a given, they were optimistic in their belief that as a distinct part of the body of Christ they were destined for heaven and would prosper on earth as long as they adhered to God's will. In his examination of cosmic optimism as an American nineteenth- to early twentieth-century worldview, Frederick William Conner writes, "The Puritan version of the tradition has importance here, however, not merely as an interesting native analogue but because the Puritans, in contrast to the general drift of eighteenth-century deism, deduced the goodness of the creation from the goodness of God rather than the reverse. Many of the nineteenth-century writers to be examined below will be found to be in either explicit or implicit agreement with this position." The nineteenth- and early twentieth-century poets Conner analyzes in relation to this tradition include Emerson, Poe, Whitman (the high point of cosmic optimism, according to Conner), Bryant, Longfellow, Lanier, Lodge, Moody, and Robinson. Where the New England Puritans exhibited doubt and darkness was on the individual level, as we shall see below with Taylor's *God's Determinations*.

---

13. Carmody and Carmody, *Republic of Many Mansions,* 19; Westbrook, *Free Will and Determination in American Literature,* 2.

The idea of the Puritans as a community manifesting cosmic optimism runs contrary to the popular image of grim-faced Puritans disdaining pleasure, but in their writing there is no shortage of affirmation, rejoicing, and thanksgiving.[14]

The different histories of Puritanism in England and America have resulted in different legacies in British and American literature—both in the degree of influence and the specific beliefs and forms of expression transmitted. It must be remembered that in England Puritanism entered a long and complex tradition of Christian beliefs and British culture. In the United States, Puritanism is the *beginning* of Christian beliefs and, to a large extent, American culture. One important distinction between the English and American versions of Puritanism is Covenant theology: "Only a restricted group even of English Puritans concentrated their thinking upon it. . . ; the New England leaders were all pupils, friends, or disciples of those who formulated it. Consequently, the intellectual history of New England must commence with some notice of these covenant or, as they were then called, 'federal' theologians." Covenant theology was the doctrinal way that Puritans found to get around the implacability of God's determination of every soul's eternal destiny. Miller explains Covenant theology in legalistic terms: "By the word 'covenant' federal theologians understood just such a contract as was used among men of business, a bond or a mortgage, an agreement between two parties, signed and sworn to, and binding upon both. . . . The federal theology appropriated this concept and fastened it upon both God and man." The even more liberal "Half-Way Covenant" of 1662 is also a New England Puritan development. In brief, half-way members were Puritan men or women who had not publicly testified to the experience of converting grace in their lives, which would signify their status as elect and thus entitle them to full participation in the devotional practices of the church.[15]

---

14. Stewart, *American Literature and Christian Doctrine,* 11; Miller, *Seventeenth Century,* 208; Conner, *Cosmic Optimism: A Study of the Interpretation of Evolution by American Poets from Emerson to Robinson,* 375, 92, 6, 135. Granted, there was a spiritual "epidemic" between 1674–75 and the mid-1680s of communal fear and insecurity that God may be withdrawing his covenant with New England. The King Phillips War, the coming of the royal governor, and various natural disasters gave rise to the jeremiads by Increase Mather and others that express anxiety and doubts about backsliding and God's wrath. Ultimately those sermons call for the people to reform and regain God's favor, but many diaries and public rhetoric do express a level of pessimism in that period, which is then transformed to hope again in the 1680s by the more positive sermons of Samuel Willard, Cotton Mather, and others. See Emory Elliott, *Power and the Pulpit in Puritan New England* (Princeton: Princeton University Press, 1975).

15. Miller, *Seventeenth Century,* 366, 375–76, 379: "They achieved this remarkable feat without dethroning His omnipotence, without circumscribing His sovereignty, by the

The single most important aspect of New England Puritanism for the development of American culture in general and American literature in particular is typology. For the Puritans, typology was a biblical hermeneutic, a theory of history, a protonationalist ideology, and an important component of their de facto literary aesthetic. While typology was not a Puritan invention, they raised it to a superior position over allegory as a way to read the Bible, which led the New England Puritans to develop a conceptualization of history that is especially important to understanding American culture, as Emory Elliott explains:

> What makes the function of typology in early American thought and writing unusual, if not unique, is, however, that the special experiences of the New England Puritans seem to have provided a remarkable continuous analogy of biblical events: Thus, in the imaginations of seventeenth-century American preachers and writers, typological interpretations of scripture provided a basis for shaping a powerful cultural vision.[16]

According to this view of history, the New England Puritans could make a much stronger case than could English Puritans that they were God's new Israelites, instructed to cross a new Red Sea (the Atlantic Ocean) to escape the persecution of a new pharaoh (William Laud, archbishop of the Anglican Church) and take possession of a new promised land (America). Bercovitch explains that in *Magnalia Christi Americana* Cotton Mather "proclaims the forward movement of redemptive history. As the representative of theocracy, the Hebrew stands not with but behind the Puritan." Furthermore, the linkage of an Old Testament type and a New England antitype (the ultimate expression of the type) could be quite specific: "The next generation . . . could sanctify Winthrop as the New England Moses—or the American Nehemiah . . . and John Cotton as the American Abraham, Joshua, and John the Divine combined." This typological identification with the Old Testament Israelites was a point frequently made in the sermons, the histories, and even in spiritual autobiographies and conversion narratives.[17]

---

plausible device of attributing the instigation of the deal to Him." On the crisis of declining membership in Puritan congregations during the latter part of the seventeenth century and the attempted solution the Half-Way Covenant represents, see, for example, chapter seven, "Half-Way Measures," in Miller, *From Colony to Province,* and Robert G. Pope, *The Half-Way Covenant; Church Membership in Puritan New England* (Princeton: Princeton University Press, 1969).

16. Elliott, "From Father to Son: The Evolution of Typology in Puritan New England," 204–5.

17. Bercovitch, *Puritan Origins,* 55; Bercovitch, "Modernity," 54. See also Bercovitch, *Puritan Origins,* 117, and Kenneth B. Murdock, "Clio in the Wilderness: History and Biography in Puritan New England," 211–15.

As a structural paradigm, typology—whether applied to the Old and New Testaments of the Bible or American history or literature or an individual's life—is both cyclical and linear, both archetypal and progressive: "The image in the mirror of providence revealed the cyclical pattern which linked all selves and circumstances despite their apparent variety. The image in the mirror of redemption was dynamic, progressive, and variegated, reflecting the different stages of the evolution of the church." Consequently, the concept and the word "progress" became the linchpin of Puritan conversion morphology, ideology, eschatology, and aesthetics. As Bercovitch notes, "And collectively, as the true church, the progress of Israel was as firmly assured as was the saint's stage-by-stage progress toward heaven." Many New England Puritans even believed that the divine plan had progressed to the point that they were literally laying the foundations of the New Jerusalem, as Karen E. Rowe explains: "This developmental pattern of progressively clearer dispensations provided the basis upon which New England Puritans claimed their covenant community as God's chosen successor to Israel and voiced their latter-day millennial prophecies." Consequently, Judgment Day was a favorite subject of Puritan writers and readers, as indicated by the enormous popularity of Michael Wigglesworth's *The Day of Doom* (1662), a Puritan epic dramatizing the second coming of Christ and separation of all souls into elect and reprobate, sheep and goats.[18]

This extension of typology from biblical hermeneutic to progressive theory of history also had ramifications for the political organization and operation of the colonies, especially the Massachusetts Bay Colony. Scholars disagree on the matter, but some believe that the Puritans hoped to establish a Holy Commonwealth and even a theocracy: political rule by church leaders. It is not difficult to find evidence that the Puritans thought of themselves as establishing a distinct community based on their beliefs. The first Governor of the Massachusetts Bay Colony, John Winthrop, expressed the Puritans' protonationalistic aspirations with a phrase that American political leaders have echoed through the centuries: "[M]en shall say of succeeding plantacions: the Lord make it like that of New England; for wee must consider that wee shall be as a City upon a Hill, the eyes of all people are upon us." Of course Winthrop is using a metaphor borrowed from the New Testament, but in other Puritan writing there are literal references to nationalist aspirations; for example, in Edward Johnson's history of the colony titled *Wonder-Working Providence of Sions* [Zion's] *Saviour:* "Proclaime to all nations, the neere approach of the most wonderfull workes that ever the

---

18. Bercovitch, *Puritan Origins,* 42, 55; Rowe, "Prophetic Visions: Typology and Colonial American Poetry," 49. For a brief discussion of *The Day of Doom*'s popularity, see Murdock, "Introduction" to Michael Wigglesworth, *The Day of Doom, Or A Poetical Description of the Great and Last Judgment, with other poems.*

Sonnes of men saw. Will not you believe that a Nation can be borne in a day? Here is a worke come very neare it" (61). At the very least, New England Puritans believed, based on Covenant theology and typology, that their colony was distinct from other colonies in the New World and that they had a special destiny in human history as designed by God.[19]

Of course there are other important particularities of New England Puritanism that could be discussed here, but focusing on the aspects mentioned above—Calvinistic predestination of the elect and reprobate, cosmic optimism, Covenant theology, typology, and progress on the personal, national, and cosmic levels—provides us with a working definition of the basic tenets of Puritanism that are relevant for this study of the Puritan traces in the life and literature of Thornton Wilder.

Edward Taylor's *God's Determinations:*
New England Puritanism in Dramatic Form

It is fortunate for the purposes of this study that there exists an example of a seventeenth-century literary work by a New England Puritan author that manifests the particular theology and ideology of the Puritans in the form of a play. Edward Taylor's works may not have had any direct influence on the American literary tradition, but his pastoral and poetic writing illustrate the cultural and literary forces that did contribute to the development of American literature, as suggested by Carol M. Bensick:

> Puritanism, let us say, as a 'problem' is a phenomenon of the nineteenth century rather than of the seventeenth. For this reason Edward Taylor's *God's Determinations Touching His Elect* is a useful document in the intellectual history of American literature. Not only is it a touchstone to Emily Dickinson, on the one side, and to the first generation Puritans, on the other; but it confirms the centrality of the particular "Varieties of Religious Experience" in America, witnessed personally by Edwards, Emerson, and Dickinson, and analyzed and dramatized by Hawthorne and Melville, James and Faulkner and their successors.[20]

19. Winthrop quoted in Harry R. Butman, *The Lord's Free People,* 100. In the introduction to his collection of New England Puritan Election Day sermons, Plumstead says that the Election Day sermon started as "a defense of theocracy" (A. W. Plumstead, *The Wall and the Garden: Selected Massachusetts Election Sermons, 1670–1775,* 7).

20. Bensick, "Preaching to the Choir: Some Achievements and Shortcomings of Taylor's *God's Determinations,*" 145. Taylor did not publish any of his poetry. The manuscripts of his literary writing were not discovered until 1937 in the Yale library. Since Thomas Johnson's publication of a selection of the papers under the title of *Poetical Works* in 1939, Taylor's reputation as a colonial poet has steadily increased with each new scholarly study.

She further comments on the representativeness of *God's Determinations:* "Taylor, who of course Hawthorne could not have read, confirms the accuracy of Hawthorne's subtle and sensitive analysis [of Reverend Dimmesdale in *The Scarlet Letter*]. What Hawthorne had to read thousands of pages by hundreds of hands to come to understand, we can glean from Taylor's poem alone."[21]

God's Determinations is comprised of thirty-six segments written entirely in verse (see Appendix for the titles of the segments). Some of these segments are in the form of dialogue and some are narration, which has led scholars studying Taylor's Puritan answer to *Everyman* to conclude that it is not a play. Regardless of which generic label is ascribed to it, *God's Determinations* is the New England Puritan literary work that comes the closest to what we think of today as fictional narrative. In addition to resembling the Medieval morality play *Everyman, God's Determinations* is also reminiscent of John Milton's epic *Paradise Lost* and John Bunyan's prose allegory *The Pilgrim's Progress.* Like those English Puritan works, *God's Determinations* tells a story that illustrates the author's religious beliefs, as Karl Keller writes: "In the case of Taylor, all his work is informed, even defined, by the Puritanism for which he gave the testimony of his life. He cannot be seen without it or outside it or beyond it or beneath it. It defines him, he defines it. Whatever form his speech may take, it derives from the language of that system. Whatever his delights and fears, they have their source in the Calvinist system of his belief." Undeniably, Taylor's work is telling a story; it thus can be analyzed as narrative, with characters, plot, and settings.[22]

Characters in Taylor's narrative include God; Satan; Christ; Justice; Mercy; Man; Soul; First, Second, and Third Ranks; and Saint. There is also a narrator for some of the poems that are narrative rather than lyrical. On the macrocosmic level, the plot of *God's Determinations* depicts, in order, God creating the universe, Man falling from grace and blaming it on his mate, the devising of a divine plan to redeem Man, Satan tempting and Christ encouraging the elect, and the elect making progress toward heaven as full members in the church. On the microcosmic level, Taylor dramatizes a Puritan Everyman ("Soul") seeking reassurance of his election. The setting is abstract throughout, but it ranges from the universe, heaven, and earth as a battlefield, and some unspecified place where Soul and Saint converse. The story Taylor is telling, then, is both macrocosmic and microcosmic, and as we shall see, it manifests the Puritan doctrines summarized above.[23]

21. Bensick, "Preaching to the Choir," 140.

22. Keller, *The Example of Edward Taylor,* 41. For a thorough examination of the generic status of Taylor's work, see my "Puritan Epic Theatre: A Brechtian Analysis of Taylor's *God's Determinations," Communications from the International Brecht Society* 19, no. 2 (1990): 58–71.

23. Bensick ("Preaching to the Choir," 139) claims "Soul is not Everyman" because conversion is not universal, but one could make the same point about Dante the charac-

The most explicit signifiers of the Puritans' Calvinistic beliefs in *God's Determinations* are the titles of the work overall and of the seventh segment ("The Frowardness of the Elect in the Work of Conversion"), both of which contain the word "Elect." There are also passages that express the idea that God determines who will be saved and who will not. For example, in addition to its title, the seventh segment suggests predestination in its opening lines: "Those upon whom Almighty doth intend / His all Eternall Glory to expend, . . ." (46). In "Christs Reply" to the elect who are doubting their election, he says, "I am a Captain to your Will; / You found me Gracious, so shall still, / Whilst that my Will is your Design" (51). Christ being captain to the elect's will also suggests the Calvinistic doctrine of irresistible grace, which is alluded to earlier in the play when Justice and Mercy each mention "Inherent Grace" (38) as they argue over what to do with fallen Man. Finally, in "The Second Ranke Accused," Satan recounts a number of biblical characters (e.g., Cain, Ahab, Judas) who were evidently ineligible for God's mercy: "Grace doom'd them down to hellish flames, although / To Court the same they steep't their Souls in woe" (68). While much of *God's Determinations* suggests that salvation is an open question, in these and other passages Taylor's Calvinism is evident.

The psychological effects of the epistemological problem of Calvinistic predestination—determining whether one's status is elect or reprobate—could be quite severe. For a series of segments beginning with "The Soule Bemoning Sorrow rowling upon a resolution to Seek Advice of Gods people" and concluding with "Difficulties arising from Uncharitable Cariages of Christians," Taylor brings the cosmic drama down to a singular representation of a Puritan believer who has been variously identified throughout the text as Soul, Mankind, Man, the elect, the saints, and First, Second, and Third Ranks. We see Soul tortured by an almost paranoid fear of falling into the trap of presuming he is elect, leading to a state of neurotic doubt and near-despair that can be overcome only by extensive persuasion from Saint, a representation of a Puritan minister. Early in *God's Determinations*, Taylor synthesizes personification allegory and an extended metaphor of military battle whereby Man is attacked by "Sin," "a thousand Griefs," and "Feare" (34), all of whom, along with God, have him surrounded so that "He knows not what to have, nor what to loose, / Nor what to do, nor what to take or

---

ter in *The Divine Comedy*, Everyman in the morality play, and Christian in *The Pilgrim's Progress*, works that are widely regarded as allegories of the human experience. Soul is not literally every person on earth, but he is every member of Taylor's congregation who had not become a full member; for its intended audience, then, Soul is every one of them. As Michael J. Colacurcio established in his article "*God's Determinations* Touching Half-Way Membership: Occasion and Audience in Edward Taylor," "The implied audience of the poem is precisely the half-way member of the Puritan congregation" (299).

Choose." He "runs like a Madman. . . . For Nature in this Pannick feare scarce gives / Him life enough, to let him feel he lives." Following a debate by Justice and Mercy, we next see Man "With Trembling joynts, and Quivering Lips" before the court of "Almighty" (34, 35). Thus Taylor depicts Soul's awareness of sin as an extreme state of fear and a paralyzing panic, which he seems helpless to escape.[24]

Whatever individual suffering may have been caused by the doctrine of predestination, for the New England Puritans as a whole it was ultimately a doctrine of hope of salvation because God had determined that they were destined for heaven—ergo, their cosmic optimism. Although much of *God's Determinations* dramatizes the pessimism of Soul in his various incarnations, he finally does attain an assurance of his election. As Bensick explains, "For *God's Determinations*—more than any generally known Puritan text—goes beyond merely showing that Puritanism didn't approve, let alone mandate, gloom."[25] Thus the tone of Taylor's play becomes jubilant, as in "The Effect of this Discourse upon the second and third Rancks":

RANK THREE
I strove to soar on high. But oh! methought
    Like to a Lump of Lead my sin
Prest down my Soul: But now it's off, she's Caught
    In holy Raptures up to him.
Oh! let us then sing Praise: methinks I soar
Above the stars, and stand at Heavens Doore. (99)

But in keeping with the Calvinistic doctrine of limited atonement, Taylor does not dramatize universal salvation in the triumphant ending in which the elect proceed to heaven:

Thus in Christs Coach they sweetly sing,
    As they to Glory ride therein.

24. Bensick explains how "crippling theoretical misconceptions were keeping Calvinists in unedifying and unproductive states of emotional paralysis" and more concretely observes that "the half-way member [i.e., Soul] is instructed to stop behaving as though he were Hawthorne's Goodman Brown." Later she connects this scene in *God's Determinations* with the American literary tradition: "The problem of counseling a victim of gloom is a significant theme in the literature of the American Renaissance. Taylor's Saint has secular progeny in Poe, as well as in Hawthorne and Melville. Saint's successors as would be therapists of gloom are the narrator in 'The Fall of the House of Usher' and George Herkimer in 'Egotism.' Kenyon in *The Marble Faun* might also be suggested" (Bensick, "Preaching to the Choir," 135–36, 144).
25. Ibid., 133.

Some few not in; and some whose Time and Place
  Block up this Coaches way, do goe
As Travellers afoot: and so do trace
  The Road that gives them right thereto;
  While in this Coach these sweetly sing,
  As they to Glory ride therein. (109)

The joyous tone of *God's Determinations* and other New England Puritan works stemmed from the understanding of the Covenant between the Puritans and God.

The most explicit reference to Covenant theology occurs near the end of *God's Determinations,* when the narrator describes the elect finally reaching assurance of election and thus eligibility for full membership in the church: "They now encovenant with God, and His; / Thus they indent / The Charters Seals belonging unto this, / The Sacrament" (104). Scholars acknowledged the presence of Covenant theology in *God's Determinations* long ago, but they detected it primarily in expository passages such as those quoted above and in legal metaphors. For example, Thomas Johnson writes that Taylor "did not purpose to give epic effects to Chaos, Heaven, and Hell, but to justify Covenant theology by way of poetic exposition in highly wrought imagery." An analysis of the plot structure of *God's Determinations* in dramatic terms demonstrates that Taylor did intend to give epic effects to Covenant theology, in part to justify it, but more importantly to reassure his half-way members of their election.[26]

In preparing to mount a production of a play, modern directors and actors break down the play's action into smaller units ("beats" being the smallest) by determining which characters embody the plot- or scene-driving volition. There are four major characters in *God's Determinations:* God (or Christ), Satan, Man (or Soul), and the narrator/speaker who strives to elevate his art to do justice to his theme. The segments in which these characters appear are organized sequentially into two large sections of supernatural and human actions, which thus might well be called "acts."[27] In the first act,

26. Johnson, "Preface" to Edward Taylor's *The Poetical Works of Edward Taylor,* 20. See also Nathalia Wright, "The Morality Tradition in the Poetry of Edward Taylor," 3, 12; Lynn M. Haims, "Puritan Iconography: The Art of Edward Taylor's *Gods Determinations,*" 85; and Keller, *Example of Edward Taylor,* 130, for discussions of Taylor's inspiration by Covenant theology and allusions to the doctrine in the text; however, in terms of emphasis, at least, Douglas Barbour ("*Gods Determinations* and the Hexameral Tradition," 215) and Colacurcio ("Touching Half-Way," 301) do not think the Covenant was of much concern to Taylor in composing *God's Determinations.*
27. While refusing to classify *God's Determinations* as literal drama, prior studies have divided its plot into acts. Norman Grabo (*Edward Taylor*) noted five acts, Haims ("Puritan

God (and his divine representatives Justice, Mercy, and Christ) battle with Satan for the soul of Mankind until Christ's final appearance "on stage" in the seventeenth segment, "Christs Reply," in which he exhorts Soul to "fight on" (64), and Satan's final speech in segment twenty, "The Third Rank Accused," in which he makes a last attempt to waylay Soul. Following this scene, there are no divine characters, either allegorical or literal, to urge Soul on, and there are no more external sources of temptation and doubt. What happens in the narrative from that point on results from Soul's volition (his desire for salvation and his nearly paranoid fear of presumption of election). Thus it can be argued that the second act begins with the very next segment, "A Threnodiall Dialogue between the Second and Third Ranks," but a more likely formal beginning of the second half of *God's Determinations* is segment twenty-four, "The Preface (To the Soul's Search)," in which Soul and Saint begin a long scene with several segments. Here there is no narrator, and the dialogue appears on the page in conventional play script format.

What previous readings of *God's Determinations* have failed to recognize is that this disjointed, seemingly haphazard construction of plot is Taylor's purposeful dramatization of Covenant theology in action; or, rather, the dichotomous structure of the action is itself a representation of New England Covenant theology as a conditional pact into which the elect enter with God. Arranging the divine characters' scenes earlier and the human characters' scenes later, Taylor dramatizes both God and the elect holding up their respective ends of the bargain, which is precisely how one Puritan understood Covenant theology: "that God had done His part and it was up to him now to do his."[28] By incarnating, as it were, the reassuring Covenant theology in which man's volition does play a part in election conditionally with God's will, the overall structure of *God's Determinations* offers the half-way members of Taylor's congregation the "ocular proof" that they can have assurance of their election and enter into full membership. In this respect, then, *God's Determinations* looks like what one would expect of a New England Puritan's attempt to write drama in accord with his doctrinal beliefs.

Given the epic scale of *God's Determinations,* one would expect to find indications of the typological linkage of biblical and New England historical events; however, apparently Taylor was not representative of New England Puritanism in this one important respect. According to the early American scholars who have published on Taylor, he did not agree with the liberalization of typology beyond a biblical context: "Where types have for Sewall historical

---

Iconography") four, and John Gatta, Jr. (*Gracious Laughter: The Meditative Wit of Edward Taylor)* three.

28. Quoted in Miller, *Seventeenth Century,* 387.

and political meaning, for Taylor they have personal meaning." Whether or not Taylor's use of typology is also an extension or broadening or recapitulating of the cyclical-but-progressive view of biblical history is a matter of interpretation, but Taylor's writing clearly manifests typological structures, as Bercovitch notes: "Taylor fuses typology and poetry, transforms hermeneutic into aesthetic."[29] *God's Determinations* dramatizes the history of the universe allegorically, the only way to represent this long and complex story without writing a massive chronicle of that history à la the Bible. Consequently there are no obvious indications of even orthodox typology—the progressive manifestation of Old Testament types to New Testament antitypes—except, perhaps, for the passage mentioned earlier in which Satan catalogued figures from the Bible who, according to him, were not imbued with inherent grace. The Old Testament and New Testament characters that together form a type and antitype are Cain (betrayer of his brother, Abel) and Judas (betrayer of Christ). But in the context of the passage (*GD,* 68) Taylor does not seem to be pointing up their typological relationship. However, there is one example of Taylor thinking in a typological way in *God's Determinations:*

> These are Gods Way-Marks thus inscrib'd; this hand
> 　　Points you the way unto the Land Divine,
> The Land of Promise, Good Immanuels Land,
> 　　To New Jerusalem above the line.
> 　　Ten thousand times thrice tribled blesst he is,
> 　　That walketh in the suburbs here of bliss. (97–98)

The Promised Land (associated with the Old Testament Israelites), Immanuel's Land (referring to Christ's time on earth: Immanuel—God with us), New Jerusalem (the culmination of history as prophesied in the New Testament book of Revelation), and suburbs of bliss (read, in relation to New Jerusalem, as Taylor's current time in which the millennium was believed to be imminent) are all metaphors, yet each vehicle of its tenor is time-specific, which is precisely the idea of a typological reading of the Bible or history: earlier events correspond to later, prophesied events.

While Taylor may not have accepted the extension of typology beyond the Bible to the events of his time, he did believe in New England Puritan eschatology—doctrine related to the end of history, the second coming of

29. Karl Keller, "'The World Slickt Up in Types': Edward Taylor as a Version of Emerson," 183; Bercovitch, *Typology and Early American Literature,* 6. See, also, Barbara Lewalski, *Protestant Poetics and the Seventeenth-Century Religious Lyric,* 407; Karen E. Rowe, *Saint and Singer: Edward Taylor's Typology and the Poetics of Meditation;* and Gatta, *Gracious Laughter.*

Christ, and Judgment Day—as suggested by the reference to New Jerusalem in the passage quoted above. Indeed there are references to Judgment Day itself in *God's Determinations*. Here, for example, Taylor employs a legal metaphor in the character Mercy's debate with Justice. In addition to alluding to Judgment Day, it also relates Mercy to Christ: "All this I'le do, and do it o're and o're, / Before my Clients Case shall ever faile. / I'le pay his Debt, and wipe out all his Score, / And till the *pay day Come,* I'le be his baile" (37, emphasis added). Thus, in contrast to Wigglesworth in *The Day of Doom,* Taylor predicts, rather than depicts, Judgment Day in order to warn the half-way members of his congregation.

Another manifestation of cosmic optimism in *God's Determinations* includes the multiple metaphors for spiritual progress Taylor uses. In writing *God's Determinations* with his congregation as audience, Taylor is so concerned that his half-way members not miss his point that he is not content to offer them one or two metaphors for spiritual progress; instead he employs nearly all of the figures typically used by the Christian poet of his time: winning a military battle, arguing a case in a courtroom, bringing guests to a feast in a coach, refinement of musical skill and instruments with which to praise God, and cultivating a garden.[30] Since all of the metaphors are eminently human activities, it would seem that Taylor's Calvinist doctrine did allow for reaching assurance of election. Choosing concrete images more for their analogous qualities to the spiritual life as Puritans understood it rather than for their ornamentation, he invites the individual half-way member to respond to whatever representation of spiritual progress will persuade her or him to become a full-fledged member of the church. He was saying, in effect, "Does it help you to comprehend reaching assurance of election as a courtroom debate and verdict? Or do you want to see it as winning a military battle? Or as an apprentice musician learning to play an instrument with which to praise God? As riding in a coach to a great man's feast? Perhaps as a flower growing? However you see it, just be sure you do see it and come into full membership." Taylor even seems to have rhetorically strategized for the more literal-minded of his half-way members, making his point about progress as the way to assurance of election by using the word itself within one of the metaphors: "Sure Grace a progress in her Coach doth ride" (99).[31]

30. For a catalog of metaphors for the spiritual life, see Lewalski, *Protestant Poetics,* 86–103.

31. Taylor scholars have viewed these extended metaphors of progress as an example of plain style: "In *God's Determinations,* however, Taylor very noticeably and significantly alters his usual handling of conceits. Relative to the rest of his poetry, the conceits of this poem are remarkably simple and thereby a further indication that Taylor here designs his imagery for the understanding of even the least sophisticated in his audience" (Daniel Patterson, *Edward Taylor's "God's Determination and Preparatory Meditations": A Critical Edition,* 16).

As we have seen, *God's Determinations* reflects the Puritan tenets identified in the previous section of this chapter. Furthermore, Taylor's morality play provides an example of what New England Puritanism in dramatic form looks like. But there are other aspects of form and style found in seventeenth-century Puritan narrative, including *God's Determinations,* and in classic American literature that we will also see in Wilder's drama and fiction nearly three centuries later.

God's Determinations and Puritan Narrative Aesthetics

New England Puritans wrote a variety of narrative works and also expository works that contained narrative. A short list of these in chronological order might include the following: *Of Plymouth Plantation* (1630–47) by William Bradford, *Wonder-Working Providence of Sions Savior* (1650–51) by Edward Johnson, *The Day of Doom* (1662) by Michael Wigglesworth, *God's Determinations* (ca. 1670) by Edward Taylor, *A True History of the Captivity and Restoration of Mrs. Mary Rowlandson* (1677) by Mary Rowlandson, *Magnalia Christi Americana* (1702) by Cotton Mather, *The Kingdom of Basaruah* (1715) by Joseph Morgan, and *Personal Narrative* (ca. 1740) by Jonathan Edwards. That most of these works would be classified today as nonfiction is a moot point: "It is quite true that the Puritans wrote no novels as such, but their histories and narratives of travel served them as novels and read today remarkably like fiction. The Puritan had developed the art of story-telling to a high degree." These writers, most of whom were ordained ministers, were not attempting to establish themselves as literary figures; instead, they were, for the most part, employing literary means to fulfill a spiritual need in their congregations or fellow colonists. The Puritan authors shared a worldview as members of a Christian sect and frontier experience as colonists; it is not so improbable, then, that they would arrive independently of one another at a more or less homogeneous aesthetic. A few studies of English and American Puritan writing have described some stylistic features of the Puritan aesthetic according to the various genres in which Puritan writers worked, though each scholar proceeds from a particular point of interest either too narrow or too broad for its schema to be imported in its entirety or exclusively into this study.[32]

32. Lawrence Willson, "The Puritan Tradition in American Literature," 38. For studies of some aspects of Puritan narrative, see Lynen, *Design of the Present;* Damrosch, *God's Plot and Man's Stories;* Peter Gay, *A Loss of Mastery: Puritan Historians in Colonial America;* Murdock, "Clio in the Wilderness"; and Daniel Shea, *The Spiritual Autobiography in Early America.* For studies of Puritan poetry, see Lewalski, *Protestant Poetics;* Peter White, *Puritan*

It is fairly evident that much of *God's Determinations* takes the form of argumentative debate. That is, the sections with Justice and Mercy in Almighty's court, Satan's accusations and the responses of Soul (in various forms), the debate between Second and Third Ranks over who needs grace more, and Saint's attempt to reassure Soul that he is one of the elect—all have two speakers of dialogue focusing on issues of doctrine. Yet the dialogue and narration are not limited to the rhetorical mode. *God's Determinations* imitates divine and human actions, and dramatic dialogue is the predominant vehicle for representing those actions.[33]

To begin with basic qualities of style and mimesis in Puritan narrative, Larzer Ziff focuses on the "characteristic combination of plainness, passion, and allegory [that] crystallized in the century 1560–1660 [and which] has ever since been a strong feature if not a separate tradition in our literature." Allegorical representation and passion (read *zeal*) for affirming their beliefs need no explanation, but "Puritan plain style" has become such a cliché in studies of Anglo-American writing that some clarification is warranted:

> To speak plainly was not primarily to speak simply, and not at all to speak artlessly. It meant speaking the Word—making language itself, as self-expression, an *imitatio Christi* because it conformed to scripture. . . . The plain stylist condemned eloquence for its own sake. He imitated the Bible's dovelike flights of language, as he imitated Christ, in order to efface the self, to sacrifice the polishings of "I" and "our" on the christic altar of scripture.[34]

In other words, plain style is plain in the sense of clear, easily understood; it does not require that writing be aesthetically unappealing. If the best way to communicate a point about doctrine was to employ a vivid metaphor, the Puritan writer would do that; if expository writing was the best way, the Puritan writer would do that. In *The Kingdom of Basaruah*, Joseph Morgan includes a definition of plain style in his first chapter: "The Laws were so plain

---

Poets and Poetics: Seventeenth-Century American Poetry in Theory and Practice; and Rowe, *Saint and Singer.* For studies of Puritan rhetoric and style, see Bercovitch, *Puritan Origins* and *American Jeremiad;* Lowance, *Language of Canaan;* and Patricia Caldwell, *The Puritan Conversion Narrative.* For some comments more generally on Puritan mimesis, see Cecelia Tichi, *New World, New Earth: Environmental Reformation in American Literature from the Puritans through Whitman,* and Sacvan Bercovitch, ed., *The American Puritan Imagination.*

33. Of the 2,132 lines in *God's Determinations,* 1,354 (or 64 percent) are in dialogue form, 320 (or 15 percent) are in monologue form (as invocation, prayer, and choral interlude), and 458 (or 21 percent) are the narrator's exposition of events. Undeniably, *God's Determinations* is an amalgamation, a pastiche of literary forms: drama, epic, lyric, allegory, and sermon, but as I argued in "Puritan Epic Theatre," the drama genre subsumes the others.

34. Ziff, "The Literary Consequences of Puritanism," 43; Bercovitch, *Puritan Origins,* 29–30.

and easie to be understood, that every Man might know them and keep them easily and perfectly to every *Punctilio*" (38). Studies of *God's Determinations* have described its verse and other aspects of composition so that we can conclude that Taylor wrote his play, like his meditations and sermons, in clearly understandable Puritan plain style, or a verse equivalent.[35]

Thus Puritan prose and poetry do contain beautiful descriptions and figurative language where appropriate, though they tend to get lost in the deluge of explanations of doctrine, interpretations of events, and so forth (after all, Puritan literature was, first and foremost, didactic). But the Puritans were against ornament for ornament's sake in their writing, just as they had attacked the formal embellishments of the Christian liturgy as practiced by both the Catholic and the Anglican churches. In fact, Puritanism originated as a protest over formal aspects of liturgy, but it evolved into a rigid iconoclasm. According to Horton Davies, some English Protestants were so iconoclastic that they even "desired to do away with all images of the Holy Trinity, the Incarnate Son of God, and the saints, as a breaking of the Second Commandment against 'graven images.'" Because the Puritans also viewed the Roman Catholic Church as the Antichrist and felt that the Anglican Church had maintained too many Catholic corruptions in its liturgy, they condemned virtually all representational elements in liturgy and worship, including the use of icons, stained glass windows, or paintings, as Thomas H. Luxon explains:

> Puritanism is obsessed with idolatry. It is an iconoclastic campaign against virtually every conceivable form of idol that insinuates itself into faith: in ritual, the surplice and the Mass; in hermeneutics, allegorical exegesis; in architecture, statues and rood-lofts; in church government, bishops, priests, or hierophants of any description; in private meditation; and in the "carnal" imagination itself, which clings perversely to those images of God forged by what Calvin called "a perpetual forge of idols"—"the human mind."[36]

This purgation of icons or imagery accounts for, to some extent at least, the abstractness of Puritan narrative, as well as the employment of allegory (as long as it was easily interpreted, as in *The Pilgrim's Progress*).

God's Determinations is, in part, a personification allegory in the tradition of *Everyman* and *The Pilgrim's Progress,* and allegory is inherently an abstract mode,

---

35. Patterson explains the concept in terms of the implied reader rather than as a style, explaining that in *God's Determinations* various modes "all contribute to the general homiletic design by conforming to the theory that words, images, and tropes must be intelligible to the understanding of the 'plain man'" (*Critical Edition,* 24). See also Alan MacGregor, "Edward Taylor and the Impertinent Metaphor," 342.

36. Davies, *Worship and Theology in England: From Cranmer to Hooker, 1534–1603,* 350; Luxon, *Literal Figures: Puritan Allegory and the Reformation Crisis in Representation,* 39–40.

but even those more famous allegories are not as schematic, rough, and disjointed as *God's Determinations.* The early critical assessment was that New
England Puritan poetry was amateurish, but more recent scholarship on
Puritan aesthetics has recognized that the roughness and plainness, as well
as the lengthy, abstract exposition, are deliberate, not compositional ineffec-
tiveness.[37] In fact, the relation of these formal characteristics to the themes
the Puritan writers were trying to convey is quite logical. The roughness of
form, for example, lends an unfinished quality to their art, which is a textual
manifestation of the Puritans' belief that the soul, history, and the universe
were unfinished; that is, everything is a work in *progress.*

Illustrating the abstractness and plainness of Taylor's allegory, the fourth
segment, "A Dialogue between Justice and Mercy," is a personification allegory of contradictory concepts within Christian doctrine (and perhaps within
the divine nature itself). Interestingly, their dramatization happens gradually, almost as if Taylor had to work his way up to mimesis even as abstract
as this. The narrator first introduces the characters Justice and Mercy at the
end of the third segment, "The Effects of Mans Apostacy," and then describes them entering the scene in a manner similar to stage directions; they
are given speeches with speaker tags in three stanzas at the beginning of the
scene (36), and finally rendered as speaking in alternating stanzas with character name headings, as in conventional play script format:

JUSTICE
I'le take thy Bond; But know thou this must doe:
   Thou from thy Fathers bosom must depart,
And be incarnate like a slave below,
   Must pay mans Debts unto [the] utmost marke
   Thou must sustain that burden, that will make
   The Angells sink into th' Infernall lake.
Nay, on thy shoulders bare must beare the Smart
   Which makes the Stoutest Angell buckling cry;
Nay, makes thy Soule to Cry through griefe of heart,
   ELI, ELI, LAMA SABACHT[H]ANI.

MERCY
All this I'le do, and do it o're and o're,
   Before my Clients Case shall ever faile.
I'le pay his Debt, and wipe out all his Score,
   And till the pay day Come, I'le be his baile. (37)[38]

---

37. See, for example, Lewalski, *Protestant Poetics;* Rowe, "Prophetic Visions"; and Haims,
"Puritan Iconography."

38. Although God is not represented anthropomorphically, Taylor foreshadows, per-

Because New England Puritan writing was utilitarian rather than aesthetic—that is, it could be considered quasiliterary as it was always first and foremost didactic—one finds in their works an overdetermination of important concepts. This overdetermination may take the form of mere repetition, as in Jonathan Edwards's sermon "Sinners in the Hands of an Angry God," or it might be that the same idea is expressed with multiple metaphors, as in *God's Determinations* and its various metaphors for spiritual progress. David Bevington explains that with the repetition of episodes in morality plays, "The hazard was monotonous elaboration, but the potential reward was a mounting persuasiveness through varied restatement of basic truths."[39] The bottom line for a Puritan writer, especially if he also happened to be a minister who wrote sermons weekly, was always that the audience not miss the point, even if that meant, in the case of narrative works, halting the narration of action for passages of doctrinal discourse, or making an urgent appeal directly to readers or listeners.

One example of where Taylor's play directly addresses its audience, thus calling attention to its own artifice à la epic theater or theatricalism, rather than disguising its artifice à la fourth-wall naturalistic theater, occurs near the end of "A Dialogue Between Justice and Mercy" as the allegorical figures shift their references to Man from third to second person. That is, suddenly they begin to address the "Humble and Haughty Souls" directly. Mercy says, presumably to the discouraged half-way members, "Though simple learn of mee; I will you teach / True Wisdom for your Souls Felicity." Justice adds, perhaps to those full members who presume their election, "You that Extenuate your sins, come see / Them in Gods multiplying Glass: for here / Your little sins will just like mountains bee," followed by this final tender appeal from Mercy: "My Dove, come hither, linger not, nor stay" (42). Is this just a slip of composition, Taylor lapsing momentarily into the direct address of the sermon, or is it the same kind of playing directly to the audience that occurs in such morality plays as *Everyman* and *Mankind*? Even in this episode, in which Taylor clearly is inventing a fictional action not directly adapted from the Bible, the Puritan doctrine and didactic purpose necessitate a disruption of the willing suspension of disbelief in order to bring about a more important belief in the audience.[40] Thus, when New England

---

haps similar to typology, that Mercy will indeed be incarnated in human form. Justice's line "ELI, ELI, LAMA SABACHT[H]ANI" is a quotation of Gospel accounts of Christ's crucifixion that is better recognized by its translation: "My God, my God, why hast thou forsaken me?" (Matt. 27:46, *KJV;* all subsequent biblical references are to the *KJV*). Taylor's implicit point seems to be that if Christ was the Word, that word is mercy.

39. Bevington, *From Mankind to Marlow: The Growth of Structure in the Popular Drama of Tudor England,* 4.

40. As Clark notes in his analysis of Puritan gravestone art, "The materiality of the

Puritan writers undertook mimesis, it mostly was abstract, self-reflexive, and didactic.

To move on to other aspects of the Puritans' narrative aesthetic illustrated in *God's Determinations,* the plot construction of New England Puritan histories or spiritual autobiographies was also a manifestation of doctrine, and Taylor's plotting was shaped by the ideas he was trying to convey, as was discussed earlier in relation to Covenant theology. His play begins with God's creation of the universe, Man's fall from grace, and his expulsion from the garden of Eden; in short, Taylor's narrative depicts the history of the universe created by God. The literary genre most associated with history is epic, as Leopold Damrosch Jr. notes: "Epic tends to confirm the order of history." Like any Puritan of higher education, Edward Taylor was familiar with examples of famous epics. The Puritans' progressive historical overview, which encompasses the major characters and action in *God's Determinations,* is in fact what gives epic totality to Taylor's Puritan "Epic Theatre."[41]

Furthermore, the plot of *God's Determinations* is structured according to the epic model, as defined in Aristotle's *Poetics.*[42] Aristotle frowned upon tragedies that employed the epic's multiple lines of action, claiming that single action plots in tragedies such as *Oedipus the King* are superior. It would be difficult to describe Taylor's play as having the strong central plot with a single protagonist characteristic of the dramaturgy of classical tragedy according to Aristotle. The plot of *God's Determinations* is comprised of four major actions initiated by four characters (thus four candidates for protagonist): one, God creates the universe and (assisted by his representatives Justice, Mercy, and Christ) salvages it after Man's fall; two, Satan tempts the elect away from Christ; three, the elect (Soul) seek assurance of election from the pious wise (Saint); and four, the narrator (an unidentified first-person voice that speaks the prologue and choral interludes, and narrates some of the action) strives to offer praise that does justice to God's greatness. None of these characters

---

sign must be recognized; otherwise, they are not signs." Clark, "The Honeyed Knot of Puritan Aesthetics," 74.

41. Damrosch, *God's Plot and Man's Stories: Studies in the Fictional Imagination from Milton to Fielding,* 119. Taylor's library contained a book cited as "Homer's Iliad" (*Poetical Works* 215). Although Gatta is more often demonstrating that the tone of *God's Determinations* rarely ascends to the lofty eloquence of the epic, he says his comic reading of *God's Determinations* "explains, for instance, why the poem seems on the one hand to follow the theme and design of the epic, even to the point of using extended Homeric similes" ("The Comic Design of *Gods Determinations touching his Elect,*" 139).

42. Although no direct evidence exists that Taylor read the *Poetics* specifically, it is reasonable to assume that he might have studied it along with Aristotle's other works while he was in school in England or America or both. See Donald E. Stanford's "Preface" to *The Poems of Edward Taylor,* xl–xli; Colacurcio, "Touching Half-Way," 313; and William Costello, *The Curriculum at Early Seventeenth-Century Cambridge,* 39, 63.

"holds the stage" long enough to unify the plot into one action. God and other divine agents exit after the seventeenth segment, "Christs Reply"; Satan enters in segment eight, "Satans Rage at them in their Conversion," and last appears in segment twenty, "The Third Rank Accused," obviously functioning as antagonist to God and his representatives; Soul metamorphoses into plurality after Saint's sermon in the twenty-ninth segment, "Difficulties arising from Uncharitable Cariages of Christians"; and though the narrator begins, interrupts, and ends *God's Determinations,* it is not always clear if the first-person singular voice that speaks the verses praising God is a continuation of the narrator who invokes the Christian muse in "the Prologue" or if it is Soul.[43]

Of course Taylor could have made any of the four characters—God, Satan, Soul, the narrator—dominate the action from start to finish as in the more common plot structure described in Aristotle's *Poetics.* He could have shown God or Christ triumphing at Judgment Day as in Michael Wigglesworth's *The Day of Doom;* or he could have made the central action be Satan's mission of sabotage in Eden, as in John Milton's *Paradise Lost;* or he could have depicted the Puritan Everyman traveling on his spiritual journey to heaven as does Christian, the protagonist of John Bunyan's *The Pilgrim's Progress;* or he could have made the narrator, after numerous unsuccessful attempts to evacuate the darkness from his soul, finally free his spirit to praise God, as in Jonathan Edwards's *Personal Narrative* or in other spiritual autobiographies with similar endings. The multiple lines of action and lack of a unified plot in *God's Determinations* is not—as some scholars have had it—another example of Taylor's artistic failure;[44] it is, rather, the minister-poet's quest to find a narrative design to match doctrinal concepts, as was discussed earlier. This brings us to another aspect of Taylor's plot structure that relates to New England Puritan doctrine.

Rather than strictly following the Aristotelian organizing principle of causality, as most western drama does, in *God's Determination* Taylor employs the episodic plot of epic. The episodic structure appears most obviously in the titles of the thirty-six segments comprising the Puritan morality play. However, the titled segments do not always correspond to the units of action. A single *agon* or scene between two characters may extend through several

43. Interestingly—and relevant to the character in Wilder's most famous play—Thomas M. Davis in *A Reading of Edward Taylor* twice identifies Taylor as the narrator with a theatrical metaphor: "Taylor as stage manager (in the first part of the poem at any rate) ... Then in his role as the stage manager ..." (33–34).

44. For example, when Grabo criticizes *God's Determinations* for "erratic structure and inconsistencies of the entire work," he is basing his evaluation on a limited, monolithic paradigm of drama (*Edward Taylor,* 161). See also Gatta, "Comic Design," 139–40, and Keller, *Example of Edward Taylor,* 134.

segments (for example, the six segments in which Saint comforts and preaches to Soul), or more than one *agon* may take place within a single titled segment (for example, "The Effect of this Reply [by Christ] with a fresh Assault from Satan"). Furthermore, the titles function in the same manner as the arguments at the beginnings of books and cantos in such epics as *The Faerie Queene* and *Paradise Lost,* as well as in Bunyan's marginal notes for *The Pilgrim's Progress* and Wigglesworth's in *The Day of Doom:* to summarize the ensuing action and, sometimes, to point up the theme of the episode.

While Puritan histories such as *Of Plymouth Plantation* and *Wonder-Working Providence* have the loosely organized episodic plot of the epic mode, it is the representation of the microcosmic drama that causes Puritan spiritual autobiographies and biographies also to take the form of episodic plots. Damrosch explains the correlation between Puritan belief and episodic plot structure: "Human life is temporal, and trying to discern the meaning of events, self-examination inevitably took on narrative form. But it was always a type of narrative intended to identify crucial moments, not a connected tale based on causal sequence." Later in his study Damrosch further explains, "A traditional Anglo-Catholic philosophy [sees time] as a coherent structure with an Aristotelian beginning, middle, and end. But Puritan thought, in its quest for the epiphanic moment and its suspicion of human interpretation, is committed to admiring the grace that rescues each separate instant from the void, rather than tracing the pattern that connects one instant with another in temporal sequence." This is easily illustrated again by Bunyan's episodes with margin summaries in *The Pilgrim's Progress,* and by the thirty-six segments, each with its own title, in *God's Determinations.* But there is also a poetic analogue to the episodic structure in the extended metaphors for progress occurring frequently throughout *God's Determinations.* Each conceit represents progress on the human scale while also relating analogously to the cosmic scale. "History is a narrative, but the narrative is built up out of timeless symbols"; surely vegetative growth, military battle, a pilgrimage, a coach ride to a feast, learning to play a musical instrument, even a courtroom debate are timeless symbols. This is also one way in which Taylor expresses the macrocosmic theme of *God's Determinations* in microcosmic form.[45]

---

45. Damrosch, *God's Plot,* 36, 60, 62. This trait is typical not only of Puritan narrative but of American narrative: "As the most ambitious of seventeenth-century historical works, Cotton Mather's *Magnalia* provides the clearest evidence that Bradford's episodic method marks the beginning of a traditional form which becomes increasingly conscious and elaborate" (Lynen, *Design of the Present,* 57). A familiar enough example of episodic plotting in classic American literature is the various gams in *Moby-Dick.*

"God's plot and man's stories," a title Damrosch derived from a sermon by the New England Puritan minister Thomas Shepard, illustrates the two levels on which Puritan narrative operates, there being many stories that represent the one plot. As Damrosch says of John Bunyan's plot construction in *The Pilgrim's Progress,* "The biographical subplot is conflated with the cosmological main plot, and this frees the self from unescapable anxiety about election. *Heilsweg* is harmonized with *Heilsgeschichte,* the individual journey of the spirit with the universal history of God's elect." That is, the macrocosmic view provides the epic history of the war between God and Satan, while the microcosmic view renders each battle on the battleground of the individual soul. This interpretation of plot in *The Pilgrim's Progress* applies to *God's Determinations* as well.[46]

The analogous relationship between providential and personal progress represented by the combination of the panoramic scope of epic and the psychological close-up of drama also determined the effect of setting in *God's Determinations,* as well as the point of view. Rowe explains how Taylor achieved a divine perspective: "Allegories that embrace typal parallels as signs within a grander providential scheme that affects all time and all men create an explosion of reference or telescopic perspective, so that one seems to share an omniscient vision comparable to God's."[47] That is, Puritan writers were sure to remind their readers of the macrocosmic background for the microcosmic foreground of their works. The effect of this dual focus in terms of a theatrical stage might be to construct the area where the actors play as a fairly realistic set (a house), but in such a way as to suggest universality (Everyhouse). The backdrop (specifically, a cyclorama) would be the star-sprinkled cosmos as created by God, rather than a landscape, the horizon, or an abstract space. To paraphrase Shakespeare's theatrical metaphor, Puritan narratives' representation of setting suggest that all the world's a stage, but they insist that the universe is a theater built and managed by God.[48]

Taylor begins *God's Determinations* on the macrocosmic scale with a magnificent description of God as creator that is not at all plain aesthetically but is perfectly clear:

46. Damrosch, *God's Plot,* 119. As Lynen notes, "Taylor was enough of a theorist to see that he could not surrender the narrow present of human understanding because he must also believe in the deity's eternal will; and he was enough of a poet to see that his dual allegiance called for narrative of a double kind" (*Design of the Present,* 62–63).

47. Rowe, *Saint and Sinner,* 241.

48. Scholars often use a theatrical metaphor to describe the Puritan worldview. For example, Davis refers to the "cosmic drama of God's activities" and then states, "Man, for all his smallness, is in fact the central figure in the drama of God's determinations" (*Reading of Edward Taylor,* 38).

Infinity, when all things it beheld,
In Nothing, and of Nothing all did build,
Upon what Base was fixt the Lath, wherein
He turn'd this Globe, and riggalld it so trim?
Who blew the Bellows of his Furnace Vast?
Or held the Mould wherein the world was Cast?
Who laid its Corner Stone? Or whose Command?
. . . . Who in this Bowling Alley bowld the Sun?
Who made it always when it rises set:
To go at once both down, and up to get?
Who th' Curtain rods made for this Tapistry?
Who hung the twinkling Lanthorns in the Sky?
Who? who did this? or who is he? Why, know
It's Onely Might Almighty this did doe.
. . . . Whose Little finger at his pleasure Can
Out mete ten thousand worlds with halfe a Span:
    Can take this mighty World up in his hande,
And shake it like a Squitchen or a Wand.
Whose single Frown will make the Heavens shake
Like as an aspen leafe the Winde makes quake. (31)

The choral interludes spoken by either the narrator or Soul also place the
events of the plot in a cosmic context:

Oh! Stand amaizd, yee Angells Bright, come run
    Yee Glorious Heavens and Saints, to sing:
    Place yee your praises in the sun,
        Ore all the world to ring. . . .
What! can a Crumb of Dust sally such praise
    Which do from Earth all heaven o're ring! (65, 66)

As modern playwrights have discovered, drama can achieve the epic scope
of longer works by employing narration in addition to dialogue. Conversely,
epic can focus in on individual episodes to represent the microcosm.

Because *God's Determinations* is an allegory, obviously Taylor never sets the
action in a particular locale, but the abundance of domestic, agricultural,
and commercial metaphors used by all the principal characters to describe
Soul's struggle ground the epic plot in the microcosmic world. In addition to
those recurring metaphors for progress previously cited, the metaphor that
spiritual life is like a physical journey also appears throughout *God's Determinations*. For example, in segment eighteen the narrator prays,

Yet, Lord, accept this Pittance of thy praise,
  Which as a Traveller I bring.
  While travelling along thy wayes,
    In broken notes I sing.
And at my journies end in endless joyes
  I'll make amends where Angells meet
  And sing their flaming Melodies
    In Ravishing tunes most Sweet. (67)

Later in the play, Taylor extends a sea-voyage metaphor (a comparison that would obviously resonate with seventeenth-century New England Puritans) for the spiritual life:

Who'le with a Leaking, old Crack't Hulk assay
To brave the raging Waves of Adria?
Or who can Cross the Main Pacifick o're?
Without a Vessell Wade from shore to shore?
. . . .
If Stay, or Go to sea, we drown. Then see
In what a wofull Pickle, Lord, we bee.
Rather than tarry, or the rough sea trust,
On the Pacificke Ocean forth we thrust.
Necessity lies on's: we dare not stay:
If drown we must, we'l drown in Mercy's Sea! (76–77)

The narrator makes clear that going off course has ultimate consequences: "while down the tide / The other scull unto eternal woe, / By letting slip their former journey so" (45). Along with the episodes dramatizing the suffering of the Puritan Everyman as he tries to find assurance from Saint that he is among the elect, the journey metaphor and other concrete conceits give Taylor's play a sense of living "Man's stories" in the here and now, though ultimately pointed in the direction of the after-life. Thus, in keeping with the Puritans' aesthetic, while *God's Determinations* is, in part, a macrocosmic morality play, in the manner of *The Castle of Perseverance*, it also is a microcosmic morality play in the manner of *Everyman*.[49]

49. Or *Paradise Lost* and *The Pilgrim's Progress*, if one prefers examples of Puritan narratives, though they are not plays and are English rather than American. This relationship of levels of reality has been discussed in Taylor's better-known work, *Sacramental Meditations:* "Providential history becomes, however, only a macrocosmic pattern for the microcosmic journey of each soul, a journey through which Taylor repeatedly travels, meditation by meditation, and one made poetic through figural narratives, personal

To review the formal characteristics of the Puritan narrative aesthetic as illustrated by *God's Determinations,* the prose or verse is written in a plain style (clearly understood, and perhaps also simplified), and significant points are overdetermined; the representation of character and events tends toward the abstract and is often allegorical or typological or both; the plots are progressive overall but episodic, resulting in a dual level of action, setting, and perspective: a microcosmic foreground presented against a macrocosmic background. These stylistic features are nearly identical to Wilder's description of classic American literature aesthetics summarized in the Introduction. This study's position is that the plays and novels of Thornton Wilder to a large extent share these formal characteristics of Puritan narrative and are thus part of a tradition extending from the seventeenth century to the twentieth.

---

applications, and recurrent images that signal the soul's transport from sin to salvation" (Rowe, *Saint and Singer* 240); see also Pearce, *Continuity of American Poetry,* 51; MacGregor, "Edward Taylor and the Impertinent Metaphor," 339; and Barbour, "*Gods Determinations* and the Hexameral Tradition," 221.

Two

Judgment Day in the Jazz Age

Eschatology and Providence in
Wilder's Early Plays and Novels

> Eschatology, the study of the final events in human history, was a major
> Puritan preoccupation. . . . In the cosmos each progressive step in the pattern
> was markedly closer to the ultimate redemption at the Day of Judgment.
>
> —Cecelia Tichi, *New World, New Earth: Environmental Reformation*
> *in American Literature from the Puritans through Whitman*

> Puritans believed in an unalterable plan underlying human history.
>
> —Leopold Damrosch Jr., *God's Plot and Man's Stories*

If Thornton Wilder is examined in the context of the period during which
he made his entrance onto the literary stage—that is, in relation to the writers
of the 1920s, dubbed by F. Scott Fitzgerald "the Jazz Age"—he is usually described as the odd man out,[1] but not because he did not measure up to their
literary achievement and potential. As Malcolm Cowley writes, "In 1926 a

---

1. Wilder himself said that he was the only American writer of the 1920s who "did not
go to Paris"; his brother, Amos Niven Wilder, published an article in a German journal
with that observation as its title: "He Didn't Go to Paris: Thornton Wilder, Middle
America and the Critics," *Literaturwissenschaftliches Jahrbuch* (Berlin) XX (1979). This
chapter was first published in slightly different form in *Thornton Wilder: New Essays*, ed.
Martin Blank, Dalma Hunyadi Brunauer, and David Garrett Izzo, and it is reprinted
here with permission.

new galaxy of writers was taking shape, with its novelists, poets, playwrights, and critics . . . . [H]ardly anyone doubted from the first that Wilder would be an important member of that galaxy." Gertrude Stein coined the famous name for American writers in the early 1920s: "the Lost Generation." A well-known prose passage to support that label is found at the end of *This Side of Paradise* (1920) where Fitzgerald writes, "Here was a new generation . . . , dedicated more than the last to the fear of poverty and the worship of success; grown up to find all Gods dead, all wars fought, all the faiths in man shaken." Though part of this generation by date of birth, Wilder did not share the expatriates' pessimistic outlook. As H. Wayne Morgan writes, "He traveled widely and was in no sense provincial, but unlike so many of the Lost Generation, he had firm roots that were never broken by the shock of social dislocation or war. They reached far back into the past and anchored him in an orderly tradition with which he could not break." In corroboration, Cowley notes, "In all his travels Wilder never had this sense of being exiled or expatriated, because there was no one place he regarded as home. . . . He ceased to be a Midwesterner, and he did not become a Californian in spite of his schooling. Today he is little more of a New Englander, but chiefly he is an American."[2]

In relation to the wasteland zeitgeist, the idea that a historical entropy was everywhere evident (in western civilization, at least), Wilder's early plays and novels also convey a sense that the end was near. However, in contrast with other literary figures of the time (e.g., Hemingway, Fitzgerald, Eliot, Yeats), for Wilder the world would end not with a whimper, but with the triumphant blast of an apocalyptic trumpet heralding not the nadir but the zenith of history. Travis Bogard's observation that "in a sense, perhaps, all of Wilder's plays are about the Day of Judgment" is especially true of his plays and novels of the 1920s. *The Angel That Troubled the Waters and Other Plays* (1928), *The Trumpet Shall Sound* (1919–20), *The Cabala* (1926), and *The Bridge of San Luis Rey* (1927) represent, both literally and allegorically, an American conceptualization of Judgment Day descended from the seventeenth-century New England Puritans.[3]

Judgment Day is not an exclusively Puritan doctrine, of course, but the interpretation of America as a sign that the last days are upon us is a particularly American notion stemming from the New England Puritans. As Tichi explains, "From the Puritan belief that the Christian Millennium would

---

2. Cowley, "Introduction" to *A Thornton Wilder Trio*, 1–2; Fitzgerald, *This Side of Paradise*, 282; Morgan, "The Early Thornton Wilder," 252; Cowley, "Introduction," 7.

3. Bogard, "The Comedy of Thornton Wilder," 361. The dates of Wilder's books parenthetically cited are of publication, but the order in which the works are listed and will be discussed is according to the chronology of composition, from earliest to latest.

originate in New England and that God intended Puritans to bear major responsibility for its site preparation came a literature fraught with millennial themes." Bercovitch cites an example of Tichi's observation: "When John Cotton speaks of America as 'the ends of the earth' he is referring not only to a specific locale, but also to Christ's second coming." Having come of age during World War One, the "war to end all wars," Wilder may well have thought then that Armageddon and the second coming of Christ prophesied in the New Testament were imminent. Given that his works published during the Jazz Age were written as Wilder himself was still close to the point in his life when the doctrines of his Congregationalist upbringing were first inculcated in him, it should not be surprising to find more frequent occurrences of religious ideas inherited from the Puritans during this period than in his later works, where they are somewhat sublimated or, when they do appear, are cast in more secular form. As we shall see, in the plays and novels of the first decade of his career, Thornton Wilder literally and allegorically alludes to and dramatizes a Puritan vision of Judgment Day.[4]

The Angel That Troubled the Waters and Other Plays

Though published in 1928, many of the "three-minute plays" collected in *The Angel That Troubled the Waters and Other Plays* were written and published in literary magazines ten years prior, while Wilder was still in college.[5] In his early study, Donald Haberman emphasizes the influence of Theodore Dreiser's *Plays of the Natural and Supernatural* (1916) on Wilder's first dramatic works. Haberman is closer to recognizing the source of the aesthetic that produced works such as Wilder's *Angel Plays* when he says, "They are in the exegetical tradition of the Protestant sermon which takes a biblical text and then expands upon it, examining some of its implications for the Christian life." Wilder himself referred to his literary efforts while at Oberlin College as "aesthetic missionary work," and in his foreword to the *Angel Plays* he writes, "The revival of religion is almost a matter of rhetoric. The work is difficult, perhaps impossible (perhaps all religions die out with the exhaustion of the language), but it at least reminds us that Our Lord asked us in His

---

4. Tichi, *New World, New Earth: Environmental Reformation in American Literature from the Puritans through Whitman*, 15; Sacvan Bercovitch, *The American Jeremiad*, 40.

5. See Richard H. Goldstone and Gary Anderson, *Thornton Wilder: An Annotated Bibliography of Works by and about Thornton Wilder*, 8–9, for bibliographical references of initial publication in college literary magazines. Quotations from *Prosperina and the Devil* and *And the Sea Shall Give Up Its Dead* are taken from *The Collected Short Plays of Thornton Wilder Volume II*.

work to be not only gentle as doves, but as wise as serpents" (*CSPTW II*, 7). Thus some of these early literary efforts were Wilder's deliberate attempts to write on religious issues.[6]

Except for those dealing with purely literary subjects (such as *Childe Rolande to the Dark Tower Came* and *The Centaur*), all of the *Angel Plays* are directly concerned with religious ideas that echo the Puritan past: predestination of the elect and reprobate, providential determination of events, a typological interpretation of the Bible and history, the imminence of Judgment Day, and the belief in the Devil as an active agent of evil. Other Wilder scholars have noticed some of these elements, yet they did not see them as having significance for understanding the origin and practice of Wilder's aesthetic.[7] Two of the more emphatically religious plays, *And the Sea Shall Give Up Its Dead* and *Prosperina and the Devil*, dramatize, at least in part, Judgment Day as a cosmic grand finale to human history, and they manifest residual Puritan beliefs and structures.[8]

And the Sea Shall Give Up Its Dead literally dramatizes Judgment Day—or, rather, a few minutes before and a few seconds after the "trial of all flesh"— as indicated by the initial and final stage directions:

> *The clangor of Judgment Day's last trumpet dies away in the remotest pockets of space, and time comes to an end like a frayed ribbon. In the nave of creation the diaphanous amphitheater is already building for the trial of all flesh. Several miles below the surface of the North Atlantic, the spirits of the drowned rise through the water like bubbles in a neglected wineglass.*

. . . .

> *The three panic-stricken souls reach the surface of the sea. The extensive business of Domesday is over in a twinkling and the souls divested of all identification have tumbled,*

6. There obviously are correspondences between Dreiser's plays and Wilder's *Angel Plays* in terms of mood, nonrealistic aesthetic, and particular themes. However, Haberman does not acknowledge the difference in religious point of view between Dreiser's plays (apparently Hindu or Buddhist) and Wilder's (explicitly Christian), nor does he consider other sources of the ideas and forms in Wilder's plays within American culture. See Haberman, *The Plays of Thornton Wilder*, 28; Gilbert Harrison, *The Enthusiast: A Life of Thornton Wilder*, 41.

7. A few studies of Wilder treat these brief dramatic pieces as shades of things to come (e.g., Travis Bogard, "The Comedy of Thornton Wilder"), but most dismiss them as apprentice work (e.g., Malcolm Goldstein, *The Art of Thornton Wilder*).

8. Traces of Puritan doctrine are sprinkled through the entire collection; while space does not permit quoting them all, the following speech shows that the Judgment Day theme was prevalent. In *Brother Fire* the title character says, "I know that there is flame to burn all evil in the Lake of the Damned" (*CSPTW II*, 48). "The Lake of the Damned" is an allusion to the New Testament book Revelation (specifically, chapter twenty), from which most Christian doctrine about Judgment Day originates.

like falling stars, into the blaze of unicity. Soon nothing exists in space but the great un-winking eye, meditating a new creation. (CSPTW II, 49, 52)[9]

What makes this play and *The Trumpet Shall Sound* characteristically American visualizations is that their image of Judgment Day owes more to New England Puritan mythography than to the Bible. In the following lines from *God's Determinations,* Taylor also uses both the eye and courtroom metaphors: "That he [Man] may Something say, when *rain'd,* although / His Say seems nothing, and for nought will go. / But while he Sculking on his face close lies, / Espying nought, the *Eye Divine* him spies. / Justice and Mercy then fall to debate / Concerning this poore fallen mans estate. / Before the *Bench* of the Almighties Breast / Th' ensuing Dialogues hint their contest" (35, emphasis added). The first American depiction of Judgment Day as a "trial of all flesh" was also the colony's first bestseller, Puritan minister and poet Michael Wigglesworth's *The Day of Doom* (1662). This apocalyptic ballad bears little resemblance to the great epics depicting heaven and hell and the saved and the damned, *The Divine Comedy* and *Paradise Lost,* but Wilder's first and last stage directions in *And the Sea Shall Give Up Its Dead* do compare to the following description of Judgment Day from Wigglesworth's *The Day of Doom:*

> Before his throne a trump is blown,
>   proclaiming the day of doom,
> Forwith he cries, "Ye dead, arise,
>   and unto judgment come."
> No sooner said but 'tis obeyed;
>   sepulchers opened are;
> Dead bodies all rise at his call,
>   and's mighty power declare.
> Both sea and land, at his command,
>   their dead at once surrender . . . (stanzas 17 and 18)

After the opening stage direction, *And the Sea Shall Give Up Its Dead* dramatizes the conversation of three souls as they rise. Even in this early short play, Wilder was working at both the macrocosmic level in the framing stage directions and at the microcosmic level in the intervening dialogue.

Furthermore, Wilder's representation of Judgment Day as a cosmic trial

---

9. One need not have experience in the theater to recognize that these stage directions are unstageable. In fact, most studies of Wilder regard the *Angel Plays* as closet drama—intended for reading, not staging. However, in their 1999 production of *The Angel That Troubled the Waters and Other Plays,* the Broadway Thesbyterians solved this problem with a theatrical device famously employed by Wilder in *Our Town:* they had a stage manager read the stage directions.

with Christ presiding as judge and prosecutor, welcoming the elect and accusing and condemning the reprobate—the latter in a procession of representative types who plead their cases which are then refuted by Christ—has no exact precedent in the Bible. Wigglesworth based *The Day of Doom* primarily on Matthew 25 and Revelation 20 and 21, as his marginal annotations indicate, but these New Testament passages do not anatomize the condemned to the extent that Wigglesworth and Wilder do. Wigglesworth frequently refers to Christ as "the Judge," and to the judgment in terms of a courtroom trial: "yet all are brought / unto this solemn trial, / And each offense with evidence, / so that there's no denial. . . . Sad is their state, for advocate / to plead their cause there's none—none to prevent their punishment" (stanzas 54, 188).[10]

To demonstrate that Wilder knew in detail the biblical basis for the belief in Judgment Day, in *And the Sea Shall Give Up Its Dead* one of the rising spirits says, "All this is the second death, and the one to be dreaded" (*CSPTW II,* 51), an allusion to Revelation 20:14, 15: "And death and hell were cast into the lake of fire. This is the second death. And whosoever was not found written in the book of life was cast into the lake of fire." While there is no direct evidence that Wilder read *The Day of Doom,* his play nevertheless takes its cue from an American iconographic tradition, paradoxically begun by iconoclastic Puritan ministers, and still appearing today in popular culture and fundamentalist church leaflets.

The dialogue of the three souls in *And the Sea Shall Give Up Its Dead* might be thought to lend itself more easily to a reading of the play as a dramatization of the Catholic belief in purgatory; however, the play's representative of Catholicism, Father Cosroe, is portrayed in such a way that it seems unlikely that *And the Sea Shall Give Up Its Dead* is an illustration of Catholic doctrine:

> I told myself, also, that after death I should sit through eternity overhearing the conversation of Coleridge and Augustine and Our Lord . . . ; there I should hear vindicated before the devils the great doctrines of *Infant Baptism* and *Sacramental Confession.* Only now have I been delivered from *these follies.* As I swayed in the meteoric slime I begged God to punish me for certain sins of my youth, moments I well remembered of rage and pride and shame. But these seemed of no importance to him: he seemed rather to be erasing from my mind the notion that my sins were of any consequence. (*CSPTW II,* 51, emphasis added)

10. Wigglesworth's poem is actually a versified explanation of various Calvinistic doctrines, including predestination and total depravity. The only dramatic structure is the debate between Christ and each class of those predestined for hell. He allows them to come forward and plead their case, and then he rationally explains why they are condemned to eternal torment rather than installment in eternal bliss as are the elect. See *DD,* stanzas 69–181.

In fact, adducing certain Catholic doctrine as erroneous ("these follies") is only one of many examples of Puritan anti-Catholicism that pervades Wilder's earlier works.[11]

Whatever Wilder's actual beliefs with regard to biblical prophecy, *And the Sea Shall Give Up Its Dead* is best understood in the context of a conceptualization of Judgment Day present in American culture since the publication of *The Day of Doom*.[12] As the "Foreword" to the *Angel Plays* makes clear, at this point in his literary career Wilder thought of himself as a religious writer on an errand: "Almost all the plays in this book are religious. . . . It is the kind of work that I would most like to do well, in spite of the fact that there has seldom been an age in literature when such a vein was less welcome and less understood. I hope, through many mistakes, to discover the spirit that is not unequal to the elevation of the great religious themes, yet which does not fall into a repellent didacticism" (*CSPTW II*, 6–7). Although Wilder was modern enough to have an aversion to "*repellent* didacticism," his works are clearly didactic—especially those published during the decadent Jazz Age.[13]

Another *Angel* play that dramatizes God's judgment of the saved and the damned is *Prosperina and the Devil*. Subtitled *A Play for Marionettes, Prosperina and the Devil* is set, interestingly enough, in 1640 Venice, the period—though not the place—when Puritanism was approaching its zenith as a cultural force in both England (with the civil war between the Royalists and the mostly Puritan supporters of Parliamentary rule) and America (following the Great Migration and the establishment of the Massachusetts Bay colony). This farcical play foreshadows Wilder's later practice of metatheater or theatricalism in *Our Town* and *The Skin of Our Teeth* by depicting the performance of a puppet show that goes awry.[14] As a prototype of the Stage Manager in Wilder's

---

11. This is not to say that Wilder was consciously prejudiced against Catholicism—at least not later in his life. Harrison recounts a 1937 conversation between Wilder and another writer who was attacking the Catholic Church; Wilder's response was, "Don't talk like that; just suppose it might be the right answer" (Harrison, *Enthusiast*, 166).

12. As Charles Berryman explains in *From Wilderness to Wasteland: The Trial of the Puritan God in the American Imagination*: "The warning of death and Hell was dramatized with such lurid intensity in *The Day of Doom* that it remained the most celebrated poem in the New World for more than a century" (177). In fact, it was "the most popular book in America, except for the Bible, for the next hundred years" (202).

13. As Morgan writes in "The Early Thornton Wilder," "He looked at the society of the 1920's and condemned it, a condemnation that ran like threads through all his early work" (245–46). Joseph Firebaugh explains Wilder's frequent objection to didacticism despite the fact that he obviously is a didactic writer: "Mr. Wilder's real objection is to *inartistic* didacticism" ("The Humanism of Thornton Wilder," 426).

14. These terms refer to, respectively, theater about theater and a theatrical aesthetic based not on life, as with mimetic art (including theater), but on theater itself. In addition, a play employing theatricalism does not try to maintain an illusion of reality, but instead acknowledges its artifice. See Oscar G. Brockett and Robert R. Findlay, *Century of*

later plays, the character in *Prosperina and the Devil* called "Manager" addresses the audience directly: "Citizens and little citizens! We are going to give you a delicious foretaste of our great performance this afternoon to which the whole world is coming. This is a pantomime about how a beautiful girl named Prosperina was snatched away by the Devil; . . ." (*CSPTW II*, 13).

In this initial speech, along with the title, there is an apparent conflation of classical and Christian mythology. We then see a more detailed mix of classical mythology, biblical figures, and contemporary (i.e., 1640) characters as evident in this stage direction: *"This is the Lake of Wrath and in it are seen floating arms and legs–all that are left, alas, of great puppets, ABRAHAM, PENE-LOPE and JEPHTHA'S daughter, MIDAS and HARLEQUIN"* (*CSPTW II*, 14).[15] In the following stage direction, there is not merely a metaphorical conjunction of different mythologies but, rather, an assertion of dual identity: *"At her elbow HERMES, the Archangel Gabriel, guides her through the Lake of Perdition"* (*CSPTW II*, 15). These passages constitute the earliest evidence in the Wilder oeuvre that he had inherited from the Puritans a typological habit of mind. Though this crucial element of Puritan thought will be discussed more in depth in Chapter Three, a brief elaboration on the explanation of typology from Chapter One is needed here in order to understand the cause and interpretation of certain passages in Wilder's early aesthetic missionary work.

Although Puritans applied typology primarily to the Bible, they expanded the textual territory they explored for the divinely placed foreshadowings of things to come. Kenneth B. Murdock explains, "It became not too difficult for thorough-going typologists or tropologists to relate the mythology and history of Greece and Rome to those of the Hebrews and to find in the classics as well as in the Bible exemplifications of the continuing providential plan of God, foreshadowed in the Old Testament and revealed in a variety of forms throughout the whole history of mankind." Thus the reference to classical figures by Puritan writers should not be mistaken for literary allusion, as Murdock points out: "This apparent jumbling of pagan mythology and the Old and New Testament is not a mere display of scraps of learning. The same device appears again and again in Puritan histories and biographies." In other words, the presence of classical elements in Puritan writing is a manifestation of the biblical hermeneutic in which types and antitypes are perceived to exist throughout history in all cultures, from the drama and

---

Innovation: A History of European and American Theatre and Drama since 1870, and John Gassner, *Form and Idea in Modern Theatre.*

15. In *God's Determinations* we find a similar description based on the eschatological doctrine: "Thou must sustain that burden, that will make / The Angells sink into th' Infernall lake" (37).

epic poetry of classical Greece to persons and events in seventeenth-century New England and literary narration about them.[16] This is why Wilder's dramatization of Judgment Day is peculiarly American; it is interwoven with specific doctrinal beliefs that distinguish New England Puritanism from English Puritanism, to say nothing of Catholicism.

To examine more specific evidence of Wilder's typological habit of mind in *Prosperina and the Devil,* the following stage directions indicate not only an awareness of the analogous relationship between the classical and Christian myths, but also their different points on a progressive time line:

> *The curtain rises with indecent haste and shows the underworld. The rivers Styx and Acheron have been replaced by a circular piece of cloth, sulfur-colored, with waves delicately embroidered about the margin. This is the Lake of Wrath . . . Beside the lake* PROSPERINA *is straying, robed in bluish black as one anticipating grief.* PLUTO— *now a medieval Satan—is stealthily approaching her. Suddenly* PROSPERINA *throws up her arms, runs to him and buries her face in his scarlet bosom.* NOAH'S ARK— *mutely protesting against the part it must play, with all its Christianized animals within it, of* CHARON'S *barge—is lowered from the proscenium and the curtain falls . . . . When the puppets are next seen* PROSPERINA *is exhibiting grief in pantomime. Her lord with affectionate gestures urges her to eat of a yellow pomegranate. Sadly she puts it to her mouth. With an odd recollection of the Garden of Eden, she tempts him into eating the remaining half. They go out cheerlessly . . . .* HERMES, *the Archangel Gabriel, guides* [DEMETER] *through the Lake of Perdition.* (CSPTW II, 14–15)

It is not only the author of the stage directions who has consciousness of the correspondences of the myths; Prosperina can only "anticipate grief" and eat the fruit "sadly" if she knows she is reenacting Eden; Noah's ark can only "protest" its part as Charon's barge if it is aware of its original function and context. This mixture of mythologies is not uncommon in classical American literature (one could easily imagine *Prosperina and the Devil* having been written by Nathaniel Hawthorne as one of the retellings of classical myths in his *The Wonder-Book*),[17] but the practice of representing the myths as historical analogs within a single figure or event originates in American literature with New England Puritan typology.

---

16. Murdock, "Clio in the Wilderness: History and Biography in Puritan New England," 214–15, 211. Sacvan Bercovitch explains how the figures relate in the typological hermeneutic: "The Bible story is 'the very thing' celebrated by the pagan poets Homer, Ovid, and Virgil; the legendary python, the old serpent, 'is the same with' both Og and Satan; and Apollo 'is the same with' Joshua who 'is' Jesus who in turn 'is the great Phoebus'. . . . In his 'plain history,' Christ antitypes Joshua-Apollo, and the victorious New England army antitypes the Israelites entering Canaan" (*The Puritan Origins of the American Self,* 65).

17. I owe this comparison to Hawthorne's *The Wonder-Book* to Professor Sargent Bush Jr.

The farcical action of *Prosperina and the Devil* also ironically reflects another tenet of Puritanism—that history is determined by Providence. As the Carmodys write, "The Calvinist God was the sovereign controller of the universe, guiding all things by his providential will."[18] Providential influence is apparent in *Prosperina and the Devil*'s plot as well. After the puppet show manager delivers his prologue to the audience, the First and Second Manipulators awkwardly animate the puppets, unintentionally deviate from the script, exchange verbal abuse, then literally bring the house down with a backstage fight. At first glance, this slapstick action would seem to suggest the opposite of a benevolent Providence in control; however, in Wilder's final stage direction the positions of the puppets manifest a Bible-based Judgment Day: "*The altercation behind the scenes grows out of bounds and one blow knocks down the stage. The Archangel falls upon the pavement and is cherished by gamins unto the third generation; the Devil rolls into the Lake;* Prosperina *is struck by a falling cloud, and lies motionless on her face;* Demeter *by reason of the stiffness of her brocade stands upright, viewing with staring eyes the ills of her daughter*" (*CSWTW II,* 15).[19]

In these ostensibly random fallings the poetic justice of Providence is revealed: Hermes (the Archangel) is cherished; the Devil is cast into the Lake of Fire, as in both the Book of Revelation and *The Day of Doom*;[20] Prosperina, struck down to a position signifying submission, and her mother Demeter (the goddess of corn, the harvest, and summer—fertility, reproduction) together recall the punishment of the serpent and Eve in Genesis: the serpent must crawl on its belly in the dust, Eve must bear children in pain and sorrow, and her desire and obedience will be to her husband. Thus in this single stage direction, biblical time is collapsed into one tableau of the Fall of Man and Judgment Day, the alpha and omega of "God's Plot."

In these microcosmic dramatic pieces Wilder wrote while still a college student, we see represented the macrocosmic finale of Judgment Day. While the *Angel Plays* dramatize their religious subjects literally, in the following analysis of Wilder's more ambitious undergraduate attempt at writing drama, we will see his first use of the allegorical mode as a way to broaden the scope of a play beyond the ephemeral circumstances of a contemporary setting and action.

18. Denise Lardner Carmody and John Tully Carmody, *The Republic of Many Mansions: Foundations of American Religious Thought,* 19.

19. In the Broadway Thesbyterians' production, actors played the puppets (without strings, but the puppeteers were visible above them). Again, imaginative staging can solve the production problems created by the young Wilder's impractical stage directions.

20. Wigglesworth represented the final punishment for the reprobate in similar terms: "His wrath is great, whose burning heat / no floods of tears can slake; / His word stands fast, that they be cast / into the burning lake" (stanza 189).

The Trumpet Shall Sound

Following his two years at Oberlin College, Wilder transferred to Yale, where he wrote his first full-length play, *The Trumpet Shall Sound.* While the play has been dismissed by the few scholars who have briefly discussed it as an unsuccessful amateur work, in its time *The Trumpet Shall Sound* was recognized both for its literary merits, receiving Yale's Bradford Brinton Award and published serially in the *Yale Literary Magazine* (1919–20), and for its theatrical potential, produced by Richard Boleslavsky at the American Laboratory Theatre in New York in 1926. While my claim is not that *The Trumpet Shall Sound* is a great undiscovered work of drama that should be revived for the stage, it is nevertheless true that Wilder's first full-length play has been neglected by Wilder scholars, who have failed to appreciate its merits and its relationship to Wilder's objectives in his more mature drama, as this comment by Mildred Kuner exemplifies: "There is little in the play, except for occasionally effective dialogue, to indicate the author's coming stage triumphs." As we shall see, Wilder was trying in *The Trumpet Shall Sound* to create a theatrical effect that he later achieved in *Pullman Car Hiawatha* (1931), *Our Town* (1938), and *The Skin of Our Teeth* (1942): to set the microcosm of present life against the backdrop of the eternal macrocosm.[21]

In *Our Town,* Wilder would stimulate the audience to activate their imaginations and enlist their empathy (thus creating universality) by having them picture the images of a small town setting—perhaps their own town—as the Stage Manager talks and points to areas of a bare stage. In *The Trumpet Shall Sound,* at least in its published form, Wilder stimulates readers to see beyond their earthly existence—or, at least, to see that there is a "Beyond"—with multilayered language. This imaginative act is suggested by the title of his drama of doomsday as it appears on the first page of each of the four acts serially published in the *Yale Literary Magazine* and in headers throughout the third and fourth acts: "*The Trumpet Shall Sound* . . . . ." The ellipsis alludes to the continuation of the apostle Paul's teaching on the resurrection of the dead in the New Testament: "Behold, I shew you a mystery; We shall not all sleep, but we shall all be changed, In a moment, in the twinkling of an eye, at the last trump: for the trumpet shall sound, and the dead shall be raised incorruptible, and we shall be changed. For

---

21. See, for example, Haberman, *Plays of Thornton Wilder,* 29–31, and Goldstone, *Thornton Wilder: An Intimate Portrait,* 37–38. No attempt has been made to give *The Trumpet Shall Sound* a thorough reading, and the few studies of Wilder's career that comment upon it in passing have misread the allegory. See, for example, Francis Fergusson, "Three Allegorists: Brecht, Wilder and Eliot"; Goldstein, *Art;* Harrison, *Enthusiast;* and Kuner, *Thornton Wilder: The Bright and the Dark.* Kuner, *Bright and Dark,* 39.

this corruptible must put on incorruption, and this mortal must put on immortality" (I Cor. 15:51–53).[22]

The New Testament allusion of the title notwithstanding, Wilder acknowledged Ben Jonson's *The Alchemist* as the source of *The Trumpet Shall Sound*'s action on the literal level: a rich man named Peter Magnus comes home after being away a long time and discovers that his servants have been unfaithful to him by renting rooms in his large house to disreputable types; upon discovery of the situation, Magnus conducts an impromptu trial, forgiving the offenses of some and punishing those of others. The three acts leading up to his return in the fourth act consist of the servants attempting to deflect one boarder's suspicions about the set-up, and Flora, the servant who hatched the plot, pleading with her lover to marry her—obviously the material of nineteenth-century melodrama. However, as the title suggests, the real subject of Wilder's first full-length play is the prophesied Judgment Day. That is, Act Four of *The Trumpet Shall Sound* allegorically dramatizes the trial of all flesh that was omitted in *And the Sea Shall Give Up Its Dead.*

"Judgment Day is coming!" is the overdetermined warning in *The Trumpet Shall Sound.* First, it is signified several times on the literal level of the narrative by characters referring to the Bible's prophecy of the event. For example, a visitor to the house says to Nestor, one of the servants who has gone along with the plan to rent out rooms to those in trouble with the law, "Don't let the master of the house come back and catch you at a high jinx! We know not the day nor the hour. Like a thief in the night. The trumpet shall sound!" (16). Such direct references are motivated by Wilder's creation of religious characters who believe in an impending Judgment Day. The most emphatically religious character is a sailor-turned-evangelist who has scripture tattooed on his body: "John Three Sixteen. I bear witness. And it is with this body, *marked,* that I shall rise again, when the trumpet shall sound" (24). Miss Flecker, another roomer (though no evangelist), says to the former sailor, foreshadowing the end of the play, "Hold your ears open, is all I ask you. Or else we'll have a little Judgment Day, like you're always talking about, right here in this drawing room, and blessed are the sheep!" (83). Even Flora, who claims to have never been in a church, refers to the second coming: "Jerusalem is where God is going to come again" (143).

In addition to such literal references to Judgment Day, several speeches and actions allegorically signify the second coming of Christ and the ensuing trial of all flesh. At the beginning of the play, when the plan to rent out

22. Again, Wigglesworth uses similar language: "The same translates from mortal states / to immortality / All that survive and be alive, / i' th' twinkling of an eye" (*DD,* stanza 19).

rooms is being implemented, Nestor says, "From now on we're as good as the masters of this house; and it'll bring us money. Perhaps old Magnus'll stay away years like he stayed away before, eh?" Another servant, Sarah Budie, who is a reluctant accomplice to the plan, replies, "His instructions to John Bowles was to be ready at any time for his return. Night and day. He said he wanted things ready for him any minute in any hour, as he said—day or night" (13). As in the speeches when characters were consciously alluding to Judgment Day, here the language of the New Testament is echoed so that it is difficult to miss the point that there will be a final day of judgment and that Magnus's return and interrogation of the servants and the people they have rented the rooms to allegorically represents that final day. Flora, the servant who masterminds the plan, even says to one resident shortly after Magnus makes his presence known in Act Four, "It's come, Mrs. Soderstrom. The last day" (194).

The Trumpet Shall Sound also contains speeches that signify Judgment Day on both the literal and allegorical levels simultaneously. Upon his return, Magnus compares his judgment as a human to the final judgment of God: "Do not forget that there is still a judgment seat to face beyond this, wiser than man's. Yes, I own it. It may even be that my verdicts will be reversed. Some of them, I say. At midnight the cry goeth forth, and we shall be snatched up. You know the text, Dexter?" (205). In the phrase "Yes, I own it" Wilder fuses the literal meaning of Magnus-the-man's affirmation of the Christian belief and the allegorical meaning of Magnus-the-representation-of-Christ's assigned role at the end of history. Another example of simultaneous allegorical and literal reference to Judgment Day occurs after Flora's suicide is discovered; Magnus laments, "Self-murder is added to her offenses. Ah, what a burden before the judgment-seat!" (206). This literary pun—that the burden *will be* before the judgment seat of Christ, that the burden *is* before the judgment seat of Christ allegorically represented on stage at the present moment—is so pointed that it might break the willing suspension of disbelief, giving emphasis to the didactic message of the play: everyone had better be ready to account for his or her time on earth because Magnus (Christ) has been given "full power to bind and unbind" (137), another echo of New Testament language.

This overdetermination of the allegorical meaning of *The Trumpet Shall Sound* has been regarded as an amateurish flaw in Wilder's play: "Understandably enough, the play failed, for the allegory is too obvious for comfort"; "It is a heavy allegory about a householder (God) who goes away on a journey, leaving his servants in charge." What is curious—even contradictory—in scholars' and critics' complaints about the obviousness of Wilder's allegory is that they also criticize it for being unclear: "It is an obvious allegory. . . . *The Trumpet Shall Sound* is ambitious, but the message is cloudy";

"The intention is blurred. The symbolism is too obvious"; the play "furnishes a rather murky evening among the better known symbols." How can the allegory be both obvious and ambiguous?[23]

It may be that the message is more disagreeable or inconsistent with post-Calvinist Christian doctrine than it is unclear. The Puritans' belief in God's determination even before the birth of every soul as elect or reprobate does seem to clash with a view of Christ as a God of mercy, but the Puritans made no apologies for this hard dogma; as Horton Davies writes, "The steel in the Puritan soul was the conviction of the truth of the doctrine of predestination."[24]

Furthermore, although all but one of the scholars who comment on *The Trumpet Shall Sound* interpret Magnus as God, none has recognized that Magnus's return represents the second coming of Christ and his judging of the elect and the reprobate, as in Wigglesworth's *The Day of Doom*.[25] When Flora speaks to her lover, Carlo, about fearing the return of Magnus, Carlo says, "He can't do any more than turn you out, can he?" She replies, "Oh, yes he can. Lots worse. (*In a frenzy:*) It's a sin! He can give us to the Devil!" (91). As further evidence that Magnus represents Christ, in Act Three he delivers a modern equivalent of Christ's speech while he clears the temple of money-lenders and merchants: "It is written, My house is a house of prayer, but ye have made it a den of thieves" (Luke 19:46). Similarly, Magnus says, "and the home of my fathers became a haven of crime" (141). Along with other dialogue echoing New Testament language, Magnus's speech is too similar to Christ's in the Gospels to believe that Wilder was not aware of the parallels he was creating between Christ and Magnus.

Scholars' failure to identify Magnus as Christ may be due to Wilder's characterization of him not as the gentle, compassionate Christ of the Gospels, but rather as an overbearing, self-righteous man who revels in his authority to pronounce judgment.[26] Literary dramatizations of Judgment Day from

23. Goldstein, *Art,* 33; Fergusson, "Three Allegorists," 554; Harrison, *Enthusiast,* 56; Kuner, *Bright and Dark,* 38; *New York Times,* 1926. Perhaps the meaning is unclear because, as Martin Blank notes, "The realistic form Wilder chose [for *Trumpet*] was inappropriate to embody his Christian allegory of justice, mercy, and spiritual rebirth" ("Introduction" to *Critical Essays on Thornton Wilder,* 5). Paul Lifton agrees that on its surface, the play is realistic: "*The Trumpet Shall Sound* is also technically a realistic play, although its allegorical overtones carry it beyond 'pure' or photographic realism. . . . There is nothing physically impossible in the play's action and nothing stylized, abstract, distorted, or anti-illusionistic in the manner of its presentation" (*Vast Encyclopedia: The Theatre of Thornton Wilder,* 56).

24. Davies, *Worship and Theology in England: From Cranmer to Hooker, 1534–1603,* 43.

25. Haberman interprets Magnus not as God but as "perhaps a kind of ironic modern St. Peter" (*Plays of Thornton Wilder,* 9).

26. Haberman writes, "Magnus has, in the tradition of the man of hubris, forgotten his own humanity in his attempt to play god" (*Plays of Thornton Wilder,* 31)—but he is God!

the elect point of view have a tendency to appear self-righteous, as Berryman notes about *The Day of Doom:* "Michael Wigglesworth obviously admired the powerful display of 'God's revengeful ire' and described the cruelty of divine wrath with great relish."[27] Magnus does express or manifest a self-righteous glee in catching his servants in the act of disloyalty, but, from a Calvinist point of view, this reads as an affirmation of God's plan; as George Santayana concisely explains, "Calvinistic principle asserts three things: that sin exists, that sin is punished, and that it is beautiful that sin should exist to be punished."[28] Furthermore, the characterization of Christ as administrator of justice is completely orthodox according to his different functions in the Passion and on Judgment Day.

The tendency in the Puritan aesthetic to overdetermine important points, as we saw with Taylor's multiple signifiers of spiritual progress in *God's Determinations,* may be responsible for one potential source of critics' confusion about the message in *The Trumpet Shall Sound.* Flora's waiting for the return of her lover may seem to represent the Second Coming of Christ, but it proves to be an allegorical red herring. She waits "day and night" for him to arrive, insists that the best room in the house be "saved" for him, and reassures herself by telling him, "You'll try and save me. Perhaps you'll be able to save me somehow" (91). In contrast to her hopes, when Carlo does come he refuses to marry Flora, telling her that as a servant-girl she is "expecting too much" (128). She tries to conduct an impromptu wedding ceremony with just the two of them, but when she addresses "Angels and God" and asks for forgiveness for "not doing it the way most people do," he exclaims, "That's blasphemous!" (144). At the end of the play he even prompts Flora to take her own life. Clearly, Carlo is not the groom come for the bride, as in Christ's metaphor in the New Testament (see Revelation 19:7).

As in *God's Determinations,* God the Father is not directly represented in *The Trumpet Shall Sound,* but in an exchange of dialogue between Magnus and

---

Similarly, Harrison says, "The master of the house, from whom we expect perfect justice, has a soul of stone" (*Enthusiast,* 56). But this was consistent with the conceptualization of God Wilder inherited from his Calvinistic father and, most likely, his teachers at Oberlin. In an archived file labeled "Untitled (Oberlin)" at Beinecke, Wilder wrote, "We were in god's hands and god was obscurely felt to be a man of property who furnished provision for the just" (2).

27. Berryman, *From Wilderness to Wasteland,* 18. Wigglesworth describes the effect of Christ's appearance contrary to the biblical portrait of Christ as a mostly gentle teacher and healer: "The Judge draws nigh, exalted high / upon a lofty Throne, / Admidst the throng of Angels strong, / lo, Israel's Holy One! / The excellence of whose Presence / and awful Majesty, / Amazeth Nature, and every Creature, / doth more than terrify" (*DD,* stanza 14).

28. Quoted in Frederick William Conner, *Cosmic Optimism: A Study of the Interpretation of Evolution by American Poets from Emerson to Robinson,* 241.

one of the police officers whom he has summoned to help him conduct his trial, God is allegorized as the "Head" (literally, the police chief); Magnus says, "Your Head gave me to understand that the disposition of these lives was entirely in my hands, however black the record of any one of them may be" (*TSS,* 192). Shortly thereafter Dexter, the officer, delivers a speech that reflects Christian theology of God the Father as the supreme figure of the godhead and Christ as the earthly representation of God: "The Head wished me to say that he greatly regretted not being here tonight as an onlooker. He is much interested in your view of it as an experiment. He will have his joke, sir: he called it your attempt to play God. (*Magnus frowns.*) He wished to see especially your disposition of cases where the law is inconclusive, the half-and-half crimes, Mr. Magnus" (193). In these two speeches Wilder is performing a kind of variation on dramatic irony—call it *allegorical irony*—in which we recognize that Dexter's report of the Head's sarcasm is actually telling the audience or reader that Magnus allegorically represents Christ. Though himself a character in the play, Magnus, when he frowns, seems to be just as displeased with the pointed reference to the play's allegorical mode as were the scholars quoted above.

To follow the development of the allegory of Judgment Day in *The Trumpet Shall Sound,* early in the play Wilder clearly establishes that the servants and the roomers, who will later be judged by Magnus, are the dead. The words "dead," "die," and "death" are repeated throughout the first act. Many of the references to death are in regard to the butler, who has literally died at the opening of the play, yet they also extend generally to the dead as all those who have died, and then more specifically to other living characters in the play. For example, Sara Budie, the housekeeper, asks, "Was you never in the house with the dead before? . . . Are the dead dead?" (11). Flora says to Nestor, her brother, "You're just as dead as John Bowles. *I* am alive" (20). Finally, Nestor says, "If this bird does turn up, whoever he is, . . . we'll see who's dead then" (20).

We have accounted for nearly all of the players in this Judgment Day play, but one. To clarify another point of confusion, scholars' complaints about the unjust judgment in *The Trumpet Shall Sound* are focused especially on Magnus's treatment of Flora, but the judgment may appear less unjust if Flora's allegorical identity is recognized: she is not merely a sinner, but the cause of sin, which is, in Christian theology, Satan or the Devil. The representation of Satan as a positive force of evil is a motif in Wilder's works that scholars have not recognized, but its pervasiveness in his oeuvre is surely another trace of the Puritan ethos inculcated in Wilder at an early age.

As with Judgment Day, the belief in Satan is a Christian (as well as a Judaic and Muslim) doctrine, but New England Puritanism had its own conceptualization of the supreme agent of evil.[29] While the Devil's presence at Judgment Day is only noted by Wigglesworth in stanza 36 of *The Day of Doom,* Edward Taylor portrays Satan in *God's Determinations* at some length attacking the Puritan Everyman character:

> Then Satan in a red-hot firy rage
> Comes bellowing, roaring, ready to ingage,
> To rend and tare in pieces small, all those
> Whom in the former Quarrell he did lose.
> But's boyling Poyson'd madness, being by
> A Shield Divine repelld, he thus lets fly:
> 'You Rebells all, I Will you gripe and fist;
> I'le make my Jaws a Mill to grin'de such grists . . .' (48)

Later in *God's Determinations,* Taylor portrays Satan abandoning this scare tactic and instead using devious logic to tempt the Elect into believing that they are actually reprobate: "Doth Mercys Sun through Peaces lattice clear / Shine in thy Soule? Then what's that Uproare there? / Look well about you, try before you trust: / Though Grace is Gracious; Justice still is just. / If so it be with you, say what you can, / You are not Saints, or I no Sinner am" (69). Taylor's multidimensional portrait of the Devil has its seeds in the Bible, of course, but not even the Bible dramatizes Satan as a character with dialogue and action as extensively as Taylor.

Wilder's early theological interest in the Devil is apparent not only in *Prosperina and the Devil* but also in *Hast Thou Considered My Servant Job?,* another of the explicitly biblical *Angel Plays.*[30] In this dramatic "paraphrase" of

29. After demonstrating the providential interpretation of history in the writings of Virginian colonists, Perry Miller comments on how Puritans both in New England and the South accounted for evil or misfortune in a providential theology:

> To men of the Reformation, to Protestants, the Devil was no abstraction; he was an ever-present force of evil, and to their eyes it seemed obvious that his last stronghold was the wilderness of America, inhabited by his imps [in other words, the Indians]. (*Errand into the Wilderness,* 114)

In corroboration of Miller, John O. King III explains, "[T]he wilderness can confront the American as a demonic otherness. Literally, in Puritan writings, America was the place of Satan" (*The Iron of Melancholy: Structure of Spiritual Conversion in America from the Puritan Conscience to Victorian Neurosis,* 1–2), and it was their errand, or mission, to overthrow the devil and make America the place of Christ, as suggested by the title of Cotton Mather's epic history, *Magnalia Christi Americana* (1702).

30. David Castronovo offers the most substantive discussion (*Thornton Wilder,* 66–67) of *Hast Thou Considered My Servant Job?* with regard to the problem of evil in a Christian worldview. After the 1920s, Wilder's treatment of evil follows a more Freudian than biblical approach (e.g., Henry in *The Skin of Our Teeth,* Uncle Charlie in *Shadow of a Doubt*),

the Old Testament book of Job, Wilder reverses the roles of Satan and God by having Satan allow Jesus to do his best to induce Judas, rather than Job, to "curse [the Devil] and die," which he does, thereby underscoring the triumph of forgiveness through Christ. As Wilder dramatizes him in this early three-minute play, Satan is bewildered by his servant Judas's repentance, which is suggested by the casting away of the thirty pieces of silver given to him to betray Christ, and by the marks of the rope on his neck from hanging himself (*CSPTW II,* 66), both events found in the Gospels. Since Wilder had already dramatized Satan as a literal character in his explicitly religious *Angel Plays,* we should not be surprised to find the Devil represented allegorically in *The Trumpet Shall Sound.*

The support for reading Flora as Satan is in the text of the play. Although Flora's motivation on the literal level of the story—unrequited love of Carlo—makes her somewhat sympathetic, her role in the plot as mastermind of the renting of the rooms and the usurper of authority in Magnus's absence signifies her nature as a schemer and a liar. The other characters in the play almost seem aware of whom she represents, as evident in the following series of speeches. Sarah characterizes Flora's actions as "Lies and plans of darkness" (12). In at least three instances, other characters refer to Flora as "wicked" (11, 14, 205). Carlo addresses her as "you devil" (129). Even Flora takes note of his nicknames for her: "Devil! Fool! Devil! Fool!" (129). Flora herself laments, "All this cleverness of mine that I've been doing bad with . . ." (128) and "Everything I do is wrong" (129). Nestor says of Flora's plan, "The thing's safe as hell. And I'll give you the credit for it, Flora. It was your idea" (13). Finally, Flora tells Carlo, "You know I've never in my life been in a church, before you took me tonight. I've tried to go a thousand times, but I've always been afraid" (143). Thus Flora is strongly associated with wickedness and the Devil.

Interpreted as a representation of Satan, Flora's fate—the prison sentence Magnus predicts and her ensuing suicide—corresponds, not as well as it might have, to Satan's being cast into the lake of fire, as in the Book of Revelation, *The Day of Doom,* and Wilder's *Prosperina and the Devil.* Another reason Wilder's allegorical representation of Satan went awry, perhaps, is that Flora's crime was too insignificant and her punishment too harsh on the literal level of the narrative.[31] Douglas Robinson describes a trap intrinsic to the subject of Judgment Day into which Wilder's first full-length play fell:

---

but even these agents of death are colored by a Puritan sensibility that sees them allegorically as the Devil or the reprobate, as will be discussed in Chapter Four.

31. A few scholars have cited this as why the play fails; for example, Kuner says, "The ending with Flora's suicide is too illogical" (*Bright and Dark,* 39).

There is a certain aesthetic satisfaction in the almost pantomimic separation of good from evil in the Book of Revelation that is lost in the Matthew passage when the damned speak and thus assume personalities. For as the judgment of the damned shifts to a quasi-realistic context, what happens is that one perversely begins to identify with them, not in repentance, as the writer desires, but in indignation. . . . It is this feature that the modern reader will find most disturbing about *The Day of Doom.* A thoughtful reading of the work is a positively frightening experience—one that frightens the reader not into moral obedience but into moral revulsion from the judgment. . . . [T]o render Christ's vindictiveness in a humanly plausible context [suggests] that divine diacrisis is human, and finally inhuman.[32]

Wilder's dramatization of Judgment Day as a drawing room trial does not read as a frightening experience to a contemporary sensibility; however, many of Wilder's characters, especially Flora, are shown to be genuinely fearful of the consequences of Magnus's return. Apart from an occasional speech that makes him appear silly, most of Magnus's speeches are solemn and authoritarian, in accordance with his divine nature as judge of humanity.[33] For example, when he enters near the end of Act Three, Magnus tells his informant, "I come here tonight, Miss Flecker, to see justice. Neither with vengeance; nor with pardon overflowing. Purest justice" (139).

Not only did previous studies miss Magnus's identity as Christ and condemn the harsh fate of Flora, they also misread the acts of judgment Magnus makes in which the roomers are separated as sheep and goats, the elect and the reprobate: "After Magnus questions each of the characters he decides that despite their wicked lives they are all worthy of forgiveness. . . . Wilder's idea might suggest that God in His infinite mercy, in the person of Magnus, can forgive even those who have committed serious sins; possibly only Flora, who has been guilty of the unpardonable sin of despair in taking her life, is beyond redemption." Kuner's description of almost-universal forgiveness is most likely based on the following speech by Magnus: "I am the owner of the house returned. Let me tell you right now that I forgive you. I am the only person injured by your intrusion and I forgive it you. As far as living in the house is concerned, you are absolved. If that is your total fault, you may return to your beds and sleep" (198). However, the speech continues, "But there are others among you whom I can forgive, but *not* absolve,—

32. Robinson, *American Apocalypses: The Image of the End of the World in American Literature,* 55.

33. The inconsistency of tone in Magnus's speeches and actions may result from the history of Wilder's dramatic conceptualizations of the play: "The idea of servants taking over their master's (God's) house in his absence first occurred to Thornton as comedy, then as a Renaissance tragedy and finally as ironic farce" (Harrison, *Enthusiast,* 56).

the thievish, the fraudulent, the blasphemers, and the filthy. These men and women it is the duty of citizenship to punish; perhaps to extirpate" (198, emphasis in original). Magnus does, in fact, order Miss Del Valle (who is apparently a prostitute) and Mrs. Miller (a shoplifter) and her young son to leave the house immediately (202, 199). Read within the Judgment Day allegory, this does not suggest forgiveness and admission to heaven, as Kuner suggests.[34] The rest of the boarders are judged as follows: Frau Soderstrom (a rich miserly woman) will be repaid her rent and must leave the next day; Carlo (Flora's lover) is allowed to leave that night but with a warning from Magnus to guard against weaknesses in his character; Sarah and Nestor's judgment is deferred until a letter allegedly confessing their unfaithfulness arrives or does not arrive; Mr. Gaylord (a crazed, older man betrayed by his daughters à la King Lear) is put to bed; Mr. Dabney (the evangelist) is allowed to stay on as a guest; Miss Flecker will be repaid her rent and is offered the job of caretaker of the house; and, finally, Magnus tells some unnamed roomers to leave the next day. Magnus has, indeed, divided the "half-and-half" into the sheep and goats, the elect and the reprobate. Allegorically, then, not everyone is welcomed into Magnus's mansion, which has many rooms.[35]

The fact that some of the characters Magnus judges favorably (i.e., Miss Flecker, Dabney, and Carlo) seem more morally reprehensible than Flora (on the literal level) has led scholars to see his impromptu trial as all too human rather than divine.[36] One explanation of the seemingly imperfect judgment in Magnus's pronouncements is that it reflects the Calvinistic doctrine of predestination, which appears to the modern sensibility like a moral arbitrariness, and—as with the famous example from stanza 181 of Wigglesworth's *The Day of Doom* in which Christ grants the reprobate infants "the easiest room in hell"—even unjust. The criticism of arbitrariness and unfairness is what, in part, led to the decline of belief in Calvinistic theology by American Protestants. As for Wilder, Goldstein says, "The tenets of Calvinism

34. Kuner, *Bright and Dark,* 38. But reviewers of the play also got it wrong. In a file at Beinecke labeled "Trumpet" is a clipping of a newspaper review in which Magnus's dispensation of judgment is characterized similarly to Kuner's: "He proves to be a forgiving judge and lets each transgressor go his way."

35. While Wigglesworth gives the most space in his ballad to justifying the damnation of the reprobate, Taylor emphasizes the elect; however, in these lines from *God's Determinations* it is clear that he too conceptualized Judgment Day as separating the saved and the damned: "You'l see both Good and Bad drawn up hereby / These to Hells Horrour, those to Heavens Joy" (98).

36. Haberman asserts that the last act in *The Trumpet Shall Sound* demonstrates the "total failure of human justice emphasized by Magnus' name and its suggestion of greatness and generosity" (*Plays of Thornton Wilder,* 30).

were too deeply imbedded in his personality to suffer even partial displacement without a struggle."[37]

Such a deterministic doctrine is suggested in various speeches throughout *The Trumpet Shall Sound*. Flora says to Carlo, defending her behavior, "But I'm only half-wrong. It's like things been planned to come out this way" (130). With regard to Miss Del Valle, police officer Dexter says, "I'm sorry, Mr. Magnus, but we never do anything with them. Of course, we find them in every haul, like this. There's nothing the force can do with them, Mr. Magnus. The Head calls them the little fish that are found in the net every time you draw it up, and that you throw back into the water as a matter of course" (201). The allegorical implication is that there are those such as Miss Del Valle who are not saved by the "fishers of men" (Matt. 4:19), but are already condemned by God. In *The Day of Doom,* Wigglesworth has Christ respond to the reprobates' protest that predestining some souls for damnation and others for salvation is unfair: "Amongst all those their souls that lose, / none can Rejection blame. / He that may choose, or else refuse, / all men to save or spill, / May this Man choose, and that refuse, / redeeming whom he will" (stanza 43).[38]

This is not necessarily to suggest that Wilder is consciously allegorizing the Calvinistic doctrine of predestination of the elect and reprobate; rather, the dichotomous structure of characters depicted literally as the elect and reprobate in Puritan narrative works such as Taylor's *Gods Determinations* or Wigglesworth's *Day of Doom* were passed down to Wilder as a cultural code that manifests itself in different terms, and when those terms occur in a context of literal or allegorical religious issues, especially within a Protestant worldview, then it is reasonable to conclude that this is a trace element of the cultural continuity unearthed in this study.[39]

That the doctrine of predestination alluded to in *The Trumpet Shall Sound* is a particularly Protestant belief is illustrated by the character of Horace Dabney, the sea captain turned evangelist who is wanted by the authorities for

---

37. Goldstein, *Art,* 22.

38. The doctrine of predestination is unorthodox, even irreligious, according to contemporary Christian theology; however, the Puritans were able, for a time, to rationalize this belief: "The unregenerate will is not really free, since it can will only evil.... He wills as he chooses, but his choice is determined by his sinful nature.... [Calvin] makes a distinction between compulsion and necessity from which it appears that man, while he sins of necessity, yet sins no less voluntarily; for he follows his inclination, albeit a predestined inclination" (Perry D. Westbrook, *Free Will and Determination in American Literature,* 3, 5, 6).

39. Emory Elliott notes, "The Puritan ideas of elect and non-elect, the calling, and the covenant became key metaphors through which Americans understood and expressed their social situation" ("The Puritan Roots of American Whig Rhetoric," 108).

abandoning his ship and leaving its passengers to drown. In Dabney's explanation of what happened on the ship we see an anti-Catholicism typical of fundamentalist Protestants from the seventeenth century to today: "I endeavored for a while to spread the grace of inspired interpretation among the passengers, but found them to be of that faith for which judgment and destruction are laid up in the book of Revelation. And I saw in a dream that my true work would lie in America at a later time" (131), and then we learn what the faith of the passengers was: "I saw clearly that my work must go on. I could not evade my heavenly appointment: my mission must go on . . . I remember quite distinctly that they had heard mass that morning from a priest of their own" (132). To underscore that these drowned passengers were Catholic, Wilder has Dabney explain that he was transporting them from Queenstown (formerly Cobh), a seaport in southern Ireland, to Boston aboard the ship *Limerick Lady.* Dabney's defense of his deed is based on his claim that his Catholic passengers were already damned; in other words, it didn't matter that he let them drown since their souls were predestined for hell anyway. Of those who sought to punish him, Dabney says, "They could not know the mysterious and religious reasons whereby I stand justified. . . . The law remains insensible to motives, often of the most elevated sort" (132). Magnus not only exonerates Dabney, he even welcomes the evangelist to stay on in his house. If Magnus is an allegorical representation of Christ, then Wilder is expressing a version of Christianity in which neither works nor free will affect one's eternal destiny, but, rather, God's determinations alone.[40]

Even Flora, the "Devil" in *The Trumpet Shall Sound,* is probably also intended to represent a member "of that faith for which judgment and destruction are laid up in the book of Revelation." First, she comes from Puerto Rico, which suggests Spanish culture and Catholicism. Second, a key distinction between Puritanism and Catholicism is the former's condemnation of iconography and the latter's employment of it. Flora's collection of superstitious objects and religious paraphernalia clearly aligns her with Catholic devotional practice. To underscore the contrast of Protestantism and Catholicism with respect to Dabney and Flora, Wilder has Flora ask Carlo, "And when they pray they kneel down?" which is consistent with Catholic devotional practice, and then she describes Dabney's church, clearly in contrast to a Catholic church: "He says his church has no candles or statues" (143). A final example of anti-Catholic bias in the play demonstrates how much the history of the Reformation was inculcated in Wilder: Flora

---

40. Walter G. Muelder puts it very succinctly: "We are free to do as we please, but we are not free to please as we please" (quoted in Westbrook, *Free Will,* 20).

tells Carlo she has some "earth from Jerusalem" sold to her by a priest (143), obviously an allusion to an old Protestant attack upon Catholicism—the charge that priests in the Middle Ages sold fake relics.[41]

In the preceding discussion of Wilder's dramatic works of the Jazz Age, we have seen both explicit and implicit (allegorical) signification of the Judgment Day theme in Puritan terms. That these efforts were not wholly successful is due, at least in part, to their being composed very early in Wilder's life, before he could even be said to have had a writing career. With his two novels of the 1920s, Wilder's literary career began in earnest. *The Cabala* (1926) was generally well received by critics and provided Wilder with an entree into the exclusive world of literary celebrities. (After its publication he was invited to a party where he met F. Scott Fitzgerald and Edmund Wilson.) *The Bridge of San Luis Rey* (1927) was an enormous success, with both the critics and the public; it became an international bestseller, allowing Wilder to retire from teaching for a time, and it won him the first of three Pulitzer Prizes. In relation to the Judgment Day theme, although neither novel dramatizes the trial of all flesh as the plays did, both of them in the course of their narration enact judgment on a selection of character types, so that the novels also manifest a Puritan eschatological conceptualization of America.

The Cabala

Wilder's first novel, written after the *Angel Plays* and *The Trumpet Shall Sound,* mixes autobiography with fantasy. The first-person narrator is a young American scholar who comes to Europe to continue his studies, just as Wilder spent the year after graduating from Yale in Rome. The narrator, who never reveals his name but is called "Samuele" by the European characters he comes to know, ends up studying a group of the elite persons of Rome referred to as "the Cabala." He sees them as representatives of a decadent, declining Europe, and in the end he gladly returns to America, "longing for the shelf of Manhattan" (144). It should be obvious to students of American literature that the plot, as related thus far, bears close resemblance to other American novels that show the modern American abroad (for example, Henry James's *The American*). Indeed, in an interview with Robert Van Gelder in 1948, Wilder said he used to think *The Cabala* was "a wholly individual performance, but now I realize that it reflected the fashion of that period. The only difference is that it was written by the son of a

41. To be fair to Wilder, there is a progressive ecumenicalism in his works, beginning with *The Bridge of San Luis Rey.*

Maine Calvinist." That difference manifests itself tonally in *The Cabala* in that Wilder does not criticize his American protagonist for his lack of sophistication in contrast to the Europeans.[42] In fact, Samuele may represent America both allegorically and typologically, if we note two possible namesakes: Uncle Sam for the United States, and Samuel, the Old Testament prophet in the Bible.

The fantastic twist on this plot is that Samuele discovers that the members of the Cabala are actually reincarnations of the gods of antiquity, and he himself is the newest incarnation of Mercury, the messenger god.[43] In the Old Testament, the prophet Samuel, too, was a messenger, bringing God's word to Saul, the first king of Israel. Thus in *The Cabala* Wilder conflates classical and biblical identities, which is characteristic of the Puritans' extended typology, as we saw in *Prosperina and the Devil.*

In fact, *The Cabala* is quite explicit about America's Puritan heritage. As quoted in the Introduction, Wilder has one of the members of the European Cabala say, "Now in America you are all descended from your Puritans, are you not, and your ideas are very different" (36). It can also be deduced that it is to the Puritans Samuele is referring when he thinks about some advice he is given: *"Never try to do anything against the bent of human nature. I came from a colony guided by exactly the opposite principle"* (54). Such statements in the novel as the following would seem to reduce "Puritan" to the cultural stereotype of Puritanism: "Heaven knows what New England divines lent me their remorseless counsels. I became possessed with the wine of the Puritans and alternating the vocabulary of the Pentateuch with that of psychiatry I showed him where his mind was already slipping . . . [and] had the energy and sincerity which the Puritan can always draw upon to censure those activities he cannot permit himself" (61–62). However, traces of the more specific features of American Puritanism already discussed in regard to the *Angel Plays* and *The Trumpet Shall Sound* may be found in *The Cabala.*

Allusions to Judgment Day occur in the text of Wilder's first novel. Samuele refers to a piece of music as "This motet for ten voices, a chorus of angels on the last day" (98). Even more directly, in describing the grave of Marcantonio, a character who, like Flora in *The Trumpet Shall Sound,* commits

42. Jackson R. Bryer, ed., *Conversations with Thornton Wilder,* 44. Castronovo compares *The Cabala* to James's novels, but he criticizes *The Cabala* for its different treatment of the material: "While Wilder directs us toward his [Samuele's] puritanical nature, he does not make him confront himself" (*Thornton Wilder,* 42). What Castronovo would apparently prefer to see is the Puritan American humbled, to have him disavow his American Puritan values. However, unlike James, Wilder compares European and American cultures in such a way as to have America appear more positive.

43. See Rex Burbank, *Thornton Wilder,* 31, for his list correlating the members of the Cabala with the Roman gods.

suicide in despair over his debauchery, Samuele observes that "the mother had contrived a false wall of stones and briars that seemed to include his grave among those of souls that the Church felt safe in recommending at the Judgment Day" (138). While Judgment Day is also a Catholic belief, what colors these allusions to the end of the world as Puritan is their association with America. At the end of *The Cabala,* Wilder implies that civilization has reached its zenith rather than its nadir, as in the zeitgeist of the post–World War I period (and expressed in such literary works as Eliot's *The Waste Land*). Traveling back to America on an ocean liner, Samuele summons the ghost of Virgil, who speaks amazingly like a Puritan: "I cannot enter Zion until I have forgotten Rome" (147), with Zion representing the New World, the site of the prophesied New Jerusalem, and Rome representing the Catholic Church, with which Protestant Reformers had broken. In their conversation Virgil describes a cyclical view of history, citing the rise and fall of empires and great cities, but after the ghost's departure Samuele expresses a progressive and finite sense of history: "The engines beneath me pounded eagerly towards the new world and the last and greatest of all cities" (148)—that is, New York. For New York to be the last and the greatest of all cities, history would have to be coming to an end. Even the European characters recognize—indeed, almost prophesy—the providential destiny of America: "He comes from the rich new country that will grow more and more splendid while our countries decline to ruins and rubbish heaps" (69).[44]

In *The Cabala* Wilder also uses allegory as he did in his first full-length play, *The Trumpet Shall Sound.* For example, the Cardinal, the de facto leader of the Cabala, is an allegorical representation not of God or Christ, but of Satan.[45] As evidence for reading the Cardinal this way, Samuele relates what a servant who witnessed a scene involving the Cardinal told him: "She [Astree-Luce] called out: The Devil is here. The Devil has come into this room. At the Cardinal!" (132). Astree-Luce, another member of the Cabala, claims the Cardinal had killed God (134), and Samuele observes, "If she had lost God, oh how clearly she had gained the Devil" (134). Astree-Luce is so

---

44. Most scholars describe Wilder's view of history as cyclical; see, for example, Burbank, *Thornton Wilder,* 93; Haberman, *Plays of Thornton Wilder,* 37; and Ethan Mordden, *The American Theatre,* 207. However, Helmut Papajewski notes that "in *The Cabala,* he has oriented the action to the eschatological" (*Thornton Wilder,* 15). Wilder's view of history will be examined in depth in Chapter Three.

45. Previous scholars have come close to this reading of the Cardinal's allegorical identity: "When [the Cardinal] brings the full force of his great intellect upon [Astree-Luce's] simple, naive faith, he becomes the epitome of evil" (Burbank, *Thornton Wilder,* 36). W. D. Maxwell-Mahon writes, "Having lost his own faith, the Cardinal sets about destroying that of Astree-Luce. It is devil's work . . . ; Astree-Luce is convinced that he is Satan himself" ("The Novels of Thornton Wilder," 37).

distraught over the Cardinal destroying her faith that she actually attempts to shoot him (134). Although the Cardinal is not as developed an allegorical representation of the Devil as was Flora in *The Trumpet Shall Sound,* he is nevertheless responsible for Astree-Luce's loss of faith and the subsequent breakup of the Cabala, and though he is filled with remorse, he dies not long after the episode.[46]

On the literal level of the novel, the Cardinal is esteemed as a figure of authority in the Church, a keen intellectual, and a member of the Cabala. But the Cardinal has allegorical significance, and the allegorical meaning corresponds to Puritan beliefs about the Roman Catholic Church. This depiction of the Cardinal as a Satanic figure is another manifestation of the Puritan ethos inculcated in Wilder as a child; in fact, most of the European characters in *The Cabala* are implicitly identified as Catholic, while Samuele explicitly labels himself American and Protestant (21–22). The anti-Catholicism of the Puritan ethos Wilder inherited may account for why Samuele never seems to express guilt or even regret over Marcantonio's suicide (which he helped bring about with his condemnation of the young man's promiscuity),[47] especially if one recalls a similar lack of remorse in *The Trumpet Shall Sound* by Dabney, the former sailor turned evangelist who played a role in the drowning of the Catholic passengers when his ship sank. This is not to suggest that Wilder was consciously prejudiced toward Catholics or Catholicism, only that there may be a cultural explanation for why the Catholic characters in many of his works of the 1920s, when he was still near his Congregationalist upbringing, are portrayed as doomed or corrupted or harmful to themselves and to others. Perhaps Wilder realized this and made amends with the respectful portrait of the Abbess in *The Bridge of San Luis Rey.*[48]

Thus in his first novel Wilder affirms a Puritan view of America through

46. Taylor also dramatized how Satan can appear to be one of God's servants at first and then reveal his true self later: "And in this nick of time the Foe, through spite, / Doth like a glorious Angell seem of Light. / Yet though he painteth o're his Velvet smut, / He Cannot yet Conceal his Cloven foot. / . . . . Off goes the Angels Coate, on goes his own; / With Griping Paws, and Goggling Eyes draws nigher, / Like some fierce Shagg'd Red Lion, belching fire" (*GD,* 52).

47. In defense of Samuele, however, Maxwell-Mahon correctly points out, "Despite its disastrous consequences, Samuele's attempt to reform Marcantonio by turning him into an Italian version of an all-American college boy is basically humanitarian" ("Novels of Thornton Wilder," 36).

48. The Puritans saw the Catholic Church as the Antichrist. They believed that Catholics were not among the elect, and thus they were not going to heaven. While this may be a controversial reading of Wilder, it would seem to account for 1) the negative treatment of Catholic characters in Wilder's early works, and 2) the growing positive treatment of Catholic characters in his later works. That is, Wilder's religious worldview became more and more ecumenical the older he became, most likely the result of his distancing himself from the beliefs of his father and himself when he was a young man. I do

the ascendancy of his narrator/protagonist over the declining Europeans. Residual traces of Calvinist and other beliefs of the Puritans can also be seen in his second novel, which likewise resonates with the Judgment Day theme.

The Bridge of San Luis Rey

Wilder's second and most popular novel, *The Bridge of San Luis Rey*,[49] which also won him his first Pulitzer Prize, is not an allegory of Judgment Day, nor does it allude to Judgment Day explicitly, yet its central concern is judgment of the principal characters. Indeed, the effect and meaning of "the sometimes obtrusive presence of the omniscient author, who judges and interprets as he narrates the histories and inner lives of the main characters" is quite similar to Act Four of Wilder's Judgment Day play *The Trumpet Shall Sound*.[50] However, it is not only the author—or the narrator, to be more precise—but also the Franciscan priest Brother Juniper who judges major and minor characters in the novel. In fact, he devises a system of evaluating the victims of "acts of God" to detect the hand of Providence at work. Like Peter Magnus in *The Trumpet Shall Sound,* Brother Juniper, though for different and disinterested reasons, conducts his own "trial of all flesh." Thus *The Bridge of San Luis Rey* examines ontological and epistemological issues of this life that have ultimate ramifications in the next life, making it like the other literary descendants of *The Day of Doom* already discussed in this chapter, despite the non–New England and non-Protestant milieu—eighteenth-century Peru in predominantly Catholic South America.

Scholars have noted that setting *The Bridge* in Peru was only a defamiliarizing technique. In an interview Wilder said, "It merely supplied the background of the story. It could have been placed in any other country just as well. Peruvian scenery and manners were not essential."[51] In the text of the

---

not point this out to criticize Wilder, because I do not think he was consciously prejudiced against Catholics; my surmise is that he began to be aware of the anti-Catholicism in his early beliefs and intentionally began to show more respect for Catholics, beginning with the Abbess in *The Bridge of San Luis Rey*.

49. "It sold more than three hundred thousand copies in the U.S. its first year and two million worldwide between 1927 and 1958" (Jackson R. Bryer, "Thornton Wilder at 100: Wilder's Literary Legacy," 26).

50. Burbank, *Thornton Wilder*, 48.

51. For example, Morgan writes, "He used historical flight as a technique, choosing to portray twentieth-century Americans in an eighteenth-century Peruvian setting that was more flexible and whose remoteness gave him the perspective he needed" ("Early Thornton Wilder," 251). Bryer, ed., *Conversations*, 6.

novel, too, are hints that Wilder was thinking of the story as closer to home. In referring to the Marquesa coming back to Peru from Spain, the narrator says that she "took ship and returned to America" (16), even though, properly speaking, it is *South* America. Later the narrator identifies South America—or Peru, at least—as "the New World" (31).

As for the Catholic context of the theological issues raised in the novel, Haberman points out that "[T]he meaning of life of the novel's characters is closer to old-fashioned Protestant individual will."[52] Though we do not have Protestant characters counterpoised to Catholic characters, as in Wilder's other works of the 1920s, there are still vestiges of Puritan prejudice toward Catholics in *The Bridge,* as in the following passage: "*I am told that in the convent the silly sisters inhale it so diligently that one cannot smell the incense at Mass*" (18). But does the following description mock only the Marquesa or Catholic devotion in general? "She hysterically hugged the altar-rails trying to rend from the gaudy statuettes a sign, only a sign, the ghost of a smile, the furtive nod of a waxen head" (31–32). Idolatry was one of the charges the Puritans made against Catholics; even the Abbess in *The Bridge* is said to have "torn an idol from her heart" (102). Except for Brother Juniper, priests are not highly regarded in the book, even by their superior: "The Archbishop knew that most of the priests of Peru were scoundrels" (81). Furthermore, the Archbishop is portrayed in terms hardly respectful: "There was something in Lima that was wrapped up in yards of violet satin from which protruded a great dropsical head and two fat pearly hands; and that was its archbishop. Between the rolls of flesh that surrounded them looked out two black eyes speaking discomfort, kindliness, and wit. A curious and eager soul was imprisoned in all this lard, but by dint of never refusing himself a pheasant or a goose or his daily procession of Roman wines, he was his own bitter jailer" (80).

Yet the novel's respect for Brother Juniper and especially the Abbess makes up for any negative descriptions of Catholicism elsewhere; more importantly, the theological issues are framed in terms closer to Puritanism than Catholicism.[53] The dominant interpretative issue in *The Bridge* is the belief in Providence; as the narrator says in his description of Brother Juniper's investigation, "Either we live by accident and die by accident, or we live by plan and die by plan" (7). The hermeneutic Brother Juniper applies to events is almost identical with that of Puritan historians such as Edward Johnson,

---

52. Haberman, *Plays of Thornton Wilder,* 33.
53. In an interview Wilder explained, "The central idea of the work, the justification for a number of human lives that comes up as a result of the sudden collapse of a bridge, stems from friendly arguments with my father, a strict Calvinist. Strict Puritans imagine God all too easily as a petty schoolmaster who minutely weighs guilt against merit" (Bryer, ed., *Conversations,* 59).

the author of *Wonder-Working Providence of Sions Savior in New England.* When disease, death, or other misfortune occurs, Johnson refers to the "rod of God" (258); good fortune he attributes to Providence. In *The Bridge,* the narrator shows us how Brother Juniper made the connection between divine intentions and historical experience: "If there were any plan in the universe at all, if there were any pattern in a human life, surely it could be discovered mysteriously latent in those lives so suddenly cut off. . . . This collapse of the bridge of San Luis Rey was a sheer act of God. It afforded a perfect laboratory. Here at last one could surprise His intentions in a pure state" (7). Johnson also interpreted "acts of God" in his history of seventeenth-century New England: "This yeare . . . the Lord caused a great and terrible Earth-quake" (185).[54]

The claim that Brother Juniper, a Catholic priest, expresses a theology closer to Puritanism than to Catholicism may seem less radical in view of the response his project elicits from his superiors: he is burnt at the stake as a heretic. Another indication that the version of Christianity *The Bridge* represents is closer to Puritanism than it is to Catholicism occurs when the narrator describes Brother Juniper's purpose with an allusion to a rather famous English Puritan poet's intention in retelling the story of the garden of Eden: "He would fall to dreaming of experiments that would justify the ways of God to man" (8)—obviously, John Milton's *Paradise Lost.*

A major tenet of American Puritanism especially, the view of history as providentially determined, colors the novel, though both early and recent commentators have argued against determinism in *The Bridge.*[55] Despite the apparent indeterminacy suggested by Brother Juniper's failure to prove God's intentions, and the titling of the frame chapters of *The Bridge* "Perhaps an Accident" and "Perhaps an Intention" ("perhaps" is one of the most repeated words in the novel), Wilder provides enough information about each of the characters for the hand of Providence to be seen in the bridge falling: "He [Brother Juniper] thought he saw in the same accident the wicked vis-

54. Note the similarity between Brother Juniper's project and the following description of a Puritan historian's methodology:

> His task as "the Lord's Remembrancer" was not to cut and trim experience to fit the curve of the providential epic, but to discover the point at which, without violating the integrity of either the Book of Nature or the Book of Scriptures, he might see them combining in one harmonious, mutually supporting whole . . . . History, as Bradford practiced it, was the continuing process in which the historian struggled to mediate between an imperfectly understood providential design and the continually unfolding realm of historical experience. (Alan Howard, "Art and History in Bradford's 'Of Plymouth Plantation,'" 266)

55. "This view of history bred a sense of resignation that especially flavored *The Bridge*" (Morgan, "Early Thornton Wilder," 252). Like most readers of *The Bridge,* Lifton says the issue of accident/intention is left unanswered (*Vast Encyclopedia,* 51). I disagree: Wilder dramatizes the answer, even while having the narrator tell us that it is uncertain.

ited by destruction and the good called early to Heaven" (101). Kuner concludes, "Pepita was a good child, so was Jaime. Therefore the accident called
the young to Heaven while they were still pure. On the other hand, Uncle
Pio had led a dissolute life and the Marquesa was an avaricious drunkard.
Therefore the accident punished the wicked."[56]

Besides, for all his skeptical commentary on Brother Juniper's quest, the
narrator expresses the alternatives to the question of Providence in such a
way that neither version denies a Calvinistic universe ruled by a sovereign
God: "Some say that we shall never know and that to the gods we are like
flies that the boys kill on a summer day, and some say, on the contrary, that
the very sparrows do not lose a feather that has not been brushed away by
the finger of God" (9). Borrowing from Shakespeare (*King Lear* 4.1.36) and
the Bible (Matt. 10:29–30), the point is the same: the gods or God controls
history; the difference lies in the point of view—tragic or reverent (in
Calvinistic terms, reprobate or elect).[57] Note the similarity of language used
by Johnson in *Wonder-Working Providence:* "and the marvellous providences
which you shall now heare, be not the very finger of God" (60–61). While the
narrator of *The Bridge*'s own stance would not allow a glib "All's for the best
in this best of all possible worlds," he does admit near the end, "But where
are sufficient books to contain the events that would not have been the same
without the fall of the bridge?" (105).[58] From one perspective, then, the accident was a fortunate fall.

The belief that Providence operates on a larger historical level is also affirmed in *The Bridge*, as seen in the Abbess's protofeminism and her care of
the mentally ill: "She was one of those persons who have allowed their lives
to be gnawed away because they have fallen in love with an idea several centuries before its appointed appearance in the history of civilization" (27). For
the Puritans, everything had its appointed appearance in God's plot, especially the establishment of a colony in New England.[59] Clearly, Wilder—or

56. Kuner, *Bright and Dark*, 76. A few students in my Wilder seminar offered during
the spring 1997 semester chose to write on the Providence issue, and they made convincing arguments in support of Brother Juniper's position. For example, Christie
Kennedy wrote, "Wilder portrays Esteban as a lost soul when Manuel dies. He even talks
about suicide, which was considered a mortal sin. . . . Wilder's account of Esteban's life
makes his death on the bridge seem part of a divine plan to save him from sadness and
the possibility of his impending tragic sin."

57. Jean Leahey, another student in the Wilder seminar, pointed out that in the passage there is also a hint of random acts by the gods (as boys randomly kill flies) versus
very precise acts by God (feather brushed from a sparrow by the finger of God).

58. Renee Semler, another student in the Wilder seminar, called my attention to the
significance of this sentence to the Providence theme.

59. Johnson describes the New England Puritans as "the forerunners of Christ's
army" and asks his readers to consider "whether the Lord hath not sent this people to
preach in the Wildernesse" (*WWP*, 60–61).

his narrator—is affirming the belief that "there's a divinity that shapes our ends, rough-hew them how we will" (Shakespeare, *Hamlet* V.ii.10–11).

The problem with deterministic explanations of history, at least when the Determiner is believed to be good, is the existence of evil in the world, in events, and in people. As demonstrated in Wigglesworth's *The Day of Doom*, it was possible for the Puritans to rationalize that the doctrine of predestination did not absolve individual souls of responsibility for their reprobate nature or behavior. Compared to Wigglesworth's hard-line Calvinism, Taylor's consideration of evil in *God's Determinations* seems much more humanistic. In Taylor's Puritan morality play the blame for the failure or delay of the allegorical character sometimes identified as "Soul" to come into assurance of election is laid upon Satan. Following the theological tradition that extends in the United States from Wigglesworth and Taylor to the present, in *The Bridge* Wilder addresses the theodicy problem with a providential worldview by including in his anatomy of souls an allegorical representation of the Devil—Uncle Pio. This study's reading of a motif of Satan figures in *Prosperina and the Devil, Hast Thou Considered My Servant Job?, The Trumpet Shall Sound, The Cabala,* and *The Bridge of San Luis Rey* is an original, albeit controversial, contribution to Wilder scholarship. The fact that there are also literal representations and references to the Devil in some of these works as well as the allegorical figures noted here suggests that this motif may have been part of a young Wilder's intentions, but it was at least part of the unconscious influence of his Puritan heritage. The prominence of Satan in the Puritan tradition (and in this study's Puritan touchstone, Taylor's *God's Determinations*) further supports this reading. These characters are, on the literal level, at least somewhat sympathetic—a fact that does not preclude their having a different allegorical significance. Since this motif ends or is transformed to a secular equivalent of the psychological deviant (e.g., Henry in *The Skin of Our Teeth,* Uncle Charlie in *Shadow of a Doubt,* George Lansing in *The Eighth Day*), perhaps Wilder consciously suppressed this more overt Puritan vestige, along with other explicit references.

In *The Trumpet Shall Sound* Wilder's allegorical representation of Satan went awry, perhaps, because Flora's crime was too insignificant and her punishment too harsh on the literal level of the narrative; in *The Bridge,* Wilder creates a more appropriate Satanic character to represent the Devil in an attempt to address the problem of evil within a providential universe. Although other characters in the novel exhibit attitudes and behaviors considered sinful in a Christian context, what distinguishes Uncle Pio is his manipulation, temptation, and destruction of others. That is, Uncle Pio is a representative of the category of souls in Brother Juniper's Judgment

scheme which "was not . . . merely bad: [but] was a propagandist for bad-
ness" (98–99).[60]

So there will be no mistaking what or who Uncle Pio represents, the summary of his life includes descriptions traditionally associated with the Devil
or Satan. The narrator says that Uncle Pio can be seen on a street in a typical posture as he "whispers, his lips laid against his victim's ear"; he is to be
left to "his underworld . . . He is like a soiled pack of cards [and the
Marquesa] doubt[s] whether the whole Pacific could wash him sweet and fra-
grant again" (67–68); "He possessed . . . that freedom from conscience that
springs from a contempt for the dozing rich he preyed upon" (70); "He
spread slanders at so much a slander . . . he was sent out by the government
to inspirit some half-hearted rebellions in the mountains so that the government could presently arrive and whole-heartedly crush them" (70); "His pretensions to omniscience became more and more plausible," and he "was
perpetually astonished that a prince should make so little use of his position,
for power, or for fantasy, or for sheer delight in the manipulation of other
men's destinies" (72–73, 73); he watches Camila give a performance, "standing at the back of the auditorium, bent double with joy and malice" (78).
When Brother Juniper conducts his research on Uncle Pio, only Camila
speaks well of him: "Her characterization of Uncle Pio flatly contradicted
the stores of unsavory testimonies that he had acquired elsewhere" (101).
(She was, of course, greatly indebted to him for her own success in life;
therefore, she could not be considered an unbiased source.) If this were not
enough, even Uncle Pio's physical appearance resembles the traditional portrait of the Devil: "With his whisp [sic] of a mustache and his whisp of a
beard and his big ridiculous sad eyes" (72).

As a deceiver of great subtlety and invention, Uncle Pio is a pretender to
and a parody of God. Thus his name—Uncle Pio, suggesting pious—is ironic.
The ostensibly affectionate title of "uncle" should not necessarily be taken at
face value either; in *Shadow of a Doubt,* "Uncle" Charlie turns out to be a serial killer, and recall that the Cardinal in *The Cabala* was a destroyer of faith
rather than a creator, and that Taylor also dramatized Satan in disguise as
an angel of light in *God's Determinations.* Furthermore, Wilder follows Milton's portrayal of Satan as one who would rather rule in hell than to serve in
heaven: "Even in this kingdom he [Uncle Pio] was lonely, and proud in his
loneliness, as though there resided a certain superiority in such a solitude"

60. Burbank is the only previous scholarly reader of *The Bridge* who has even come
close to this view of Uncle Pio: "Until he meets Camila, Pio is totally unscrupulous"
(*Thornton Wilder,* 45). On the literal level, Uncle Pio is a lover of theater, literature, and his
creation, Camila Perichole. But those literal traits do not preclude his allegorical identity
as the devil.

(73). This allegorical Satan even has his own version of Calvinistic predestination:

> He divided the inhabitants of this world into two groups, into those who had
> loved and those who had not. It was a horrible aristocracy, apparently for
> those who had no capacity for love (or rather for suffering in love) could not be
> said to be alive and certainly would not live again after their death. They were
> a kind of straw population, filling the world with their meaningless laughter
> and tears and chatter and disappearing still lovable and vain into thin air. . . .
> He regarded love as a sort of cruel malady through which *the elect* are required
> to pass in their late youth and from which they emerge, pale and wrung, but
> ready for the business of living. (83, emphasis added)

From a Puritan perspective, then, on the literal level of the narrative Uncle
Pio's untimely death would not seem to bode well for a blissful afterlife since
he has not made progress during his life on earth, as Camila tells him: "You
don't seem to learn as you grow older, Uncle Pio" (89). That Uncle Pio is cat-
egorically different from Camila in the state of his soul is evident in the narrator's comment that "One day an accident befell that lost him his share in
her progress" (91). Camila's slow conversion from her former selfish life is
confirmed by the implication (though it is fairly oblique) that it will be she
who takes over the charitable work of the Abbess (caring for the mentally ill
and other unfortunates): "She [the Abbess] disappeared a moment to return
with one of her helpers, one who had likewise been involved in the affair of
the bridge and who had formerly been an actress. 'She is leaving me,' said
the Abbess, 'for some work across the city'" (107). For Camila to have gone
from cafe singer, to honored actress, to member of the social Cabala in
Lima, to comforter of the poor and sick, attests to the progress of grace in
her life. Uncle Pio was responsible for her ascension in the world, but her
spiritual growth was solely the result of the accident of the bridge, an act of
God which, as we have seen, had fortuitous as well as tragic effects. For the
Puritans, the proof was in the progressive manifestation of their election.
Wilder plots such a trajectory for Camila, but not for Uncle Pio.[61]

The Bridge also affirms progress on the historical level, as is evident when
Wilder employs dramatic irony (relying on the reader's knowledge of the advances made in the twentieth century for the care of the mentally ill, the

---

61. One might argue, as one of my students and a Wilder scholar have in unpublished
responses to this reading, in a more traditional interpretation of Uncle Pio, that he was
redeemed by his love for Camila. Space does not permit an analysis of Uncle Pio's motives for wanting to teach first Camila and then her son Jaime (was it for their sake or his
own?). If, in his beliefs, Wilder did indeed have sympathy for the "Devil," that wouldn't
change the fact that he (Uncle Pio, in this case) is still the Devil.

physically handicapped, and so forth) in the Abbess's hopeful musing on what could be done for the suffering of those she cares for as best she can:

> The Abbess would stop in a passageway and say suddenly: "I can't help think- ing that something could be done for the deaf-and-dumb. It seems to me that some patient person could, . . . could study out a language for them. You know there are hundreds and hundreds in Peru. Do you remember whether anyone in Spain has found a way for them? Well, some day they will." Or a little later: "Do you know, I keep thinking that something can be done for the insane. I am old, you know, and I cannot go where these things are talked about, but I watch them sometimes and it seems to me . . . In Spain, now, they are gentle with them? It seems to me that there is a secret about it, just hidden from us, just around the corner." (106)

Of course she is right; sign language, Braille, and psychoanalysis and other theories and methods of psychiatry are just a century or so away. In some ways, then, things do get better; the kind of charity people like the Abbess used to do as a matter of their religious beliefs becomes institutionalized; so ciety itself becomes more charitable.

Thus *The Bridge* shows us a world in which there are no real accidents, nor the free reign of evil; judgment and the appropriate reward or punishment occur within the providence that presides over the events of our lives; prog- ress is made on the historical and personal levels (at least for the elect); and all of this is discernible—even provable, though Brother Juniper paid with his life for trying to provide the proof that each soul must find for him- or herself. As the Abbess tells herself near the end of the novel when all loose ends have been tied up, all plot lines resolved, "'Learn at last that anywhere you may expect grace.' And she was filled with happiness like a girl at this new proof that the traits she lived for were everywhere, that the world was ready" (106). The very last lines of *The Bridge* are more bittersweet in tone as they remind us of the deaths of the five travelers on the bridge and allude to the death and being forgotten "predestined" for us all; yet the narrator al- lows the Abbess to pronounce an acceptance of this aspect of the human condition: "But the love will have been enough; all those impulses of love re- turn to the love that made them. Even memory is not necessary for love. There is a land of the living and a land of the dead and the bridge is love, the only survival, the only meaning" (107). If "all those impulses of love return to the love that made them" is interpreted as a reference to the elect going to be with God after death, a theology Wilder expressed in the final line of stage directions at the end of *And the Sea Shall Give Up Its Dead,* then the last line of *The Bridge* is as affirmative as the cosmic optimism of the New England Puritans.

The similarity of particular aspects of this worldview in *The Bridge of San Luis Rey* to Puritan doctrine and Puritan writers' ways of expressing their beliefs in narrative works is no coincidence. In this his last work of the 1920s, we see the young author finding the combination of theme and form, shaped in part by the Puritan legacy in his familial and American heritage, that would later bring him his greatest artistic and popular success in *Our Town*. Thornton Wilder may not have believed in Judgment Day by that time, but the belief in Judgment Day was in him and thus, as we have seen, was also in his early drama and fiction written in the moral wilderness of the Jazz Age.

Three

The Puritan's Progress

Typology and Plain Style in Wilder's 1930s Drama and Fiction

The image [of life as a voyage] was as old as Christianity, but the Puritans made it their own, elaborating details of the voyage and emphasizing far more the "progress" of the Christian pilgrim than his heavenly destination.

—Michael Walzer, *The Revolution of the Saints:*
A Study of the Origins of Radical Politics

Anyway it's no news to you that I am a slow-poke plodder in so many ways, still stuck in the literal XIXth century; but very proud every time I feel I have made progress.

—Wilder to Gertrude Stein, September 23, 1935, quoted in Donald Gallup, ed.,
The Flowers of Friendship: Letters Written to Gertrude Stein

Most studies of Wilder's life and oeuvre conclude that his shift to American subject matter in the 1930s resulted from an attack on his earlier works, especially his novel set in classical antiquity, *The Woman of Andros.* Left-wing critic Mike Gold criticized Wilder's literary expression of timeless themes of the human condition set in exotic locales of the past as bourgeois escapism.[1]

1. Gold, "Wilder: Prophet of the Genteel Christ." For accounts of what was to be only the first of two major critical controversies concerning a Wilder work, see Gilbert A. Harrison, *The Enthusiast: A Life of Thornton Wilder,* 144; Richard H. Goldstone, *Thornton Wilder: An Intimate Portrait,* 77–83; and David Castronovo, *Thornton Wilder,* 14–15.

Wilder coveted acceptance not only by the literary and critical community, but also by the larger intellectual establishment. He knew or had met Archibald MacLeish, Hemingway, Fitzgerald, Stein, Edmund Wilson, Shaw, Freud, and Sartre. His desire to be part of the community of great writers, critics, and thinkers of his time may account not only for the Americanization of his narratives, but also for the secularization of themes in his works of the 1930s.[2]

Despite the ostensible satire of fundamentalism in his only novel written during the decade, *Heaven's My Destination* (1935), Wilder's statements in his journal and the general worldview of his later works simply do not bear out the conclusion of those scholars who think that he had disavowed the religious beliefs of his youth. If Wilder did purposely recast his religious faith into more fashionable terms in interviews, lectures, and some of his works, the plays and novel of the 1930s still reflect a worldview and aesthetic bearing a strong resemblance not only to his 1920s drama and fiction, but also to the Puritan work Wilder had read as a boy, *The Pilgrim's Progress* by John Bunyan. As H. Wayne Morgan points out, Wilder's "Christianity was not that preached by Billy Sunday, whose strident commercialism was only another form of materialism to him. Wilder never really spelled out his view of Christianity, possibly because he thought that like all of life, it was never complete. Like the tradition he supported, it was a growing thing."[3] The development of Wilder's aesthetic can be seen as paralleling the overall evolution of both Puritanism and the Puritan narrative tradition in American literature. While the direct expression of Puritan ideas was repressed, the forms of Puritanism (in its literary, social, and theological manifestations) continued to reveal themselves symptomatically in both American culture and Wilder's writing.

In Wilder's drama and fiction of the 1930s, the most prominent feature of the legacy of Puritanism is a faith in progress on the personal, social, and universal levels. Sacvan Bercovitch and other authors of Puritan continuity

2. A case could be made that Wilder's great enthusiasm for his relationship with Gertrude Stein was not, as most studies have asserted, because of all that she taught him; rather, perhaps it was because she, one of the intellectual and literary elect (or elite, if you prefer) of the times, admired Wilder and his works. In other words, some of his feelings toward Gertrude Stein were closer, perhaps, to gratitude for her acceptance of him than for his having learned anything crucial from her.

3. Morgan, "The Early Thornton Wilder," 248. In the 1930s, Wilder still identified himself with Puritan antecedents; in a 1935 letter to Stein, he referred to himself as "John Calvin Wilder" (Edward Burns and Ulla E. Dydo, with William Rice, eds. *The Letters of Gertrude Stein and Thornton Wilder,* 50). Even as late as 1953 Wilder told an interviewer, "High moral standards and ethical meditation are typical of our brand of American Puritanism. As a Protestant, I am a practicing Christian" (Jackson R. Bryer, ed., *Conversations with Thornton Wilder,* 57).

studies have argued that the nineteenth-century understanding of progress, at least in America, has an antecedent in the Puritan concepts of history—providential determination of events, typology, and eschatology. For example, Mason I. Lowance Jr. writes, "This conflation of sacred and secular images of historical progress constituted an important achievement for the Puritans and their followers." Indeed, a subtle yet pervasive legacy of New England Puritanism in modern American culture is a national optimism and assurance based on the presumption that progress is always ongoing. As Karen Rowe states, "The reservoir of types provided the sustaining power of a God-sanctioned myth, one which placed the Puritan migration and each saint's spiritual journey within providential history and millennial revelation. Those imaginative visions of America's grand destiny resonate today, even in a world significantly altered from the theocracy of the Massachusetts Bay Colony."[4] A brief look at a seventeenth-century history of colonial New England illustrates that progress—or the perception of progress—on the universal, social, and personal levels was part of the Puritan worldview.

Published in 1654, *Wonder-Working Providence of Sions Saviour in New England* by Edward Johnson attests to the fact that it was not only Puritan ministers who subscribed to an eschatological interpretation of the colonizing of New England. Unlike most of the authors of Puritan works studied by early American literature scholars, Edward Johnson was not a minister; however, he was a militant Puritan who was very much involved with the colonizing of New England and therefore well versed in the Bible, Puritan doctrine, and the "plantation," as they called it, of new settlements during the peak period of Puritan immigration to New England.[5] The belief that the Puritans were on a mission from God—or an errand into the wilderness, as they called it—is everywhere evident in Johnson's narration of events, from the establishment of the Massachusetts Bay Colony to the Pequot War. In particular, we find the word "progresse" regularly employed throughout the book. For example, Johnson uses progress on the literal level to describe a journey, as when describing one leader "who with a holy and humble people made his progresse to the North-Eastward, and erected a Towne about six miles from Ipswich called Rowly" (183). Johnson also uses progress to signify advancement in learning on the individual level, as in the following: ". . . knowing likewise that young students could make but a poor progresse in learning . . ." (200). On a social level, Johnson would describe the history of the founding

4. Lowance, *The Language of Canaan: Metaphor and Symbol in New England from the Puritans to the Transcendentalists,* 16; Rowe, "Prophetic Visions: Typology and Colonial American Poetry," 64.

5. See the introduction to J. Franklin Jameson's edition of Johnson's history of the years 1628 to 1651, *Wonder-Working Providence of Sions Savior.*

of churches in terms of progress: "After this manner have the Churches of Christ had their beginning and progresse hitherto" (218). Finally, Johnson would use the term in a more cosmic context: "The Summer after the blazing starre (whose motion in the Heavens was from East to West, poynting out to the sons of men the progresse of the glorious Gospell of Christ . . ." (40). Thus New England Puritan writers' use of the word and concept of progress on multiple levels of experience, in contrast to John Bunyan's use of it only on the allegorical level, helped support an ideological as well as a theological optimism about the future.

Similarly, Wilder's use of the term "progress" almost always resonates with spiritual or moral significance. However, progress is not only a theme in the works of his thirties; it is also the form of the works themselves. Before the progress or development of Wilder's aesthetic is examined in *The Long Christmas Dinner and Other Plays in One Act* and in the novel *Heaven's My Destination,* it is necessary to discuss previous scholarly readings of Wilder's conceptualization of time and history to demonstrate that progress in his works is to be understood in the Puritan sense of the pilgrim's progress, an errand into the wilderness, and God's plot.

Every major study of Thornton Wilder discusses to varying extents his view of the history of western civilization or of the universe itself. Most scholars describe the shape of time or history in Wilder's works as cyclical; a few see it as static; a couple emphasize the downturn of the wheel, stopping just short of classifying his view as entropic.[6] Some scholars acknowledge Wilder's optimism and his desire to see history as progressive; their qualification of progress in his works perhaps tends to reflect their own more skeptical viewpoints.[7] Even the most extensive study of the treatment of time in

6. Rex Burbank reads *The Skin of Our Teeth* as a denial of progress: "Wilder's historical view rejects the theory of progress; for the circular form . . . indicates that history will follow a similar cycle" (*Thornton Wilder,* 93). Ethan Mordden paraphrases Wilder's message in *The Skin of Our Teeth* as "We'll make it. . . . It's all cycles. . . . There's always rebirth" (*The American Theatre,* 207), but of *Our Town* he says, it is "a work of despairing sorrow" (*American Theatre,* viii) because the movement is toward death. For other readings of Wilder's texts with regard to the shape and tone of history, see also Travis Bogard, "The Comedy of Thornton Wilder"; Bernard Hewitt, "Thornton Wilder Says 'Yes' "; Castronovo, *Thornton Wilder;* and Edmund Fuller, "Thornton Wilder: The Notation of the Heart."

7. No major study unequivocally labels Wilder's theory of history as progressive; Donald Haberman grants that the minute changes in the repetitions "can suggest some sort of progress" (*"Our Town": An American Play,* 37), but he relies too much on Gertrude Stein's view of history, even though in his earlier study he quoted Wilder on the progressive theme in *The Skin of Our Teeth:* "The play held all the implications that were real to me: man's spiral progress and his progression through trial and error'" (*The Plays of Thornton Wilder,* 24). See also, Linda Simon, *Thornton Wilder, His World;* Louis Broussard, *American Drama: Contemporary Allegory from Eugene O'Neill to Tennessee Williams;* and Bernard

Wilder, Mary Ellen Williams's *A Vast Landscape: Time in the Novels of Thornton Wilder* (1979), sees Wilder's conception of time as cyclical rather than progressive. Patricia R. Schroeder comes the closest to defining accurately the particular theory of history manifested in Wilder's works—she even identifies its source as the Puritans—but she does not make the connection to typology, which encompasses both cyclical and linear views of history.[8]

If one examines all of the evidence, there is no question that Wilder believed in progress. In a scene from *The Emporium,* an unfinished play from which fragments of scenes were first published in his journal, we find a powerful statement of a progressive vision. In one scene the head of an orphanage says to an assembly of boys, "The generations of men are like the generations of leaves on the trees. They fall into the earth and new leaves are grown the following spring. The world into which you have been born is one of eternal repetitions—already you can see that. But there is something to which you *can* belong—you *do* belong: I am not yet empowered to tell you its name. It is something which is constantly striving to bring something new into these repetitions, to lift them, to color them, to—" (*JTW,* 303–4, emphasis in original). Struggling to define the meaning of this play, Wilder writes in his journal, "It is about the Wheel of Being; the endless repetitions of the life-forms; but the Emporium is, precisely, the evidence of pressures from Elsewhere to introduce a qualitative change into the mechanical repetitions. . . . Those children . . . are the effort to alter and 'redeem' the wheel" (*JTW,* 325). Harrison describes another of Wilder's unfinished projects with a similar theme: "He had put aside *The Emporium* because a new idea had suddenly come to mind . . . its theme, the eternal movement of social betterment . . . [or as Wilder put it,] 'the quiet, absurd, obstinate drive toward better things.' "[9] Finally, commenting directly on the issue of progress in his journal notes on one of the Norton lectures on nineteenth-century American literature, Wilder writes,

---

Grebanier, *Thornton Wilder,* for other brief, skeptical acknowledgments of Wilder's progressive view.

8. Williams, *A Vast Landscape: Time in the Novels of Thornton Wilder,* 1. In *The Presence of the Past in Modern American Drama,* Schroeder writes, "The attitude of the early Puritan settlers toward history contains the seeds of a confusing dualism that still pervades and perhaps defines American literature" (21). Regarding Wilder, she notes, "This difference between time as it passes and time as characters perceive it is at the heart of Wilder's dramatic experiments; one might even call it the central conflict of his plays. . . . He was able to proclaim the intrinsic significance of each moment and simultaneously to explore the place of the moment, once past, in shaping the unfolding patterns of history" (54).

9. Harrison, *Enthusiast,* 289.

Now where in our thought-world do we get the feeling for the minute specifications of individuality, the acceptance of the interest and dignity of unique occasions? From two things: (1) The Christian dispensation, whereby every individual is of vast importance in the eyes of God and, derived from it: (2) The *doctrine of progress.* No two individuals have ever been the same, no two happenings have ever been the same; but they are not haphazard in their differential: there is a relation between them all, and that is the *forward movement* of society. The death of Joan of Arc is a milestone. The repudiation of Falstaff is a tiny increment in the moral development of a prince. The plays of Chekhov are plays about sloth—but they ring with a half-ironic, half-agonized assertion that *the world will get better and better.* . . . Possibility = the modern Western world: liberty and *progress;* the unique occasion tremulous with what A.N. Whitehead called the injection of the teleological movement of the universe into every moment of consciousness. (*JTW,* 107–8, emphasis added)

As explained in Chapters One and Two, typology is both cyclical and progressive; certain figures recur, but with each recurrence the figure—be it a person, an event, an object, or other—is more perfectly realized: "From Calvin to Samuel Mather, Puritan Reformers came gradually to view all history less as dualistic (the Gospel as opposed to the Law) and more as a continuum of progressively clearer revelations of God's will, each new dispensation more brilliantly anticipating the day of judgment." An example of a New England Puritan linking events from the Bible to recent events that could have been seen as merely cyclical occurs in Samuel Danforth's famous Election Day sermon, "A Brief Recognition of New England's Errand into the Wilderness." Danforth analyzes three instances of the people of God going into the wilderness: Moses and the Israelites, John the Baptist, and the New England Puritans. Each "errand into the wilderness," according to Danforth, marks an important step in God's plan for the salvation of the human race.[10]

Although Wilder had an unusually direct link with Puritanism, it is unlikely that he was aware of the source of the particular view of history within his works.[11] But, as Karl Keller writes of another writer influenced by the "New England Mind," "We do not need to think that Emerson believed in

10. Rowe, "Prophetic Visions," 52. Danforth's sermon and his preface to the published version of it are collected in A. W. Plumstead, *The Wall and the Garden: Selected Massachusetts Election Sermons, 1670–1775.*

11. However, Wilder would surely have heard of Jonathan Edwards, and the theory of history Edwards, an especially conservative Puritan, employed corresponds to these definitions of typology and to Wilder's shape of history: "The paradigm that should be used, therefore, to illustrate Edwards' view of history would be the spiral, progressively moving forward toward a teleological end point, rather than either the linear or the circular pattern" (Mason I. Lowance, "Sacvan Bercovitch and Jonathan Edwards," 62).

the assumptions behind typology, for it was already the frame of his mind. Typology was not what he thought about but the way he thought about things in general." The way Wilder thought about American history was clearly typological; time and history, though cyclical, were progressive, as will be demonstrated in the following analysis of three plays from *The Long Christmas Dinner and Other Plays in One Act—The Long Christmas Dinner, Pullman Car Hiawatha,* and *The Happy Journey to Trenton and Camden*—and in his novel *Heaven's My Destination.*[12]

Travis Bogard describes each of these three plays from *The Long Christmas Dinner and Other Plays* as "a journey play," and *The Long Christmas Dinner* itself "involves a progress through time." But what kind of journey are these plays about? What is the point of the journey? What play does not involve a progress through time? What is the view of time that serves as plot for these plays? Bogard does not answer these questions, nor have other scholars sufficiently understood that in these three significant plays from the 1931 collection of one acts, *progress* is both the point and the plot, the affirmative tone and the shape of time and history in an elect American society.[13]

The Long Christmas Dinner

Wilder dramatizes a debate about the nature of time in *The Long Christmas Dinner:* is it progressive or static?[14] Whenever characters make references to time, opposite points of view are expressed, but the dramatic irony created by the audience or reader viewing an accelerated montage of a family's history—ninety years are represented passing—suggests that both perceptions are true: things change (mostly for the better) and things stay the same. This seeming contradiction is possible in a typological theory of history. That is, a finite number of types appear again and again, giving the impression of

12. Keller, "Alephs, Zahirs, and the Triumph of Ambiguity: Typology in Nineteenth-Century American Literature," 285. The discussion of *Our Town* and *The Skin of Our Teeth* is relevant to this point as well; see Chapter Four.

13. Bogard, "Comedy of Thornton Wilder," 360. The other three one-act plays included in this collection—*Queens of France, Love and How to Cure It,* and *Such Things Only Happen in Books*—are farces and conventionally realistic in form, though underestimated in literary merit by Wilder scholars before Christopher Wheatley's insightful reading of them; see his "Thornton Wilder, the Real, and Theatrical Realism" in *Realism and the American Dramatic Tradition,* ed. William W. Demastes, 139–55 (Tuscaloosa and London: University of Alabama Press, 1996). Because they do not address issues of religious faith, American history, or the nature of the universe, none of the three light one-acts manifests traces of Puritanism, and thus they are not discussed here.

14. Peter Szondi describes *The Long Christmas Dinner* as "a secular mystery play about time" (*Theory of the Modern Drama: A Critical Edition,* 91).

mere repetition or stasis; however, with each repetition there is a development of the type and an overall progress toward antitypal fulfillment.

The scenery of *The Long Christmas Dinner*—birth portal left, long dining table center, death portal right—and the movement of characters from the birth portal toward the death portal to represent the span of their lives would seem to symbolize an entropic rather than a progressive view of time. However, the play dramatizes time functioning as healer and restorer. For example, a mother says after a child is stillborn, "Only time, only the passing of time can help in these things (20)."[15] Time also seems to run according to debits and credits, as implied by the juxtaposition of two deaths, Lucia and Cousin Brandon, with the birth of twins (15) maintaining a balance between birth and death.

The characters' perception of time in *The Long Christmas Dinner* would seem to differ according to geography, gender, and generation. Illustrating the geographic perspective, Charles says, "Time certainly goes very fast in a great new country like this," to which Ermengarde replies, "Well, time must be passing very slowly in Europe with this dreadful, dreadful war going on" (18). Earlier in the play the perception of time differs by gender. Roderick, representing the masculine interest in enterprise, comments, "No time passes as slowly as this when you're waiting for your urchins to grow up and settle down to business," to which his wife, Lucia, speaking from her maternal instincts, replies, "I don't want time to go any faster, thank you. I love the children just as they are" (9). When their son Charles grows up and has his own son, Roderick II, we see a generation gap in perception of time: "You gotta get drunk in this town to forget how dull it is. Time passes so slowly here that it stands still, that's what's the trouble" (21); Roderick II's aunt Genevieve, however, sees time as passing quickly: "My mother died yesterday—not 25 years ago" (23). Thus Wilder has given theatrical expression to the concept of relativity, that the perception of time is dependent upon the observer's point of view.

As to what happens over the course of time, much of *The Long Christmas Dinner* suggests continuity or cycles. For example, the potential for doubling of roles by actors can create a visual signification of the idea that life is static, nothing changes.[16] "It'll all be the same in a hundred years" (7), pronounces Cousin Brandon near the beginning of the play, and various kinds of repeti-

15. Since there were several editions of *The Long Christmas Dinner*, I have decided to quote from the recently published *The Collected Short Plays of Thornton Wilder Volume I*, which contains all of the plays from the original edition of *The Long Christmas Dinner and Other Plays in One Act*.

16. The Samuel French acting edition lists parts for twelve actors, but one play sourcebook cites ten.

tions would seem to support that statement: year after year characters cry at the Christmas sermon, others comment on the beauty of ice coating the tree branches, the family's Christian names repeat (three sets of Roderick and Lucia), the Christmas dinners themselves, and, finally, births, marriages, and deaths. All of these repetitions in the play would seem to confirm that things are essentially the same, generation after generation.

Yet there are many subtle indications of change in the Bayard family and in the outside world, most of which constitute progress: examples cited in the dialogue range from having to cross the Mississippi River on a raft (5), to crossing by bridges and ferries (18); from a single paved street and walking on boards, to more than one paved street and sidewalks (12); from a new house (4) and a new factory (9), to another new house (24) and many factories (22); from a single servant (6), to specialized servants such as a butler (16) and cook (24); from only the wealthy having leisure time for such recreational activities as tennis, to the middle class having it as well (17); from regarding stained glass windows in church as a sin of the Catholic church, to incorporating them into a Protestant church (19); from temperance, to uneasy acceptance of drinking (6); and finally, from prosperity as a sign of evil (4, 9), to wealth as a confirmation of one's virtue (12, 24). Of course, such details are mere references in conversation at the Bayard family's dinner table—and a few of them are complaints (soot from factories, for example)—but for the most part the changes alluded to represent familial and social steps forward.

The Long Christmas Dinner ends where it began: with a Lucia and Roderick Bayard, a Mother Bayard in a wheelchair, a first Christmas dinner in a new house, and an old woman remembering the distant past. There is repetition, then, but there is also progress: the Bayards are "The first family of this city" (21) and have a "Bayard aisle" in church (24); they can cable their children living abroad; the Bayard house has two servants now, not just one. Even in the death of the last character on stage new life is signified: the aged Ermengarde murmurs, as she totters through the death portal, the names of yet a third set of the male and female Christian names of the Bayards, "Dear little Roderick and little Lucia" (25), whose births had been anticipated in a letter read aloud just prior to her exit. Though there is death, there is also new life, continuation of life, and improvements in life. From birth through love and procreation to death, the emphasis for Wilder, the *affirmation* for Wilder, is that each generation is not only a reproduction of the previous generation, but it is also an improvement upon the original.

Although the characters themselves are unable to transcend their own perspective to apprehend the overall effect of time, Wilder bestows upon the audience watching or reading *The Long Christmas Dinner* a more omniscient point of view by the use of dramatic irony. For example, when Lenora says to her baby, "Stay just as you are" exactly as Lucia had, which demonstrates continuity of the desire for stasis, Genevieve "repeats dryly. 'Stay just as you are'" (17) because she is bitter over her mother's early death. The point is not merely a theory of relativity: Wilder has dramatized that things and people do not stay just as they are; yet there is also the dramatic irony of seeing gender roles remain the same, family rituals remain the same, and so on, so that there is at least some continuity or repetition or cycles.[17] One way to make sense of these contradictions is to recognize the Puritans' typological view of time and history—repetition with variation achieving slow, gradual progress—as an American habit of mind passed down from generation to generation.

The cyclical component of typology is not present within *The Happy Journey to Trenton and Camden*, the next journey play of *The Long Christmas Dinner and Other Plays* to be discussed; however, progress dominates the theme and the structure of this one-act play as well. In addition, *The Happy Journey to Trenton and Camden* illustrates the degree to which Wilder's dramaturgy and theatrical style resemble the Puritan aesthetic of plain style.

The Happy Journey to Trenton and Camden

Almost every book-length study of Wilder analyzes this one-act play, along with *Pullman Car Hiawatha*, as an "anticipation" of the techniques and ideas Wilder employed in *Our Town*. As in the more famous full-length play, *The Happy Journey* is to be acted on a bare stage without any scenery, and it employs a character called "The Stage Manager" to impersonate minor characters: "*No scenery is required for this play. Perhaps a few dusty flats may be seen leaning against the brick wall at the back of the stage. / The Stage Manager not only moves forward and withdraws the few properties that are required, but he reads from a type-script the lines of all the minor characters*" (85). Although the Stage Manager character does not speak in his own voice and the stage directions inform us that "He should never be obtrusive nor distract the attention of the audience from the central action," his very presence in the play, along with the absence of scenery, rules out any possibility of a realistic theatrical production of *The Happy Journey*. While the Stage Manager may be forgotten as he "smokes, reads a newspaper, and eats an apple through the course of the play,"[18] the

17. Szondi has a similar perception of *The Long Christmas Dinner*, saying that it shows a "constant duality of change and stability" (*Theory of the Modern Drama*, 91).

18. These stage directions are quoted from the acting edition published by Samuel French, 4.

audience cannot ignore his presence when he moves the platform representing the family car around on stage and when he assumes the roles of, in order, Mrs. Schwartz, Mrs. Hobmeyer, Caroline's friends saying good-bye as the car departs, Mrs. Adler, and the gas station attendant, especially when he makes little or no adjustment in his appearance or sound: "He reads [the lines of all the minor characters] clearly, but with little attempt at characterization, scarcely troubling himself to alter his voice, even when he responds in the person of a child or a woman" (85). The effect is to call attention to the artifice of the play (here with the Stage Manager holding the script, rather than direct references to "this play" as in *Pullman Car Hiawatha* and more famously in *Our Town* and *The Skin of Our Teeth*).[19]

Wilder's employment of these devices effectively prevents the creation of an illusion of reality and the audience's suspension of disbelief. John Gassner labeled this kind of anti-illusionist drama "theatricalism"; Bertolt Brecht and others called it "epic theatre." Both terms have been applied to Wilder as the first American playwright to employ this mode. Due to the prominence of Brecht in the modern theater and studies of it, one might assume that Wilder's dramaturgy was influenced by Brecht's. The Wilder scholar who has considered this question in depth is Douglas Wixson Jr.; in "The Dramatic Techniques of Thornton Wilder and Bertolt Brecht: A Study in Comparison," he writes, "There is much evidence to argue Wilder's familiarity with German drama from an early age, especially the drama of Brecht. This study will mention some of the evidence without attempting to argue Brecht's influence." Twenty-five years later, in "Thornton Wilder and the Theater of the Weimar Republic," Wixson again notes parallels between the two playwrights but still does not argue influence; in fact, he quotes a letter from Wilder in which the author rejects Brechtian influence. Similarly, Paul Lifton, author of the most recent book-length study of Wilder's dramaturgy and possible sources for it, concludes, "In all likelihood, the resemblances between the two playwrights' dramaturgical styles are the result of coincidence rather than direct influence."[20]

19. The self-reflexivity in the text is not merely an imitation of Pirandello. John F. Lynen sees textual self-reflexivity as an American characteristic stemming from the Puritans: "American symbolism is symbolism of a particular kind, and what distinguishes it is the peculiar self-consciousness which is characteristic of Puritan experience, and which makes the symbolic process itself the center of attention" (*The Design of the Present: Essays on Time and Form in American Literature,* 44). Recall that Taylor "breaks the fourth wall" a few times in *God's Determinations.*

20. Wixson, "The Dramatic Techniques of Thornton Wilder and Bertolt Brecht: A Study in Comparison," 112; Wixson, "Thornton Wilder and the Theater of the Weimar Republic," 311; Lifton, *Vast Encyclopedia: The Theatre of Thornton Wilder,* 95–96. Lifton goes on to say that although it is possible Wilder saw the original production of *The Three-Penny*

John Gassner describes Wilder's shift in style as a "simplicity of subject and style combined with modernistic structural departures from realism," noting that Wilder is "at once a radical and a traditionalist. . . . But returning to tradition in the twentieth century was an innovation, and Wilder's manner of returning to it was personal and unique . . . [and] amounted to a *minor revolution in American theatre.*"[21] Wilder himself said in his author's note to *The Happy Journey,* "The form in which this play is cast is not an innovation but a revival. The healthiest ages of the theatre have been marked by the fact that there was the least literally representative scenery. The sympathetic participation of the audience was most engaged when their collaborative imagination was called upon to supply a large part of the background" (84). But is this a modernist approach Wilder learned from Pirandello and other twentieth-century European playwrights, as Wilder scholars have deduced, or was it an aesthetic inherent in American culture stemming from the Puritans?[22]

In his preface to *Three Plays,* Wilder himself assesses the theatrical style of both his one-act plays and *Our Town:* "I am not an innovator but a *rediscoverer* of *forgotten* goods and I hope a remover of obtrusive bric-a-brac" (xiv, emphasis in original). The significance of this statement to understanding the effect of the cultural legacy of Puritanism on Wilder's writing cannot be overstated: removing the obtrusive bric-a-brac of realistic scenery is the Reformation and especially Puritanism applied to theatrical style. That is, Wilder was doing for theater what the Puritans did for church liturgy—purify, simplify, reform: "The Puritan ideal was to revive the simplicity and vitality of the

---

Opera in Germany during his theatrical tour of 1928, there is no record of it; furthermore, "Nor is there any record of Wilder's having attended any of the American productions of Brecht's plays during the years when he [Wilder] was writing his own major dramatic works (1930–1942)" (*Vast Encyclopedia,* 96). One thing that Wilder scholars are aware of that Brecht scholars, modern drama scholars, and even American drama scholars are usually not is that the forms and styles Wilder employed most famously from 1938 to 1942 in *Our Town, The Merchant of Yonkers,* and *The Skin of Our Teeth* he had previously used in *The Long Christmas Dinner and Other Plays in One Act,* published in 1931.

21. Gassner, "The Two Worlds of Thornton Wilder," 317, 318, 319, emphasis added. In a relatively recent study, *The Simple Stage: Its Origins in the Modern American Theater,* Arthur Feinsod devotes an entire chapter to Wilder; he concurs with Gassner that Wilder's use of the simplified stage was momentous in American theater history: "Even though his ideas for stage simplicity are all borrowed, they blend into a simplicity that is radical, unique, and innovative" (213).

22. It is undeniably true that the origin of Wilder's aesthetic is complex and has many wellsprings; Lifton's exhaustive study demonstrates that emphatically. However, the European sources of his aesthetic have been repeatedly identified in Wilder studies; there doesn't seem to be much point in retracing that well-traveled path. Instead, this study provides the first in-depth examination of the *American* wellsprings of Wilder's aesthetic.

Apostolic church."[23] In order to understand better that the way Wilder chose to write his first mature drama could just as well have come from colonial American aesthetics as from modern European drama, additional historical background on Puritanism is necessary.

Puritanism is generally associated with Reformation theology (Calvinism) and church polity (Congregationalism), but it originated in the historical context of Elizabeth I restoring Anglicanism as the state religion after her sister Mary had attempted to reinstate Catholicism: "Puritans demanded the complete purification of the Anglican Church of all relics of Catholicism, regarding ornaments, rites, and vestments retained." One such rite was Holy Communion, then still a part of the regular Sunday liturgy, but the Puritans "aimed at the simplest celebration of the Lord's Supper" to correct what they believed was a corruption of this sacrament: "The Anglican emphasis on the primary role of the Sacraments was partly responsible for the ever-present dangers in the Church of England of sacerdotalism and the 'sacristy mind,' or of a *play-acting* in the form of ritualism." Interestingly, Davies again chooses a theatrical metaphor in describing the purified liturgy: "It was, to change the metaphor, a bare stage—like the Elizabethan theatre—so that the provocative images of Scripture could make their own impact on the tabula rasa of the sensitive imagination without the tinsel trappings, or merely distracting stage decor."[24]

Wilder too could associate theater and Puritanism. Wixson quotes from an unpublished essay about German director Max Reinhardt, for whom Wilder wrote *The Merchant of Yonkers* in 1938: "This is the high Barock [*sic*] thought-world which never tires of depicting the supernatural as woven into the daily life of man. It sprang to one of its greatest manifestations in this soil and is renewed annually at Salzburg, '*a light set upon a hill*.'"[25] Wilder is describing a modern theater director with the famous phrase of John Winthrop aboard the *Arabella* at the time of the largest migration of Puritans to the Massachusetts Bay Colony. Winthrop's metaphor is in reference to the

23. Bard Thompson, *Liturgies of the Western Church*, 317. Although I did not read Feinsod's study *The Simple Stage* until the summer of 2003, he does seem to share my view that one of several sources for this aesthetic was the Puritans: "In this association between the simple and the transcendent, one can also chart Wilder's spiritual lineage to an American Puritanism in which austerity in everyday living manifests spiritual purity; and from Transcendentalism, especially the Thoreauvian vein" (*Simple Stage*, 191). Feinsod writes further that theater artists saw the simple stage as "promising purification and a kind of spiritual cleansing" (*Simple Stage*, xix), which is parallel to the Puritans' and Wilder's intentions.

24. Winton U. Solberg, *Redeem the Time: The Puritan Sabbath in Early America*, 28; Davies, *Worship and Theology*, 74, 69 (emphasis added), 286.

25. Wixson, "Thornton Wilder and Max Reinhardt: Artists in Collaboration," 13 n. 24, emphasis added.

Puritan example to the rest of the Protestant world; Wilder's is to the Austrian and German culture that produced the director Max Reinhardt.

Even Puritan architecture emphasized a minimalist approach quite similar to the bare stage of *The Happy Journey, Pullman Car Hiawatha,* and, of course, *Our Town:* "When they came to build their own meeting houses, the houses were scrubbed, white, bare, as austerely naked as they should be in the sight of God, stripped of all its disguises and pretensions." This simplification of form also extended to their sermons and ultimately to all Puritan writing, coalescing into "plain style." As discussed in Chapter One, clarity of the lesson rather than aesthetic appeal was the guiding principle in Puritan writing, as Paul Lindholt explains: "The Puritans of New England likewise strove to elevate their independent acts, to memorialize their city on a hill by means of stirring documentaries. More homely in their literary style, less willing to exploit verbal flourishes learned from pagan pens, they grappled, as did Milton, with matters of effective *stagecraft*. God's altar needed not their polishing, or so they argued to defend the metrically primitive but doctrinally pure translations for the *Bay Psalm Book*."[26]

Thus the force that led to the abstract form in these plays by Wilder is older and broader than modern European drama. Granted, previous scholarship has established that Wilder had witnessed nonrealistic theatrical style in Pirandello's plays in the 1920s, but rather than seeing the effect of that experience as imprinting this style on the tabula rasa of Wilder's aesthetic sensibility, I suggest that it was more like two tuning forks vibrating in harmony. That is, Pirandello's nonrealistic theatrical style in such plays as *Six Characters in Search of an Author* (1921), *Each in His Own Way* (1924), and *Tonight We Improvise* (1930), though for different reasons, consists of narrative forms similar to the branch of the American literary tradition stemming from the New England Puritans.

Furthermore, a fundamental error has persisted in scholarly comparisons of Pirandello's famous play *Six Characters in Search of an Author,* of which Wilder saw the original production, and Wilder's bare stage and central character of the Stage Manager. With Pirandello's play, the stage is bare because the literal action of *Six Characters* is that of a theatrical company beginning to rehearse a play; having the stage nearly bare of scenery and props is a matter of realistically representing the setting of the play. Similarly, the Stage Director character in Pirandello's play is literally a producer-director of the production that the company is mounting; in short, he is a completely realistic character who never breaks the fourth wall to address the audience directly. Wilder's Stage Manager is not a realistic character; his presence is

26. Davies, *Worship and Theology,* 75; Lindholt, "Arts and Letters: Iconoclasm as a Puritan Art," 464, emphasis added.

never actually explained, and he constantly breaks the fourth wall.[27] Now that a possible native source of the theatrical plain style of Wilder's 1930s plays has been examined, we can proceed with the analysis of *The Happy Journey* and then *Pullman Car Hiawatha*.

As in *The Long Christmas Dinner*, *The Happy Journey* focuses on a single American family. While they are given their particularities, Wilder wrote them abstractly enough to be a representative family. That is, the character-izations of the Kirby family—Ma, Pa, Caroline, and Arthur—are quite realis-tic, and yet they are also idealized into types: Mother, Father, Daughter, and Son. In short, the Kirbys are Everyfamily or, at least, Every American family of this time period. Furthermore, their journey is meant to be seen as the journey of life, and the play encompasses all phases of it, from birth to death, like *The Long Christmas Dinner*. Thus, in *The Happy Journey* Wilder is closer to the allegorical form of the morality play, which Taylor also took up in *God's Determinations*. But unlike the realistic theatrical vehicle of his earlier alle-gory *The Trumpet Shall Sound*, this abstract mimesis of character and action better suits Wilder's microcosmic and macrocosmic themes.

Another aspect of the Puritan narrative aesthetic *The Happy Journey* utilizes is an episodic plot. As discussed in Chapter One, the episodic structure em-ployed in Taylor's *God's Determinations* (also in Bunyan's *The Pilgrim's Progress*) was one of the legacies of Puritan narrative in classic American literature. Unlike *The Long Christmas Dinner*'s temporal journey dramatizing the prog-ress of a family and—albeit obliquely—the United States, *The Happy Journey* dramatizes the geographic journey of a family from northern to southern New Jersey. Although Wilder does not mark the episodes of the journey with titles, as did Taylor in *God's Determinations*, or as a modern dramatist like Brecht does in *Mother Courage and Her Children* (1941), such events as waiting for a funeral procession to pass by, reading a billboard sign along the high-way, stopping at a hot dog stand, and so on constitute separate incidents as the Kirby family progresses toward its ultimate destination of Camden. The only causality in *The Happy Journey* is what happened to the Kirbys' oldest daughter, Beulah, which prompted the journey to visit her.

Everything is so underplayed in *The Happy Journey* that indications of the kind of universe in which the play takes place are found only in the ostensi-bly pointless details of the family's banal conversation as they drive to

27. Even Feinsod misses this distinction when discussing Pirandello and Wilder, though he understands it in one of the plays in *The Long Christmas Dinner and Other Plays*. Feinsod notes that *Love and How to Cure It* takes place "on an empty stage, but not as a neutral, imaginatively fluid space for action to occur, but rather as an actual site" (*Simple Stage,* 196). The same is true of *Six Characters in Search of an Author,* but not of *The Happy Journey, Pullman Car Hiawatha,* or *Our Town*. While the bare stage in those three plays by Wilder is "a neutral, imaginatively fluid space for action to occur," it is not in Piran-dello's play.

Camden. The Puritan worldview is only hinted at by minute indications of the Kirbys' belief in Providence, which range from the trivial to the didactic to the stoic; for example, Ma Kirby will not allow Arthur to have an early morning paper route because it would deprive him of the "sleep God meant him to have" (92). In response to Arthur's satire of her constant referral to her faith, Ma says, "God has done a lot of things for me and I won't have him made fun of by anybody. . . . Where'd we all be if I started talking about God like that, I'd like to know! We'd be in the speak-easies and night-clubs and places like that, that's where we'd be" (93). Finally, trying to comfort Beulah, who is recovering physically and emotionally from losing her first baby in childbirth, Ma says, "God thought best, dear. God thought best. We don't understand why. We just go on, honey, doin' our business" (101). The tone of *The Happy Journey* toward the Kirbys' faith is quiet respect, as indicated by the directions in the "Note to the producer" of the Samuel French acting edition to play these characters neither farcically nor piously, but with simplicity, sincerity, and dignity. The note also explains that Wilder considered naming the play "The Portrait of a Lady," since he views Ma's "humor, strength, and humanity [as] constitut[ing] the unifying element throughout."[28]

As in *The Pilgrim's Progress,* the most obvious signifier of progress in *The Happy Journey* is the journey from Newark to Camden, but there are many subtle details in the characters' speeches during the ride to suggest other levels of progress. Like *The Long Christmas Dinner, The Happy Journey* alludes to the growth of industrialization as social progress in a reference to a factory replacing a farm (94). Individual maturation is suggested in the instructions Ma gives to her children and their responses. Beulah, the Kirbys' oldest child, represents a rite of passage with her initiation to birth and death, as with members of the Bayard family in *The Long Christmas Dinner* and the Gibbs and Webb families in *Our Town.* Beulah also represents the progress of the family in socioeconomic terms: "It's an even nicer street than they used to live in. . . . It's better than our street. It's richer than our street.—Ma, isn't Beulah richer than we are?" (99).

There also seems to be an allusion to the progress of Christianity in terms of Protestants and Catholics learning to peacefully co-exist. Ma's instinctive liking of the gas station attendant is only temporarily cooled by his oblique profession of faith:

MA. My husband and my boy are going to stay at the Y.M.C.A. I hear they've got a dormitory on the top floor that's real clean and comfortable. Had you ever been there?

28. Acting edition of *Happy Journey* published by Samuel French, 4.

STAGE MANAGER. [playing the attendant] No. I'm Knights of Columbus myself.

MA. Oh.

STAGE MANAGER. I used to play basketball at the Y though. It looked all right to me. (*HJTC,* 94).

After they leave the station, Ma Kirby says that the attendant was a nice young man though too thin, which she would like to remedy with a few of her meals. Citing two organizations originally affiliated with Protestant and Catholic versions of Christianity (Y.M.C.A. stands for Young Men's Christian Association, which was Protestant affiliated, and the Knights of Columbus is a Catholic organization) is the most oblique of references to the historical division out of which Puritanism itself was born (in other words, the Reformation), but it is in keeping with the understated dramaturgy of this play.[29]

The progress *The Happy Journey* most affirms is national progress. The litany of "better" and "best" in the speeches of this representative family reflects an American egocentrism that was an anthem first sung by the Puritans, as Karl Keller suggests: "The typological structure applied, in the early American mind, wherever there was a situation involving partial and total fulfillment. In time the structure of types turned faith in Christ into national and personal egocentrism."[30] The Kirby family gives voice to an American elitism that may well be a legacy of Puritan Covenant theology, their belief that they were God's new Israel, new chosen people: "He's just the best driver in the world" (87); "We think it's the best little Chevrolet in the world" (89); "I was born in New Jersey. I've always said it was the best state in the Union" (95); "I live in the best street in the world because my husband and children live there" (99). Not that these comments are totally free of irony; Wilder's tone may be affirmative, but he is not naive. At one point on the journey the Kirby children are ecstatic with patriotism as they sing the praises of George Washington for being first in war, peace, and the hearts of his countrymen; Ma's dry, undercutting response is, "Well, the thing I like about him best was that he never told a lie" (96). As the stage directions tell us, "The children are duly cast down" (96). The point would seem to be that the new generation represents a decline in values, but in the context of so much

29. If this seems like reading too much into the dialogue, then why would Wilder have the Garage Hand mention that he was Knights of Columbus and Ma reply curtly with an "Oh"? This information is completely irrelevant to the literal point of the episode. In this case I think Wilder was consciously representing the Protestants' and Catholics' aversion to each other in America, which has been much less violent though no less pervasive than in Europe.

30. Keller, "Alephs, Zahirs," 276–77.

affirmation of the American dream, which is what *The Happy Journey* finally represents (as well as an updating of *The Pilgrim's Progress*), Ma Kirby's comment may be read as the usual complaint of parents about their children or of the older generation about the younger.

Like *The Long Christmas Dinner, The Happy Journey* is a testimony to the doctrine of progress and its incarnation in American society. *Pullman Car Hiawatha,* one of the most direct manifestations of American Puritanism as it survived into the twentieth century (surpassed only by *Our Town* and *The Skin of Our Teeth*), is another paean to progress on the individual, social, and universal levels.

Pullman Car Hiawatha

Like *The Long Christmas Dinner, Pullman Car Hiawatha* is associated with Christmas, with the action taking place in the early morning hours of December 21, 1930, on board a train traveling from New York to Chicago. As in *Our Town,* a Stage Manager begins the play by verbally "setting the scene" on a bare stage: "This is the plan of a Pullman car. Its name is Hiawatha and on December twenty-first it is on its way from New York to Chicago. Here at your left are three compartments. Here is the aisle and five lowers" (42). As in *The Happy Journey,* no scenery is used apart from chalk lines on the floor and pairs of chairs to represent the berths of a Pullman car. As the play progresses, the Stage Manager calls characters forth and dismisses them when they have delivered their speeches—in other words, he speaks and acts out what is normally "invisible text" in a play manuscript, the stage directions written by the playwright.

The Stage Manager performs the very minor parts in the play, again as in *The Happy Journey* and *Our Town;* in addition, he and other characters break the "fourth wall" by addressing the audience directly, and he also refers to "the purposes of this play" (42), as do certain characters who express a desire to be in the play (e.g., the ghost of a construction worker who had been killed while working on the bridge over which the train is passing at the moment). Having this Stage Manager, unlike the one in *The Happy Journey,* directly address the actors and the audience in his own character was completely alien to American theater in 1931. Of *Pullman Car Hiawatha*'s theatrical style Wixson notes, "This was bold, experimental drama, a revolution in American stagecraft."[31]

The abstract mimesis of the Puritan aesthetic is evident in *Pullman Car*

31. Wixson, "Thornton Wilder and Max Reinhardt," 4.

Hiawatha's characters, most of whom, as Burbank notes, are types meant to represent a cross section of society, if not the entire spectrum of the human race.[32] These types include businessmen, a grandmother, a doctor, a nurse, a porter, and so on. Wilder also uses allegory to disrupt the illusion of reality and to suggest the universality of the human condition. In addition to characters representing the planets Saturn, Venus, Jupiter, and The Earth, and the hours Ten O'clock, Eleven O'clock, and Twelve O'clock (Wilder uses both sets again in *The Skin of Our Teeth*), *Pullman Car Hiawatha* contains the following allegorical characters as described on the cast of characters page of the Samuel French acting edition: "Grovers Corners, represented by a Grinning Boy," "The Field, represented by Somebody in Shirt Sleeves," "Parkersburg, Ohio, represented by a Farmer's Wife and Three Young People," and "The Weather, represented by a Mechanic." These characters announce their identities to the audience at the Stage Manager's direction, then quote famous poets or espouse proverbial morality. That the audience is meant to be included in this world is indicated when The Field says, "I represent a field you are passing between Grovers Corners, Ohio and Parkersburg, Ohio" (50).[33]

The abstract representation of the train and the typical characters indicates the microcosmic setting of Wilder's play; the macrocosmic setting is suggested by the characters of the planets, two archangels, and the God-like Stage Manager, who literally orchestrates the figures and events into a universal harmony of motion and sound—the music of the spheres:

> *The planets appear on the balcony. Some of them take their place halfway on the steps. These have no words, but each has a sound. One has a pulsating, zinging sound. Another has a thrum. One whistles ascending and descending scales. Saturn does a slow, obstinate . . . M–M–M–M–*
> STAGE MANAGER. Louder, Saturn.—Venus, higher. Good. Now, Jupiter.— Now the earth. *He turns to the beds on the train.* Come, everybody. This is the earth's sound.
> *The towns, workmen, etc. appear at the edge of the stage. The passengers begin their "thinking" murmur.*
> STAGE MANAGER. Come, Grovers Corners. Parkersburg. You're in this. Watchman. Tramp. This is the earth's sound. *He conducts it as the director of an orchestra would. Each of the towns and workmen does his motto.* (53–54)[34]

32. Burbank, *Thornton Wilder,* 61.

33. This initial use of the name "Grover's Corners" would be, in typological terms, the type that would be more fully realized later in *Our Town.*

34. At one point, Taylor conflates two of his motifs in *God's Determinations*—traveling in a coach and trying to praise God with instrument and voice—creating imagery and metaphor similar to Wilder's in *Pullman Car Hiawatha:* "In Heaven soaring up, I dropt an

Admittedly, the Stage Manager conducting the universe as if he were God is not necessarily Puritan or even Christian, but the language resembles that of one of Wilder's earlier attempts at dramatizing the macrocosm in *The Angel That Troubled the Waters and Other Plays,* which was more overtly Christian. In *And the Servant's Name Was Malchus,* Christ stares out of a window of heaven as "The stars weave incessantly their interlocking measures . . . fulfilling happily and with a faint humming sound the long loops of their appointment" (*CSPTW II,* 107). The following speech and stage directions from *Pullman Car Hiawatha* echo Wilder's earlier description of cosmic harmony:

> STAGE MANAGER. All right. All right.—Now we'll have the whole world together, please. The whole solar system, please. *The complete cast begins to appear at the edges of the stage. He claps his hands.* The whole solar system, please. Where's the tramp?—Where's the moon? *He gives two raps on the floor, like the conductor of an orchestra attracting the attention of his forces, and slowly lifts his hand. The human beings murmur their thoughts; The Hours discourse; the Planets chant or hum.* (58)

Clearly, Wilder has given the Stage Manager godlike powers to control the microcosmic and macrocosmic levels of reality represented on the stage.

What sort of cosmos does the Stage Manager preside over? What kind of God does he represent? First, unlike the Stage Manager in *Our Town,* he is not the folksy-but-also-slightly-bored narrator; he is not one of the people, except when he speaks as a minor character (the occupant of the Upper Five berth, for example); he is not even a representation of a harsh judge on Judgment Day, as was Peter Magnus in *The Trumpet Shall Sound.* Rather, the Stage Manager of *Pullman Car Hiawatha* is closer to the portrait of God as creator in the first book of the Bible: Genesis. After explaining the layout of the Pullman car to the audience, the Stage Manager suddenly says, "All right! Come on, everybody!" (42) and the actors simultaneously appear, an act of creation as performative as "And God said, 'Let there be light,' and there was light" (Gen. 1:3). After his virtuoso conducting of the cosmic orchestra, the Stage Manager waves them away and pronounces, "Very good" (59), echoing the language of God satisfied with his creation, again in Genesis. We saw in Chapter One Taylor's depiction of God creating the universe at the start of *God's Determinations.*

Eare / On Earth: and oh! sweet Melody! . . . And listening, found it was the Saints who were / Encoacht for Heaven that sang for Joy. / . . . And if a string do slip by Chance, they soon / Do screw it up again: whereby / They set it in a more melodious Tune / And a Diviner Harmony. / For in Christs Coach they sweetly sing, / As they to Glory ride therein" (109).

Contrary to Malcolm Goldstein's assessment,[35] the Stage Manager in *Pullman Car Hiawatha* is omnipotent, and he is also omniscient. He commands the riders of the train to think for the audience; when the porter falters in his thinking aloud, the Stage Manager encourages him and then comments, "That's right" (46), confirming to the Porter his own thoughts. The Stage Manager also translates the German speech of the ghost of the worker and explains how he was killed years ago during the construction of the bridge (51). He prompts the "hours of the night," who speak excerpts from the works of great western thinkers (Plato, Epictetus, St. Augustine) as if they were his own words (52–53). The Stage Manager knows all, then, though he tells only enough to give the audience a taste of his God's-eye-view.

Though not a God of judgment as in *The Trumpet Shall Sound,* the Stage Manager would seem to preside over a Calvinistic universe. Once he announces the arrival at the "theological position of Pullman Car Hiawatha" (54), the play begins to demonstrate an affinity with the theology of Wilder's 1920s works, which were overtly concerned with many of the same doctrinal issues as seventeenth-century Puritan works by Taylor and Wigglesworth. For example, the speech of the character "Grovers Corners" expresses a liberalized version of total depravity: "There's so much good in the worst of us and so much bad in the best of us, that it ill behooves any of us to criticize the rest of us" (50). The doctrine of irresistible grace is dramatized when two archangels descend to the Pullman car and summon Harriet, a woman who has died of an illness during the trip; despite all her protests, their whispered replies to her imply that she is one of the elect:

> I wouldn't be happy there. . . . I'm ashamed to come with you. I haven't done anything with my life. Worse than that: I was angry and sullen. I never realized anything. I don't dare go a step in such a place. . . . But it's not possible to forgive such things. I don't want to be forgiven so easily. I want to be punished for it all. I won't stir until I've been punished a long, long time. I want to be freed of all that—by punishment. I want to be all new. . . . But no one else could be punished for me. (56)

Her desire for punishment and the archangels' rejection of that as an option also demonstrate that the theological position of *Pullman Car Hiawatha* is not Catholic—there is no purgatory here. There may be a hell, however, as the action and dialogue leave open the possibility that not everyone will join Harriet in heaven. The Insane Woman begs to be taken now, but the archangels merely nod at her assumption that she must wait. Also, Harriet,

35. Goldstein, *The Art of Thornton Wilder,* 77.

overwhelmed by emotion, says, "Let's take the whole train. . . . Can't we all come? You'll never find anyone better than [her husband] Philip" (57), but the archangels remain silent as they lead her up the stairs. On the other hand, it may be that the others, the Insane Woman included, have not reached their appointed time. The Stage Manager does indicate there is a schedule of some kind when the planets and hours enter prematurely and he says that it is not time for them yet (50).

The central metaphor of *Pullman Car Hiawatha,* that life is like taking a trip on a train, expresses the structure and theme of progress, providentially determined on all levels. The physical traverse—"We're tearing through Ohio" (46)—symbolizes a metaphysical pilgrimage with the same goal as Wilder's next major work, the novel *Heaven's My Destination.* Wilder's inspiration for *Pullman Car Hiawatha* specifically may have come from an adaptation of *The Pilgrim's Progress,* which also uses the train device: Nathaniel Hawthorne's "The Celestial Railroad."[36]

Progress on the individual level is demonstrated in *Pullman Car Hiawatha* by the Insane Woman: "I'm grateful for being so much better than I was. The old story, the terrible story, doesn't haunt me as it used to. A great load seems to have been taken off my mind" (55). Harriet also progresses spiritually, even if the most important step comes after her life has ended: "I never used to talk like this. I was so homely I never used to have the courage to talk. Until Philip came. I see now. I see now. I understand everything now" (58). Harriet, a self-admittedly undeserving recipient of saving grace, also represents election on a national scale: "Oh, I'm ashamed! I'm just a stupid and you know it. I'm just another American.—But then what wonderful things must be beginning now. You really want me? You really want me?" (57). However far America has traveled from its Puritan origins, Wilder suggests we are still on the right track. In addition, there is a progress of a cultural tradition broader than America's in *Pullman Car Hiawatha* represented by the order of recitation of the great philosophers of western civilization (52–53): Ten O'clock—Plato (ancient Greece), Eleven O'clock—Epictetus (classical Rome), and Twelve O'clock—Augustine (Medieval Christendom). Had Wilder added One O'clock, it might well have been Martin Luther or John Calvin to represent the Reformation.

Furthermore, Wilder seems to intend for there to be a rhetorical or intellectual progress in the audience's understanding of *Pullman Car Hiawatha.*

---

36. I owe this connection to Professor Sargent Bush Jr. The difference between Wilder's and Hawthorne's modernization of Bunyan is that Hawthorne's treatment parodies *The Pilgrim's Progress,* perhaps to satirize the beliefs of his ancestors, whereas Wilder's, though also tongue-in-cheek, is nevertheless a reaffirmation of the Puritans' cosmic optimism.

After we hear the passengers thinking aloud about their reasons for being on the train, thus dramatizing the microcosm, the Stage Manager says, "So much for the inside of the car. That'll be enough of that for the present. Now for its position geographically, meteorologically, astronomically, theologically considered" (49). The allegorical characters (e.g., Parkersburg, Ohio) deliver their speeches representing the geographical and meteorological positions; the actors playing the planets represent the astronomical position; then the Stage Manager announces, "Now shh—shh—shh! Enter the Archangels. (*To the audience*) We have now reached the theological position of Pullman Car Hiawatha" (54). The Archangels Gabriel and Michael enter from above, interact briefly with the Insane Woman, then confront the deceased Harriet; after her initial reluctance, she agrees to go with them, then stops to say goodbye to the world (which Wilder will have Emily do in Act Three of *Our Town*). Finally, the Stage Manager creates a theatrical macrocosm: "Now we'll have the whole world together, please. The whole solar system please" (58). With all the characters murmuring, chanting, or humming, Harriet presents what must be the theological position of "Pullman Car Hiawatha" (the train and the play): "I was not ever thus, nor asked that Thou / Shouldst lead me on, and spite of fears, / Pride ruled my will: Remember not past years" (58).[37] The Stage Manager pronounces this "Very good" and announces their arrival at the Chicago train station, subtly suggesting the Puritan eschatological view of having reached the zenith, here represented by the University of Chicago (where Wilder taught in the 1930s): "See the University's towers over there! The best of them all," and the Porter confirms, "This train don't go no further" (59).

Embodying most of the elements of the Puritan narrative tradition—abstract representation, allegorical and type characters, microcosmic and macrocosmic setting, a God-like figure, Calvinistic theology, progressive structure and conceptualization of history and life as progressive—*Pullman Car Hiawatha* reads like a direct descendent of Taylor's *God's Determinations*. In this third play from *The Long Christmas Dinner and Other Plays,* the Puritan influence on our national image is woven into a text that manifests a unity of content and form in signifying the doctrine of progress.

These three one-act plays are significant, then, not only for understanding the evolution of Wilder's career as a writer, but also for tracing the progress of Puritanism within American culture. His use of a bare stage is the theatrical equivalent of Puritan plain style; his act of purifying the theater of

37. The elevated style of Harriet's speech—she is quoting John Cardinal Newman's 1833 hymn "Lead kindly Light"—suggests she, at least, has reached a theological position.

modern realism reenacts the Puritans' purifying the rites of worship in the church. Thus, although *Our Town* is the most famous example of an abstract and purified stage and dialogue, Wilder had employed the style seven years earlier in *The Long Christmas Dinner and Other Plays*.[38] With his theatrical reformation underway in the early 1930s, Wilder then set his sights on the novel.

Heaven's My Destination

As *The Long Christmas Dinner and Other Plays* was Wilder's first mature dramatic work to concentrate on America as a literary subject, so too *Heaven's My Destination* was his first novel with American settings, characters, and actions. Not surprisingly, then, as in the one-act plays, progress is not only the theme but also the form of Wilder's novel, suggesting that the narrative expression of his imagination was not rooted in genre, but in a more fundamental source of form and structure. As Edmund Fuller writes, "This fourth novel is startlingly different, in manner, method, and material, from the other novels. Its tone is that of his plays, and I have wondered if, at some stage in its gestation, it may have hovered between the two forms." Other scholars have also commented on the generic ambiguity of *Heaven's My Destination,* taking note of the quantity and quality of dialogue in the novel.[39]

To clarify why Wilder wrote generically hybrid works (narrators in plays, dialogue representing much of the action in novels), some definitions of narrative terms are in order. Both Wilder and his brother Amos use the term "fabulist" to describe the kind of writer he was.[40] Whatever sense of fabulist either of them intended, the early twentieth-century Russian formalist meaning of the root *fable* or *fabula* as *story* (i.e., an action) versus *syuzhet* (i.e., plot, the way the story is presented), regardless of the genre—fiction, drama, poetry—applies to Wilder's narrative aesthetic. That is, Wilder conceived stories whose presentation was not determined primarily by their genre—novel

38. Szondi offers this assessment of *Our Town:* "Hardly another work of the modern theater is at once so bold in the formal realm and of such moving simplicity in the statement it makes as Thornton Wilder's *Our Town*" (*Theory of the Modern Drama,* 83). Despite Szondi's praise, American drama scholars in the past couple of decades have failed to credit Wilder's importance.

39. Fuller, "Notation of the Heart," 214. One other scholar is Hermann Stresau, *Thornton Wilder,* 28. Even this ambiguity of genre has precedent in seventeenth-century Puritan writing. As seen in Chapter One, the narrative mode of Taylor's *God's Determinations* in various places resembles *Everyman* (dramatic allegory), *The Pilgrim's Progress* (prose narrative allegory), and *Paradise Lost* (epic poem).

40. Thornton Wilder, "Thornton Wilder," in *Writers at Work I,* 118; Amos Niven Wilder, *Thornton Wilder and His Public,* 16.

or drama—but, as we have seen, by the Puritan narrative aesthetic, which had persisted in the American literary tradition. Thus his drama and fiction tell much the same kind of story using many of the same narrative and rhetorical strategies as the works of the Puritan writers Taylor, Wigglesworth, Morgan, and Johnson.

For example, in the same way Judgment Day was overdetermined in Wilder's first full-length play, *The Trumpet Shall Sound,* so, too, progress is overdetermined in *Heaven's My Destination;* more specifically, progress is signified by the word "progress" itself; by symbols of progress in the story; by progress in the protagonist George Brush's development as demonstrated by a progressive though episodic plot and Brush's own belief in progress; by an intertextuality with John Bunyan's *The Pilgrim's Progress;* and, finally, by the progress in Wilder's own career to which the book itself and its epigraph testify, as we shall see later in this chapter. This overdetermination of progress makes *Heaven's My Destination* even more quintessentially American than other characteristics of the novel examined by previous studies of Wilder.[41]

Besides the use of the word "progress" itself near the beginning of *Heaven's My Destination* as part of the phrase "in progress" (1), there are signs or symbols of progress within the narrative of the protagonist George Brush, a traveling salesman who rides on trains from town to town. (In that respect, he could be one of the young businessmen on board the train in *Pullman Car Hiawatha.*) Two recurring signifiers of progress in George's story are education and evolution. The fact that George Brush works for a publisher of textbooks is only the most obvious way in which he is associated with education. George doesn't just spew forth a company spiel; he personally testifies to the educational quality of the textbooks he sells (he has worked out all the problems in the math book and done the lessons in the language primer) as he visits many colleges and other schools. He talks and thinks a lot about his own college education, about the courses and teachers he had. He visits a camp and not only talks with the college students who work there during the summer, but also washes dishes and sings with them because he still feels he is one of them (43–45).

Of course, one might argue that George's persistent naïveté undermines

---

41. Goldstein cites three particularly American elements that *Heaven's My Destination* dramatizes: the struggle against fundamentalist evangelism, the freedom to move about the country, and the old joke about the traveling salesman and the farmer's daughter (*Art of Thornton Wilder,* 82–94). No less than Gertrude Stein herself described *Heaven's My Destination* as "the American novel" (quoted in Goldstone, *Intimate Portrait,* 100). In Book of the Month Club Editorial Board, comp., *The Well-Stocked Bookcase: Sixty Enduring Novels Published by Americans between 1926–1986,* Wilfred Sheed counts *Heaven's My Destination* as "one of the most American novels ever written" (33).

the effectiveness of the higher education he received, except that in the purely vocational purpose of education he is a shining example; that is, Brush is the company's best salesman. The fact that he is a better salesman of educational textbooks than of the fundamentalist Christianity he witnesses to on the train, in hotels, and everywhere he goes perhaps suggests that the problem is either with the "product" rather than the seller, or with the "hard-sell" method George employs, as does an even more fundamentalist evangelist he encounters later in the book (91–95). George is only beginning to apply the same comparative tests to his religious beliefs that he does to the textbooks he sells, as indicated by his knowledge, albeit superficial, of Ghandi's teachings (146). The point is, it's a start. And George is always making a new start on his self-improvement, as suggested by the new year's resolutions he makes yearly on his birthday rather than January first, which are initially composed in rough draft along with a list of his vices and virtues (5). This periodic self-examination and inventory-taking of character goes back not just to Benjamin Franklin's famous plan for perfection in the *Autobiography*, but to the Puritan founders, whose method for determining their election was self-examination over time, culminating in a public conversion narrative to effect their acceptance into the congregation as full members.[42]

Although George is narrowly educated when we first meet him, the fact that he was a good student—he "got the highest grades of anybody" (48)—gives us hope for his continued growth. He recalls one college professor's exasperated statement that he had a closed mind and would never get anywhere; George's response indicates his commitment to continuing his education: "I don't want to live if I've got a closed mind and can't get anywhere—anywhere in thinking, I mean. But I don't believe what he said anymore. I keep getting new good ideas all the time. I learn things as I go" (50). One way Wilder shows us that George's education is ongoing after he has completed his formal education is by dramatizing his persistence in thinking about what he doesn't immediately comprehend. For example, George is so troubled at not understanding the merit of *King Lear*, which a college professor told him is the "greatest work in English literature," that he decides to commit it to memory (71). Of course we are meant to laugh at the simplemindedness of his approach, but we cannot doubt his sincerity in wanting to continue to understand, to learn, to make progress.

---

42. As Leopold Damrosch Jr. explains, "For the Puritan the self is all-important not because it *is* one's self but because it represents the sole battleground of the war between good and evil. . . . But the self is duplicitous and complex, requiring the most stringent analysis. . . . The truth can only emerge from a sustained scrutiny of behavior over a period of time, and thus the need for temporal narrative is born" (*God's Plot and Man's Stories: Studies in the Fictional Imagination from Milton to Fielding*, 4).

The other major signifier or symbol of progress in *Heaven's My Destination* is the theory of evolution, to which George, as the kind of Christian who believes the Bible should be read literally, is adamantly opposed—at least in the beginning. The fundamentalist abhorrence of evolution is satirized here not from the point of view of the atheist; rather, Wilder shows the irony of those who believe in providential and personal progress but reject a theory that provides a biological paradigm for their beliefs. Unlike other descendants of the Puritans, Congregationalists did not resist the revelations of scientific inquiry, as demonstrated by this statement from *Progressive Religious Thought in America: A Survey of the Enlarging Pilgrim Faith,* which was written by John Wright Buckham in anticipation of the tercentenary of the landing of the Pilgrims on Plymouth rock:

> If only it could come to be recognized universally among Christians that progress is the true and normal life of theology. . . . Progress means something very different from fluctuation, or the renunciation of convictions once firmly and clearly grasped. To abandon a conviction once formed is one thing; to reinterpret and enlarge it is another. Progress means, not the former, but the latter. It means the recognition of the law of development—whose counterpart in the sphere of nature is evolution—as the very nature of the spiritual life. True development is never a destructive but always a conserving process.[43]

Early in *Heaven's My Destination* George meets a college girl who in many ways resembles himself, and he is initially quite taken with her. Then, learning that she is studying to become a teacher of biology (Darwin included), George is shocked and disappointed, but also declares, as he often does, that he needs to think it through (52–53). Again, Wilder makes his protagonist open to change and to progress in his beliefs, unlike truly closed-minded religious zealots who condemn to hell all those who believe differently. Later in the novel, George discusses evolution with George Burkin, who, as Mildred Kuner points out, functions as Brush's doppleganger, but is also, as Michael Vivion notes, "an unabashed Satan figure" in a long line of Satan figures we have seen in *Prosperina and the Devil, The Trumpet Shall Sound, The Cabala,* and *The Bridge of San Luis Rey.* On the literal level of the narrative, Burkin is a left-wing documentary filmmaker who travels around middle America looking through the windows of houses in typical residential neighborhoods for confirmation of his Marxist condemnation of capitalist culture. This episode ends even more badly than the one with the college girl: Brush angrily denounces Burkin and his ideas, as Burkin does Brush and

---

43. Buckham, *Progressive Religious Thought in America: A Survey of the Enlarging Pilgrim Faith,* 310–11.

his, and they part company on bad terms. At this point in the novel George would not appear to be making any progress intellectually. However, *Heaven's My Destination* concludes with the report of George encountering yet another believer in evolution, a waitress who reads Darwin in her spare time, but in this episode his response indicates that *he* has evolved: George arranges to put her through college. As George Greene writes, "Yet by the close of his embattled year he has advanced."[44]

Previous studies are more or less evenly divided between reading this ending and the novel overall straightforwardly or ironically.[45] But clearly Wilder means for us to see that his protagonist is making progress, which was also an intense Puritan preoccupation, as Davies explains: "They were interested in the stages of the redeemed soul's progress: election, vocation, justification, sanctification, glorification."[46] Commenting on the structure of *Heaven's My Destination,* Wilder said in a newspaper interview that "The action is episodic, but the episodes are not unrelated; each has its bearing on the development, the education, of the hero." The novel's narrator makes this point explicitly: "Many unusual adventures befell him during these weeks. Of the great number we select three that illustrate certain stages in his education" (91). In one of these further episodes, George gets an absurd taste of his own medicine when he meets an older version of himself—an evangelist who aggressively witnesses to unwilling listeners on trains. He tells the evangelist, "You don't do any good making them mad" (94). Following this, he goes to meet a former roommate who is dying in a hospital; the roommate doesn't want him to preach at him, and George says, "I won't. I've learned not to. That's one of the things I've learned" (112). Although Papajewski and Goldstein characterize the episodic structure of the novel as repetitious without growth, we have seen in the episodes discussed above that the repetition manifests progress.[47]

George himself believes in progress on all levels: the personal, the global,

---

44. Kuner, *Thornton Wilder: The Bright and the Dark,* 119; Vivion, "Thornton Wilder and the Farmer's Daughter," 43; Greene, "The World of Thornton Wilder," 573.

45. Burbank, *Thornton Wilder,* 69; Kuner, *Bright and Dark,* 114, 122–23; Haberman, "The Americanization of Thornton Wilder," 23–27; and Firebaugh, "Farce and the Heavenly Destination," 12, read the conclusion of *Heaven's My Destination* and the novel's overall tone as positive; Streasu, *Thornton Wilder,* 54; Helmut Papajewski, *Thornton Wilder,* 53, 59; Goldstein, *Art of Thornton Wilder,* 92, 164; and David Castronovo, *Thornton Wilder,* 110–17, as negative.

46. Davies, *Worship and Theology,* 68. In *God's Determinations,* Taylor's Puritan Everyman says to Saint in expressing his fear that he is not one of the Elect, "Such as are Gracious grow in Grace, therefore / Such as have Grace, are Gracious evermore. / Who sin Commit are sinfull: and thereby / They grow ungodly. So I feare do I" (86).

47. Quoted in Simon, *Thornton Wilder, His World,* 95; Papajewski, *Thornton Wilder,* 60; Goldstein, *Art of Thornton Wilder,* 89–90.

and the providential. He explains after a quarrel with another of his fellow roomers at a boardinghouse, "I guess the best of friends quarrel every now and then. It doesn't mean that they're any the worse persons; it only means that human nature isn't raised up yet to what we hope it's going to be.... Sometime the day's coming when there aren't going to be any quarrels, because in my opinion the world's getting better and better" (83). He later retreats from this ameliorative view: "Well, I think the world's in such a bad way that we've all got to start thinking all over again.... I'm trying to begin all over again at the beginning" (102), but he maintains that, overall, the movement is forward, as illustrated by a scene with Roberta, the farmer's daughter of Wilder's novelized extension of the old joke. George has been searching for Roberta to do the right thing by marrying her; when he finds her he says, "I know I'm kind of funny in some ways ... but that's only these earlier years when I'm trying to think things out. By the time I'm thirty all that kind of thing will be clearer to me, and ... and it'll all be settled" (172).

This is not to say that George never experiences doubt about progress: "I believe in God, all right; but why's he so slow in changing the world?" (116). In his greatest crisis, near the end of the novel, George even rejects the concept of personal progress: "I made the mistake all my life of thinking that you could get better and better until you were perfect" (183). What restores his faith is the gift from a priest he has never actually met, though they know of each other through a mutual friend. Previous studies have noted that Father Pasziewski is a kindred spirit, that he is, like George, another "fool in Christ,"[48] but they haven't accounted for why hearing that a Catholic priest is praying for him and receiving the priest's deathbed gift of a spoon are enough to bring George out of his depression.

As discussed in Chapter Two with regard to *The Trumpet Shall Sound* and Wilder's other works published in the 1920s, one aspect of Puritanism that has persisted in Protestant American culture is anti-Catholicism. Of course, the feelings were mutual in Europe during the Reformation, the Counter Reformation, and continuing in official Catholic doctrine until the time of Vatican II in the early 1960s. Thus, that a Catholic priest would care personally for a fundamentalist he had never met; that George-as-fundamentalist does not reject the priest's best wishes, prayers, or gift; and that Father Pasziewski would establish a kind of communion with him from his deathbed to George's deathbed (for that is the state in which George and the doctors believe him to be), all attest to Wilder's growing ecumenical spirit,

---

48. "George turns his back on the materialistic aspect of the Dream. He is Wilder's idea of the fool in Christ, a mythic character whose ideals and goals reflect a pure version of the Puritan spirit in America" (Vivion, "Farmer's Daughter," 41).

which, as discussed earlier in this chapter, was also evident in *The Happy Journey* when the Catholic garage hand and Protestant Ma Kirby hit it off despite their religious differences. While the ecumenical movement has not been accepted by all Christian denominations as a sign of the progress of Christianity, the unity of the Church is prayed for weekly in the Catholic liturgy. Thus the gift of something as simple as a spoon represents a progress of recognition of similar beliefs and values between fundamentalist Protestants and Roman Catholics; it is a lesson in tolerance and acceptance of differing beliefs, which is the primary lesson George needed to learn, as America itself has had to learn, and is still learning.[49]

As John Henry Raleigh explains in his introduction to a 1960 edition of *Heaven's My Destination,* "Counterpointing this fully developed and concrete Protestantism is a muted, rather vague and off-stage Catholicism. As in American history, it has been Protestantism that has been the chief actor, while Catholicism has waited in the wings. Thus Father Pasziewski is never even seen." Raleigh apparently did not understand why the priest has a positive effect on George: "Yet, strangely enough, it is Father Pasziewski who 'saves' Brush." But Raleigh does appreciate the significance of the effect: "They [news of the priest's death and the reception of the spoon] turn him away from despair (the only unforgivable sin in Catholic theology)." Raleigh concludes that Brush "is finally a Protestant man triumphant, slightly liberalized."[50]

The most erudite and subtle indication of progress in *Heaven's My Destination* is the intertextuality between Wilder's novel and what could almost be called the original source from which it was adapted: John Bunyan's *The Pilgrim's Progress.*[51] As noted earlier in this study, although *The Pilgrim's Progress* is an English Puritan work, it was enormously popular in colonial New England and subsequently throughout the United States. Bunyan's aesthetic is similar to the American Puritan aesthetic as described in this study, but it is not identical.[52] Space does not allow a lengthy comparison of the two

49. Though it can't be proven definitively, I suspect that the spoon was a "Puritan spoon," which *The Random House Dictionary of the English Language,* 2d ed., defines as "a silver spoon having an ovoid bowl and a straight, flat, completely *plain* stem" ("Puritan spoon," emphasis added). The problem is that the entry dates the term to 1955, twenty years after *Heaven's My Destination* was published.

50. Raleigh, "The American Quixote: George Brush," in the "Introduction" to Thornton Wilder's *Heaven's My Destination,* 11, 12.

51. Papajewski, *Thornton Wilder,* 52; Kuner, *Bright and Dark,* 193; and Harrison, *Enthusiast,* 145, have briefly commented on the relationship between Wilder's and Bunyan's books, but they did not support the connection with any detailed analysis.

52. Damrosch analyzes *The Pilgrim's Progress* as a precursor to the English novel, which is more realistic than the American novel, as Richard Chase has argued in *The American Novel and Its Tradition.*

works, and perhaps an in-depth demonstration of the similarity of the texts would be forced at times anyway, but enough analogies between the two works can be cited to conclude that at least in his first American novel Wilder's debt to Puritanism, the Puritan aesthetic, and a particular Puritan text is conscious and direct rather than unconscious and diffused through his family and American culture and literature.[53]

First, Wilder's title *Heaven's My Destination* describes the narrative as a journey similar to Bunyan's title, *The Pilgrim's Progress,* and the goal is the same (Bunyan calls it "The Celestial City"). Second, the summaries of events at the beginning of each chapter, an antiquated practice by the time of *Heaven's My Destination*'s publication (1935), correspond to Bunyan's marginal annotations of the events in *The Pilgrim's Progress,* first published in 1678. A more substantive intertextuality between Wilder and Bunyan is that many episodes in *Heaven's My Destination* correspond not only in content, sometimes quite specifically, to episodes in *The Pilgrim's Progress,* but also to their position within the two works' plots. For example, George's encounter with the banker and police chief in Armina corresponds to Christian's encounter with Mr. Worldly-Wiseman of the town of Carnal Policy and Mr. Legality; George's receiving a telegram in code is identical in function to Christian's visit to the House of Interpreter; George's early bout of depression parallels Christian's wallowing in the slough of despond; George's staying in a barn (where, as the joke goes, he is intimate with the farmer's daughter) is analogous to Christian's stay at Palace Beautiful with Discretion and other virgins who feed him, listen to his adventures, but not *etc.* (it is a pious story, after all); George and Burkin's incarceration is similar to Christian and Faithful's imprisonment; and, finally, George's rescue from his near-death malaise by Father Pasziewski's gift matches Christian's salvation from despair by Hopeful's encouragement while wading through the river of death. The specificity of the similarity between recurring incidents in *Heaven's My Destination* and *The Pilgrim's Progress* could not be duplicated in a comparison of Wilder's novel to, say, *Everyman* or *The Castle of Perseverance,* though perhaps it could with *God's Determinations* had Taylor's work been discovered before Wilder wrote *Heaven's My Destination.*[54]

53. As a renowned author in his early fifties, Wilder still lived with Bunyan, mentioning him in his journal as evidence that allegory, though an inferior form of narration, can be done (*JTW,* 157); and in the midst of his attempt to write *The Emporium,* he called it "a Pilgrim's Progress" (*JTW,* 52).

54. In more abstract terms, *God's Determinations* is a "depression play" with a happy ending, as are both *The Pilgrim's Progress* and *Heaven's My Destination.* Wilder even said that *Heaven's My Destination* was "in every paragraph a depression novel" (Harrison, *Enthusiast,* 149), which Castronovo quotes (*Thornton Wilder,* 114), but he does not find the double reference to George's state of mind and America's economic "slough of despond" convincing.

Another similarity of *The Pilgrim's Progress* and *Heaven's My Destination* is that both are allegories. Although Wilder's allegorical representation isn't as obvious as Bunyan's personification, the characters in the book are clearly one- or two-dimensional types, as were the characters in *The Long Christmas Dinner* plays, and George himself is a representative of America, which the text signifies in many ways. First, Brush is the first of three major Wilder characters to be named "George" (the other two are George Gibbs in *Our Town* and George Antrobus in *The Skin of Our Teeth*), undoubtedly after George Washington. Second, his profession—traveling salesman—is the quintessential American occupation in twentieth-century literature.[55] As Vivion explains, "George's dual role as traveling salesman and evangelist allow the forces of materialism and spirituality opportunity for full interplay. The salesman/evangelist duality also makes him a combination of two American folk-heroes, and, as such, he approaches myth because he represents two of America's most sacred beliefs: Money and God." Finally, in one passage George tells Burkin how he received an autograph from a famous Italian singer touring America who had gotten to know him enough to write, "To my good friend, the true American George Busch, child of Walt Witmann's [*sic*] hopes" (160).[56] Goldstein concludes that although we may deny it, George Brush is "one of us." Wilder himself regarded George as representing America: "George Brush is a sort of short history of the American mind raised by exaggeration into humor: idealistic, but unclear; really religious, but badly educated in religion."[57]

Occasionally Wilder does make the allegory as heavy-handed as Bunyan (or his own earlier allegory, *The Trumpet Shall Sound*). For example, George reports that one girl he was interested in made the mistake of *smoking* in front of him; this incident took place in the fictional town of *Sulphur Falls,* Arkansas, and he sums up the incident by saying, "It wasn't only me she lost" (24), implying, apparently, that she lost her soul, which will fall to the place full of sulfur and smoke—hell. Another example of pointed allegory is that Roberta, the farmer's daughter with whom George spent the night, is living and

---

55. Wilder's use of the traveling salesman as a representative American predates both Eudora Welty's in "Death of a Travelling Salesman" (1941) and Arthur Miller's *Death of a Salesman* (1949); however, the traveling evangelist representative of America, a character type to which George Brush also belongs, was depicted most famously by Sinclair Lewis in *Elmer Gantry* (1927). Burbank (*Thornton Wilder,* 64) thinks that *Heaven's My Destination* is Wilder's answer to Lewis's satirical novel.

56. Vivion, "Farmer's Daughter," 41. The assessment might be questioned because it comes from a foreigner, as suggested by her misspelling of both their names, but one of the most cited definitive studies of American culture, *Democracy in America,* was also made by a non-American on tour—Alexis de Tocqueville.

57. Goldstein, *Art of Thornton Wilder,* 84; Harrison, *Enthusiast,* 148.

working under the assumed name Lily, and one of the prostitutes in the Kansas City bordello George mistakes for a legitimate boardinghouse is also named Lily. In Wilder's works (most famously, in *The Skin of Our Teeth*), the name "Lily" is code for "fallen woman" and temptress, probably derived from Lilith, the witch-like first mate of Adam not included in the Christian Bible. An allegorical cliché used in *Heaven's My Destination* is the apple as the forbidden fruit (25); George is offered one during his explanation (read confession) of his fall from grace with Roberta (the third "big secret disappointment" in his life).

All of the preceding interpretations of Wilder's allegory should be readily apparent to the scholar, but like Bunyan, Wilder encourages his readers to look for allegorical meanings by means of a built-in lesson on decoding. In *The Pilgrim's Progress,* Bunyan includes the House of Interpreter episode relatively early in the narrative; similarly, in *Heaven's My Destination* Wilder begins Chapter Three with George receiving a telegram from his boss at the publishing house: "JUDGE LAKE MORGAN CAMP SETTLE GUTENBERG ALDUS CAXTON GIVE HIM THE WORKS SKIES THE LIMIT EINSTEIN," which the narrator explains wasn't "so difficult of interpretation as it appears to be" (29). Part of the interpretation is as follows: "'Settle Gutenberg Aldus Caxton' meant that Brush was to persuade [Judge Corey at Lake Morgan Camp] to recommend [to the educational committee of the Oklahoma state legislature] certain textbooks published by his house. The names of the great printers served as code convention for Caulkins' *First Year Algebra*, Mademoiselle Desfontaines' *Les Premiers Pas*, and Professor Grubb's *A Soldier with Caesar*" (30).

Wilder also plays with names similar to Bunyan's personification allegory in characters such as Mr. Worldly-Wiseman or Evangelist. Again providing an internal reading lesson, Wilder has George see an advertisement for social activities at Camp Morgan that reads, "Girls, extend your acquaintance. Our Name-Badge Dances introduce everyone" (31). At the camp, he stays in a tent named "Felix" (32), meets a girl named "Mississippi Corey" (38), and picks up his home state as a temporary nickname—"Michigan" (58). This allegory isn't as blatant as that in *Pullman Car Hiawatha*, where Wilder represented places (a field, Grover's Corners) with actors, but it does call attention to unusual naming and thus names in general.

Furthermore, in the Armina episode in chapter one of *Heaven's My Destination,* the criticism of materialistic society lies not only in the action but in the decoding of characters' and the town's names and a few common nouns. To begin with, there is no town in Oklahoma named "Armina"—not that appears in any recent map index. In the context of the story of a fundamentalist by an author imbued with Puritanism, it is difficult not to associate the fictional name "Armina" with Arminianism, the anti-Calvinistic belief that, along with antinomianism, seventeenth-century New England Puritans saw as a straying from the path of truth.[58] Secondly, this episode serves as the major evidence for those studies (e.g., Burbank, *Thornton Wilder,* 69) that place *Heaven's My Destination* in the tradition of *Gulliver's Travels, Candide, Tom Jones,* and *Huckleberry Finn* as a criticism of a materialistic and corrupt society by means of the encounters an innocent protagonist has with representatives of the norm who often bear allegorical names. In that vein, Wilder seems to be focusing directly on how certain aspects of Puritanism have been secularized in a Franklinesque conversion to capitalism in American culture at large.[59]

George goes to Armina to withdraw his savings from a bank already in trouble: "Beside the door the president sat in his smaller pen, filled with despair. Short of a miracle, his bank had little over a week to live. Banks had been failing all through these states for months, and now even this bank, which had seemed to him to be eternal, would be obliged to close its doors" (11). When George declares that he only wants his *principal* because he doesn't "believe in interest" (11), the president of the bank tries to explain to him, "The interest represents those profits, which we share with you," to which George replies with the kind of wordplay we expect in allegorical works, "I don't believe in profits like that" (12); obviously, George means that he believes in prophets like Isaiah and Jeremiah. George himself makes a connection between his economic ideas and his religious beliefs, as he explains to the president: "You see, the fact that I had this money here was a sign that I lived in fear. . . . No one who has money saved up in a bank can really be happy. All the money locked up here is being saved because people are afraid of a rainy day. They're afraid, as they say, that worst may come to worst. Mr. Southwick, may I ask if you're a religious man?" (13). The narrator informs us that Mr. Southwick had been a deacon of the First Presbyterian Church for twenty years, and then reports that Mr. Southwick has George arrested. This possible vestige of the Congregationalist/Presbyterian rivalry helps make the episode's point that zeal is felt now for the doctrines

58. Arminianism was a theology espoused by Jacobus Arminius; it was in direct conflict with the doctrine of Calvinism that Christ's sacrifice was only for the elect, not everyone, as Arminius believed. Antinomianism was the belief that Christians were not required to adhere to Old Testament law since they were under the Covenant of Grace. See Perry Miller's *The New England Mind: The Seventeenth Century* for a more in-depth explanation of these theological conflicts in Puritan New England.

59. Sacvan Bercovitch says, "Socially and economically, the Puritan vision issued in a federal nation 'under God,' committed to progress as prophecy, contract as covenant, expansion as destiny, and (through the primacy of personal faith) the divine right of self-possessive individualism" ("The Modernity of American Puritan Rhetoric," 60).

of capitalism rather than Calvinism, of savings rather than salvation, of the accruement of interest rather than of "any real interest left in wanting to see the sun come up on the next day" (27), of socioeconomic progress rather than spiritual progress. George is *arrested* here, but, ironically, it is the moral development of America that has come to a halt. The jail's photographer, who comments that George's "spirals" (fingerprints) stand for "character," repeatedly calls him "Mr. Brown" (the Puritans—or "Pilgrims"—who were on the *Mayflower* were also known as Brownists).[60]

It is not only the Armina episode in *Heaven's My Destination* that functions as a parable of the corruption of Puritan doctrine in America; the Camp Morgan episode also makes use of wordplay to suggest how Puritanism has been secularized. When George reports that his first big secret disappointment is never being *elect*ed to any of his college's literary societies, and he dissuades a real estate salesman distraught over the Great Depression from committing suicide for the *insurance,* it is legitimate to read these terms in the same way as the conversion of Calvinistic predestination of God's chosen people, the elect, to election in a fraternity, a socioeconomic elite, and as the substitution of insurance for assurance of what happens after death.[61] Thus, in patterning so much of *Heaven's My Destination* after *The Pilgrim's Progress*—the title, plot summaries, episodes, overall progression, the representative protagonist, the allegorical method—Wilder has signified progress with a demonstration of the progress of the Puritan narrative tradition in America.

A final way in which *Heaven's My Destination* signifies progress is as a turning point in Wilder's career. As mentioned at the beginning of this chapter, most studies of Wilder cite *The Long Christmas Dinner and Other Plays* or *Heaven's My Destination* or both as his turning toward American subjects as the result of Mike Gold's attack on Wilder's third novel, *The Woman of Andros*. However, Wilder denied that simplistic cause-effect interpretation of his development: "I think you would find that the work is a gradual drawing near to the America I know. . . . I began, first with *Heaven's My Destination,* to approach the American scene. Already, in the one-act plays, I had become aware of how difficult it is to invest one's contemporary world with the same kind of imaginative life one has extended to those removed in time and place. But I

60. If this double reading of words seems far-fetched, take another look at *The Pilgrim's Progress* or any allegory. In *The Language of Allegory: Defining the Genre,* Maureen Quilligan says that wordplay is a definitive characteristic of allegorical texts (35). Besides, the Puritans, Quakers, Dunkards, and other Protestant sects formed during the Reformation were named such by their detractors in a manner similar to personification allegory.

61. Other traces of disguised Calvinism in the text of *Heaven's My Destination* include a definition of a self-predestined reprobate: "A criminal is a human being who thinks that the whole universe hates him" (244); and the ascension of grace over law: "Nobody's strong enough to live up to the rules" (290).

always feel that the progression is there and visible; I can be seen collecting the practice, the experience and courage, to present my own times."[62]

Wilder felt this way about his career and *Heaven's My Destination*'s place in it not only at the time of the *Paris Review* interview (more than twenty years after the publication of *Heaven's My Destination)*; he also seemed to have self-consciously written *Heaven's My Destination* as a step in his progress toward becoming the kind of writer he wanted to be (which may or may not support the interpretation that he was wounded by Gold's attack). The evidence for this is found in the novel's epigraph, which itself is another affirmation of progress but also demonstrates progress in the particularly Puritan way of typology. The epigraph reads, "Of all the forms of genius, goodness has the longest awkward age." Virtually every scholarly reading of *Heaven's My Destination* has noted that Wilder was quoting himself from *The Woman of Andros*. Haberman even recognizes that "The epigraph also connects the two novels: Wilder was writing of his own artistic awkward age for the 'kind of work . . . he would most like to do well': portray religious experience."[63] However, Haberman does not mention that the occurrence of the line in *The Woman of Andros* is also an adaptation from Wilder's foreword to his collection of three-minute plays, *The Angel That Troubled the Waters and Other Plays,* published the year before *The Woman of Andros:*

> It is a discouraging business to be an author at sixteen years of age. Such an author is all aspiration and no fulfillment. . . . Such fragments as he is finally able to commit to paper are a mass of echoes, awkward relative clauses and conflicting styles. In life and literature mere sincerity is not sufficient, and in both realms the greater the capacity *the longer the awkward age.* Yet strange lights cross that confusion, authoritative moments that all the practice of later maturity cannot explain and cannot recapture. He is visited by great depressions and wild exhilarations, but whether his depressions proceed from his limitations in the art of living or his limitations in the art of writing he cannot tell. An artist is one who knows how life should be lived at its best and is always aware of how badly he is doing it. (*CSPTW II,* 3–4, emphasis added)

Here Wilder is both apologizing for the amateurishness of the work to follow but also defending its publication on the basis of inspiration over craft. That he uses the language from this preface again in *The Woman of Andros* when Chrysis simultaneously chides and compliments an earnest but naive pro-tégé—"It is true that of all forms of genius, goodness has the longest awkward age" (55)—and then as *Heaven's My Destination*'s epigraph, which, like all epi-

---

62. Wilder, *Writers at Work,* 104.
63. Haberman, *Plays of Thornton Wilder,* 39.

graphs, suggests the major theme of the work, reflects the same progressive repetition of types (i.e., typology) found in the Bible, Puritan narratives, and elsewhere in Wilder's oeuvre. In addition, what Wilder says in the excerpt from the *Angel Plays* foreword about depression in the artist's life relates to his later assessment that *Heaven's My Destination* was "in every paragraph a depression novel." His statement should be read as referring both to the historical period of economic crisis in the United States and elsewhere, which is when *Heaven's My Destination* takes place, and to mental depression, of which George Brush suffers two major bouts, and which Bunyan had allegorized as the "slough of despond" in *The Pilgrim's Progress*. In this sense, then, *Heaven's My Destination* is part of the trail we are following of the Puritan's progress through the texts of Thornton Wilder, who—as a twentieth-century descendent of the Puritans—also marks the path Puritanism has taken in American culture.[64]

64. Harrison, *Enthusiast,* 149. An early article on Wilder concludes in similar terms: "I think of Thornton Wilder's career as a journey, from self-absorption toward dialogue, unresolved but still, happily, undismayed, with the permanent enigmas" (George Greene, "The World of Thornton Wilder," 584).

Four

Dramatic Jeremiads

Wilder's Revival of the Puritan Rhetoric of Crisis

American writers have tended to see themselves as outcasts and isolates, prophets crying in the wilderness. So they have been, as a rule: American Jeremiahs, simultaneously lamenting a declension and celebrating a national dream. Their major works are the most striking testimony we have to the power and reach of the American jeremiad.

–Sacvan Bercovitch, *The American Jeremiad*

Thornton Wilder's plays and novels have been described by scholars as sermons,[1] and Wilder himself thought of his Norton lectures on American Literature, delivered at Harvard in 1950, as "lay sermons," the American form he believed was the most suitable for his subject (*JTW,* 249). Wilder recognized that he was working within an intrinsically American genre, though he intuited rather than fully understood its appeal: "I shall say . . . that the most popular and flourishing literary genre of the Americans, and all too congenial to them, was that sorry, now disuete [*sic*], thing, the Sermon. (Development: the moralizing tendency in Americans; why? etc. Its impress effect on American prose style–) So: my obligation to furnish sermons" (*JTW,* 249).

The historical and literary studies of Perry Miller and other scholars of early American literature suggest one possible answer to Wilder's question: the moralizing tendency of Americans, the popularity of the sermon as a lit-

---

1. See, for example, Donald Haberman, *The Plays of Thornton Wilder,* 28.

128

erary genre in America, and the influence of both on American literature are legacies of the New England Puritans. As with any literary genre or mode or style, sermons and rhetoric do not exist in a vacuum. Rather, "rhetoric functions within a culture. It reflects and affects a set of particular psychic, social, and historical needs."[2]

Our national medium today is television, but in seventeenth-century New England it was the pulpit, and there were several varieties of sermons according to different services and public occasions. The jeremiad, the earliest form of American social criticism, was adapted by the New England Puritans to advance their cause of becoming "a city upon a hill," and it was further developed by American colonists in the years immediately preceding the American Revolution, as Bercovitch and other scholars have demonstrated. Bercovitch describes the American jeremiad as "a mode of public exhortation that originated in the European pulpit, was transformed in both form and content by the New England Puritans, persisted through the eighteenth century, and helped sustain a national dream through two hundred years of turbulence and change. . . . The jeremiad has played a major role in fashioning the myth of America."[3]

The notoriety of this particular type of sermon preached by New England Puritan ministers is one of the more conspicuous legacies of the Puritan past to American culture at large. The popular usage of the term "jeremiad" as a protracted lament or complaint against society in general or against a current event or condition in particular, however, is an oversimplification of the rhetorical strategies employed by seventeenth- and eighteenth-century colonial ministers and politicians.[4] Rather, the jeremiad, as preached in America, "intertwines lamentation with optimism." Since the word "jeremiad" is derived from the Book of Jeremiah in the Bible, New England Puritan preachers of jeremiads acted the role of prophets, and their sermons were akin to "Old Testament prophecy, a scriptural genre that devotes itself as much to diagnosing the spiritual condition of an age as to predicting the future."[5]

---

2. Sacvan Bercovitch, *The American Jeremiad*, xi. For book-length studies of the sermon as genre in relation to the American literary tradition, see, for example, Harry S. Stout, *The New England Soul*, and David P. Hall, *The Faithful Shepherd*.

3. Bercovitch, *American Jeremiad*, xi.

4. Although the New England Puritans did not originate the jeremiad, they did adapt it for their protonationalist purposes. In the second half of the eighteenth century, after the heyday of Puritanism had passed, Whig orators again adapted the jeremiad for the more secular purpose of supporting the American Revolution; see Emory Elliott, "The Puritan Roots of American Whig Rhetoric," and David Minter, "The Puritan Jeremiad as a Literary Form," in *The American Puritan Imagination: Essays in Revaluation,* ed. Sacvan Bercovitch, 45–55.

5. Richard L. Johannesen, "The Jeremiad and Jenkin Lloyd Jones," 161; George P. Landow, "Elegant Jeremiahs: The Genre of the Victorian Sage," 21. For other uses of the jeremiad similar to this study's, see also Dolan Hubbard, "David Walker's *Appeal* and

Bercovitch argues that the impetus for preaching the jeremiad was an actual or perceived communal crisis; it was enacted as a ritual response to affirm the Puritans' intentions of creating a theocracy in the New World: "My focus is on the affirmative energies through which the jeremiad survived the decline of Puritan New England, and, in what amounted to a nationwide ritual of progress, contributed to the success of the republic."[6] As Bercovitch and other scholars have delineated them, the definitive components of the American jeremiad include a lament of the current crisis, an invocation of a golden age in the past, and a reaffirmation of the mission of God's chosen people.[7] These elements were simple enough to have been employed by many writers for a wide range of purposes. In *The American Jeremiad,* Bercovitch demonstrates the continuity of the jeremiad through the development of American culture and American literature, as it informed the works of such nineteenth-century writers as Emerson, Thoreau, Hawthorne, Melville, and Whitman.[8] The jeremiad lived on, then, not only in the form of a sermon,

---

the American Puritan Jeremiadic Tradition," *Centennial Review* 30, no. 3 (Summer 1986): 331–46; John A. Murray, "The Hill Beyond the City: Elements of the Jeremiad in Edward Abbey's 'Down the River with Henry Thoreau,'" *Western American Literature* 22, no. 4 (February 1988): 301–6; Maurice A. Mierau, "Carnival and Jeremiad: Mailer's *The Armies of the Night,*" *Canadian Review of American Studies* 17, no. 3 (Fall 1986): 317–26; Johannesen, "Jeremiad and Jenkin Lloyd Jones"; and my "American Jeremiah: Edward Albee as Judgment Day Prophet in *The Lady from Dubuque,*" *American Drama* 7, no. 1 (Fall 1997): 30–49.

6. Bercovitch, *American Jeremiad,* xiv–xv. Bercovitch uses the term "ritual" in the sense employed by anthropologist Victor Turner: an active agent in the conservation or revolution of a society at any given point in its development. See Victor Turner, *Dramas, Fields, and Metaphors: Symbolic Action in Human Society* (Ithaca: Cornell University Press, 1967).

7. In the section on the jeremiad in his essay "New England Puritan Literature" within *The Cambridge History of American Literature Volume 1: 1590–1820,* Emory Elliott writes,

> Overall, the jeremiads had a complicated, seemingly contradictory, communal function. On the one hand, they were designed to awaken a lethargic people. On the other hand, in their repetitive and ritualistic nature, they functioned as a form of reassurance, reinscribing proof that the saints were still a coherent body who ruled New England in covenant with God and under His sometimes chastising and yet ultimately protective hand. The tension between these competing, yet finally reconciled, purposes gives the jeremiads their literary complexity and power. (258–59)

8. Elliott also notes the influence of the jeremiad not only on classical American literature but also on some twentieth-century works: "From presidential addresses to works of literary artists, the jeremiad appears as a fundamental structure in the American expression. *Moby-Dick, The Narrative of the Life of Frederick Douglass, Life in the Iron Mills, Walden, The Great Gatsby, The Grapes of Wrath, Gravity's Rainbow*—these works and many others have all been called jeremiads because they seem to call for a return to a former innocence and moral strength that has been lost" ("New England Puritan Literature," 263).

but also as an American rhetoric, which writers (especially those who lived in or near New England where ties to the Puritan past were more direct) would access, consciously or unconsciously, as part of the cultural inheritance of rhetorical modes available to them.

Beginning in the 1930s, when he had reached his own thirties, Thornton Wilder wrote explicitly about American subjects and themes in both his drama and fiction (as we saw in Chapter Three with the discussion of *The Long Christmas Dinner and Other Plays* and *Heaven's My Destination*). Toward the end of the decade, the Great Depression was fresh in the national memory, and World War Two was escalating to apocalyptic dimensions that would soon draw the United States into the global conflict; there was an urgent need for reassurance. Because it was a responsive, even an occasional genre, the American jeremiad was perfectly suited for delivering an affirmative message in this time of crisis.[9] Especially in *Our Town* but also to varying degrees in *The Skin of Our Teeth, The Matchmaker,* and *Shadow of a Doubt,* Wilder translated rhetoric into drama to enjoin Americans to persevere through the recent and current crises of the Great Depression and World War Two, and to recommit themselves on the microcosmic level to daily life and on the macrocosmic level to the progress of history, as seen from a Puritan point of view. We shall see how Wilder's native literary tradition provided an affirmative rhetoric that could easily be adapted to the stage.[10]

Our Town

Thornton Wilder's most famous and most American play, *Our Town,* can almost be read as a literal jeremiad in that its non-Aristotelian dramaturgy bears a close resemblance in form to a sermon with illustrative episodes, and its most prominent character, the Stage Manager, expresses a critical yet finally affirmative vision of life directly to the audience, like a minister preaching the gospel to his or her congregation. Wilder's brother, Amos Niven

9. As Bercovitch explains, "The American jeremiad was a ritual designed to join social criticism to spiritual renewal, public to private identity, the shifting 'signs of the times' to certain traditional metaphors, themes, and symbols" (*American Jeremiad,* xi).

10. Although the notion of adapting the rhetoric of the sermon to drama may strike some readers as unlikely, given the Puritan attacks (in sermons and pamphlets and books) on the theater during the English Renaissance, the pairing is not as strange as it may appear, as David Leverenz notes: "The theater and the sermon were two major genres that reveal their conflicted seventeenth-century world more when set side by side than when taken separately for the whole" (*The Language of Puritan Feeling,* 24). In other words, though apparent opposites, the sermon and the play are really two sides of the same (performative) coin.

Wilder, was a minister, and the Wilders came from a family line that included several ministers (for example, Thornton and Amos's maternal grandfather was a Presbyterian minister). In fact, Thornton himself may have heard the call to ministry; in a 1935 letter to Gertrude Stein, he wrote, "I should have been a preacher." Others seem to have recognized Wilder's suitability for that profession as well; according to Gilbert A. Harrison, the first Congregational Church of Los Angeles wanted Wilder "to preach at their evening service." The Stage Manager, whom Wilder himself played in the original production of *Our Town* when Frank Craven took a two-week vacation, assumes the identity of a minister in the second act of the play, delivering a sermon at Emily and George's wedding: "In this wedding I play the minister. That gives me the right to say a few more things about it . . . that's why I'm in the ministry" (74–75).[11] Both as minister in Act Two and as narrator throughout the play, the Stage Manager's purpose is clearly didactic as he summons actors playing secular authorities and representative characters to perform scenes that illustrate the ultimately affirmative worldview of *Our Town*.

One might argue that Wilder's dramaturgy takes its cue from another form of oratory, the academic lecture; the Stage Manager does call on Professor Willard from the state university to give background information on Grover's Corners. Certainly by the time Wilder wrote *Our Town* he was an old hand at lecturing, not just from his two teaching positions, first at the Lawrenceville School in New Jersey during the 1920s, then at the University of Chicago during the 1930s, but also from the lecture tours he went on in 1929 and in the early 1930s. Wilder said in the cover story of the January 12, 1953, issue of *Time*, "Teaching is a natural expression of mine. It is part of my inheritance." The article goes on to tell about Amos Parker Wilder's renown as a public speaker, and also his in-the-home lectures on morality: "Mr. Wilder was always fearful for his children's spiritual safety, and was forever lecturing them on how to defend themselves against a wicked world." Thornton Wilder was described in similar terms earlier in the *Time* article: "He puts on no airs, and has an immense interest in human beings, young and old, whom he treats with fatherly didacticism." A character based on Wilder's father appears in *Our Town* in the form of Editor Webb, who, at the Stage Manager's request, lectures on the town's political-cultural bent in Act

---

11. Edward Burns and Ulla E. Dydo, with William Rice, eds. *The Letters of Gertrude Stein and Thornton Wilder*, 9; Harrison, *The Enthusiast: A Life of Thornton Wilder*, 194. Wilder repeated the role of the Stage Manager in a few subsequent summer stock productions of *Our Town*, as well as a 1946 Theatre Guild Radio adaptation. Scholars have noted that the character was a stand-in for Wilder himself; see, for example, Richard H. Goldstone, *Thornton Wilder: An Intimate Portrait*, 119–20.

One, and who has been away giving a lecture at his alma mater in Act Three.[12]

However, if we read Wilder's own attempt to historicize the lecture in *American Characteristics and Other Essays,* we are brought back to the sermon: "Discourses have been delivered in all times and ages; but the lecture as we understand it, *the secularization of the sermon* and the popularization of the academic address, is probably a product of the middle-class mind. . . . Yet there is a wide difference between an Old-World and a New-World lecture, and the difference arises from those American characteristics which are precisely the subject of these lectures" (*AC,* 3, emphasis added). It may be true that, as Arthur H. Ballet writes, "people do not go to the theatre to hear sermons or to be told that the only truth they can comprehend is that the end of all life is death and that in death they will achieve life," but they did come out to hear Wilder's sermon, perhaps because of his stature in the public eye. In both *Our Town* and *The Skin of Our Teeth,* Wilder has characters refer to him as the author of the play, no doubt capitalizing on his Pulitzer Prize recognition and popularity as both novelist and dramatist.[13]

Apart from such formal similarities of *Our Town* to a sermon, Wilder's play reproduces the rhetorical strategy of the American jeremiad, as delineated by Bercovitch and others. Elliott's summary of the rhetorical moves of the jeremiad concurs with those of Bercovitch and Johannesen: "Taking their texts from Jeremiah and Isaiah, these orations followed—and reinscribed—a rhetorical formula that included recalling the courage and piety of the founders, lamenting recent and present ills, and crying out for a return to the original conduct and zeal." Although Bercovitch stresses the affirmative message of the jeremiad, he acknowledges the prominence of the sermon's tone of lament: "Perry Miller stressed the dark side of the jeremiad. I argue that this was a partial view of their message, that the Puritans' cries of declension and doom were part of a strategy designed to revitalize the errand; [however], even when they are most optimistic, the jeremiads express a profound disquiet." In one of the most famous New England Puritan jeremiads, "A Brief Recognition of New England's Errand into the Wilderness," the minister Samuel Danforth, preaching the Election Day sermon[14] for the year 1670, laments the state of the theocracy:

12. "An Obliging Man," 44.

13. Ballet, "In Our Living and in Our Dying," 248. It should not be surprising that a play adapting a particular rhetorical form would rely on *ethos,* one of the triumvirate of Aristotle's *Rhetoric.* In Landow's catalog of devices employed by late nineteenth-century British authors whom he labels "Elegant Jeremiahs," one device is "an essential reliance upon *ethos,* or the appeal to credulity" ("Elegant Jeremiahs," 24).

14. Elliott, "New England Puritan Literature," 257; Bercovitch, *American Jeremiad,* xiv. For a relatively brief explanation of the Election Day sermon, see the "Intro-

Is not the temper, complexion, and countenance of the churches strangely altered? Doth not a careless, remiss, flat, dry, cold, dead frame of spirit grow in upon us secretly, strongly, prodigiously? They that have ordinances are as though they had none; and they that hear the Word as though they heard it not; and they that pray as though they prayed not. . . . Yea and in some particular congregations amongst us is there not instead of a sweet smell, a stink; and instead of a girdle, a rent; and instead of a stomacher, a girding with sackcloth; and burning instead of beauty? . . . Pride, contention, worldliness, covetousness, luxury, drunkenness, and uncleanness break in like a flood upon us and good men grow cold in their love to God and to one another.[15]

Danforth goes on to consider the possible causes for the Puritans' "coolings, faintings, and languishings,"[16] liberally quoting the Bible to draw parallels between the New England Puritans and Old Testament Israelites or New Testament Jews.

Our Town contains overt expressions of lament, though in this first example from Act Two the complaint is in the subdued, folksy manner of the Stage Manager. On the advent of street traffic in town, the Stage Manager— now acting the role of Mr. Morgan the druggist—expresses the traditional harangue against the detriments of progress and laments the passing of the good ol' days: "I tell you, you've got to look both ways before you cross Main Street these days. Gets worse every year. . . . Yes, sir. There are a hundred and twenty-five horses in Grover's Corners this minute I'm talking to you. State Inspector was in here yesterday. And now they're bringing in these auto-mo-biles, the best thing to do is to just stay home. Why, I can remember when a dog could go to sleep all day in the middle of Main Street and nothing come along to disturb him" (67–68).

Another complaint about the changing times is offered in response to Mrs. Gibbs's report in Act One that residents in one section of the town have begun to lock their doors at night: "They're all getting citified, that's the trouble with them" (42). Later, at the beginning of Act Three, the Stage Manager confirms that all of "our town" has become "citified": "Everybody locks their house doors now at night. Ain't been any burglars in town yet, but everybody's heard about 'em" (86).

The most vehement of the laments in *Our Town* is uttered by Simon Stimson, the alcoholic choir director who commits suicide: "(*With mounting violence, bitingly*) Yes, now you know. Now you know! That's what it was to be

duction" to A. W. Plumstead, *The Wall and the Garden: Selected Massachusetts Election Sermons, 1670–1775.*

15. Danforth, "A Brief Recognition of New England's Errand into the Wilderness," 68–70.

16. Ibid.

alive. To move about in a cloud of ignorance; to go up and down trampling on the feelings of those ... of those about you. To spend and waste time as though you had a million years. To be always at the mercy of one self-centered passion, or another. Now you know—that's the happy existence you wanted to go back to. Ignorance and blindness" (109). Though less bitter, other members of the dead and even the Stage Manager agree that people are, for the most part, blind and unaware.

A more moving and ultimately more profound lament in *Our Town* is not even spoken; it is dramatized in George's lying prostrate before Emily's grave near the end of the play, but it is the most universal lament of them all: that we, our loved ones, everything living, dies. As *New York Times* theater critic Mel Gussow writes, "*Our Town* may be the most misunderstood and misinterpreted of American plays. It is not, as is often assumed, a hymn to small-town life at the turn of the century. . . . The primary subject of *Our Town* is not love and marriage but life and death. . . . In *Our Town* as in *Waiting for Godot,* one is born astride the grave." Wilder himself was born astride the grave; his twin brother, Theophilus, was stillborn. Perhaps this accounts for why death is rampant in all of Wilder's works,[17] but especially in *Our Town.* For example, the Stage Manager predicts the deaths of three characters—two of them major—at the beginning of the play; thus, like an Old Testament prophet (such as Jeremiah) or, as we shall see later, like Esmeralda in *The Skin of Our Teeth,* the Stage Manager predicts the future in the form of characters' fate, their death.

At the beginning of Act Two, the Stage Manager again alludes to dying and death in several ways but most obliquely when he says, "The First Act was called the Daily Life. This act is called Love and Marriage. There's another act coming after this: I reckon you can guess what that's about" (48). In the first act, the Stage Manager warns Professor Willard, lest he ramble on too long, "A few brief notes, thank you, Professor,—unfortunately our time is limited" (21). This statement, "our time is limited," resonates beyond the

17. Gussow, "Theater View: The Darker Shores of Thornton Wilder," H7. Though a comprehensive analysis of Wilder's treatment of death is not offered here (such a study would be valuable), the ubiquity of death in his plays and novels belies any claim that Wilder does not address the darker aspects of the human experience. To offer a few examples of death in Wilder's oeuvre, in *The Angel Plays,* we see death as life after life from a conventional Christian perspective. Of course *The Bridge of San Luis Rey* deals in depth with the deaths of the five victims of the accident, and on the effects those deaths had upon friends and family. In *The Woman of Andros* characters learn to accept death as part of life, but from a pre-Christian perspective. The death of characters is dramatized onstage in *The Long Christmas Dinner* and *Pullman Car Hiawatha.* Even the airy light farce *The Matchmaker* has three major characters whose spouses have died. *The Ides of March* presents the last days before Caesar's assassination, which looms fatally throughout the novel.

performance of the play; as "our town" allegorically represents all our towns, so does "our time" stand for all our time on earth, which is limited by death.[18] Of course, a jeremiad would not be used to protest a timeless, universal, and unchangeable truth such as human mortality; however, what Wilder was responding to in writing *Our Town*—a global economic depression and escalating world war—was causing the death of many people short of their natural life span. Most of the deaths in *Our Town*—Emily's, Mrs. Gibbs's, Wally's, Simon Stimson's, Joe Crowell's—are also short of their natural life span, and therein lies much of the sorrow and lament of the play.

Although the jeremiad is a complaint against the present, the past is also prominent in the Puritan rhetoric of crisis. As Peter Gay writes, "The jeremiads were implicit histories, the histories were explicit jeremiads." However, in keeping with the didacticism of their aesthetic, Puritans did not write history in the sense of an objective record of events: "The jeremiad was a stylized history, designed to shame the present generation out of its erring ways by recalling the surpassing virtues of its fathers." In other words, the point of praising the past in the jeremiad was to support its criticism of the present. In his jeremiad, Danforth begins to compare the present dire spiritual conditions in New England to the first generation of Puritans and quotes from The Lamentations of Jeremiah: "But who is there left among you that saw these churches in their first glory and how do you see them now? Are they not in your eyes in comparison thereof as nothing? 'How is the gold become dim! how is the most fine gold changed!'[Lam. 4:1]." Earlier in his sermon Danforth recalls the golden age of New England before the declension and praises its excellence:

> O what a reverent esteem had you in those days of Christ's faithful ambassadors that declared unto you the word of reconciliation! . . . What holy endeavors were there in those days to propagate religion to your children and posterity, training them up in the nurture and admonition of the Lord, keeping them under the awe of government, restraining their enormities and extravagances, charging them to know the God of their fathers and serve him with a perfect heart and willing mind, and publicly asserting and maintaining their interest in the Lord and in his holy covenant and zealously opposing those that denied the same?[19]

Clearly Danforth is not waxing nostalgic here; rather, he is basing his social criticism of the present on the exemplary past. The American jeremiad's

---

18. It is subtle points such as this that must have made Edward Albee refer to *Our Town* as "one of the most existential plays [he'd] ever come across" (personal interview).

19. Gay, *A Loss of Mastery: Puritan Historians in Colonial America,* 69, 67; Danforth, "Brief Recognition," 68, 66–67.

dynamic of time (along with New England Puritans' typological view of the past, all history, and time itself) helps to explain the complex function of time and history in *Our Town.*

From the beginning of *Our Town* to the end, the narrative regresses from the present (i.e., 1938), most notably in Act Three when the newly dead Emily chooses to revisit a "happy day" of her life. She goes from 1913 on the day of her funeral to 1899 on her twelfth birthday. Transported back to that day by the Stage Manager, Emily's nostalgic reaction to what she sees provides the praise of the past in Wilder's dramatic jeremiad: "Oh, that's the town I knew as a little girl. And, *look,* there's the old white fence that used to be around our house. Oh, I'd forgotten that! Oh, I love it so!" (101, emphasis in original). Later Emily both celebrates the youth of the past and laments the decline we all face: "I can't bear it. They're [her parents] so young and beautiful. Why did they ever have to get old? Mama, I'm here. I'm grown up. I love you all, everything.—I can't look at everything hard enough" (105). Like Danforth and other Puritan Jeremiahs, Wilder encourages his audience to recall a time when individuals, family, and the community as a whole were as we wish they would be in the present. But for Danforth, the community was limited to the Puritan colonies in New England; for Wilder, the community is all of America and more.

Despite its abstract theatrical style, *Our Town* is emphatically rooted in the concrete American setting. Many signifiers of American history are found in the play's dialogue: the Pilgrims, the Indians, the Constitution, the Louisiana Purchase, the Civil War, the Monroe Doctrine, World War One, the Lindbergh flight. Also, the American way of life is signified by references to the rights granted by the Constitution, historical developments, and the mundane: representative democracy, open elections, freedom of religion, pluralistic immigrant population, the family farm, patenting of new technology, Ford automobiles, baseball, the *New York Times,* high school, the drugstore soda fountain, small town gossip, and so forth. Even some of the names are as American as . . . George Washington (George Gibbs) and Emily Dickinson (Emily Webb). Wilder even refers back to the year Danforth preached his jeremiad. In fact, in the opening speech of Act Three of *Our Town,* the Stage Manager refers as far back in American history as the Pilgrims, who were, of course, Puritans: "Over there are the old stones—1670, 1680. Strongminded people that came a long way to be independent. Summer people walk around there laughing at the funny words on the tombstones . . . it don't do any harm. And genealogists come up from Boston—get paid by city people for looking up their ancestors. They want to make sure they're Daughters of the American Revolution or of the *Mayflower*" (*OT,* 86–7). It is the text's saturation with American codes as well as the dramatization of the daily life that early commentators praised. Esteemed theater critic Brooks Atkinson wrote, "Mr. Wilder has looked straight into the heart of an American village. . . . It is an idealized portrait. His characters are the salt of the earth. His love for them is overflowing with compassion. Far from being depressed, I came away from the theatre exalted by the bravery, kindliness and goodness of American people." Jed Harris, the director of the original production, said that "it might very well be the best American play ever written." Writing in 1956, Ballet pronounced *Our Town* "the great American drama."[20]

Some theatergoers and literary scholars have mistaken Wilder's setting *Our Town* around the turn of the century as an exercise in nostalgia and sentimentality.[21] Undeniably, the action of *Our Town* takes place before the onslaught of the global upheavals of the twentieth century—the world wars and the Great Depression; in comparison, the turn of the century would appear to be a golden age, the citing of which is part of the American jeremiad's rhetorical strategy. However, Bercovitch's explanation of Cotton Mather's method of writing history in *Magnalia Christi Americana*—which "In an age of jeremiads . . . [was] the greatest jeremiad of them all"—describes Wilder's strategy as well: "History is invoked to displace historicism," which can also extend to spatial as well as temporal displacement.[22]

In *Our Town,* anthropological or historical truth would seem to be the objective as explained by the Stage Manager: "So—people a thousand years from now—this is the way we were" (33). However, in the introduction to *Three Plays,* Wilder explains his intention: "*Our Town* is not offered as a picture of life in a New Hampshire village. . . . It is an attempt to find a value above all price for the smallest events in our daily life" (*TP,* xii). A subtle indication that a particular town is not what we are meant to see is that there is no town named Grover's Corners in all of the United States, let alone New Hampshire, and the precise longitude and latitude given for the location of the town (4) would put it in the Atlantic Ocean.[23] In Act Three, Emily's moving speech is not a farewell to American culture and lifestyle at the turn of

20. Atkinson, *Broadway Scrapbook,* 91–92; Gottfried, *Jed Harris: The Curse of Genius,* 165; Ballet, "In Our Living," 243.

21. See, for example, George R. Stephens, "*Our Town*—American Tragedy?" and Mary McCarthy, *Sights and Spectacles, 1937–56,* for derisive comments on *Our Town*'s emotional effect on the audience, also regarding Emily's death and reliving part of a day from her childhood. But see also Ballet's article that prompted Stephens's denial that *Our Town* is a tragedy. Ballet claims that *Our Town* has sentimentality "without sententiousness; it has romance without romanticism, and innocence without naiveté" ("In Our Living," 248).

22. Gay, *Loss of Mastery,* 65; Bercovitch, *Puritan Origins,* 5.

23. Michael V. Williams seems to think the location of the coordinates was an error on Wilder's part, but it is more likely that Wilder intended it to reinforce his theme of universality. See "Errors in Thornton Wilder's *The Eighth Day*."

the century, but a farewell to the details of daily life that are, for the most part, universal and timeless: "Mama and Papa," "clocks ticking," "sunflowers," "food and coffee," "new-ironed dresses," "hot baths," and "sleeping and waking up" (108). Thus, as an American jeremiad in dramatic form, *Our Town* is not meant to apply only to the current American crisis, but to the whole world's.[24]

Not surprisingly, in *Our Town* Wilder achieves what he said Emily Dickinson achieved in her poetry: to keep one's eye simultaneously on the particular, in this case a New England small town at the turn of the century, and the general: our world, life, the timeless human condition. To confirm that this is what Wilder intended in *Our Town,* in an interview he said, "The play is a close examination of the life at a New Hampshire village in which the audience may well come to feel toward the close that the whole world has been presented in microcosm." Wilder's dual focus—on the immediate community and the world as a whole—was also part of the Puritan sensibility. The American jeremiad, like the Puritan errand into the wilderness itself, operated at two levels: "Winthrop emphasized the universalist aspect of the Protestant outlook, but the 'national' or 'federal' aspect—the sense of the importance of this people in this locale—was there as well." We have already noted the American particulars in *Our Town;* now for the general.[25]

In *Our Town* Wilder refers to even further back in time than the European colonization of North America to demonstrate that the aspects of daily life he depicts are universal, true not only for every generation, but also for every age and culture. In Act One, the Stage Manager discusses how family life in ancient Greece and Babylon must have been the same as in Grover's Corners: "Y'know—Babylon once had two million people in it, and all we know about 'em is the names of the kings and some copies of wheat contracts . . . and contracts for the sale of slaves. Yet every night all those families sat down to supper, and the father came home from his work, and the smoke went up the chimney,—same as here" (33). Immediately following this speech the church choir begins to sing "Blessed be the ties that bind." Wilder is reminding future generations, as well as his own, that growing up, marrying, living, and dying are what tie and bind us to other members of the human race, even if we disagree about the abstractions of ideology or religion. *Our*

24. Responding to the popularity of *Our Town* as well as *The Skin of Our Teeth* in Germany after the war, Wilder said, "It seems that *Our Town* also is a dramatic war play" (Jackson R. Bryer, ed., *Conversations with Thornton Wilder,* 45).

25. In his essay "Emily Dickinson," Wilder writes, "The imagination of this spinster withdrawn into a few rooms in Amherst was constantly aware that the universe surrounded every detail of life. . . . Emily Dickinson, in all appearances the loneliest of beings, solved the problem in a way which is of importance to every American: by loving the particular while living in the universal" (*AC,* 63). Gottfried, *Jed Harris,* 166; Sacvan Bercovitch, "The Modernity of American Puritan Rhetoric," 50.

Town is also a universal jeremiad, then, and in it Wilder laments that we are always losing the larger perspective of community in which "our town" really means "our world."[26]

Like Puritan ministers in their jeremiads, Wilder in *Our Town* is working to make the audience conscious of time and the relationship between the past, the present, and the future. The interruptions by the Stage Manager and the subsequent jumps in time reflect one of the things Emily comes to realize: "I can't. I can't go on. It goes so fast. We don't have time to look at one another" (108). Similarly, the audience's disorientation caused by the jumps in time is a theatrical means of stimulating an epiphany in the audience: they suddenly realize that a lot of time has passed—whether a few hours (as in Act One) or a few years (Act Two) or many years (Act Three)—and perhaps this helps them share in Emily's realization. The jumps in time start out short, but then grow longer by the end of the play when Emily goes back fourteen years. However, there is an overall chronological progression within the space of the day; the Stage Manager begins the play at early morning—5:45, to be exact (6)—and ends the play late at night—"Eleven o'clock in Grover's Corners" (112). What has been a series of days—"an ordinary day" (Act One), "a special day" (Act Two), "a sad day" (Act Three), and "a happy day" (Emily's twelfth birthday, which she revisits at the end of Act Three)—have been amalgamated into one day, dramatizing that each day is ordinary, special, sad, and happy; that is the universal day. Thus this single day is Everyday, a microcosm of a life.[27] The audience, like Emily, is "saddened but wiser in the ways of life and death. . . . [They] learn, as Emily must, to accept the life cycle." In fact, Emily's epiphany is the climax of the play, corresponding to the *anagnorisis* (usually translated from the Greek as "recognition" or "discovery") that tragic heroes experience before dying or beginning great suffering, according to Aristotle in his *Poetics*.[28]

Another way in which the climactic scene of *Our Town* recalls the past is by borrowing from Wilder-the-writer's past, or his past work, to be more precise. In his third novel, *The Woman of Andros*, Chrysis, the protagonist, is a Christ-

26. Bernard Dukore writes, "Its continuing popularity both in and outside America demonstrates the *ourness* of *Our Town*" (*American Dramatists, 1918–1945,* 141). *Our Town* is generally recognized in Wilder scholarship as an *Everyman*-type allegory; see, for example, Haberman, *Plays of Thornton Wilder,* 75–76.

27. As Atkinson writes of *Our Town,* "Mr. Wilder's scheme of playwriting distinguishes between what is mortal and what is immortal in the chronicle of normal living. There go all of us, not 'but for the grace of God,' but 'by the grace of God.' This is the record of the simplest things we have all been through. Grover's Corners is Our Town—the days and deaths of the brotherhood of man" (*Broadway Scrapbook,* 87).

28. Ballet, "In Our Living," 248. Ballet concludes, "Like its Greek predecessors [Greek tragedies, he means], *Our Town* is concerned with the great and continuing cycle of life; out of life comes death and from death comes life. This cycle is man's closest understanding of eternity" (245).

like character in that she teaches her disciples with parables. One day she tells her followers a fable about a hero slain in battle who is granted his wish from "The King of the Dead" to return to earth "to live over again that day in all the 22,000 days of his lifetime that had been least eventful; but it must be with a mind divided into two persons,—the participant and the onlooker" (34–35). Like Emily, the hero returns to his youth to find that neither he nor his parents truly appreciated their time together. His epiphany is described in terms very similar to Emily's: "Suddenly the hero saw that the living too are dead and that we can only be said to be alive in those moments when our hearts are conscious of our treasure; for our hearts are not strong enough to love every moment. And not an hour had gone by before the hero who was both watching life and living it called on Zeus to release him from so terrible a dream. The gods heard him, but before he left he fell upon the ground and kissed the soil of the world that is too dear to be realized" (36).[29]

That such an insight need not have come from twentieth-century existentialism, could even have come from the Puritan tradition in America, is illustrated by the closing paragraph of eighteenth-century Puritan minister Jonathan Edwards's "The Beauty of the World." Edwards's prose passage sounds like Emily when she asks the Stage Manager, "Do any human beings ever realize life while they live it,—every, every minute" (108): "Corollary. Hence the reason why almost all men, and those that seem to be very miserable, love life, because they cannot bear to lose sight of such a beautiful and lovely world. The idea, that every moment whilst we live have a beauty that we take distinct notice of, brings a pleasure that, when we come to the trial, we had rather live in much pain and misery than lose."[30] Thus Wilder's use of the past, whether of America's, western civilization's, or his own, is always purposeful—that is, didactic, if also deeply moving.

The perspective needed for what will prove to be *Our Town*'s affirmative vision of history and of current events in light of the perceived shape of history can be achieved only by the older generation, or by a historian, or by God.[31]

29. In these two quotes from Wilder's earlier work we again see the typological habit of mind he inherited from the Puritan narrative tradition. Wilder *shows* Emily's speech directly and thus more powerfully, whereas in *The Woman of Andros* the epiphany is *told* in indirect discourse so that there is more distance from it. Thus Emily's speech is, in typological terms, the antitype or more perfect incarnation of this concept in relation to the earlier work's, which constitutes the type. This is analogous to the typological reading of the relationship between the Old and New Testaments of the Bible.

30. Quoted in Elliott, "New England Puritan Literature," 306.

31. Atkinson believed this more distant perspective to be indigenous to the New England milieu itself:

His detached and speculative point of view conveys the New England rhythm. From Cotton Mather through the Concord cosmologists, Longfellow and Lowell to Edwin Arlington Robinson and Robert Frost, the New Englander has tuned

In fact, a few scholars have interpreted the Stage Manager as God or a god-like character in his apparent omniscience, as when he refers as far back as ancient Babylon and as far forward as "a thousand years from now" (33).[32] That is, with the device of the Stage Manager, Wilder was able to achieve the same effect on stage as he had in his novels: "The sole motive of the omniscient novelist is to arouse in the reader the emotion of omniscience" (*JTW*, 64). As Atkinson notes, the effect is "profoundly moving. . . . In the deepest sense of the word, *Our Town* is a religious play." Wilder appeals to emotion, then, but pathos is a legitimate rhetorical strategy, according to rhetoricians as far back as Aristotle. Furthermore, Wilder's comment shows that it is the omniscient point of view, a device more intrinsic to fiction than to drama, that he was trying to create in the theater: "The Stage Manager role which Frank Craven plays in *Our Town* was a 'hang-over from a novelist technique.'"[33] Recalling that Wilder's works from the 1930s also manifested an ambiguity of genre, *Our Town* is thus comprised of both narration and drama like Brecht's epic theater and Pirandello's theatricalism, but also like Edward Taylor's *God's Determinations*. The incorporation of a narrator in a play can thus provide the omniscient perspective usually precluded in theatrical performance that occurs in an actual present. Omniscience, knowing all that has happened and will happen, is well suited to the eschatological vision of the Puritan writers who viewed past and current events in the context of God's plot. In this respect, *Our Town* is a tour de force of style, structure, and form. For example, the juxtaposition of future, past, and present—the major rhetorical strategy of the American jeremiad—is achieved in one sentence when the Stage Manager yokes together the three major time tenses: "First automobile*'s going to come* along in about five years—belong*ed* to Banker Cartwright, our richest citizen . . . liv*es* in the big white house up on the hill" (5, emphasis added).

---

himself to the infinite. Perhaps it is the age of the culture of the Puritan heritage, . . .—whatever the reason, the New Englander is aware of something mightier than his personal experience. The long point of view . . . comes naturally to him. (*Broadway Scrapbook*, 85)

32. Thomas P. Adler states that the Stage Manager "possesses a god-like omniscience, overseeing the progression of history as God would" (*Mirror on the Stage: The Pulitzer Plays as an Approach to American Drama*, 124). Many theater critics and scholars (e.g., Ballet) have compared the Stage Manager to a Greek chorus; however, though the chorus had much the same function as the Stage Manager with regard to narration and commentary, since it usually represented the townspeople it was not imbued with omniscience as the Stage Manager is. See Douglas C. Wixson Jr., "Thornton Wilder and Max Reinhardt: Artists in Collaboration" for a more extended discussion of the Stage Manager as God reading, though he argues that Wilder borrowed allegorical characterization from European theater.

33. Atkinson, *Broadway Scrapbook*, 91–92; Bryer, ed., *Conversations*, 23.

Thus far we have seen how *Our Town* follows the rhetorical pattern of the American jeremiad in its lamentation of the present and its invocation of the past. The last movement is the reaffirmation of the errand, the call for a renewal of progress. In his jeremiad to the New England Puritans of 1670, Danforth again compares them to the Old Testament Israelites but now for the purpose of encouraging them to recommit themselves to God's mission for them:

> And having thus shown them their spiritual uncleanness, he encouraged them to go on with the work in hand, the building of the temple, promising them from this day to bless them. . . . Use II. Of exhortation to excite and stir us all up to attend and prosecute our errand into the wilderness. To what purpose came we into this place . . . ? We came not hither to see "a reed shaken with the wind." Then let us not be reeds—light, empty, vain, hollow-hearted professors, shaken with every temptation—but solid, serious, and sober Christians, constant and steadfast in the profession and practices of the truth . . . , holding fast the profession of our faith without wavering.[34]

Later, Danforth repeats this call to begin again, reaffirming the purpose for which they came to New England: "Labor we to redress our faintings and swervings and address ourselves to the work of the Lord. Let us arise and build and the Lord will be with us and from this day will he bless us."[35] Along with the praising of the past when the New England Puritans first began the Lord's work, this encouragement gives the American jeremiad its optimistic outlook for the future.

Similar to how the jeremiad has been misrepresented as pure harangue, some readers and audience members have missed the affirmation of life in *Our Town*. For example, Ethan Mordden thinks the tone of the play with regard to aging and dying is one "of despairing sorrow." Similarly, after seeing *Our Town* Eleanor Roosevelt was "moved and depressed 'beyond words.'"[36] As mentioned above, in Act Three Simon Stimson repudiates life; however, Wilder does not permit Stimson's "jeremiad" against life to go unchallenged. Mrs. Gibbs, seemingly still playing the role of mother, chides him as if he were her child: "Simon Stimson, that ain't the whole truth and you know it" (109). Similar to Emily saying in Act One that the moonlight was "terrible" and "wonderful," one of the dead says in Act Three, "My, wasn't life awful— and wonderful" (93). This is the truth about life that Wilder conveys in this dramatic jeremiad: it is both awful and wonderful.

34. Danforth, "Brief Recognition," 71.
35. Ibid., 75.
36. Mordden, *The American Theatre*, viii; Roosevelt quoted in Atkinson, *Broadway Scrapbook*, 90. In a 1966 letter to a friend, Wilder noted about *Our Town* that "the last act of my play suggests that life—viewed directly—is damned near Hell" (Bill Slocum, "The Legacy of Thornton Wilder," 4).

Of course, it is ironic that the realization of how wonderful life is comes only in death, after life has been lost. However, *Our Town* accepts death as natural, as part of the life cycle. Though death is ubiquitous in the play, it is balanced by new life. For example, at the beginning of Act Two, the Stage Manager counters each indication of decline and death with growth and birth:

> Summers and winters have cracked the mountains a little bit more and the rains have brought down some of the dirt. *Some babies that weren't even born before have begun talking regular sentences already;* and a number of people who thought they were right young and spry have noticed that they can't bound up a flight of stairs like they used to, without their heart fluttering a little. All that can happen in a thousand days. *Nature's been pushing and contriving in other ways, too: a number of young people fell in love and got married.* Yes, the mountain got bit away a few fractions of an inch; millions of gallons of water went by the mill; *and here and there a new home was set up under a roof.* . . . Most everybody in the world *climbs* into their graves *married.* (47–48, emphasis added)

Emily's death is itself partially balanced by the mention of her and George's son—"Oh, Mr. Carter, my little boy is spending the day at your house" (96)—and perhaps as well by the baby Emily died bringing into the world: "Why just then for a moment I was thinking about . . . about the farm . . . and for a minute I *was* there, and my baby was on my lap as plain as day" (98, emphasis in original).[37] We saw how Wilder employed this balancing of death with new life in his earlier play *The Long Christmas Dinner* when baby carriages were rolled onstage from the birth portal shortly after characters exited through the death portal, and we will see him balance life and death again in Act Three of *The Skin of Our Teeth* when the war has ended and Gladys exits the bomb shelter holding a baby.

It is also ironic, some have said melodramatic, that Emily, the character in *Our Town* who seems to value life the most, is the one who dies in the end. However, Emily's (and our) tragedy is not that she dies; it is that, as she says, "Oh, earth, you're too wonderful for anybody to realize you" (108). Thus, as is often the case in classical and Shakespearean tragedy, the hero affirms life even as she loses it. This is, finally, the meaning of Act Three: though Emily dies, we live. Life goes on, for example, on the familial level: "The earliest tombstones in the cemetery up there on the mountain say 1670–1680—they're Grovers and Cartwrights and Gibbses and Herseys—same names as are around here now" (6). Thus Emily's epiphany in the cemetery also drama-

---

37. Whether the "baby" is her first child, the little boy referred to on the previous page, or the second child with whom she was pregnant when she died is ambiguous. That Wilder leaves us hanging as to the fate of Emily's second child was pointed out to me by Todd Pelletier, a student in my Wilder seminar, spring 1997.

tizes the possibility of a progress of understanding of the meaning or value of life, the affirmative message Wilder wants us to hear.

Even in his description in Act Three of what happens to the dead, the Stage Manager employs a quasi-oxymoron, mixing life with death: "They get weaned away from earth" (88). In the metaphor "weaned," life itself is the mother's milk from which death takes them, but that makes death equal growth, maturation, *progress* in the vehicle of the metaphor.[38] As with the description of life as both awful and wonderful, Wilder at the very least provides a balanced view of death, and since the point is to accept death as part of the life cycle, the sorrow and resulting negative tone related to death is ultimately subsumed under an overarching affirmative tone or vision in *Our Town* similar to the American jeremiads preached by the New England Puritans.

If one reads the text closely, it is evident that Wilder has tried to balance the tone between optimism and pessimism throughout *Our Town*. As he will do at the beginning of *The Skin of Our Teeth*, on a few occasions Wilder has the Stage Manager refer to the mundane event of the sun rising. When he allows Emily to relive her twelfth birthday, he says, "We'll begin at dawn" (100). "The sun's coming up" (100) is a part of daily life that is taken for granted— except perhaps for such times as Wilder was writing in, when fear and doubt of the continuation of things might even extend, at an extreme, to the sun coming up again. Wilder is reassuring his 1938 audience that the sun, peace, and prosperity will reappear. At the end of the play, Wilder nudges the tone (the audience, really) back toward life. In the Samuel French acting edition of *Our Town*, the Stage Manager says, in spite of all the emphasis on death, "Tomorrow's going to be another day" (86). Again, people in the late 1930s may have doubted this, but Wilder, employing a long view of human history, of God's plot, reassures his audience and readers that life will go on.

As an American jeremiad "preached" to the world, *Our Town* must call for a recommitment to the human errand. As Bercovitch writes, "In contrast to traditionalist rituals, the New England Puritan jeremiad evokes the mythic past not merely to elicit imitation but above all to demand progress." In Wilder's drama, fiction, and lectures on nineteenth-century American literature, the most prominent feature of the legacy of Puritanism is a faith in progress on the personal, national, and macrocosmic levels.[39]

---

38. Interestingly, Taylor also used nursing from the mother's breast as a metaphor for spiritual matters in *God's Determinations:* "Those who suck Grace from th' breast, are nigh as rare . . ." (46).

39. Bercovitch, *American Jeremiad*, 24. The following description of the Puritans' purview indicates how much Wilder, especially in *Our Town*, was attuned to the oldest and deepest sensibility in American culture: "Even as [John Cotton and his contemporaries] urged each man to search into the minutest details of his life, they insisted upon the over-

We saw in Chapter Three that Wilder's view of history and time is neither entropic nor purely cyclical but rather progressive overall, a view of history corresponding to the New England Puritans', which was based on typology. This view of history is evident in *Our Town* as well. Here, as in *The Long Christmas Dinner,* Wilder's typological view of history may be misread as contradictory observations on the effects of time passing, often resulting from the different perspectives of characters belonging to younger and older generations. Are things getting better with time, getting worse, or staying the same? This issue is represented in microcosm in *Our Town* by Simon Stimson, the choir director of the Congregational Church in Grover's Corners and also the town drunk. As the women return from choir practice, they disagree over the current state of his condition:

MRS. SOAMES. But it's getting worse.
MRS. WEBB. No, it isn't, Louella. It's getting better. (40)

Later, the Constable and Editor Webb echo Mr. and Mrs. Gibbs's summation of Stimson's crisis: "I don't know how that's goin' to end" (44). Act Three reveals how it did end—in his suicide—but it is only from the perspective of a whole life that we know that; as we live it, we are unsure. In "Thornton Wilder Says 'Yes,'" Bernard Hewitt comments on the function of Stimson-like characters in Wilder as opposed to other playwrights: "The ugly side of American small-town life is not entirely missing from *Our Town.* Simon Stimson, the drunken, disappointed organist, is there. In a play by Tennessee Williams or William Inge, he would be stage center." Simon Stimson is an indication that Wilder was not oblivious to those who were living less than blessed lives. In fact, the Samuel French acting edition of *Our Town* makes this even more emphatic with the following stage directions: Simon "lifts his head in pleading agony" (35).[40]

Yet there may be hope for Simon. The progress or spiritual growth of one's soul is the subject of the work from which Wilder said he took the dialogue of the dead in Act Three, *The Purgatorio* in Dante's *The Divine Comedy* (*TP,* xii).[41] Dante the pilgrim is taking an epic journey from hell to heaven,

---

arching plan which explained the social pattern of their lives, and so allowed them to fuse the particular, the social, and the cosmic" (Bercovitch, *American Jeremiad,* 42).

40. Hewitt, "Thornton Wilder Says 'Yes,'" 114. Stimson's continued bitterness in death, as represented in Act Three, may also indicate that Wilder had difficulty shaking off the sensibility, inherited from the Puritans, which divides the human race into the elect and the reprobate, with Stimson perhaps corresponding to the latter in *Our Town.*

41. However, the tone of the dialogue in this scene bears far more resemblance to American representations of a dialogue among the dead, such as Emily Dickinson's #976

but all of the souls he encounters in Purgatory are also on a journey, one of penance for and purification from sin, so that they too will eventually reach heaven. Although Wilder said in his preface to *Three Plays* that he did not mean Act Three of *Our Town* "as a speculation about the conditions of life after death" (xii), the Stage Manager nevertheless seems to subsume death within the continuity of something that extends beyond the boundaries of corporal existence. That is, in one of the most moving speeches from *Our Town,* the Stage Manager affirms progress on the metaphysical or spiritual level:

> Now there are some things we all know, but we don't take'm out and look at'm very often. We all know that *something* is eternal. And it ain't houses and it ain't names, and it ain't earth, and it ain't even the stars . . . everybody knows in their bones that *something* is eternal, and that something has to do with human beings. All the greatest people ever lived have been telling us that for five thousand years and yet you'd be surprised how people are always losing hold of it. There's something way down deep that's eternal about every human being./ *Pause.*/ You know as well as I do that the dead don't stay interested in us living people for very long. Gradually, gradually, they lose hold of the earth . . . and the ambitions they had . . . and the pleasures they had . . . and the things they suffered . . . and the people they loved. They get weaned away from earth— that's the way I put it,—weaned away. And they stay here while the earth part of 'em burns away, burns out; and all that time they slowly get indifferent to what's goin' on in Grover's Corners. They're waitin' for something that they feel is comin'. Something important, and great. Aren't they waitin' for the eternal part in them to come out clear? (87–88, emphasis in original)[42]

While such speeches do not demand progress per se as in the American jeremiad, they do affirm the idea of progress on the personal level. Simon, Mrs. Gibbs, and the other members of the dead are waiting for a progression of their souls, the "something eternal" that the Stage Manager refers to. Mrs. Gibbs even instructs Emily in this: "When you've been here longer you'll see that our life here is to forget all that [their lives on earth], and think only of what's ahead, and be ready for what's ahead. When you've been here longer you'll understand" (99). That Emily's understanding will continue to progress

---

"Death is a dialogue between" or #449 "I died for Beauty," than it does to a Medieval Italian Catholic work. As implied earlier, Wilder may have named his heroine after Emily Dickinson. There was also Wilder's earlier dramatization of a dialogue among the dead discussed in Chapter Two: the three souls in *And the Sea Shall Give Up Its Dead.*

42. Again, here we can see that in *God's Determinations* Taylor expressed spiritual progress in terms of purifying the Soul, similar to Wilder's: "If in the fire where Gold is tri'de, / Thy Soule is put, and purifi'de, / Wilt thou lament thy loss? / If silver-like this fire refine / Thy Soul and make it brighter Shine; / Wilt thou bewaile the Dross?" (64).

over time is surely one of the most profound and affirmative literary characterizations of death in the twentieth century; though it is subtle, the implication of Mrs. Gibbs's speech lifts us to the level of the sublime.[43]

In addition to individual progress, the Stage Manager's wedding sermon in Act Two—along with dramatic and expository testimonies of "Gradual changes in Grover's Corners"—provide subtle references in *Our Town* to authentic improvements that represent progress in the larger setting of society or the human race as a whole. At one point, the Stage Manager mocks the notion that "we're more civilized now,—so they say" (77), but only in the context of a tongue-in-cheek discussion and dramatization of marriage as an invention of women.[44] The Stage Manager's statements testifying to progress on various levels of experience are more plentiful, though understated for the most part as with everything else in the play. References to a new hospital, the town's population growth, the increase in the value of antique furniture, patented farm equipment, and the Ford's adaptation to farmwork suggest subtle, even mundane advances; nevertheless, they do represent improvements in the quality of life. Furthermore, the Stage Manager's view of nature is clearly evolutionary: "It's like what one of those European fellas said: every child born into the world is nature's attempt to make a perfect human being. Well, we've seen nature pushing and contriving for some time now. We all know that nature's interested in quantity; but I think she's interested in quality too " (75). To paraphrase, life not only expands, it improves.

Finally, Wilder's dramatic jeremiad affirms progress on the macrocosmic level of God's plot. Like Puritan ministers interpreting events during the colonization of New England as manifestations of a Providential design, Wilder has set the human microcosm against a macrocosmic background.[45] He said that in *Our Town* he was attempting to portray "the life of a village against the life of the stars" (*AC,* 102). A speech by the Stage Manager realizes this intention near the end of the play: "There are the stars—doing their old, old crisscross journeys in the sky. Scholars haven't settled the matter yet, but they seem to think there are no living beings up there. Just chalk . . . or fire.

---

43. This is perhaps on a par with St. Paul's "For now we see through a glass, darkly; but then face to face: now I know in part; but then shall I know even as also I am known" (1 Cor. 13:12).

44. Wilder knew his Freud. He could even paraphrase (see *Writers at Work,* 114–15) the theory of the origin of marriage in Freud's *Civilization and Its Discontents,* which he parodies in Act Two of *Our Town* in Editor Webb's wedding day advice to George Gibbs and again in Act Two of *The Skin of Our Teeth* in Mrs. Antrobus's address of the convention of mammals.

45. Malcolm Goldstein describes the perspective in *Our Town* similarly: "The scenes devised by Wilder are moments of eternity singled out for our attention and played against the panorama of infinity" (*The Art of Thornton Wilder,* 102).

Only this one is straining away, straining away all the time to make something of itself" (111). Before the infinity of the cosmos, the finitude of life on earth is acted; what we are witnessing, what we are living—from a Puritan perspective—is the progress of the elect earth across this stage of the universe. The last bit of business performed by the Stage Manager before he says goodnight to the audience is to wind his watch, a small action that culminates a motif of clocks, watches, and time in *Our Town*. This moment, subtle as any, along with the Stage Manager's final speech that "The strain's so bad that every sixteen hours everybody lies down and gets a rest. . . . You get a good rest, too" (111–12), is Wilder's assurance that we can go on, his affirmation that we *should* go on. Wilder seems to be saying, in effect, entropy and inertia are physical laws, yes, but progress is an existential law: things run down—watches, families, civilization—but we can "wind them up" again if we so choose.

Thus the conflicting views of time and history given voice by Wilder in *Our Town* make sense if recognized as features of the American jeremiad. Like the Puritan ministers who lamented the decline of the theocracy but also called for recommitment to the errand, Wilder's portrait of an American golden age, at least what appears to be one from the vantage point of 1938, calls for us to recommit ourselves in the most fundamental ways to life and to living, day by day, during the errand of our lives.

The Matchmaker

In the same year in which *Our Town* appeared, *The Merchant of Yonkers* was unsuccessfully produced on Broadway; seventeen years later Wilder rewrote it as *The Matchmaker,* and it was a huge hit.[46] The Puritan imprint is not as evident in *The Matchmaker* as it is in Wilder's other works, possibly because in adapting an Austrian adaptation (*Einen Jux will er sich machen* [1842] by Johann Nestroy) of an English farce (*A Day Well Spent* [1835] by John Oxenford) Wilder did not connect as strongly with his native culture and aesthetic. However, there are traces of Puritan attributes, including the American jeremiad, that we have observed in his previous plays and novels. Their presence can be accounted for because Wilder did successfully Americanize the setting,

46. Although *The Merchant of Yonkers* and *The Matchmaker* are two separate plays (both were published under their respective titles), *The Matchmaker* was only a slight revision of the earlier work. All references to the play in this study will use the later title (except in quotations of studies that chose to use the original title) and quote from the later text as reprinted in *Three Plays. The Matchmaker* was later adapted as the Broadway musical and then the Hollywood film *Hello, Dolly!*

characters, and ideas of the story, as testified to by theater critic Alexander Woollcott: "He thought he was writing an adaptation from the Viennese but all unbeknownst to himself his good American ancestry took possession of him and what he really wrote was a pure Charles Hoyt farce of the 1885 vintage. If this had been given to any American stock company prior to 1900, it would have presented no problem." Scholarly opinion agrees with Woollcott; for example, Kuner says that *The Matchmaker* "belongs essentially to this 'discovery of America' phase of Wilder's career." Maria P. Alter has a similar view of the effect of Wilder's central character on the rest of the play: "Wilder invented a new character, the vivacious, witty, and incomparable Dolly Levi, who thinks on her feet and gives the farce its American flavor." Alter also refers to her as "the charming all-American Dolly Levi, an American busybody[; she] is a sort of artist in her own way, who tries to improve life around her and gives the farce American optimism and authenticity." Even Wilder attested to his having culturally transformed the source play: "Imagine an Austrian pharmacist going to the shelf to draw from a bottle which he knows to contain a stinging corrosive liquid, guaranteed to remove warts and wens; and imagine his surprise when he discovers that it has been filled overnight with very American birch-bark beer" (*TP,* xiii).[47]

The American milieu of *The Matchmaker* is established by beginning the action in Yonkers, New York, and then transporting the characters to Manhattan in the rest of the play. Manhattan was also the setting of Wilder's first full-length play, *The Trumpet Shall Sound.* Other similarities with that earlier play include a rich man named Horace Vandergelder—the merchant of the original title of the play—who, like Peter Magnus, goes on a trip and leaves servants in charge, but they jump at the chance for freedom, disobeying his orders to keep his store open till the usual closing time. In the fourth acts of both *The Matchmaker* and *Trumpet,* a rich man confronts a woman named Flora, but in the earlier play Flora commits suicide, whereas here the character named Flora is a friend to all lovers, helping them overcome obstacles to their being together. Thus, while in *Trumpet* one Flora dies for love, in *The Matchmaker* another Flora lives for love.[48]

There are allusions in *The Matchmaker* to the conservative Protestantism that has been so prevalent in American culture from the seventeenth century to the present. Cornelius Hackl refers to his attending church twice on Sundays (291) and later confesses to Irene Molloy, "Irene, the Hackls don't

47. Woollcott quoted in Donald Gallup, ed., *The Flowers of Friendship: Letters Written to Gertrude Stein,* 353; Kuner, *Bright and Dark,* 138; Alter, "The Reception of Nestroy in America as Exemplified in Thornton Wilder's Play *The Matchmaker,*" 38.

48. It is almost as if Wilder felt bad about the fate he had given his earlier heroine and here resurrects her, still unrequited but not despairing.

dance. We're Presbyterian" (358). Prior to this, Cornelius and Barnaby Tucker sing "Tenting Tonight," an old revivalist song that will be sung in Act One of *The Skin of Our Teeth* (*SOT,* 45). Vandergelder, the antagonist of the play, seems to be a Satanic character along the lines of the Cardinal in *The Cabala* and Uncle Pio in *Bridge,* as suggested by Wilder himself in a reference to Vandergelder as a "miser-monster-demonic creature."[49] However, Dolly saves Vandergelder when she manipulates circumstances so that he sets his eyes on her for a wife (so love redeems even the Devil, perhaps, as some commentators feel is the case in *The Bridge of San Luis Rey*).

Though characters do address the audience directly as in *Our Town, The Matchmaker* does not seem to follow the sermon form and intention of Wilder's earlier dramatic jeremiad. In fact, *The Matchmaker* is subtitled "a Farce in Four Acts" (251), and the play is such a broad farce that scholars have tended to give it short shrift in their studies.[50] Yet this lightest of Wilder's three major full-length plays does have didactic intentions, as a few previous critics have noted, though none as in depth as David Castronovo. He reads *The Matchmaker* as a "social parable" in which there is a faint criticism of capitalism: "But for all its buoyancy, *The Merchant of Yonkers* deals with the darker side of human nature—capitalistic greed, exploitation, denial of vital possibilities, and neurosis." He calls Dolly "an interfering and generous spirit" and "anti-laissez-faire." Wilder even has one character in *The Matchmaker* sound almost like a radical Marxist:

> There was a time in my life when my chief interest was picking up money that didn't belong to me. The law is there to protect property, but—sure, the law doesn't care whether a property owner deserves his property or not, and the law has to be corrected. There are several thousands of people in this country engaged in correcting the law. For a while, I too was engaged in the redistribution of superfluities. A man works all his life and leaves a million to his widow. She sits in hotels and eats great meals and plays cards all afternoon and evening, with ten diamonds on her fingers. Call in the robbers! Call in the robbers! (365)

Of course, the speech is, like the entire play, tongue-in-cheek, but as Castronovo concludes, "For a play that has earned a reputation as a trivial farce,

49. Wilder quoted in Martin Blank, "Broadway Production History," 63.
50. The tendency of scholars and theater critics to not take *The Matchmaker* seriously may be due to their greater familiarity with *Hello, Dolly!* However, one does find exceptions where critics distinguish between the two. For example, in a review of a production of *The Matchmaker* directed by Emily Mann at the McCarter Theatre in Princeton, New Jersey, Ted Otten comments, "Everyone knows the story in its more popular musical version, *Hello, Dolly!* The play, however, has more depth, humor, and humanity" (133).

The Merchant of Yonkers offers a clever assessment of life in a competitive society." This was also true of the Armina episode in *Heaven's My Destination,* in which George Brush causes a run on a bank. Castronovo's reading of Dolly and the play makes clear that in writing *The Matchmaker* Wilder was indeed responding to the Great Depression, in that much of the play subtly comments on economic and social conditions: "Instead of presenting a cynical or bitter character, Wilder has managed to offer Dolly as a buoyant, worldly-wise woman whose major social mission is to get the juices of the capitalist system flowing." Thus *The Matchmaker* warrants inclusion in this study's examination of Wilder's drawing upon American sources for his response to the crisis state of America and the world in the late 1930s and early 1940s.[51]

The initial movement of the American jeremiad is the most pronounced element of the rhetorical pattern in this play. In Act One, Vandergelder complains, "Joe—the world's getting crazier every minute. Like my father used to say: the horses'll be taking over the world soon" (261). Still lamenting the present and also citing a golden age in the past, Vandergelder says to his store clerks Cornelius and Barnaby, "When I was your age I got up at five; I didn't close the shop until ten at night, and then I put in a good hour at the account books. The world's going to pieces" (290). In Act Two, Vandergelder repeats himself, this time more vehemently: "The world is going to pieces! I can't believe my own eyes!" (331). For all her optimism, even Dolly states near the end, "Yes, we're all fools and we're all in danger of destroying the world with our folly" (409). In spite of the farcical plot and tone of the play, such statements must have resonated with audiences in 1938 with the approach of World War Two and the memory of the Great Depression, which is alluded to by Malachi Stack, a ne'er-do-well who asks Vandergelder for a job: "That's right, Mr. Vandergelder. It's employers there's a dearth of. Seems like you hear of a new one dying every day" (267).

The other rhetorical movements of the jeremiad are present in *The Matchmaker* but only faintly. In her Act Four "sermon," Dolly cites a personal golden age: "Oh, it won't be a marriage in the sense that we had one"; followed by a declension: "After my husband's death I retired into myself"; then a recommitment to the errand of life: "But there comes a moment in everybody's life when he must decide whether he'll live among human beings or not—a fool among fools or a fool alone. . . . [T]hat night I decided to rejoin the human race"; and finally a determination to make progress: "I'm marrying Horace Vandergelder for his money. I'm going to send his money out doing all the things you [her deceased first husband, Ephraim Levi] taught me. . . . Money, I've always felt, money—pardon my expression—is like ma-

51. Castronovo, *Thornton Wilder,* 107, 94, 95, 98.

nure; it's not worth a thing unless it's spread about encouraging young things to grow" (408–9).[52]

Although as the protagonist of *The Matchmaker,* Dolly is a more concrete and complex character than the Stage Managers in *Our Town* and *Pullman Car Hiawatha,* she functions in much the same way, directing the actors to speak and referring reflexively to the play:

> *To audience.*
> There isn't any more coffee; there isn't any more gingerbread, and there isn't any more play—but there is one more thing we have to do . . . . Barnaby, come here.
> *She whispers to him, pointing to the audience. Then she says to the audience:*
> I think the youngest person here ought to tell us what the moral of the play is.
> *Barnaby is reluctantly pushed forward to the footlights.* (415)[53]

Indeed, Dolly's function as a Stage Manager in realistic human form proves to be *The Matchmaker*'s strongest manifestation of New England Puritanism. That is, both aesthetically and thematically, Dolly Levi, Wilder's major addition to the original story, can be seen in typological relationship with other elements in Wilder's earlier and later plays and novels. The earliest occurrence of the Stage Manager type expresses Wilder's providential interpretation of events in *The Cabala:* "As by the click of some invisible stage manager, Miss Grier entered" (*C,* 61).[54] What is merely a simile in this first novel by Wilder—that events in our lives are controlled by someone or something like the characters and incidents in a play are controlled by a stage manager—is incarnated in his plays as a character called the Stage Manager, first in both *Pullman Car Hiawatha* and *The Happy Journey,* and then in *Our Town,* as a god- or author-like being who controls the scenes that are acted out for the audience and who explains the significance of the action. In the strict use of typological terminology, then, the simile in *The Cabala* is the *type* to *Our Town*'s Stage Manager character in the plays, which would be the *antitype.* But then Wilder wrote *The Matchmaker,* making Dolly, a more fully realized character than the Stage Manager, the antitype. In Wilder's next play, *The Skin of Our*

52. Linda Simon also reads Dolly's climactic and didactic speech as a homily: "Her monologue in the last act is nothing less than one of Thornton's amiable sermons" (*Thornton Wilder, His World,* 149).

53. Wilder scholars previously noted Dolly's similarity to the Stage Manager; for example, Haberman writes, "She, like Wilder himself, is able at will to call to life and endow with personality the other characters of the play, like the Stage Managers in *Pullman Car Hiawatha* and *Our Town*" (*Plays of Thornton Wilder,* 19).

54. Unless one counts the Manager in the three-minute play *Prosperina and the Devil,* which was published in *The Angel that Troubled the Waters and Other Plays* after *The Cabala,* though written before.

Teeth, the Stage Manager is reduced to a one-dimensional character who appears only briefly twice in the play; therefore, Dolly represents the furthermost development of this figure in Wilder's oeuvre up to the 1940s.

Like the Stage Manager, Dolly also may be read allegorically, even though, as Kuner notes, she is "the most realistically drawn character in the play." Castronovo's description of her as a "New Deal Planner" raises and broadens the significance of her powers to the presidential if not the providential level. But Dolly also seems omniscient, omnipotent, and benevolent—she, like the Stage Managers, is a godlike character. Her benevolence and power to effect good have been noted in studies of *The Matchmaker;* for example, Haberman writes, "All the characters have been 'saved' by Mrs. Levi, but they are worth saving."[55] It is also worth noting that Levi was the tribe of priests in Biblical Israel. Dolly describes herself as "a woman who likes to know everything that's going on; who likes to manage things" (375)—like a stage manager. As with the Stage Manager, Dolly can play various roles, can be whatever the moment requires.[56] Like *Our Town*'s Stage Manager, she has ideas about nature: "Nature is never completely satisfactory and must be corrected" (277). Finally, she describes herself as an arranger: "I am a woman who arranges things" and just before this line she assures Ambrose that "everything will be arranged" (276); by the end of *The Matchmaker* she has fulfilled her own prophecy.

Thus, despite the fact that Wilder adapted *The Matchmaker* from European sources, and that it seems to be only a light farce perfectly suited for adaptation as a Broadway musical rather than a serious didactic work, faint traces of the American jeremiad as well as other aspects of the writings of Wilder's New England Puritan forbears do manifest themselves in the text. Had Wilder limited himself to merely translating the dialogue and substituting an American setting for the European one of the original, there probably would have been even fewer trace elements of Puritanism. But when he decided to add a major character named Dolly Levi,[57] the part of his aesthetic that stems from the New England Puritan mind was activated, and the Puritan rhetoric of crisis again took dramatic form.

55. Kuner, *Bright and Dark,* 140; Castronovo, *Thornton Wilder,* 99; Haberman, *Plays of Thornton Wilder,* 21. In "The Role of Gender in Wilder's *Three Plays,*" a paper written for my spring 1997 seminar on Wilder, Renee Semler says of Dolly, "She, like the Stage Managers of Wilder's other works, directs and controls the characters in such a way that [she] continuously pushes them forward in motion" (12).

56. In his review of the McCarter production of *The Matchmaker,* Ted Otten notes of Elizabeth Franz's performance, "This Dolly is a chameleon, changing from situation to situation" ("McCarter opens season with *Matchmaker*").

57. Haberman makes a point of saying that Dolly is Wilder's invention, not Nestroy's (*Plays of Thornton Wilder,* 113).

The Skin of Our Teeth

In his next play after *The Matchmaker,* Wilder "preaches" a jeremiad in which New England Puritan ideology and aesthetics are manifested in their purest form since the seventeenth century. Even the venue where *The Skin of Our Teeth* was first produced manifests a trace of the Puritan past: the Plymouth Theater.[58] In addition, with *The Skin of Our Teeth* Wilder's progress as an American dramatist reaches its climax. His next novel and play return to classical subjects: *The Ides of March,* published in 1948, and *The Alcestiad,* first produced in 1955 under the title *A Life in the Sun.* When Wilder wrote *The Skin of Our Teeth* in 1942, western civilization was faced with its greatest modern challenge, the second world war. An artistic response to the crisis that could transcend any one nation's point of view was sorely needed, as suggested by early commentators on the play: "In 1942 when this country was rallying from the defeat at Pearl Harbor, Thornton produced his finest play, *The Skin of Our Teeth,* a thrilling reminder of man's ability to survive"; "Rather call it a bulletin issued from the sickroom of a patient whose health we are all pardonably interested, a bulletin signed by a physician named Thornton Wilder."[59] At a time when the world seemed doomed to repeat the tragedies of the past, the cosmic allegory and the historical vision inherent in the American jeremiad were just what was needed to reaffirm the progress of human civilization. In *The Skin of Our Teeth,* the continuation of God's plot is affirmed even on the brink of Armageddon.

Despite the gravity of the times, the tone of most of *The Skin of Our Teeth* is farcical, and the theatrical style and dramaturgy in some ways are similar to the nonrealistic style of *Our Town.* Act One begins on the global scale: a voiceover newsreel-like presentation called "News events of the world" informs the audience that after the sun rose "The society for Affirming the end of the World at once went into a special session and postponed the arrival of that event for twenty-four hours" (5). The choice of the word "affirming" for an awareness that the end of the world may be imminent subtly alludes to Puritan eschatology.[60] Using a dramatic analogy, Bercovitch ex-

58. The fact that the first colony of Puritans in the New World was at Plymouth, Massachusetts, and that the theater in which *The Skin of Our Teeth* debuted was named the "Plymouth" would seem to most people a meaningless coincidence. However, in a cultural criticism hermeneutic informed by psychoanalytic literary criticism, Marxist literary criticism, semiotics, and so forth, this would not be a mere coincidence, because there are no coincidences according to that school of thought. Everything in cultural production is linguistic cause and effect, following the endless chain of signifiers, to paraphrase Jacques Lacan.

59. Edward Weeks, "The Peripatetic Reviewer," 296; Alexander Woolcott, "Mr. Wilder Urges Us On," reprint in *Long, Long Ago,* 245.

60. As during World War One, Judgment Day was again on the Christian mind, especially the Puritan-influenced Christian mind. To illustrate, a *Time* magazine reference to

plains how the Puritans' sense of their errand or progress in the New World was seen within the divine progress of history toward the millennium when they would witness "the imminent renovation of all things in 'a new heaven and a new earth.' A new beginning, then, and a newly urgent sense of an ending; and intermediate between these, at once linking them in time and confirming the overall design, like an apocalyptic play-within-a-play, was the story of New England."[61] *The Skin of Our Teeth* is also an apocalyptic play-within-a-play, in that it doesn't simply break the fourth wall, acknowledging the audience in the manner of *Our Town;* it is actually a double narrative: the story of the Antrobus family in the play and the story of a theater company putting on the play. The question in both plots is, will the action continue or will it end? Furthermore, *The Skin of Our Teeth* asks, "If human history is the longest running play in . . . well, history, is that play a comedy or a tragedy? A farce or Theater of the Absurd?" The cataclysmic events in the story of the Antrobuses—the Ice Age, Noah's flood, and world war—as well as the interruptions of the performance of that story, suggest that the end of the world is indeed near. However, in *The Skin of Our Teeth* we see Armageddon, Doomsday, the end of history, the end of the world—all of them eternally deferred: Apocalypse (not) Now. In Puritan terms, God's plot will continue, but man's stories must continue to progress as well. To help ensure they do, Wilder again employs the Puritan rhetoric of crisis to encourage America and the whole world to march onward.

Sounding the first movement of the American jeremiad, Sabina, the maid of the Antrobuses, laments the current state of things: "The whole world's at sixes and sevens, and why the house hasn't fallen down about our ears long ago is a miracle to me" (8). The fracturing of the set—flats are flown up or lean outward in conjunction with her speech—seems only to confirm that the end is near. The literal crisis in Act One is the prehistoric Ice Age. Mrs. Antrobus, in a less melodramatic tone than Sabina, offers an explanation for freezing temperatures in the middle of summer: "The earth's getting so silly, no wonder the sun turns cold" (20). In a more serious tone, Mrs. Antrobus's lament over the loss of her other son, "Abel" (41), recalls George falling prostrate in front of Emily's grave in *Our Town;* as in all of his works, Wilder

---

The Skin of Our Teeth summarized the plot in similar terms: "Its action spread over 5,000 years, took in the Flood, the Ice Age and Armageddon" ("An Obliging Man," 48). We also know that in an early draft of *The Skin of Our Teeth* Wilder used the title "The Ends of the Worlds" (Burns and Dydo, *Letters,* 268 n. 5). Even in 1937 when he was forty and apocalypse was again in the air, Wilder could write to Stein, "I feel like some brand-new Chinese convert . . . , saying that a Christian must turn his back on his family, expect the end of the world at any minute. . . ." (Burns and Dydo, *Letters,* 156).

61. Sacvan Bercovitch, "The Ends of American Puritan Rhetoric," 173.

brings both the idea and the emotion of death on stage. Maintaining the tone of lamentation, Mr. Antrobus, hearing that his son Henry has thrown a stone at a neighbor boy, possibly killing him, also attributes the sun turning cold to punishment for what sounds like the Calvinistic doctrine of total depravity: "No wonder the sun grows cold. . . . Myself all of us, we're covered with blood" (43, 44).[62] These speeches would seem to be more apropos of a tragedy or a historical pessimism than what one would expect from a work that manifests the Puritans' cosmic optimism, but Wilder oscillates the tone of the dialogue and action between tragedy and comedy throughout *The Skin of Our Teeth*, and in all three acts actors appear to step out of character to call attention to the fact that the audience is watching a play; we observed this same self-reflexivity in *Our Town*, *The Matchmaker*, and *Pullman Car Hiawatha*.[63]

But it is not only the characters of the narrative of the Antrobus family who express the lament of the American jeremiad in *The Skin of Our Teeth;* it is also expressed by the actors in the play-about-putting-on-the-play. Sabina—or rather Miss Somerset, the actress playing Sabina—is the character who most functions like *Our Town*'s Stage Manager, narrating and commenting on the action (though less frequently and in a parodic manner). Wilder has Miss Somerset appear to stop acting so that she can tell the audience how she longs for a return to a recent golden age of theater: "Oh—why can't we have plays like we used to have . . . good entertainment with a message you can take home with you. . . . I took this hateful job because I had to. For two years I've sat up in my room living on a sandwich and a cup of tea a day, waiting for better times in the theatre. And look at me now: I—I who've played *Rain* and *The Barretts of Wimpole Street* and *First Lady*—God in Heaven!" (11). This lament is made in response to the state of the medium of the lament; in other words, Sabina "preaches" a "jeremiad" on dramatic jeremiads.[64]

62. Critics and Wilder himself have pointed out that we are meant to see these laments as a response to the real state of crisis in the world in 1942. For example, the 1943 Pulitzer Prize committee commented on *The Skin of Our Teeth,* "Mr. Wilder's play is eminently of the hour and of the chaos of the present" ("1943 Pulitzer Prizes"). In his preface to *Three Plays,* Wilder wrote, "It was written on the eve of our entrance into the war and under strong emotion and I think it mostly comes alive under conditions of crisis" (xiii).

63. Adler calls *The Skin of Our Teeth* "the seminal text of self-consciousness in the American theatre" (*Mirror on the Stage,* 130).

64. This may have been Wilder's parody of Eleanor Roosevelt's harangue against the New York theater and theater critics after her unpleasant experience of seeing *Our Town*. Mrs. Roosevelt was taking issue with New York theater critics' pan of a play by Katherine Dayton, who had previously written a play the First Lady liked very much—*First Lady,* to which Wilder has Sabina refer nostalgically. Sabina's speech also echoes where Mrs. Roosevelt wistfully asks, "Sometimes we need a pleasant evening, so why must we have all our plays in the same vein? Why can't the critics have standards for different types of plays and give us an idea of the kind of evening we may have if we go to this play or that?" (Roosevelt quoted in Atkinson, *Broadway Scrapbook,* 90).

There is a Stage Manager in *The Skin of Our Teeth,* but he is reduced to a minor character who appears briefly only twice in the play. Most of the Stage Manager's functions in Wilder's previous incarnations are delegated to other characters: "In *The Skin of Our Teeth* the role of the Stage Manager evolves into characters stepping out of their roles." The Fortune Teller predicts the future, Sabina addresses the audience and refers to the author and the play and what it is about, and Antrobus calls to offstage characters.[65] The Stage Manager even has a name: Mr. Fitzpatrick or, even more mundanely, "Fitz" (73). In another example of the play's reflexivity, Wilder makes an intertextual joke on this Stage Manager; when "Miss Somerset" refuses to play the seduction scene in Act Two, Fitz—called on stage by the actor playing Mr. Antrobus—tells her, "Miss Somerset! Go to your dressing room. I'll read your lines" (75). This speech recalls the Stage Manager characters in *Our Town, Pullman Car Hiawatha,* and *The Happy Journey to Trenton and Camden,* all of whom speak the lines of minor characters without any attempt at realistic representation.[66]

In Act Two of *The Skin of Our Teeth* Wilder dramatizes belief in divine retribution by setting the action at a world convention that will be interrupted by a universal flood. Invoking a golden age, as we saw in *Our Town,* Mrs. Antrobus bemoans the decadence of the day and recalls the progress made up to that point in the area of institutionalizing monogamy and the family: "I only bring up these unpleasant memories because I see some signs of backsliding from that great victory [marriage]. Oh, my fellow mammals, keep hold of that" (54). When Antrobus sees his daughter Gladys wearing red

65. The previous quotation is from a paper by Paul Cappucci, a graduate student who did an independent study with me on Wilder, Tennessee Williams, and Edward Albee during the spring 1993 semester. Sabina's Stage Manager–like function in *The Skin of Our Teeth* was never more apparent than in the recent New York Shakespeare Festival production in Central Park. Played by Kristin Johnston, whom audiences recognized from the popular television sitcom *Third Rock from the Sun,* Sabina dominated the first and second acts. (In Act Three the interruptions of the action are limited to just two times, and only once by Sabina, when the actors playing Henry and Mr. Antrobus seem to lose control and actually begin to fight one another.)

66. Since the function of the earlier Stage Managers continues to occur, it could be argued in one sense that this is a further development of the Stage Manager type, but only if one uses a term such as "development," which does not necessarily mean improvement or progress toward the ideal, which is the Puritans' progressive view of recurring types in history. Furthermore, keeping in mind that the Stage Manager from first use as a simile in *The Cabala* through the one-act plays and to *Our Town* is an allegorical representation of God, one cannot argue that *that* meaning recurs in *The Skin of Our Teeth;* none of the characters performing Stage Manager–like actions—Sabina, Antrobus, or Mr. Fitzpatrick—can be read as godlike. However, the stage managers in *Pullman Car Hiawatha* and *Our Town,* along with Dolly Levi in *The Matchmaker,* can be read as godlike, as we have seen.

stockings, he shouts, "Have you gone crazy? Has everyone gone crazy?" (81). A final example of the lament of the American jeremiad is also the most literal and direct: in Act Two a fortune teller on the boardwalk in Atlantic City where the convention of the mammals and other orders takes place predicts illness, afflictions, bad luck, and an apocalyptic flood to the passersby, who jeer at her: "Charlatan! Madam Kill-joy! Mrs. Jeremiah!" (59). But Esmeralda the Fortune Teller is not merely a prophetess of doom; as the most Jeremiah-like spokesperson in this dramatic jeremiad, she laments and warns but also affirms a providential stay of chaos: "You know as well as I do what's coming. Rain. Rain. Rain in floods. The deluge. But first you'll see shameful things. Some of you will be saying: 'Let him [Antrobus or Man] drown. He's not worth saving. Give the whole thing up.' I can see it in your faces. But you're wrong. Keep your doubts and despairs to yourselves. Again there'll be the narrow escape. The survival of a handful. From destruction,—total destruction" (59). As with the precarious structure of the Antrobus house in Act One, the Fortune Teller's assessment of the crisis is corroborated here by a stage prop that serves as a metaphor for the signs of the times, a weather signal: "One of those black disks means bad weather; two means storm; three means hurricane; and four means the end of the world" (61). When the fourth black disk appears, the Antrobuses again rise to the occasion, saving the human race and other species by gathering them two by two into a boat.[67]

In Act Two, Wilder is obviously drawing upon the biblical account of the great flood as described in Genesis, which every study of *The Skin of Our Teeth* has pointed out. However, those studies have not understood that the way in which Antrobus is represented in Act One as Adam, in Act Two as Noah, and in Act Three as a modern Everyman is an unusually pure modern example of New England Puritan typology. That a wedding ring with the inscription, "To Eva from Adam Genesis II: 18" (6) was found in the theater where this play is showing, that Antrobus was once a gardener (7), that Henry has a red scar in the shape of a "C" on his forehead because his old name is "Cain" (24), that Sabina's name in her temptress role in Act Two is changed to Lily (Lilith), that Mrs. Antrobus thinks the coming storm would best be spent "in a good stout boat" (69), that the rival orders of species have sent delegates to the convention "two by two"—this all reflects Wilder's typological view of human history: the biblical types of characters and events recur, but as part of an overall progression—God's plot.[68] Just as the New

67. The fourth black disk may be an abstract allusion to the Four Horsemen of the Apocalypse.

68. One might argue that the play is almost a selective adaptation of the Bible; even the title is derived from the Old Testament Book of Job: "My bone cleaveth to my skin and to my flesh, and I am escaped with the skin of my teeth" (19:20, KJV).

England Puritans saw themselves as seventeenth-century antitypes to the Old Testament characters (e.g., Bradford to Moses, Winthrop to Nehemiah), in Act Three, Antrobus, now the twentieth-century New Jersey inventor called to serve in the war, becomes the antitype (the zenith, the culmination) to Adam and Noah; it is his mission to begin again after a fall from grace and the resulting punishment. The playful metatheatricality assigned primarily to the actress playing Sabina enables Wilder to explain to the audience how the play is working: "The author hasn't made up his silly mind as to whether we're all living back in caves or in New Jersey today, and that's the way it is all the way through" (11). Her complaint about the play's ambiguity of time is close to being a parodic definition of typology.

As in *Our Town,* Wilder also employs the allegorical mode in *The Skin of Our Teeth* to signify the universality of his message. The titles of the plays share the first-person plural possessive pronoun "our," extending from a small town or single family to the whole world or the human family. As stated in the *Time* cover story on Wilder, "*Our Town* is the life of the family seen from a telescope five miles away. *The Skin of Our Teeth* is the destiny of the whole human group seen from a telescope 1,000 miles away."[69] Furthermore, "Antrobus," as Haberman points out, is close to the Greek word for "Man," *anthropos.*[70]

Although the Antrobus family and individual members of it are repeatedly described as typical Americans (Wilder gives us yet another major character named George), the characters' many didactic and reflexive statements make it clear that the Antrobuses represent everyone. For example, Sabina says the play is "all about the troubles the human race has gone through" (11), and the Fortune Teller explains to the audience, "They're coming—the Antrobuses. Keck. Your hope. Your despair. Your selves" (60).[71] The 1998 New York Shakespeare Festival production in Central Park heightened the

69. "An Obliging Man," 48. Karen E. Rowe explains how Puritan writers achieved the divine point of view despite the limitations on the narrator (only God could be omniscient): "Allegories that embrace typal parallels as signs within a grander providential scheme that affects all time and all men create an explosion of reference or telescopic perspective, so that one seems to share an omniscient vision comparable to God's" (*Saint and Singer: Edward Taylor's Typology and the Poetics of Meditation,* 241).

70. Haberman, *Plays of Thornton Wilder,* 82. Similarly, in his prose allegory *The Kingdom of Basaruah* (1715), Joseph Morgan, another New England Puritan minister who also worked in a variety of genres, wrote that the people of Basaruah were descended from "Antropos" (35).

71. Previous studies agree that allegorically Wilder has it both ways. For example, Burbank states that the characters are "allegorical figures on three levels: as Americans, as biblical figures, and as universal human types" (*Thornton Wilder,* 90). Travis Bogard writes, "Its many specific identifications, however, combine to make it the archetype of all families in all times. It becomes 'Every Family,' the norm of the concept" ("The Comedy of Thornton Wilder," 367). Mitchell writes of *The Skin of Our Teeth* that "its characters have never been described as fully fleshed out. Sometimes they seem a bit too

universality theme by casting an African American actress and a Hispanic actor in the roles of Gladys and Henry Antrobus, while Mr. and Mrs. Antrobus were played by Caucasian actors.[72]

The potential for a pessimistic reading of *The Skin of Our Teeth* lies in the characters' voicing an uncertainty about the outcome of the crisis, which could allegorically suggest an open-ended paradigm of history: "Every night it's the same thing. Will he come back safe, or won't he? Will we starve to death, or freeze to death, or boil to death or will we be killed by burglars?" (13).[73] However, *The Skin of Our Teeth*, like New England Puritan jeremiads, affirms progress. The play is full of references and allusions to inventions: the wheel, the alphabet, prime numbers, the needle, the telegraph, food processing, silk, marriage, social progress in the rights of women (including the education of women), philosophical ideas, and great works of literature. This is not to say that Wilder ignores negative products of the progress of civilization: in each act Cain's weapons grow more sophisticated (stones, slingshots, guns). Yet for all that goes wrong through the ages, Wilder suggests that the human race is in the *process* of getting it right. Even the name of the fictional New Jersey town where the Antrobuses live suggests progress: "Excelsior," the Latin word traditionally translated as "ever upward."[74]

In order to affirm that the episodes of history signify progress rather than mere cycles, Wilder fuses the biblical codes of progress as ordained by God

---

close to allegorical figures . . . for anybody to accept except Puritans. Of course the world is chock full of Puritans, and the play has had endless productions" ("Life Viewed as a Totality versus Gobblydegarble," 2).

72. Even the casting of John Goodman as Mr. Antrobus suggested universality. Goodman is famous for playing an average ordinary husband and father in the television show *Roseanne*, and he played Fred Flintstone in the live-actor feature film inspired by the animated television series. To underscore this association of his role as a stone-age hero, the wheel Goodman carried onto the set in Act One appeared to have been cut from white limestone like wheels in *The Flintstones*. Similarly, the scene designer of another production of *The Skin of Our Teeth* made the set suggest the universality theme; instead of painting the flats to look like an ordinary living room, he painted on the flats facsimiles of famous drawings or paintings spanning the history of the human race (e.g., the first flat was the famous bison drawings found in a cave in France; the last flat was Dali's "The Persistence of Memory," with the famous melting clocks).

73. Bogard denies progress in *The Skin of Our Teeth*, claiming the characters "perform before a symbolic setting a deliberately unconvincing enactment of man's progress through the ages" ("Comedy of Thornton Wilder," 367).

74. Adler is one of very few scholars or critics who see *The Skin of Our Teeth* as affirming progress; he describes it as expressing "an optimistic philosophy of spiral progression" (*Mirror on the Stage*, 130). Wilder said of an earlier draft of the play that it was too negative because of his "assumption that the aspirational side of life can be taken for granted . . . [his] unshakable sense that work and home and society move on towards great good things" (Burns and Dydo, *Letters*, 381). He went on to say in that letter, "But the chief thing is to inform all that with the tone of warmth and courage and confidence about the human adventure which I had taken too much for granted" (Burns and Dydo, *Letters*, 382).

with the biological codes of evolution as theorized by Darwin. In Act Two, the justification on the literal level of the action for the gathering of the animals two by two is the six hundred thousandth annual convention of that "great fraternal order—the Ancient and Honorable Order of Mammals, Subdivision Humans" (49), which has just elected Antrobus as its president. Whether applying Calvinistic determinism or Darwinian natural selection, the human race is the chosen species.[75] In a clever speech by the Announcer at the beginning of Act Two, Wilder conflates biological taxonomy with biblical typology: "This great celebration of the order of the mammals has received delegations from the other rival orders,—or shall we say: esteemed concurrent orders: the WINGS, the FINS, the SHELLS, and so on. These Orders are holding their conventions also in various parts of the world, and have sent representatives to our own, two of a kind" (50). Wilder then spoofs but nevertheless affirms evolution in Antrobus's address to the convention, which resembles an American jeremiad in that jeremiads were often what amounted to a "state-of-the-covenant address":[76]

> My friends, we have come a long way. During this week of happy celebration it is perhaps not fitting that we dwell on some of the difficult times we have been through. The dinosaur is extinct—/*Applause*/—the ice has retreated; and the common cold is being pursued by every means within our power.... Before I close, however, I want to answer one of those unjust and malicious accusations that were brought against me during the last electoral campaign. Ladies and Gentlemen, the charges were made that at various points in my career I leaned toward joining some of the rival orders,—that's a lie. As I told reporters of the Atlantic City Herald, I do not deny that a few months before my birth I hesitated between ... uh ... between pinfeathers and gill-breathing,— and so did many of us here,—but for the last million years I have been viviparous, hairy and diaphragmatic. *Applause. Cries of 'Good old Antrobus,' 'The Prince chap!' 'Georgie,' etc.* (51–52)[77]

75. The two systems of belief are not that different in form: "Far from being mutually exclusive, then, orthodox Calvinism and orthodox Darwinism tend almost to fortify one another" (Perry D. Westbrook, *Free Will and Determination in American Literature,* 121). With Wilder, the word "elect" is almost always used punningly in the Calvinistic sense as well as the literal. Evidently, he never did quite detach himself from the idea of the elect as "a cabala," as demonstrated by Sabina's speech in Act Two, possibly alluding to T. S. Eliot's "The Hollow Men": "Everybody in the world except a few people like you and me are just made of straw. Most people have no insides at all. . . . There's a kind of secret society at the top of the world,—like you and me,—that know this. The world was made for us" (198).

76. Bercovitch, *American Jeremiad,* 4.

77. Frederick William Conner explains in his study that this blending of scientific, social, and sacred points of view into a cosmic optimism was native to the nineteenth century (and thus could easily have reached Thornton Wilder through his parents, teachers, and so on); in his most succinct definition, Conner writes, "To restate the simple argu-

The providential view of progress would appear to be challenged in Act Three of *The Skin of Our Teeth* when the Stage Manager and the actor playing Antrobus stop the performance and inform the audience that the actors appearing as the philosophers/hours of the night have taken ill from food poisoning: "Ladies and Gentlemen, an unfortunate accident has taken place" (92). However, this backstage accident has no serious effect on the overall design of Providence, and it may be "perhaps an intention," as with the bridge collapsing in *The Bridge of San Luis Rey* or the providential results of the backstage accident in *Prosperina and the Devil* discussed in Chapter Two. After the announcement, ushers, cleaning ladies, and others who know the speeches from watching rehearsals step up to take the places of the ailing actors, perhaps expressing an egalitarian view of the human race and history. The stand-ins are even able to explain and appreciate the author's intention better than the Stage Manager: "Just like the hours and stars go by over our heads at night, in the same way the ideas and thoughts of the great men are in the air around us all the time and they're working on us, even when we don't know it" (95).

Completing the rhetorical movement of the American jeremiad, Act Three of *The Skin of Our Teeth* affirms a recommitment to the human errand as the Antrobuses return to daily life after the end of the war: Gladys has a newborn baby to feed; Mrs. Antrobus declares, even though she knows they face more tests, more crises, "I could live for seventy years in a cellar for seventy years and make soup out of grass and bark without ever doubting that this world has a work to do and will do it" (107); Mr. Antrobus momentarily loses his desire to go on after a confrontation with his son Henry, who Sabina reveals was "the enemy" in the war.[78] However, inspired by his books

---

ment of cosmic optimism once more, if one accepted the fact of evolution and believed that God was both benevolent and omnipotent, one could not escape the conclusion that the evolutionary process must also be good" (*Cosmic Optimism: A Study of the Interpretation of Evolution by American Poets from Emerson to Robinson*, 245–46).

78. Responding to a speculation that Henry might represent Germany during World War Two, Wilder said, "But really I was not thinking particularly of Germany, I had in mind Ur and Chaldea" (Mitchell, "Live Viewed," 2). Ur and Chaldea are characterized as sinful in the Old Testament. Other scholars also see Henry and other destructive elements in the play as representing evil on an abstract and universal level rather than on a level of current events. For example, Mary McBride writes, "Pitted against Antrobus, and inherent in his nature, are evil forces with basic qualities commonly attributed to both the Satan of Christian theology (including Milton's Satan) and the demons of pagan creeds" ("Misanthropic Diabolism—Antagonist to Man: A Study of Evil in Thornton Wilder's *The Skin of Our Teeth*," 1). She sees Henry/Cain and Sabina as Antrobus's "diabolical antagonists." Sabina is also "Satan the tempter" ("Misanthropic Diabolism," 4) and "reconciled evil" as opposed to Henry—quoting Wilder himself—as "strong unreconciled evil" ("Misanthropic Diabolism," 5). Finally, Castronovo describes Henry as a wartime "embodiment of the death instinct" (*Thornton Wilder*, 144).

and the great ideas they contain, Mr. Antrobus is soon ready to begin again: "All I ask is the chance to build new worlds and God has always given us that. And has given us [*opening the book*] voices to guide us; and the memory of our mistakes to warn us. . . . We've come a long ways. We've learned. We're learning. And the steps of our journey are marked for us here" (119).

This moving final speech by Antrobus asserts several ideas relevant to the discussion of New England Puritan thought in Wilder's works: that human history continues by God's grace, that the crises and catastrophes do not destroy everything so that civilization does not have to start over from nothing, and that what does survive from the preceding ages indicates previous steps and helps humankind make further progress.[79] The pageant of the hours of the night—a projection of Antrobus's thoughts as he reads the great thinkers Aristotle, Plato, Spinoza, and the author of the Book of Genesis—represents the touchstones of civilization with which Antrobus will begin a new society. The last excerpt recited by Mr. Tremayne is a familiar text given new power by all that has preceded it: "In the beginning, God created the Heavens and the Earth; and the Earth was waste and void; And the darkness was upon the face of the deep. And the Lord said let there be light and there was light" (121). The sudden blackout and re-raising of the lights on the set, appearing as it did at the beginning of Act One, visually signifies "genesis." Sabina repeats the opening speech of the play, which some scholars have suggested indicates mere repetition, but there have been too many signs of progress in *The Skin of Our Teeth* to see the shape of its representation of history as cyclical; it is typological, repetition with progress.[80] Thus *The Skin of Our Teeth* is Wilder's attempt to reassure the world that this crisis too will pass, that the war will end. Sabina's announcement at the beginning of Act Three that the war is over surely was encouraging to audiences in 1942. Wilder has Sabina finish the play with an optimistic farewell: "This is where you came in. We have to go on for ages and ages yet. You go home. The end of this play isn't written yet. Mr. and Mrs. Antrobus! Their heads are full of plans and they're

79. Along with one line from Wilder's next full-length play, *The Alcestiad*—"Let everybody see that a new knowledge has been given to us of what gods and men can do together" (71)—this speech by Antrobus is probably the most direct expression in Wilder of the Puritans' Covenant theology discussed in Chapter One.

80. Atkinson's reading of the end concurs with my own: "Although the third act is no match for the stunning act that opens the play, it recovers its dynamic faith in the capacity of the human race to go on saving itself by the skin of its teeth, and it offers—in off-hand fashion—two or three sublime reasons for retaining hope in the future" (*Broadway Scrapbook*, 213). He goes on to write, "[R]emembering what they accomplished in the days of their youth, they begin again, each time with a little more knowledge to start with, each time with a wider vision. The basic story of *The Skin of Our Teeth* is profoundly moving because it is true. There, by the grace of God, go the lot of us" (*Broadway Scrapbook*, 214).

as confident as the first day they began" (121). At a time when it seemed that man's stories were about to bring history to an apocalyptic end, Wilder's dramatic jeremiad expressed faith in the ongoing progress of God's plot.

Civilization teetered on the brink of chaos at mid-century, and some despaired that the end was near, but the American jeremiad was "preached" once again in response to a cultural crisis. Only a cosmic optimism as strong as Wilder's, as strong as the Puritans', could maintain faith in the human race, because—as the Antrobus family's story reminds us—history is made up of one challenge after another, the collective effect of which has been to progress along a path determined by a benevolent Providence. In *The Skin of Our Teeth*, cosmic optimism can be summed up by the old theatrical saying: the show must go on.

Shadow of a Doubt

As the author of *Our Town*, Thornton Wilder has become so completely identified with a nostalgic, affirmative portrait of the American small town populated by good, honest people that it is difficult to imagine an odder partnership than that of Wilder and Alfred Hitchcock. But they did collaborate on the making of the 1943 film *Shadow of a Doubt*, which is about a psychopathic serial killer eluding a nationwide manhunt by hiding out with his unsuspecting sister and her family. The pairing of Wilder and Hitchcock seems odd only because the representation of the dark side in Wilder's works has been missed or dismissed as unconvincing.

As the title of the film suggests, Wilder and Hitchcock's examination of a typical American family finds only a *shadow* of a doubt that all is essentially well and that the violent state of the world is only temporary; and who would have been better qualified to write what would be, in the end, an affirmative view of America as incarnated in a representative American family than Thornton Wilder? The issue of authorship of the screenplay for *Shadow of a Doubt* is still very much an open one. Some critics credit Hitchcock mostly, while others give Wilder a larger share in the creation of the narrative. However, there is ample evidence that Wilder's contribution to the film was substantial, as indicated not only by his top billing in the screenplay credit, but also by the additional credit that appears in between the producer and director credits: "We wish to acknowledge the contribution of MR. THORNTON WILDER to the preparation of this production."[81]

81. According to Blank, Wilder wrote producer Sol Lesser that 80 percent of the film was his (Martin Blank, "Wilder, Hitchcock, and *Shadow of a Doubt*," 413).

As the account in Harrison reveals, Hitchcock sought Wilder's vision for his film: "Because the locale of *Shadow of a Doubt* was a small town, 'the name of Thornton Wilder, who had written *Our Town,* was the first to be considered,' the ponderous Mr. Hitchcock told an interviewer." In fact, Hitchcock valued Wilder's contribution so much that in order for Wilder to continue working on the script as long as possible, Hitchcock rode with him on a train from Hollywood to Florida, where Wilder was to begin voluntary service in the army.[82]

Some Hitchcock scholars also assign Wilder a large role in the composition of the screenplay. John Russell Taylor calls Hitchcock and Wilder's work "one of the most harmonious collaborations of [Hitchcock's] working life." He further writes that

> Wilder and [Hitchcock] would talk in the morning, then Wilder would go off by himself in the afternoon and write bits and pieces in longhand in a high school notebook. He had such a clear idea of the milieu and the characters that he never wrote consecutively, but just scenes here and there, as the mood took him, until the outline screenplay was completed . . . [He] wrote the last pages of the script on the train to his military service, with H[itchcock] accompanying him across-country to Florida to complete the collaboration *en-route.* H[itchcock] would have liked Wilder to make the last revisions possible, but obviously that was not possible.[83]

This episode is further detailed in *CineBooks' Motion Picture Guide:*

> To finish the script, Hitchcock boarded a cross-country train to Florida (where Wilder was to begin his training) with the writer and patiently sat in the next compartment while Wilder emerged to give him another few pages of copy. The great playwright finished the last page of *Shadow of a Doubt* just as the train was coming to his stop, and he used the train upon which he and Hitchcock traveled as his model in creating the setting for Cotten and Wright's final struggle.

Curiously, although in his later study of Hitchcock Donald Spoto gives Wilder little credit for the screenplay, his descriptions of the Puritan element in the film in his earlier study of Hitchcock are similar to the continuity argument applied to Wilder in this study:

82. Harrison, *Enthusiast,* 222; Goldstone, *Intimate Portrait,* 167. The train trip repeated the director's first overture to Wilder to work on the film: "So anxious was Hitchcock to begin working with Wilder before 23 May, Stewart continued in her telegram, that he was willing to fly to New York and then return with Wilder" (Burns and Dydo, *Letters,* 388).

83. Taylor, *Hitchcock: The Life and Times of Alfred Hitchcock,* 185.

But the clearest parallel lies with that authentically American Puritan view of man and his world as flawed, weak and susceptible to corruption and madness. This view, found in our earliest writers—Jonathan Edwards, Edward Taylor, Cotton Mather—reached its most dramatic development in the hands of Herman Melville, Nathaniel Hawthorne and Edgar Allan Poe. . . . [Hitchcock's] dark view of man more closely resembles the New England Puritan view.

Furthermore, in his earlier book Spoto does at least imply that Wilder had some influence: "Thornton Wilder's scenario, supervised and finalized by Hitchcock himself, in a sense reveals the dark side of *Our Town*."[84]

Authorship aside, *Shadow of a Doubt* is universally regarded as one of Hitchcock's best films, and Wilder scholars are beginning to examine the screenplay as a Wilder work of some note.[85] Though working in a medium more intrinsically realistic than theater and collaborating with a director whose films were often expressionistically Freudian in their representation of deviant behavior (e.g., *Psycho*), Wilder's screenplay draws upon the Puritan narrative tradition and dramatizes the rhetoric of the American jeremiad to make *Shadow of a Doubt* an affirmative response to the national and global crisis.

Without a minister-like character such as the Stage Manager in *Our Town* or characters who at times appear to speak to the audience as actors do in *The Skin of Our Teeth,* in *Shadow of a Doubt* Wilder delivers the lament, invocation of the past, and reaffirmation of the errand—the definitive rhetorical components of the American jeremiad—solely through dramatic means: plot, character, and dialogue.[86] The opening scene introduces the audience to Uncle Charlie (played by Joseph Cotten) as a man who is being pursued by two other men (perhaps criminals, perhaps police—we don't know yet). Learning of Uncle Charlie's plan to visit his sister's family, which includes "Young Charlie," we are next shown images of what looks to be an average small town—Santa Rosa, California—and an average family—the Newtons. Young Charlie, who is the eldest child of Joe and Emma Newton, turns out to be a young woman (played by Teresa Wright) recently graduated from

84. Spoto, *The Art of Alfred Hitchcock: Fifty Years of His Motion Pictures,* 134; Spoto, *The Darkside of Genius: Life of Alfred Hitchcock,* 140. Interestingly, some Hitchcock critics praise and blame Wilder for both the strengths and the weaknesses of the screenplay (e.g., Rohmer and Chabrol), while others blame only Hitchcock (e.g., Phillips), but all agree that this was Hitchcock's most American film, due to his collaboration with Wilder.

85. See Blank, "Wilder, Hitchcock, and *Shadow of a Doubt*."

86. One Hitchcock scholar describes the film's mode in terms close to this study's: "Rhetorically, *Shadow of a Doubt* takes the form of a theatrical demonstration that is also a serious lesson" (William Rothman, *Hitchcock—The Murderous Gaze,* 179).

high school. Like Emily in *Our Town,* Young Charlie is said to have been the smartest girl in her class at school, having won a debate. Indeed there are many similarities between *Our Town* and *Shadow of a Doubt,* beginning with the towns themselves.

The California setting is attributed more to the film industry's location in Hollywood, but it should also be recalled that Wilder spent a substantial part of his childhood in Berkeley, California. However, the original choice for the town in *Shadow of a Doubt* was, according to Blank, Hamden, Connecticut, where Wilder and his family lived in the "The House *The Bridge* Built" beginning in the late 1920s. There are allusions to more familiar Wilder territory in the film; for example, according to Wilder's film treatment of *Shadow of a Doubt* in his papers at Beinecke, the opening scenes take place in Jersey City and Passaic, New Jersey. Regardless of the west coast setting, Hitchcock and Wilder scholars agree that Santa Rosa is the equivalent of Grover's Corners; for example, Spoto notes, "Santa Rosa looks . . . no different from Grover's Corners, even as the horror unfolds," while Blank states that if Santa Rosa is Grover's Corners forty years later, we see "the last days of innocence before World War II."[87]

Besides the obvious similarity between dramatic genres, there are also stylistic and technical similarities between *Shadow of a Doubt* and *Our Town.* William Rothman describes the scenes in the film that show two neighbors discussing murder plots as "vaudeville turns [that] stop Hitchcock's show. But for Hitchcock to allow his show to be stopped by a framed piece of theater is also for him to show his own hand. And these characters are stand-ins for philosophical positions in a complex discourse that is, at one level, a reflection on the film itself," which sounds very much like both *Our Town* and *The Skin of Our Teeth.* Rothman describes Hitchcock's shooting of the scene on the train at the beginning of *Shadow of a Doubt* again almost as if it were on a stage: "The camera moves in to frame a black curtain that shields a compartment from our view. Charles, masquerading as the sick 'Mr. Otis,' is behind this curtain, which serves as an emblem of his mystery and capacity for theater." Furthermore, Rothman writes, "It's as though Charles . . . also manifests a power to direct the camera," making him sound like the Stage Manager. Later, Rothman describes Uncle Charlie as "directing" Young Charlie to push him off the train—an unconscious death wish. Even the minister's eulogy is reminiscent of the Stage Manager's "something eternal" speech in Act Three of *Our Town:* "He came into our community. . . . The beauty of their souls, the sweetness of their character, live on with us for-

---

87. Blank, "*Shadow of a Doubt*"; Spoto, *Art of Alfred Hitchcock,* 140; Blank, "Wilder, Hitchcock, and *Shadow of a Doubt,*" 415.

ever." But it is *Shadow of a Doubt*'s similarity to *Our Town* and *The Skin of Our Teeth* in appropriating the Puritan rhetoric of crisis that makes the film part of the Wilder canon and part of his response to global crisis.[88]

Early in *Shadow of a Doubt*, Young Charlie sounds the lament of the American jeremiad, which she generalizes beyond her own ennui: "Have you ever stopped to think that a family should be the most wonderful thing in the world and that this family's just gone to pieces. . . . We just sort of go along and nothing happens. We've been in a terrible rut. . . . What's going to be our future?"[89] Trying to encourage her with a sign of the family's economic progress, her father says, "Come now, Charlie, things aren't as bad as that. The bank gave me a raise last January." However, Charlie isn't concerned with materialism; she speaks more in terms of spiritualism: "Money. How can you talk about money when I'm talking about souls. . . . Guess we'll just have to wait for a miracle or something. All I'm waiting for now is a miracle." Her father thinks she is "just under the weather," but for Charlie the crisis is more serious, as indicated by the language she uses: "I know a wonderful person who'll come and shake us all up—just the one to save us. . . . All this time there's been one right person to save us." Wilder calls attention to this language by having Charlie's mother remark on her choice of words: "Have you gone crazy? What do you mean 'save us'?" which also introduces a motif in the film overall: has Young Charlie, later Uncle Charlie, and—allegorically—the world gone crazy?

The religious underpinning of Young Charlie's crisis is further developed when she learns that at the same time she had decided to telegram Uncle Charlie to come save them, he had telegrammed them that he was coming for a visit. She asks the telegraph clerk if she believes in telepathy and then says to herself as she walks down the street, barely containing her joy, "He heard me, he heard me." At this point in the film it seems as if Uncle Charlie will be a Christ figure on the allegorical level; as Rothman notes, "To Charlie, Charles *is* divine."[90] However, the dramatic irony created by the opening scene of Uncle Charlie being pursued perhaps by the police has the audience already skeptical about just how divine this worldly relative is.

Uncle Charlie arrives in Santa Rosa and is welcomed to the small community as a successful businessman from the east, the member of his and Emma's family who made it big. But Uncle Charlie brings secrets and danger

---

88. Rothman, *Hitchcock*, 184, 187, 190, 240; *Our Town* quoted in Rothman, *Hitchcock*, 243.

89. To my knowledge, the script of *Shadow of a Doubt* has never been published. The dialogue is transcribed here from the MCA Home Video videocassette of the Universal film.

90. Rothman, *Hitchcock*, 187.

with him from the outside world, as shown when he tears out an article from the evening newspaper that had alarmed him and then tries to cover up having done so. That something is disturbing him deeply is confirmed when, like Young Charlie, Uncle Charlie expresses the jeremiad lament and invocation of the past as a golden age in response to being shown photographs of his sister and himself as children: "Everybody was sweet and pretty then, the whole world. Wonderful world. Not like the world today. Not like the world now. 'S great to be young then." The opening scenes of Wilder's screenplay thus establish that the two principal characters in the film share first names and an inexplicable bond, which will ultimately fuse their two personal crises on the narrative level into one world crisis on the allegorical level.[91]

In *The American Jeremiad,* Bercovitch explains how allegorical representation became a subsequent form of the jeremiad in nineteenth-century American literature: "The symbol [of America] set free titanic creative energies in our classic writers, and it confined their freedom to the terms of the American myth. . . . It is true that as keepers of the dream they could internalize the myth. Like the latter-day Puritan Jeremiahs, they could offer themselves as the symbol incarnate, and so relocate America—transplant the entire national enterprise, en masse—into the mind and imagination of the exemplary American." In *Shadow of a Doubt,* the entire national enterprise is transplanted into the exemplary American family. The day after Uncle Charlie's arrival, his sister Emma Newton announces that two men employed by the government to take a national poll are going to interview the Newtons as a "typical American family," despite her having told him that they were not a typical family. This scene introduces another issue: how typical or representative are the Newtons, especially Uncle Charlie and Young Charlie? This uncertainty creates an ambivalent tone in the film toward being "typical." She is called a "strange girl" by Uncle Charlie; his opinions are said to be "not average" by Young Charlie. The handsome young detective posing as the poll-taker (played by MacDonald Carey) responds to Young Charlie's uncertainty about the value of being an average girl in an average family: "Average families are the best. Look at me; I'm from an average family." In the era of this film, a police officer would have represented, for the most part, society at its best, a protector of the public good.[92]

After the detective reveals who he really is and tells Young Charlie that he

---

91. To underscore this relationship between them, Young Charlie is so enamored with her uncle that she says to him, "We're like twins."

92. Bercovitch, *American Jeremiad,* 180. Of course that image of policemen was beginning to change in cinema with the advent of film noir, but 1942, when Wilder and Hitchcock were writing *Shadow of a Doubt,* was still too early for the more cynical view of policemen and police work to have established itself.

and his partner think Uncle Charlie is the notorious "Merry Widow Murderer," the detective's affirmation of average families is seen as a contradiction to Uncle Charlie's naturalistic view: "Horrible. Faded, fat, greedy women. . . . Are they alive, human? Or are they fat, wheezing animals? And what happens to animals when they get too fat and too old?" The dark side of Wilder's microcosmic portrait in *Our Town,* expressed by Simon Stimson's bitter condemnation of humanity in the cemetery scene of Act Three, is echoed in the following speech by Uncle Charlie, when the possibility that he is the killer is brought out in the open between him and Young Charlie for the first time: "What do you know, really? You're just an ordinary little girl living in an ordinary little town. . . . [on an] ordinary little day [with] ordinary little dreams, and I brought you nightmares. You live in a dream. You're a sleepwalker, blind. How do you know what the world is like? Do you know the world is a foul sty? Do you know if you ripped the fronts off houses you'd find swine? The world's a hell; what does it matter what happens in it?"[93]

Wilder's juxtaposition of Uncle Charlie's condemnation of the ordinary with the defense of average, ordinary people as expressed by the detective and Young Charlie may once again be a remnant of the Calvinistic Puritans' dichotomy of the human race; that is, Young Charlie is elect, Uncle Charlie is reprobate.[94] Evidence for reading this dualism in Puritan terms occurs in a later exchange between the two Charlies. Uncle Charlie sneers, "How's church, Charlie? Count the house? Turn anybody away?" Young Charlie replies, "No, room enough for everyone." He retorts, "Show's been running for such a long time, thought attendance would be falling off." Clearly, Uncle Charlie is no supporter of organized religion. In addition to representing the reprobate, Uncle Charlie may also function as another of Wilder's allegorical representations of Satan, as we saw in an earlier Satanic character in *The Bridge of San Luis Rey* (a character who was an admirer and user of women and also named Uncle—Uncle Pio). As the Merry Widow Murderer, Uncle Charlie does represent a type who commits malicious violence, even if the modern classification is "pathological" rather than "evil."

To further support this reading of Uncle Charlie, Hitchcock scholars have

93. In "The Second Ranke Accused," where Satan accosts the Elect, Taylor employs a style and rhythm similar to Uncle Charlie's: "Your Faith's a Phancy; Fear a Slavery./ Your Hope is Vain, Patience Stupidity./ Your Love is Carnall, selfish, set on toyes:/ Your Pray'res are Prattle, or Tautologies./ Your Hearts are full of sins both Small and Greate:/ They are as full as is an Egge of meate./ Your Holy Conference and talkings do/ But for a Broken Piece of Non-Sense go" (*GD,* 69).

94. In discussing another film in comparison to *Shadow of a Doubt,* Hitchcock said, "This picture [*Strangers on a Train*], just like *Shadow of a Doubt,* is systematically built around the figure 'two'" (François Truffaut, *Hitchcock,* 147). In addition, Spoto provides a lengthy list of pairs in the film (*Dark Side of Genius,* 263).

interpreted him in much the same way. For example, James McLaughlin compares Uncle Charlie to Dracula; Gene D. Phillips notes Uncle Charlie's Satanic qualities; and Eric Rohmer classifies Uncle Charlie as a "damned man" and Young Charlie as an "angel." Even Hitchcock understood the character as symbolizing evil. Near the beginning of the film in the shot showing the arrival of Uncle Charlie's train, a massive cloud of black smoke blocks out the sun and casts the train station in shadow. In an interview with Hitchcock, François Truffaut asserts, "The black smoke implies that the devil was coming to town"; Hitchcock replies, "Exactly."[95] Smoke is a visual motif linked to Uncle Charlie throughout *Shadow of a Doubt:* we see him smoking cigarettes several times, once blowing smoke rings; the train he rides on smokes, and the car in the garage smokes the second time Uncle Charlie tries to murder Young Charlie. In the context of this reading of Wilder's works, one might even interpret Uncle Charlie running from the law as a reprobate running from a wrathful Calvinist God, since we saw the police serve that allegorical function in *The Trumpet Shall Sound.* Finally, as noted before, Uncle Charlie resembles Simon Stimson in his bitterness and his view of people and life. He also sounds like Henry (Cain) in *The Skin of Our Teeth;* at least in Act Three, Henry could be a younger Uncle Charlie.

Wilder's resolution of the conflict between the two Charlies combines with the final speeches of the film to form the American jeremiad's call for a renewal of the errand by reaffirming the everyday, ordinary life, as in *Our Town,* and the national and global enterprise, which had been interrupted first by the Great Depression and then by World War Two. After failing at two earlier attempts to kill Young Charlie, who has come to suspect that he is indeed the Merry Widow Murderer, Uncle Charlie tries to throw her off a train, a symbol of personal and national progress Wilder employed previously in *Pullman Car Hiawatha* and *Heaven's My Destination.* In the ensuing struggle, she shoves Uncle Charlie onto a parallel track in the path of another train. Symbolically, Good does finally crush Evil underneath the wheels of (moral) progress. The film then cuts to the Congregational church in Santa Rosa in which Uncle Charlie's funeral service is taking place (apparently the town was not informed as to his true identity). Wilder dramatizes, and as an American Jeremiah even prophesies, that such exceptions to the American and human norms as Uncle Charlie and Hitler will eventually fall, and the world will continue on the right track.[96] The brief denouement of

95. McLaughlin, "All in the Family: Alfred Hitchcock's *Shadow of a Doubt*," 142; Phillips, *Alfred Hitchcock,* 105; Rohmer, *Hitchcock: The First Forty-Four Films,* 72; Truffaut, *Hitchcock,* 111.

96. Blank concludes that in Uncle Charlie Wilder was "exploring the fascist mind and preparing himself for his own encounter with evil when he went to war" ("Wilder, Hitchcock, and *Shadow of a Doubt,*" 415).

Shadow of a Doubt reinforces the optimism of the plot resolution. As the funeral oration for Uncle Charlie is spoken in the background, Young Charlie tells the detective, "He thought the world was a horrible place. He couldn't have been very happy ever. He didn't trust people; seemed to hate them; hated the whole world. He said that people like us had no idea what the world was really like." The detective replies, "It's not quite as bad as that. Sometimes it needs a lot of watching; seems to go crazy every now and then . . . like your Uncle Charlie." The detective's moral to the story signifies the return to ordinary daily life, reaffirming that Uncle Charlie was indeed an aberration.[97]

Thus, in *Shadow of a Doubt,* Wilder reassures the moviegoing audience that the twentieth century's mid-life crisis (two world wars and a depression within a twenty-five-year period) was only *temporary* insanity. The typical American family within the story has, in a sense, been purified; the human race and the world as represented by the typical American family and the typical small town have been ritually affirmed in the last of Wilder's dramatic jeremiads.

As an American Jeremiah, Thornton Wilder did not despair that the human story was nearing a tragic conclusion; rather, he affirmed in a particularly American manner the continuing progress of God's plot—the providential determination of history. Wilder's dramatic jeremiads did not merely lament the current state of affairs; they also testified to the progress made in the past and reaffirmed, not just for America, but for the entire human race, the errand into the temporal wilderness—the future.

97. Rothman points out that the detective doesn't speak for Hitchcock when he says the world is all right, it just needs watching (*Hitchcock,* 244); right—he speaks for Wilder.

Five

Cold War Wilderness

The Dark Night of Wilder's Puritan Soul

If the historian is still to be allowed to point to a controlling "myth" of America, then that myth is one of estrangement and bewilderment and the accompanying idea of the wilderness rather than that theme threaded through so many of the classical studies of American culture, the myth of the garden. The wilderness, and all of the psychological implications that the word "wilderness" allows, has provided American writing, especially American autobiographical writing, with a distinctive character of trauma from the seventeenth century to the present, whereas the garden rests as a pastoral retreat where no effort or will need be applied, where no work, in other words, need occur and therefore no change, the wilderness can confront the American as a demonic otherness. Literally, in Puritan writings, America was the place of Satan.

–John O. King III, *The Iron of Melancholy: Structures of Spiritual Conversion in America from the Puritan Conscience to Victorian Neurosis*

Following World War II his later plays of *The Seven Ages of Man* and *The Seven Deadly Sins* reveal a darker tone and the playwright creating new ways to capture the mood of cynicism, anxiety and self-indulgence he observed in postwar Americans. He seems to be conscious of a growing amount of crudeness and aggression in the world. Or are these simply the work of an older playwright with a different sensibility? Whatever their emotional or philosophical impetus these one-acts are edgier, and there is a hardness to the edge, a sharpness.

–Tazewell Thompson, "In Search of Wilder," in *Wilder Rediscovered*

In the 1950s Thornton Wilder was a highly regarded American writer, having had five novels published and six original plays or translations of others' plays produced in New York.[1] He had won three Pulitzer Prizes and various other awards. And he was revered abroad, as the many translations and productions of *Our Town* and *The Skin of Our Teeth* in postwar Europe attest. Even *The Merchant of Yonkers*, his farce that had failed critically and commercially in 1938, was successfully revived as *The Matchmaker* in 1954, vindicating his opinion that the production, not the script, had caused the play's initial failure. Thus, by the time he had reached his fifties, Thornton Wilder was sitting atop the literary and theatrical worlds. Why, then, did his personal and professional mood sour during the 1950s when he should have been able to survey his accomplishments and pronounce, like the Stage Manager in *Pullman Car Hiawatha*, "Very good"?

There are several potential causes, both personal and historical, of Wilder's darker outlook after the war. One possibility would be that it resulted from what he saw and heard during his tour of duty in World War Two, or perhaps it was prompted by the invention and use of the atomic bomb on the Japanese cities of Hiroshima and Nagasaki. It could have been the persecution of left-wing intellectuals and artists by Senator McCarthy and HUAC, which Arthur Miller famously represented in the form of the Salem witch trials in his play *The Crucible*, itself a testament to the continuity of Puritanism in American culture. On a personal level, Wilder's mother, who had been his inspiration from childhood, died in 1946, as did his friend Gertrude Stein. Also, his sister Charlotte had to be institutionalized beginning in 1941. A few Wilder scholars attribute his darker mood to a downswing in his writing career; according to Goldstone, *The Ides of March* (1948) was ignored by serious literary critics,[2] and the 1955 British production of *The Alcestiad*, his Greek tragedy trilogy, was panned, and thus didn't transfer to Broadway. Some studies have suggested that Wilder's more pessimistic outlook was the result of disappointment that he hadn't written more plays and novels. More specifically, he could have been frustrated with his failure to bring his play *The Emporium*

---

1. In addition to *The Trumpet Shall Sound, Our Town, The Merchant of Yonkers,* and *The Skin of Our Teeth,* Wilder translated Obey's *Le Viol de Lucrèce* for a 1932 production, and he adapted Ibsen's *A Doll's House* for a 1937 production. See Martin Blank, "Broadway Production History."

2. "The indifferent reception to his novel rendered a serious injury to Wilder's morale. . . . By the early summer of 1948, aged fifty-one, he had the depressing sense that his day had come and gone" (Richard H. Goldstone, *Thornton Wilder: An Intimate Portrait,* 221). But the novel itself was already manifesting Wilder's darker mood; Mildred Kuner saw *The Ides of March* as "the only one which bore traces of skepticism, even a pessimism, seldom associated with Wilder" (*Thornton Wilder: The Bright and the Dark,* 28).

and other projects to completion.[3] It also has been suggested that Wilder was denied the Nobel Prize because of Joseph Campbell and H. M. Robinson's accusations that *The Skin of Our Teeth* was plagiarized from James Joyce's *Finnegans Wake*.[4]

Although exactly what was wrong with Wilder after he returned from the war is not perfectly clear, the comments of others and of Wilder himself make it seem like some sort of malaise or depression. In a letter to his family, he wrote that he had told Archibald MacLeish that he "was a shattered man." Wilder's letter to Stein of July 20, 1945, doesn't explain the exact cause, but it ends with an ominous suggestion of a cure: "The doctors say I must take six months to a year's rest. . . . What's my sickness? I don't know. Everything and nothing . . . There's nothing organic the matter. There's nothing that a revolver can't cure."[5] In a later letter Wilder described his condition in terms of mental health: "I seem only now to be emerging from a long torpor and misanthropy and paralysis of the will. My outward health soon recovered . . . [,] but the psychological effects have dragged on for a long time." An amateur diagnosis of Wilder's postwar condition might be that he was depressed, but it seems to have been related to the state of the world, not merely the vicissitudes of his career or personal life. In a 1961 *New York Times* interview, Wilder told Arthur Gelb, "Because we live in the twentieth century overrun by very real anxiety, we have to use the comic spirit. No statement of gravity can be adequate to the gravity of the age in which we live."[6]

3. In response to my letter querying him about the possible cause of Wilder's postwar malaise, Donald Gallup wrote,

> Certainly Thornton's failure to complete *The Emporium*—and other projects!—must have played a part in any "malaise" he was feeling. And he continued to be unhappy with himself over the hours and days squandered on Joyce and Lope de Vega. The time spent self-indulgently on those fascinating projects became, doubtless, after the war, an even more persistent cause for regret as he came gradually to recognize that the years before him were limited. (Letter to the author, January 28, 1998)

4. Virtually every book-length study of Wilder discusses this controversy; for a summary, see Gilbert A. Harrison, *The Enthusiast: A Life of Thornton Wilder*, 230–34. Suffice it to say here that my point about the supposed influence of Gertrude Stein on *Our Town* applies to Wilder's alleged plagiarism of Joyce as well. Everything he needed in order to write *The Skin of Our Teeth* he had already demonstrated in his earlier works, all of which were published by 1935: his novels *The Cabala, The Bridge of San Luis Rey,* and *Heaven's My Destination;* and the plays *The Long Christmas Dinner, The Happy Journey to Trenton and Camden,* and, especially, *Pullman Car Hiawatha. Finnegans Wake* was first published in its entirety in 1939.

5. Edward Burns and Ulla E. Dydo, with William Rice, eds., *The Letters of Gertrude Stein and Thornton Wilder,* 322 n. 3, 323. This is the same "cure" that the protagonist of *The Wreck on the Five-Twenty-Five,* composed circa 1957 as part of the play cycle *The Seven Deadly Sins,* reveals he had been contemplating (*CSPTW I,* 152).

6. Burns and Dydo, *Letters,* 330; Wilder quoted in Martin Blank, "Introduction" to *Critical Essays on Thornton Wilder,* 23 n. 129.

One other possibility, suggested in a letter from Wilder's sister Isabel to Stein, is that Wilder was not writing while supporting the war effort overseas: "I can only add that it is for the best that he is not going to Paris. He is still far from well, though his improvement is noticeable. Now if he can only get discharged from the Army and have three months or six to write his play [*The Alcestiad*], he will be a whole man again. To do his own work for a year on end will cure him, nothing else." Nevertheless, after he wrote *The Alcestiad,* Wilder's worldview still seemed uncharacteristically grim. That is, his postwar works *The Ides of March* and *The Alcestiad* do not manifest an outlook that could be characterized by the term "cosmic optimism," and given that they appeared seven years apart, Wilder's darker vision was not a phase limited to the years immediately after the war. Indeed, one could argue that *The Ides of March* and *The Alcestiad* dramatize a cosmic pessimism.[7] It is almost as if life were imitating art: Wilder seemed as disillusioned as his character George Antrobus was when he returned from the war in Act Three of *The Skin of Our Teeth.* However, Wilder did not regain his enthusiasm for work and life as easily or as quickly as Antrobus.[8]

What may seem contradictory in the context of this study is the possibility that this more pessimistic tone in Wilder's postwar works originated within the Puritan heritage itself. Although on the communal level the Puritans' outlook was characterized by cosmic optimism, except for periods in which hard times were interpreted as God's displeasure with the acts of the saints, it was on the individual level that Puritan theology had a negative impact on Puritan psychology. As with other aspects of Puritan theology, ideology, and aesthetics, the dark night of the Puritan soul is illustrated by Edward Taylor's *God's Determinations.*

The Dark Side of Puritanism

Although Puritans often expressed their confidence in being God's chosen people, the writings of the seventeenth and eighteenth centuries show

7. Burns and Dydo, *Letters,* 325. *The Ides of March* and *The Alcestiad* are not analyzed here not only because of their more pessimistic tone, but also because in his last full-length play and his first novel in thirteen years, Wilder wrote narratives with classical settings and characters, as in his 1930 novel, *The Woman of Andros.* These texts are not totally devoid of Puritan traces, but they are too few and insubstantial to warrant the space needed for close reading.

8. For further speculation about the cause of Wilder's postwar condition, see Goldstone, *Intimate Portrait,* 204–10, 235–44. However, Malcolm Cowley's point concerning such speculations about Wilder's state of mind should be well taken: "What I wanted to write was a philippic against the type of academic reviewer who sets himself up in business as an amateur psychiatrist" (Letter to Thornton Wilder, October 21, 1975, Thorn-

occasional doubt in that belief or in an individual writer's own election. As David Leverenz writes, "It is easy to find images of the wrathful patriarchal God . . . ; yet that God, like Puritan language, is curiously two-faced: a wrathful father to sinners, a nurturing mother to saints." That is, certain passages in Puritan writing manifest a fear and despair that could be quite pessimistic. In fact, a dark night of the soul, as Taylor dramatized in *God's Determinations,* was to be expected in every Puritan who was truly elect: "For the elect, life will indeed be a constant struggle to maintain their state of grace, though they can be assured of successful perseverance to the end. One of the responsibilities—in fact, one of the 'evidences' that one is chosen—is that one will be the object of assaults by Satan."[9]

Furthermore, Puritans saw a connection between a real Devil and a depressed state of mind: "Melancholy served as the devil's last effort to haunt those whom he could not allure." It is important to note that King uses "melancholy" in the seventeenth-century sense, most famously employed in Robert Burton's *Anatomy of Melancholy,* which is close to the modern concepts of depression or neurosis. King demonstrates in his study that the central metaphor of the errand into the wilderness "has provided American writing, especially American autobiographical writing, with a distinctive character of trauma from the seventeenth century to the present . . . [that] accounts for the idea of a distressed American character." King delineates how the cultural paradigm of the wilderness was both without and within the Puritan pilgrim: "The wilderness, most simply, is the place where spiritual conversion occurs"; it is either "conceived externally as wilderness and desert or internally as bewilderment and desertion." Thus King attributes the darker mood or tragic mode or melancholy tone of much of American literature to the Calvinistic theology of the Puritans; however, unlike scholars who have made the same point, he argues from a psychoanalytic point of view. But even Sacvan Bercovitch, proceeding from a New Historicist approach, describes in almost pathological terms the Puritans' wrestling with their Calvinistic doctrines: "The struggle entailed a relentless psychic strain; and in New England, where the theocracy insisted upon it with unusual vigor—where anxiety about election was not

---

ton Wilder Papers, Beinecke Rare Books and Manuscripts Library, Yale University). Cowley was referring to Goldstone's book.

9. Leverenz, *The Language of Puritan Feeling,* 2; Perry D. Westbrook, *Free Will and Determination in American Literature,* 18. For other studies that have examined the emotional complexities of Puritan writing, see Daniel B. Shea Jr., *The Spiritual Autobiography in Early America* (Princeton: Princeton University Press, 1968); Patricia Caldwell, *The Puritan Conversion Narrative: The Beginnings of American Expression* (Cambridge: Cambridge University Press, 1983); and King, *Iron of Melancholy.*

only normal but mandatory—hysteria, breakdowns, and suicides were not uncommon."[10]

Karl Keller sees Edward Taylor not as representative of a monolithic tradition of cosmic optimism, but of a strain of gloominess in our cultural unconscious manifested in certain American writers of the nineteenth century:

> In time [the Connecticut Valley Way] came to give a dark cast to Puritanism. We can look back and see that there develops a Hooker—Taylor—Edwards tradition of the long, deep journey into the self that contained an energy that inevitably produced art in each—and later in others: Emily Dickinson, Hawthorne, Melville. Taylor is important to that emerging tradition for the exemplary way he used language to move deeper into himself. We can also look back and see the development of a concept of tragedy in the Valley, a concept always latent in Puritan thought but seldom admitted to or explored. . . . The tragic sense, unique to the Valley and absolutely missing as the thought to the east of Amherst moved from Covenant theology to Unitarian liberalism and Transcendentalism, that led Emily Dickinson, as it had led Taylor, to face the realities of human experience and entertain the possibility of an inhumane cosmos. [Taylor's poetry is] one example of the hard work of the first century that went into what Hawthorne, Melville, and Emily Dickinson were to identify as the very grain of the American character. . . . When Taylor writes . . . , the "darker" side of American literature has its beginning.[11]

The microcosmic scene between Soul and Saint in *God's Determinations* dramatizes the emotional burden of Calvinistic theology, but the narration of the macrocosmic level, God's plot, also manifests Puritan angst.

In the most abstract terms, conversion begins with conviction of guilt for sins, but Taylor's portrait of Man as he begins his spiritual journey is no mere acknowledgment and regret for wrongdoing; instead, in "The Effects of Man's Apostacy" (*GD,* 34–35) Man is attacked by Sin, "a thousand Griefs," and Feare, all of whom, along with God even, have him surrounded so that "He knows not what to have, nor what to loose, / Nor what to do, nor what to take or Choose" (35). He "runs like a Madman . . . . For Nature in this Pannick

---

10. King, *Iron of Melancholy,* 36, 2, 2; Bercovitch, *The Puritan Origins of the American Self,* 23. In *Errand into the Wilderness,* Perry Miller makes a similar point:

> Yet the spectacle of these men struggling in the coils of their doctrine, desperately striving on the one hand to maintain the subordination of humanity to God without unduly abasing human values, and on the other hand to vaunt the powers of the human intellect without losing the sense of divine transcendence, vividly recreates what might be called the central problem of the seventeenth century as it was confronted by the Puritan mind. (74)

11. Keller, *The Only Kangaroo among the Beauty: Emily Dickinson and America,* 46, 59, 138.

feare scarce gives / Him life enough, to let him feel he lives" (35). Following a debate by Justice and Mercy, we next see Man "With Trembling joynts, and Quivering Lips" (43) before the court of Almighty. Thus Taylor depicts the Puritan awareness of sin as an extreme state of fear (of punishment, damnation) and a paralyzing panic, which Man seems helpless to escape. That is, throughout the rest of the narrative the protagonist seeks to overcome these debilitating emotions, but he continually returns to this original state of fear until near the end of the work, where he finally experiences the elation of assurance. The evidence for this apparent lack of progress lies in the recurrence of the word "fear" in the text (too many instances to cite) and the confrontation of the allegorical character Feare even as Soul enters the gate to church fellowship, after which "joy conquours Fear" (104). Yet it is difficult for the reader to forget the extremity of Man's fear, even after he has been encouraged by Christ and the Saint; from a twentieth-century perspective the Puritan mind seems neurotically obsessed with self-analysis of guilt and thus in a depressed state.

This "between a rock and a hard place" aspect of Puritan doctrine has been noted in the works of other Puritan writers as well. Regarding Thomas Hooker, Sargent Bush Jr. has said, "He creates a peculiar dilemma between heaven and hell, grace and damnation, the Word and the world. . . . Hooker manages to convey the eternal truth that while there is life there is pressure and tension between these opposing forces. His words give a feel for as well as a literal analysis of this tension." But what was tension for Hooker is torture for Taylor. *God's Determinations* even uses the image of being stretched on the rack at several points to suggest this dichotomous structure of the doctrine, which William J. Scheick sees best illustrated in Taylor's work by the jawbones metaphor. In the following passage Satan predicts that Man will be crushed, eaten alive by Christ on the top and Satan on the bottom: "'He [Christ] will become your foe; you then shall bee / Flanckt of by him before, behinde by mee. . . . What will you do when you shall squezed bee/ Between such Monstrous Gyants Jaws as Wee?'" (49). For those who might fear they are reprobate (damned) like Man/Soul in *God's Determinations,* every day is Judgment Day.[12]

Undoubtedly there would have been ample cause of fear and depression for the average seventeenth-century Puritan struggling for survival against the wilderness and worrying about the consequences of not being admitted to church membership; however, the Puritan doctrine itself must have been

---

12. Bush, *The Writings of Thomas Hooker: Spiritual Adventure in Two Worlds,* 183. See Scheick, "The Jawbones Schema of Edward Taylor's *Gods Determinations,*" in *Puritan Influences in American Literature,* ed. Emory Elliott, 38–54.

partially or even largely responsible for the difficulty of achieving spiritual assurance and the resulting abatement of fear and depression. Therefore, Wilder's own dark night of the soul may have been part of his cultural/psychological "programming" inherited from the Puritans.

Of course Wilder wasn't the only postwar writer with a pessimistic view of civilization and the universe as a whole. In popular culture, film noir was having its heyday during the 1940s and 1950s. In the late 1940s, Eugene Ionesco began writing plays that would later be christened Theatre of the Absurd; Samuel Beckett followed Ionesco's lead in the 1950s. The implicit philosophical outlook of both these Paris-based writers is nihilistic. But if Wilder's macrocosmic view had soured, what about his opinion of the microcosm, of the United States that he had praised throughout his works of the 1920s, 1930s, and 1940s? An examination of *Our Century,* an obscure dramatic piece written almost immediately after Wilder's return from the war, answers this question. We will see that this one-act play still manifests textual traces of American Puritanism, but it expresses a more cynical view of America than any of Thornton Wilder's earlier works.

Our Century

Written and produced for the Century Association's centennial celebration in 1947, *Our Century* is a twenty-page, one-act play in three scenes. The title would seem to indicate that the subject was the very club of which Wilder was a member, but it could, of course, refer to the twentieth century, which is often called "the American Century," as well. To legitimize analyzing this slight work, Wilder himself alludes to the Bible in *Our Century* when a waiter takes away a club member's plate of food and the member comments, "The Lord giveth and the Lord taketh away." The four waiters then reply in unison, "Blessed be the name of the Lord" (16), parodying the book of Job (1:21). Shortly thereafter one member refers to their attendance at "Vestry meetings of St. Polycorp's" (17).[13]

Despite its farcical tone, *Our Century* exhibits a few of the traces of Puritanism discussed in Wilder's earlier works. For example, the four major characters—members of the Century club, a kind of American cabala—are named Matthew, Mark, Luke, and John—businessmen antitypes to the New Testament types of the Gospel authors-apostles. Given that these characters can

---

13. *Our Century* was published in a limited edition of one thousand copies by the Century Association in 1947. Quotations are from copy number 857, which I discovered in the University of Wisconsin–Madison's library in 1989 when I was doing my initial research on Wilder from a Puritan perspective.

hardly be considered more than abstract types themselves, one might argue
that they dramatize a failed American typology in which instead of a progressive reincarnation of significant figures we see a regressive diminishment
to nothing more concrete than names: Matthew, Mark, Luke, John.[14] Their
stature as a controlling elite or elect is indicated early in the play, as
Matthew says to the others, "It looks as though it's up to us to settle the fate
of New York City" (1). The ensuing inane dialogue expresses the Puritan
ideas that are rendered with high seriousness elsewhere in Wilder:

> JOHN: That's one of the fine things about the Century Club. The effective
> work of our great country is not done in committee or in the legislative bod-
> ies in Washington; but it's done right here. I thought that was very good,
> Matthew,—the way you settled the fate of the United Nations at lunch.
> MATTHEW: . . . . And if we have time this afternoon, we'll just be able to set-
> tle the fates of the Southern Pacific Railroad—
> MARK: —and Columbia University.
> JOHN: Yes, our good old Century club is the powerhouse of the Nation. When
> men of world-wide influence,—like yourself, Matthew—
> MATTHEW: —and men who mold public opinion the world over, like you
> Mark—
> MARK: —Thank you, Matthew,—and men who are the true power behind
> thrones, like you, John—
> JOHN: That's very kind of you, Mark—Nor do we forget the giants of art like
> our friend, LUKE!!!
> LUKE: Very happily put, John.—Yes, little do those New Yorkers, out in the
> street, hurrying by engaged in their little self-centered occupations—little, I
> say, do they realize that their fates and the fates of their loved ones are de-
> termined within these historic walls. (1–2)

Although the determinations in this exchange are not God's, the characters'
biblical names and repetition of the word "fate" resonate beyond the literal,
microcosmic perspective, as with *The Cabala, The Bridge, Pullman Car Hiawatha, Our Town,* and *The Skin of Our Teeth,* despite the silliness of the dialogue. The skit's status as farce is further evidenced by the slapstick humor
from the start of *Our Century* to the finish. For example, all four elderly members of the club are asleep at the opening; one will wake up, shout something

14. I make this argument in my article "'Good, Better, Best, Bested': The Failure of
American Typology in *Who's Afraid of Virginia Woolf?*" in *Edward Albee: A Casebook,* ed. Bruce
Mann (New York and London: Routledge, 2003), 44–62. In Albee's masterpiece a child-
less middle-aged couple named George and Martha (after George and Martha Washington, Albee acknowledged) are appalled at the young generation in the form of Nick
and Honey, who are ontologically less substantial than their hosts, thus representing a
downward trend of individuality and other American values.

for the sake of Mark, who is hard of hearing, and then fall back asleep (1). Or Luke wakes up, adjusts his teeth, then falls back asleep (2).

Based on the stereotype of the dour Puritan, one might think that the Puritan aesthetic would be unable to produce the farcical tone in *Our Century*. However, one scene in *God's Determinations* illustrates the versatility of the dramatic form Taylor chose for representing Puritan behavior and suggesting its psychological cause. In "A Threnodiall Dialogue Between the Second and Third Ranks," Taylor lampoons the too-humble half-way members of his congregation in repartee that reveals the exaggerated self-doubts of the Puritan Everyman, now represented as Second and Third Ranks:

SECOND
There's not a Sin that is not in our Heart,
And if Occasion were, it would out start.
There's not a Precept that we have not broke,
Hence not a Promise unto us is spoke.

THIRD
Its worse with us: The Preacher speaks no word,
The Word of God no sentence doth afford;
But fall like burning Coals of Hell new blown
Upon our Souls, and on our Heads are thrown.

SECOND
Its worse with us. Behold Gods threatonings all;
Nay, Law and Gospell on our Heads do fall.
Both Hell and Heaven, God and Divell Do
With Wracking Terrours Consummate our Woe.

THIRD
We'le ne're believe that you are worse than wee,
For Worse than us wee judge no Soul can bee.
We know not where to run, nor what to doe;
Would God it was no worse with us than you.

SECOND
Than us alas! what, would you fain aspire
Out of the Frying Pan into the Fire? (74)

This satirical one-upmanship continues as each Rank tries to top the other in laying claim to supreme unworthiness of grace. The choice of a gently mocking caricature of the half-way members, rather than a pulpit-thumping, Juvenalian lashing of those uninitiated Puritans for whom it had been necessary to devise a half-way covenant in the first place, testifies to Taylor's compassion and his "stage" savvy in providing a little comic relief from the gravity of the rest of *God's Determinations*.[15] If a seventeenth-century Puritan minister could employ humor for his solemn purpose, then one of his twentieth-century literary descendants could as well. Indeed, we have already seen in Chapter Four that Wilder did present serious ideas in the actions of farcical characters in *The Matchmaker* and *The Skin of Our Teeth*.

Our Century also includes the Puritan code of the elect in the guise of democratic election, as in *Our Town* and *The Skin of Our Teeth*. In the second scene the four senior members are appalled when a new, younger member comes in; they are certain that a mistake has been made: "They elected a man who's been black-balled by eight members. . . . You see, they thought they were electing old what's-his-name's son. You know—remarkable fellow. All American football back in '30; wrote the best novel of the last twenty years; deciphered the Littite inscriptions; climbed Mt. Everest; and won the Congressional Medal" (8). As in the first scene where the word "fate" was used five times (in two and a quarter pages), in the second scene the word "elect" in some form is used four times (in five pages). In another example, after John asks what the procedure is when a wrong man has been told he is a member of the club, Matthew replies, "He gets a letter informing him of the error. But, of course, that's not enough to clear the reputation of the Club. He's probably nipped around ringing doorbells and informing his friends of his election. We can't have *that,* can we?" (10).

Given Wilder's previous use of typology and allegory, along with the presence of the four gospel authors living in present-day New York in this play, one cannot help reading the new member as a Christ figure. Luke summons a servant named Thomas (as in Doubting) to check out the new member; Thomas confirms that the young man, who for no apparent reason has said nothing since arriving on stage, is indeed a member. Failing to elicit any response from the young man or to provoke his departure, the four senior members leave the room. Again without any explanation, "The New Member rises as though dizzy; then trying to climb into chair cushions, finds a revolver and shoots himself" (11), a kind of senseless self-crucifixion that

---

15. Taylor's use of comic techniques in *God's Determinations* to uplift the spirits of his half-way members has been thoroughly analyzed by John Gatta, first in his article "The Comic Design of *Gods Determinations Touching his Elect*" and then in chapter four of his book *Gracious Laughter: The Meditative Wit of Edward Taylor*. But Gatta goes too far in his attempt to demonstrate tonal unity in *God's Determinations* by reading humor into virtually every segment. For example, I find "The Third Rank Accused" to be a chilling portrayal of Satan's subtlety, not the "comic reduction from his traditional epic stature" in the utterance of "wry quip[s]" ("Comic Design," 132, 133).

Wilder himself was perhaps considering a couple of years prior when he wrote the above-quoted letter to Stein. The allegorical implication of the action of this scene is that had these modern men been the disciples in gospel times, they would not have allowed even Christ into their circle.

In the final scene of *Our Century,* Matthew, Mark, Luke, and John enact a last supper, complete with bread and wine, but sans Christ. The concerted attempt of the club members to deceive their wives and then to keep them out of the club with a high-pressure water hose suggests that Wilder may be satirizing such exclusive clubs as the Century Association. One passage confirms that Wilder was calling attention to this kind of exclusivity. After Luke is informed that the White House is on long distance, the following exchange occurs:

> LUKE: Tell them I'll call back in November '48.
> MARK: Serves them right.
> MATT: Funny though, this Club was Democratic once.
> LUKE: Just—once. (17)

With the national references, this dialogue may also allegorically criticize America for deviating from its original egalitarian ideals, thus continuing the jeremiad lament and citation of a golden age that we saw in Wilder's dramatic works of the late 1930s and early 1940s, but here missing the affirmation of the errand into the wilderness. It is also possible that the exclusive Century Association is Wilder's metaphor for the exclusive fundamentalist Christianity that he gently satirized in *Heaven's My Destination.* One can only speculate what members of the Century Club must have made of such an incoherent play.[16] Suffice it to say here that it does not present an image of a Puritan-based America in an affirmative tone. In fact, one could almost view it as Puritan Theatre of the Absurd.[17]

16. Actually, in *The Century, 1847–1946,* a club member did describe *Our Century* and the audience of club member's reactions to it. The member calls it "a delicious, maliciuos playlet by Centurion Thornton Wilder" (292). Of the audiences for three performances of *Our Century,* he states that the first two were "explosive in [their] enthusiasm," but they "preserved shreds of decorum," though the second audience less than the first. Finally, "The midnight audience was composed entirely of howling dervishes" (293). Apparently the club members perceived no serious satire in Wilder's farcical skit.

17. As oxymoronic as the phrase "Puritan Theatre of the Absurd" seems, recall that Wilder worked with Hitchcock, a director whose philosophical perspective would seem to be closer to absurdism than to Puritanism. Furthermore, if one considers the abstract dramaturgy and farcical characters and action in Ionesco's *The Bald Soprano* or *The Chairs,* or Beckett's *Waiting for Godot* or *Endgame, Our Century* appears to be in keeping with those early absurdist plays. A few scholars have briefly noted that Wilder deserves some credit for having paved the way for the Theatre of the Absurd, but none have cared to

But if not anticipating that theatrical movement, then in *Our Century* Wilder may have anticipated the cultural revolutions that would begin with the Civil Rights movement and the Beats in the 1950s, and would explode in the 1960s with continued agitation for equal rights by African Americans, women, and gays; movements against the military draft and the Vietnam War; and the youth movement overall tied to the rise of rock 'n' roll. Indeed, each scene of *Our Century* is titled "OUR CENTURY / As [. . .] Imagine It"; the subjects of the verb "imagine" are, respectively, "Our Sons," "a New Member," and "Our Wives" (1, 7, 15). In the second scene Luke says, "Oh, Matthew . . . the new generation . . . (*all look at stranger*) push, push, push . . . nothing makes them uncomfortable; it's impossible to embarrass them. Brass, solid brass" (11). The generation gap is a prominent theme in the next Wilder works to be examined.

Our Century was obviously not a major or serious work, and it is therefore not as valid an illustration of Wilder's darker mood as his last dramatic project that was never completed: the two cycles of one-act plays titled *The Seven Deadly Sins* and *The Seven Ages of Man,* on which he worked between the late 1950s and early 1960s. Most of them are realistic depictions of twentieth-century American characters and mores in which the New England Puritan ethos and aesthetic disappear to dramatize not the American Dream reflected in television programs of the 1950s like *Father Knows Best* and *Leave It to Beaver,* but the American Nightmare. Since the *Sins* and *Ages* plays do not manifest the Puritan codes of Wilder's earlier works, there is no need to analyze all of the individual texts in depth; however, taken as a whole they should be accounted for in this study of the progress of the Puritan cultural and literary legacy in Thornton Wilder's life and oeuvre.[18]

The Seven Deadly Sins and *The Seven Ages of Man*

It is indicative of Wilder's aesthetic independence that at a time when European theater was in a nonrealistic phase that became known as the

---

pursue this issue in any depth. See Gideon Shunami, "Between the Epic and the Absurd: Brecht, Wilder, Durrenmatt, and Ionesco," 52; Ethan Mordden, *The American Theatre,* 200; Malcolm Goldstein, *The Art of Thornton Wilder,* 129; and David Castronovo, *Thornton Wilder,* 158.

18. Of course sinning is a concern of Puritanism, but the specific origin of Wilder's idea for this play series—"the Seven Deadly Sins"—is based upon Catholic theology (previously expressed in dramatic form in Medieval morality plays like *The Castle of Perseverance* and the Renaissance tragedy by Christopher Marlow, *The Tragical History of Doctor Faustus*). The Puritans did not dichotomize sin into that which is mortal and that which is venial; rather, they subscribed to the Calvinistic doctrine of total depravity.

Theatre of the Absurd, thanks to Martin Esslin's 1961 book of that title, Wilder opted for realistic characters, actions, and settings for the majority of the one-act plays that were loosely to dramatize the two themes of sinning and aging. In fact, only one of the plays is written in the abstract, presentational style of his major plays—*The Drunken Sisters.* According to Gallup, the plan for the completed *Sins* cycle was set by 1959: *The Drunken Sisters* (Gluttony), *Bernice* (Pride), *The Wreck on the Five-Twenty-Five* (Sloth), *A Ringing of Doorbells* (Envy), *In Shakespeare and the Bible* (Wrath), *Someone from Assisi* (Lust), and *Cement Hands* (Avarice). The *Ages* cycle never reached that point of development, not even in journal notes, but four plays were recovered from the Wilder archives: *Infancy, Childhood, Youth,* and *The Rivers Under the Earth* (Middle Age). Thus we have eleven of a projected fourteen one-act plays, only a few of which were published or staged until recently.[19]

Although it is too soon after their publication to have a record of scholarly analysis of the eleven one-act plays, apart from a few comments in earlier studies of Wilder based on reading them in manuscript,[20] John Guare's introduction to *Collected Short Plays* provides an indication of the plays' relationship to Wilder's other dramatic works. Referring specifically to the *Sins* cycle, Guare comments, "These seven plays are filled with the people who have not escaped by the skin of their teeth. These are the people of *Our Town* who lived long enough to learn the price you pay for staying smugly in your own Grover's Corners. Emily said, 'Oh life, you are too wonderful.' I know what these seven plays are. These are the plays if Emily had lived."[21] Guare's speculation as to how Emily would have been changed had she lived is, of course, debatable. (Perhaps she would have been overflowing with appreciation

---

From that point of view, everyone is equally guilty of being sinful; the only difference between souls is in those whom God has predestined for salvation and those for damnation.

19. Donald Gallup, "Introductory Note," in *The Collected Short Plays of Thornton Wilder Volume I,* ed. Donald Gallup and A. Tappan Wilder, 109–10. Two of the plays—*Bernice* and *The Wreck of the Five-Twenty-Five*—were performed along with *The Happy Journey to Trenton and Camden* in Germany in 1957 and subsequently published in *Yale Review* in 1994 and 1997, respectively. Three others—*Infancy, Childhood,* and *Someone from Assisi*—were performed in New York City at the Circle in the Square Theater in 1962, billed as *Plays for Bleecker Street* under Jose Quintero's direction; *Childhood* had been published in *Atlantic Monthly* in 1960. The remainder of the plays languished in Wilder's journal and other papers at the Beinecke Library at Yale until edited for publication in *The Collected Shorter Plays of Thornton Wilder Volume I* in 1997.

20. See, for example, Goldstone's *Intimate Portrait* and Castronovo's "Strange Discipline: Wilder's One-Act Experiments," in *Critical Essays on Thornton Wilder,* ed. Martin Blank, 108–15, and "Thornton Wilder and the One Deadly Sin," in *Thornton Wilder: New Essays,* ed. Martin Blank, Dalma Hunyadi Brunauer, and David Garrett Izzo, 443–54.

21. Guare, "Introduction" to *Collected Short Plays of Thornton Wilder Volume I,* ed. Gallup and Tappan, xix.

for the minutiae of daily life as a result of her epiphany that most people are blind to all that there is to experience and savor.) The character from *Our Town* who almost certainly would have written plays such as these is Simon Stimson, for they do dramatize characters who "move about in a cloud of ignorance . . . , trampling on the feelings of those . . . of those about [them]. . . . To be always at the mercy of one self-centered passion, or another. . . . Ignorance and blindness" (*OT,* 109).

As discussed at the beginning of this chapter, the reason for this difference in tone between earlier Wilder works and the cycle plays is unclear, but Guare speculates that it may be that America had changed, not Wilder; that is, he sees Wilder's mood as a reflection of the times: "The ignorance and blindness is what the optimist Wilder faced in these later plays, plays in which he struggled to find a language to reflect the despair of postwar America. . . . What's exciting about these last unpublished plays is seeing a writer trying to find a new vocabulary, a new diction, a new way of reflecting life after the war, after the dreadful fact of the atom bomb. . . . [T]he plays [were] searching out a language for the despair, the fear, the pessimism that is America's guilty secret."[22]

While virtually every other assessment of these plays regards them as just another uncompleted project in Wilder's postwar period, Kuner sees a symmetry in his career with this final foray into the theater: "Significantly, his latest, uncompleted cycle of plays, *The Seven Deadly Sins,* like *The Trumpet Shall Sound,* rests on a theological base; despite the passage of almost half a century between the two works, his signature tune is still the religious parable." And yet there is virtually no mention of religion or things metaphysical in these eleven plays, except for *Someone from Assisi,* which is about the Catholic saint, Francis of Assisi, though even in this play the focus is not on the ideas of religious faith.[23]

Two plays in the *Sins* cycle, *Bernice* and *The Wreck on the Five-Twenty-Five,* set the tone for the rest of the cycle. According to Gallup, they were conceived virtually together in 1956, and Wilder himself referred to them as dark works: "and, oh, Muse, I want one or two in lighter vein to go with these

22. Ibid, xxvi.
23. Kuner, *Bright and Dark,* 39. In 1960 Wilder wrote in his journal, "But it is not the problems of religion that are occupying me these days, but the dogmas of property, leisure, and social position" (288). One of the *Sins* plays in particular illustrates this new interest of Wilder's. In *A Ringing of Doorbells* (Envy), a character bitterly attacks the privilege of class: "Come on, Mother, she doesn't know what we're talking about. She was born ignorant . . . and her daughter went from one dance to another dance . . . and her children would have the same thing. And what right did you have to a life like that? None at all. You were born into the right cradle. That's all you did to earn it" (*CSPTW I,* 167–68). That speech is as left-wing as any by a contemporary Marxist.

horrors."[24] Rooted firmly in the microcosm, the Americans of these plays are discontent with their daily lives, but their attempts to change their circumstances only result in suffering—for them and those closest to them. While none of these characters fear that they are literally predestined for damnation by a Calvinist God like Taylor's protagonist, in these two plays we see the American dream turn to Puritan nightmare.

Bernice

Bernice is set in 1911—around the same time as much of *Our Town*. Coinciding with Wilder's childhood, the turn of the century is also approximately the period in which *The Matchmaker* and *The Trumpet Shall Sound* take place. It is almost as if Wilder were returning to that "golden age" he reminded audiences of in his two 1938 plays, *Our Town* and *The Matchmaker*, but now foregrounding the bleaker view that was mostly kept in the background before.[25] The situation—a wealthy man returns to his house from which he has been absent and has a conclusive interaction with his servant—is initially reminiscent of *The Trumpet Shall Sound;* however, on this play's judgment day it is the servant who pronounces sentence upon the master.

The action of *Bernice* primarily consists of the conversation between the main characters, Walbeck, a caucasian man of 47, and Bernice, an African American woman of 50. Through their dialogue the audience not only discovers exactly why Walbeck's wife left him and where he has been for eight years, but also that Bernice's background proves to be similar to his in some ways. Once again, the Christian name Wilder gives to his protagonist, who might have once been the all-American husband/father/businessman, is George, but this time he is a criminal, not an idealized portrait of a middle-class man. After Bernice guesses that he was in prison at Joliet, he tells her why: "I cheated two or three hundred people out of money" (*CSPTW I*, 132).[26] His time in prison does not seem to have resulted in repentance or rehabilitation; his speeches and actions demonstrate that he is enraged by his conviction and incarceration and all that resulted, as suggested by his violently

24. Wilder quoted in Gallup, "Introductory Note," 106.
25. Indeed, the argument could be made that the more pessimistic outlook of these plays from the late 1950s is less a fundamental change than a matter of degree or emphasis. John Guare also implies that the worldview in Wilder's more famous earlier works is more negative than is generally perceived: "These later plays of Thornton Wilder will only reveal the darkness in the early plays" ("Introduction," xxvii).
26. All references to the *Sins* and *Ages* plays in this chapter are to *Collected Short Plays of Thornton Wilder Volume I*, ed. Gallup and Tappan.

overturning a table and ripping up and throwing a letter from his daughter into the fireplace. When Bernice announces she has dinner prepared, he tells her to eat it herself and to bring him a bottle of rye instead. If this were George Antrobus, he would set about rebuilding his life. If he were George Brush, he might go through a period of discouragement but then would continue on his journey through life to his final destination. If he were George Gibbs—who knows what George would have been like after Emily's death, but since he already had a child to care for, one can imagine that he would have immersed himself in the daily responsibilities of a farmer and a father, probably remarrying a few years later. George Walbeck, however, merely wants to drink.

Bernice sounds like Ma Kirby from *Happy Journey:* "I'm the best cook in Chicago . . . . I've got some tomato soup that's the best tomato soup you ever ate" (130).[27] But we soon learn that Bernice, too, spent time in prison—for murder. Interestingly, she describes the effects of her crime and incarceration as fatal for her as well as her victim; of the person she was before she went to prison, Bernice says, "She's dead. When I changed my name she became dead" (133). Thus Bernice seems to have started over, except that it is not with the affirmative feeling of the Antrobuses in *The Skin of Our Teeth.* Leading her children to believe that she is literally dead, she has cut herself off completely from her life before the crime, and she and Walbeck both seem to be cut off from the spiritual view of existence simply because there are no references to that dimension of life, a rarity for a Wilder work. In fact, Ethel Waters's description of the play is consistent with Wilder's more pessimistic outlook in the *Sins* and *Ages* plays: "She complained that there was no God in *Bernice.*"[28]

Despite the distance these revelations create between the characters and the audience, Bernice and Walbeck are meant to be broadly representative, as suggested by Bernice's line, "Well, everybody's done something" (132), which sounds like a colloquial definition of original sin or total depravity. Later she says, "I hate people who don't know that lots of people is hungry and that lots of people has done bad things" (136). Furthermore, Bernice's view of lives not scarred by criminal offenses such as theirs is not an acknowledgment of superiority, moral or otherwise: "No, Mr. Walbeck, don't ask me to throw your daughter back into the trashy lives that most people live" (136). As a morality play of sorts, *Bernice* represents the deadly sin of pride, and Wilder gives us plenty of evidence that both characters are im-

27. In the original production of *Bernice,* the actress who played Bernice, Ethel Waters, also played Ma Kirby in the evening's performance of *The Happy Journey to Trenton and Camden.*

28. Gallup, "Introductory Note," 107.

bued with pride to their and others' detriment: the livery driver describes Walbeck as "too big and mighty to talk to anybody" (128). We can see Bernice's pride, though not a destructive pride, in her self-determination: "Bernice Mayhew was the name I gave myself" (132). But she also describes herself and Walbeck as proud in the negative sense: "We did what we did because we were that kind of person—the kind that chooses to think they're smarter and better than other people" (137). And the wage of this sin is alienation: "And people that think that way end up alone. We're not *company* for anybody" (137). In fact, Bernice sees their interaction with others as having a negative effect upon them: "It's not good for other people to have to do with persons who are in a disgrace; it brings out the worst in them" (133). The extent of Walbeck's alienation is evident when he says, "I haven't opened any letters for six months" (128). Bernice pronounces their alienation appropriate—what's best for those who cared about them—if not necessarily a just punishment: "We're a stone around their necks now! If we were with them we'd be a bigger stone. Sometimes I think death come into the world so we wouldn't *be* a stone around young people's necks. Besides you and I—we're alone" (136–37). However, there may be a sinful or, at least, a selfish motivation behind this as well. At one point Bernice expresses a sentiment about the living's relationship with the dead that is similar to the end of *The Bridge of San Luis Rey:* "Have you noticed that we gradually forgive them that's dead?" (134). This is the only hint of redemption or hope for these characters in *Bernice,* but it is not a redemption based upon personal transformation.

Toward the end of *Bernice* Walbeck is presented with the opportunity to rebuild his life, though in a warped manner: his teenage daughter is coming to offer to live with him, to cook and clean and take care of him—what Wilder had Emily propose to her father in Act Two, "Love and Marriage," of *Our Town* to show she had wedding jitters. Bernice persuades Walbeck to do as she did: to cut his daughter free to live her own life by pretending to be suffering from a fatal illness, which ironically he is, though his illness is spiritual or, at least, psychological, rather than physical. Bernice concludes the play by telling Walbeck to "go upstairs and hide yourself. You's almost dead. You's dyin'" (137), and he complies. This has to be the grimmest ending to any narrative Wilder has written.[29]

29. In fact, Wilder's endings may be what leads some critics to characterize him as a sentimental writer. No matter how much suffering has been dramatized in the plot up to the denouement, Wilder almost always makes the final action or speech or narration affirm life in some way, despite the sorrow and despair that has preceded the conclusion.

The Wreck on the Five-Twenty-Five

The setting for *The Wreck on the Five-Twenty-Five* is specifically "Today" (138), which is very unusual for a Wilder play: only in *The Skin of Our Teeth* is it explicitly stated that the action takes place in the present of the original production; among his last novels, only *Heaven's My Destination* is set in the same period the book was published.[30] And how is present-day (i.e., 1957) suburbia characterized in *The Wreck?* Early in the play a teenage girl says, "Mr. Brown had preached a sermon about the atom bomb . . . and about how terrible it would be" (141). Like other post-Hiroshima writers, Wilder was trying to come to grips with an age that had witnessed the creation of the means to destroy all life on the planet.[31]

The opening action of *The Wreck* is similar to *The Skin of Our Teeth:* Mrs. Hawkins and her daughter Minnie are waiting for Mr. Hawkins to return from working in the city. What sets the plot in motion is that Hawkins has telephoned to tell them he won't be home on the 5:25 train as usual. Mrs. Hawkins's reaction to this break in routine makes Hawkins sound as if he is alienated from his family: "He hasn't telephoned for years" (139). Then she launches into a housewife's "jeremiad" about men and their desire for change: "Men! . . . They think they want a lot of change—variety and change, variety and change. But they don't really. Deep down, they don't. . . . It's as though he thought he were in a kind of jail or prison" (139). Indeed, Hawkins sees himself in a rut, thus his "hoping that something big and terrible and wonderful will happen—like a wreck, for instance" (142).[32]

What is interesting is that the 5:25, a symbol of routine, does almost wreck, metaphorically, due to Hawkins's disruption of his routine, as the Hawkins's neighbor Mr. Forbes tells Mrs. Hawkins: "The old five-twenty-five wasn't the same without him. Darn near went off the rails" (145). It is almost as if Hawkins has caused a chain reaction of routines being disrupted. His daughter comments to her mother, "Mama, you're talking awfully funny tonight"

30. Ostensibly, *The Cabala* is also set in Rome of the present, but since the dying John Keats is there as well as characters who are actually the gods of antiquity, classifying the setting as contemporary is problematic.

31. Castronovo says that *The Wreck* is about "concealed impulses, suppressed action, and the seething violence that lies below the crust of bourgeois culture"; later he writes, "Altogether, the play is one of Wilder's most pessimistic examinations of civilization" ("Strange Discipline," 110, 111). However, he doesn't seem to regard the advent of the nuclear age and the Cold War as having provoked a reconsideration on Wilder's part; he says the reference to nuclear holocaust is "the latest version of a falling bridge or the ice age" (*Thornton Wilder,* 153).

32. Wilder employed this oxymoronic description in *Our Town,* where the moonlight, childbirth, and life itself are described as terrible and wonderful.

(140), and Mrs. Hawkins responds, "I'm not myself tonight . . . I guess I'm not myself because of your father's phone call—his taking a later train, like that, for the first time in so many years" (140). When Mrs. Hawkins looks out the window into her neighbor's house, she comments, "I can't understand why Mrs. Cochran is acting so strangely. And Mr. Cochran has been coming in and out of the kitchen" (141). In the gender roles of the age of Eisenhower, a husband did not spend much time in the one part of his home/castle over which he was not king. Hawkins's simple action of taking a later train impacts upon those with whom he interacts daily, like the tipping of the first in a line of dominoes. Or, in the nuclear age, like the first splitting of an atom that sets off a chain reaction that leads to explosion and massive destruction of life—the ultimate "train wreck."

Rather than the affirmation of the daily life, as he dramatized in *Our Town,* in *The Wreck* Wilder seems to acknowledge that those daily structures, routines, and rituals are confining and, finally, unfulfilling—at least for some. Mrs. Hawkins concludes her harangue with "He simply wishes the whole world were different—that's the trouble with him" (142). Minnie seems to have similar feelings as her father: "I'm just . . . interested. Most nights *nothing* happens" (144), expressing a longing that is essentially the same as Barnaby's epilogue from *The Matchmaker:* "And the sign that something's wrong with you is when you sit quietly at home wishing you were out having lots of adventure" (*M,* 415). But Mrs. Hawkins does not share this longing for adventure or change: "Our lives are just as exciting as they ought to be, Minnie"; when her daughter replies, "Well, they are tonight," Mrs. Hawkins chides her, "They are all the time, and don't you forget it" (144). But this dissatisfaction is not limited to Minnie and her father; as Mrs. Hawkins points out, "Minnie, the world is full of people who think that everybody's happy except themselves. They think their lives should be more exciting" (144). Thus, as has usually been the case in Wilder, the protagonist represents a group of people rather than a unique individual. Furthermore, having Mrs. Hawkins observe her neighbor Mrs. Cochran in the process of cooking dinner in anticipation of the return on the train of Mr. Cochran demonstrates that the Hawkins's routine is really the middle-class family's routine in postwar America.

Despite Mrs. Hawkins's precise diagnosis, it is unclear just what Mr. Hawkins's problem is, as it was with Wilder himself during the postwar period. We get hints as to the source of the disturbance in the text; for example, the problem, as Mrs. Hawkins perceives it, is progressive, like a disease: "I declare, Minnie, every year your father makes worse jokes. It's growing on him. . . . I declare, he's getting worse. . . . People will be beginning to think he's *bitter*" (141). Hawkins explains what is behind his fantasy of a train wreck: "We're so expert at hiding things from one another—we're so cram-filled with things we can't say to one another that only a wreck could crack us open" (149). In this speech it seems that Hawkins has had an epiphany about alienation similar to Emily's realization of the unappreciated treasures of daily life. In fact, Hawkins tells his wife and daughter that he "got a message. A message from beyond the grave. From the dead" (149). Hawkins reveals that one of his clients has left him a sum of money in her will because he took the time just to listen to her, to be friendly with her during their mundane business interactions, but it would seem to be the epiphany, rather than the bequest of money, that gives Hawkins the courage to break his daily routine. He realizes that the routine is the source of alienation, which inspires him to stand on the street in front of his house looking through the windows to watch his wife and daughter as they go about their business, an action similar to the leftist documentary filmmaker George Burkin's behavior in *Heaven's My Destination*.[33]

The action of *The Wreck* may not present much of a crisis, but Wilder has merely chosen to underplay rather than to melodramatically depict what is disturbing this American Everyman. When Hawkins says, "Oh, Bennsville . . . breathes there a man with soul so dead—" (148), is he implying a self-comparison, a man with soul so dead as his? Castronovo reads Hawkins as Wilder's attempt to "convey a new version of his obsession with the lonely, self-destructive, and dangerous individual," of which George Lansing (another George!) in *The Eighth Day* is the same type.[34] In 1957 Wilder commented on *The Wreck* in his journal, saying, "I should have found earlier a symbol of spiritual desperation" (*JTW*, 261). Just how desperate is Hawkins? Near the end of the play Mrs. Hawkins asks her husband, "Were you planning to go away, Herbert?" and he answers, "Far away" (150–51). After a telephone call from the police, Hawkins reveals to her that he was caught carrying a revolver without a permit; in explanation, he tells her, "I thought that maybe it was best . . . that I go away . . . a long way" (152), suggesting that he may have been contemplating suicide.[35] Mrs. Hawkins then seems to mock his earlier statement that life in the towns he sees from the train during his commute must be more exciting; she takes complete control of the situation when she responds to the confession of his plan to "go away":

33. Wilder may have derived the action in both the novel and the play of staring through windows to observe families going about their daily lives, especially in the play with the voyeur being the husband and father of the family, from Nathaniel Hawthorne's tale "Wakefield."

34. Castronovo, *Thornton Wilder*, 153, 154.

35. Linda Simon also interprets the last lines of *The Wreck* as suggesting that Hawkins contemplated suicide (*Thornton Wilder, His World*, 228).

MRS. HAWKINS. (*Looking up with the beginning of a smile*) To Bennsville?
HAWKINS. Yes.
MRS. HAWKINS. Where life's so exciting. (*Suddenly briskly*) Well, you get the
license for that revolver, Herbert, so that you can prevent people looking in
at us through the window, when they have no business to. —Turn out the
lights when you come. (152)

Mrs. Hawkins is no ditz; she knows what is going on with her husband,
though she probably wasn't aware of how extreme his state of mind was until
the day on which the action takes place. Her reaction, though, suggests she
is more of a down-to-earth, let's-not-bother-with-such-foolishness-as-philoso-
phizing-about-life type like Mrs. Antrobus in *The Skin of Our Teeth* or Ma
Kirby in *Happy Journey* or either mother in *Our Town*. Wilder shows respect
for that figure of woman (it was based on his own mother), but in *The Wreck*
he may be criticizing her a little, too, for her contribution to her husband's
ennui. She is happy with a predictable routine, normality, conventionality,
the daily grind (for her it isn't a grind) and thinks her husband's discontent
with all of that is just foolishness or a midlife crisis at most, with which she
has no patience either.

The question is, what is the tone of this ending? The facial expressions of
the actors playing Mr. and Mrs. Hawkins in the production at the Wilder
symposium at Yale in 1997 suggested that Hawkins's crisis had passed and
they were both glad of it, but that is an interpretation of the director, Liz
Diamond, for the text gives us no such indication. Equally valid would be a
pessimistic interpretation in which we understand that Hawkins is, as he
says, living in a kind of jail (his middle-class lifestyle) and that Mrs. Hawkins
is his jail keeper. In the 2001 Centerstage production of *The Wreck* in Baltimore, Maryland, the actor playing Hawkins gave a final pained look around
the living room of his house, and then followed his wife off stage, creating a
less optimistic tone than in the Yale production.[36]

Wilder is reminding us, then, of the lesson he tried to teach in *Our Town:* to
realize life, every every minute, or more than we normally do, at least, because it all does go by so fast that "we don't have time to look at one another"
(*OT,* 108). If he saw his fellow Americans' lives even more overwhelmed by a
socioeconomic determinism than they were during the Great Depression—a

36. Simon sees the tone of the end as ambiguous: "His wife convinces him that life is
still worth living, but the monotony of the man's existence does not change, and probably will never change. For Thornton, his solitary commuter represented the Americans
haunted by a feeling of the insignificance of the proverbial seventy years they are per-
mitted to live" (*Thornton Wilder, His World,* 228). Goldstone comments, "The optimistic
note that characteristically ends Wilder's plays is absent; rather we are left chilled and
uneasy as the play comes to its abrupt, but inevitable conclusion" (*Intimate Portrait,* 235).

time of crisis—it is no wonder that these snapshots of American life in the 1950s do not attest to progress, do not affirm the American Dream but decry it. This might be the first movement of the American jeremiad, except that unlike the drama of the late 1930s and early 1940s, the *Sins* plays do not recall a former exemplar with which to shame the present generation, nor do they call for progress by affirming the American dream and life itself. In these plays Wilder is writing jeremiads in the common usage of the term: all diatribe. As Castronovo says, "It is yet another example of the way in which Wilder was on close terms with the darker side of the human condition."[37]

We must remember, of course, that *Bernice* and *The Wreck* are part of the cycle *The Seven Deadly Sins,* which is an inherently negative theme. Although the entire *Sins* cycle is pessimistic, no other play is as dark in its vision of mainstream America as *Bernice* and *The Wreck.* We shall see in briefer analyses of selected *Sins* and *Ages* plays just how much Wilder developed his view of the dark side of America during the early stages of the Cold War.

In Shakespeare and the Bible takes place in 1898, a decade later than *The Matchmaker,* and the strongest character in the play, Mrs. Mowbrey, presents herself so that she sounds like Dolly Levi, except that the earlier character's matchmaking was of hearts, whereas Mrs. Mowbrey only brought together bodies for money in her former profession. Now her purpose is not so carnal—or so she says: "I also want to help people. I want—so to speak—to adopt some. Not *young* children, of course, but young men and women who want bringing out in some way or other. I have a gift for that kind of thing. . . . I love to see young people *happy*" (175). The young heroine of the play may appear to be an innocent morally and in terms of experience, but Katy reveals she has as much of a dark side as the other characters in the *Sins* plays: "When things seem all wrong to me, I do something worse than have a temper. I turn all cold and stormy inside. It's as though something were dead in me" (182). And this is before Katy learns what her aunt's former profession was, which is the word "in Shakespeare and the Bible" (186), and that her fiancée was one of her aunt's clients. The end result is that she breaks off her engagement with the ambitious young lawyer, which was perhaps Mrs. Mowbrey's plan all along.

Similarly, in *Cement Hands,* the heroine's lawyer-uncle may also be an anti-matchmaker, scheming to break up his niece's engagement.[38] As with the other *Sins* plays, more than one of the seven deadly sins is exhibited by *Cement Hands.* For example, illustrating wrath, Blake's niece arrives to announce, "I'm furious at you. I'm so furious I could cry" (213), and she won-

37. Castronovo, *Thornton Wilder,* 154.
38. Lawyers do not come off well in the *Sins* plays; for example, the one in *Bernice* is named "Mr. Mallison" (125), which obviously sounds like malice.

ders if the demonstration of her wealthy fiancée's "cement hands"—the deadly sin of avarice in the form of never carrying money with him to leave as tips—is an attempt to break up their engagement (221). One gets the sense that, in Puritan terms, there simply are no elect characters in these plays; they all appear to be reprobate.[39]

The four plays of the *Ages* cycle—*Infancy, Childhood, Youth,* and *Rivers Under the Earth* (Middle Age) are not as obviously dark as the *Sins* plays, as one might expect from the different themes, but their view of human nature as the source of human suffering is no less grim. Even when the tone is comedic or nostalgic and the story fanciful, there is a fundamental pessimism about human nature itself that we had not seen in Wilder's earlier works.

In the first *Ages* play, *Infancy,* in direct contrast to the image of the contented housewife and doting mother of such 1950s' television shows as *Leave It to Beaver* and *Father Knows Best,* Mrs. Boker and Millie (currently a nanny but later as a wife/mother to be) do not paint a joyful picture of caring for babies. Mrs. Boker confides in Millie, "I don't have to tell you what life with a baby is: (*Looking around circumspectly*) It's *war—one long war*" (240). Later, Millie says, "I hate babies. (*Toward Tommy*) I hate you—sticking your crazy face into my business—frightening Officer Avonzino, the only man I've talked to in six months. I hate you—always butting in. I have a right to my own life, haven't I? *My own life!* I'm sick to death of squalling, smelling, gawking babies" (245). And the babies understand how the adults really feel about them: "We're in the way, see?" (246). Nor are these babies innocent and adorable; like the adults, they whine about what they want: "I can't say it . . . boody-fill . . . Why don't they *teach* me to say it? I want to LEARN and they won't teach me," and "Time's going by. I'm getting owe-uld. And nobody is showing me *anything*. I wanta make a house. I wanta make a house. I wanta make a bay-beee. Nobody show-ow-ow-s me how-ta" (236). The babies' personalities reek of Freud, as Moe tells Tommy he hates his father, and gets angry with his mother for leaving him alone to be "with that *man*" (244). The little Oedipus even expresses a death wish for his father: "I'll shut my eyes and do nothing. I won't eat. I'll just go away-away. Like I want Daddy to do" (246).[40]

Given the inherent progressiveness of the *Ages* cycle theme, one might expect Wilder to suggest that things will improve with time, but that is not what Millie tells Tommy and Moe: "You're going to grow up to be *men,* nasty,

---

39. Speaking of Uncle Charlie from *Shadow of a Doubt* and a character in a "Wrath" manuscript fragment, Castronovo notes, "Both of them want to destroy 'our town,' the contemporary pluralistic society that Wilder celebrated so memorably in *Happy Journey,* among other midperiod works" ("Strange Discipline," 111).

40. Castronovo describes the babies in *Infancy* as "curious, aggressive, grasping, sexually aware monsters out of Freud" (*Thornton Wilder,* 79).

selfish men. You're all alike" (246), which is confirmed theatrically by having grown men acting the roles of the infants. Near the end of the play, Officer Avonzino also depicts a bleak portrait of human nature and the experience of growing into adulthood: "All you babies want the whole world. Well, I tell you, you've got a long hard road before you. Pretty soon you'll find that you can cry all you want and turn every color there is—and nobody'll pay *no* attention at all. Your best days are over; you've had'm. From now on it's all up to you—George Washington, or whatever your name is" (249). Thus, far from the image of a natural state of innocence at birth and parents lovingly nurturing their adorable babies, Wilder shows us human nature young and old as consistently selfish and unsatisfied.

As the generation gap would become the major cultural theme of the 1960s, the second and third *Ages* plays are consistent with *Infancy* in their doubt that there can be a meeting of minds between generations. Toward the end of *Childhood*, Caroline, the oldest child, says to her father, who is playing the role of a bus driver in his children's game, "Besides, we've found that it's best not to make friends with grown-ups, because . . . in the end . . . they don't act fair to you" (268).[41]

The protagonist of *Youth* is Lemuel Gulliver from Jonathan Swift's *Gulliver's Travels*. In this fanciful literary play Wilder creates an eighteenth-century *Lord of the Flies*, which shows human nature to be less ambitious, altruistic, or educable than the characterization and action in his earlier works might have suggested. Wilder depicts Gulliver in his forties, once again shipwrecked, this time cast up on an island on which there is no one older than twenty-nine. The young men and women who meet him react in horror, seeing in Gulliver's appearance and his words—or, rather, his ideas—confirmation of their opinion of what happens to people once their youth is over. Then it is Gulliver's turn to be horrified when he learns why no one over twenty-nine lives on the island: when they turn thirty, they are executed, taking the 1960s saying "Never trust anyone over thirty" to an absurd extreme.[42] *Youth* ends

---

41. Goldstein sees *Childhood* as dramatizing the "touching failure of the generations to reach each other in spirit" (*Art of Thornton Wilder*, 155). Kuner also sees the point being the "lack of communication between generations, not in a physical way, as Wilder demonstrated in *Infancy*, but in a psychic one, [that] is the threat that runs through *Childhood*" (*Bright and Dark*, 190).

42. Val Smith thinks *Youth* is an eponymous satire: "As the play was conceived in the 1960s, amid the rebellion of a youthful population who had discovered for the first time its social and political clout, 'Youth' might well have been Wilder's satirical meditation on the excesses of America, or as he refers to it in the play, 'The Country of the Young'" (*Wilder Rediscovered*, ed. Joel A. Smith, 62–63). However, if "Youth" was composed in the same period as the other *Sins* and *Ages* plays, in the late fifties and early sixties, the youth movement would not have yet reached its radical stage.

somewhat optimistically when Gulliver persuades a young builder and a servant girl to free him and steal a boat to escape the island, but one of
Gulliver's last lines suggests entropy rather than evolution: "The childhood
of the race . . . You have slipped five–ten thousand years . . ." (292). He does
go on to assert that the island society will eventually stop killing thirty-year-
olds, and will do away with other corruptions in their sociopolitical system (a
rigid class structure, patriarchal values and rule), but in the context of what
has come before, his prophecy is about as convincing as the Marxist predic-
tion that one day government will fall away and humanity will live in harmony without the need of laws or means of enforcing them. That human
nature will not conform to such abstract ideals, whether they come from religion or political and economic theory, is implied when the young Duke
asks Gulliver, "Among those twenty countries [Gulliver had visited] was
there *one* that was not governed by old men—governed, misgoverned, bur-
dened, oppressed by old men? By the pride and avarice, and the lust for
power of old men?" (282). The Duke is completely unaware of his hypocrisy
as he demonstrates pride, avarice, and so on.[43]

Finally, *Rivers Under the Earth* is included in *Collected Short Plays* to represent
middle age, though the editors admit it is uncertain whether Wilder wrote it
as one of the *Seven Ages of Man*. This quiet, thoughtful play may appear to depict a family closer to the families in the earlier, more affirmative plays; however, though more subtle than the other *Sins* and *Ages* plays, its portrait of
human nature and life is still rather dark. In fact, the action takes place literally in the dark, as the characters spend part of the play groping around the
Wisconsin lake and woods where they have come for a summer vacation.
The family is again the perfect balance of gender and generation: mother
and father, son and daughter. But as in *Infancy* their relationships are colored
by Freudian ideas about the latent sexual attraction between mother and
son and father and daughter. We also see sibling rivalry rankle between the
children. Through characters remembering earlier vacations on this site, the
psychological process of repressing traumatic events is also demonstrated,
almost as if Wilder wrote *Rivers Under the Earth* as an illustration of psychoanalytic theory. During an earlier vacation, the parents realize "Francesca

43. The language here creates a link between the two play cycles; indeed, one can read
each of the *Ages* plays as demonstrating one of the seven deadly sins, and many of the
Sins plays as illustrating something about one of the ages. This would make it possible to
stage both the *Sins* and *Ages* cycles as complete and with a dramaturgical uniformity, if
one substituted, say, *Infancy* for the mythological *The Drunken Sisters* for gluttony, and, say,
Rivers Under the Earth for the historical *Someone from Assisi* for lust (though it would be, in
part, an Oedipal lust). Completing the *Seven Ages of Man,* however, would be trickier, especially if one tried to follow Shakespeare's speech from *As You Like It* (II:vii:139–66), which
shifts from "ages" to "occupation" back to "ages."

had learned about death. . . . You sat soothing her and reading aloud to her until the sun rose" (304). This time "Tom learns about old age" (302), specifically with regard to his mother.

Introducing a discordant note into the peaceful, nostalgic mood the parents feel and the idealistic dreams of the children, Tom tells his mother, "Last month I thought maybe I'd be one of those new physicists. I'd find something that could stop every atomic bomb" (306). This one speech reminds us of the atomic age context in which Wilder was writing, and he underscores the ominous implications of this technological progress with the naïveté of the rest of Tom's speech: "I think others'll get there [stopping the atomic bomb] before me . . . Besides, that's not hard enough. Any Joe will be able to find that one of these days. I want something harder . . . something nearer," and then he reveals that what he has in mind is medically deferring old age (306–7). Incredibly, Wilder seems to be suggesting that the impetus for the stay-forever-young dream stems from the Oedipal feelings of the young, not the regrets of the old. More important, though, is the dropping of the reference to the atomic bomb near the climax of the play, so that the calm, smooth surface of the mood is "troubled," as when a stone is thrown into a lake or an angel stirs a pool of heavy waters; in these plays of our sins and ages, there is no healing, whether divine or human.

Despite the American characters and settings of most of the plays of *The Seven Deadly Sins* and *The Seven Ages of Man* cycles, the vestiges of Puritanism so prevalent in Wilder's earlier works disappear. The Americans in these plays do not seem chosen by God to be an example to the world. Technological progress has given competing imperialistic governments the means to bring about the end of all human progress, with nuclear weapons. Neither death nor life are providential. In fact, only one of the eleven plays even refers to God. In *Someone from Assisi*, a deranged old woman describes how she is treated: "They throw stones at me. They kick me. Everywhere people hate people. . . . The world is *bad*. . . . Nobody is kind anymore" (196). When the eponymous saint enters, he expresses much the same view, though including himself, the convent's Mother Superior to whom he is speaking, and all others as part of the problem: "Who can measure the suffering—the waste—in the world? And every being born into the world—except One [Jesus Christ]—has added to it. You and I have made it more and more" (200). When the deranged woman says, "God must weep," the future saint simply affirms, "Yes" (207). In contrast to his earlier works, Wilder seems to be showing us that it isn't the Devil, but the Devil in us, that causes our suffering.

Since most of these last plays of Thornton Wilder are written in a realistic theatrical style, perhaps this suggests that the nonrealistic aesthetic of the earlier drama somehow "conjured" the Puritan codes that are best expressed by an abstract mimesis, allegorical characters, microcosmic episodes set against a macrocosmic backdrop, and so forth. Or perhaps Wilder finally succeeded in throwing off his Puritan "baggage," as some scholars have characterized it. That reading of Wilder and his works might hold up if this were the end of the story; however, the last chapter of Wilder's life and career climaxes with a final grand expression of the Puritan vision of America and the cosmos.

Six

Covenant Reborn

Wilder's Reaffirmation of the American Errand

> The vision of the Puritan Jeremiahs recalls still another reason for the rise of colonial literary studies. . . . The emigrants thought of themselves as a "new Israel" on an "errand" to found a "city on a hill." . . . The New World . . . was the modern counterpart of the wilderness through which the Israelites reached Canaan.
>
> —Sacvan Bercovitch, *The American Puritan Imagination*

If Thornton Wilder's darker vision in *The Seven Deadly Sins* and *The Seven Ages of Man* seemed puzzling, even more puzzling was the return of his optimistic faith in the progress of civilization and the affirmation of America in his novel of the 1960s, *The Eighth Day*. Developments in world and domestic affairs that might have caused Wilder's postwar malaise had grown worse, and Wilder himself was ten years older by the time *The Eighth Day* was published in 1967. The proliferation of nuclear arms and the heating up of the Cold War had brought the world to the brink of nuclear holocaust in 1962 during the Cuban missile crisis. President John F. Kennedy had been assassinated. America's involvement in the Vietnam War had escalated under President Lyndon Johnson. The youth of the day were opting for a lifestyle epitomized by the hedonistic slogans "Sex, drugs, and rock 'n' roll" and "Tune in, turn on, and drop out"—about as far from the stereotypical Puritan values of faith, family, and hard work as a culture can get. If ever there had been a time in the twentieth century up to that point when circumstances would cause people to lose faith in the American way of life, the decade of the 1960s was that time.

Yet Wilder did not lose faith; or, to be more precise, after perhaps having lost his faith in America during the 1950s, somehow he regained it during the 1960s. And not only did the optimistic and affirmative tone in his writing return, as we shall see in the ensuing analysis of *The Eighth Day,* but so did the Puritan codes and structures that were so prevalent in his novels and plays up to the works of the late 1940s and 1950s. How to account for this? One way is to take the telescopic perspective, as Wilder himself had done in such works as *The Bridge of San Luis Rey* and *The Skin of Our Teeth,* to the 1960s and all that was happening then. While the advent of nuclear physics gave us the capability of destroying all life on the planet, it also brought an alternative power source to coal and oil burning. The Cold War may have spurred the proliferation of nuclear weapons, but it also spawned the space race, which brought many benefits, not the least of which was extending the "errand into the wilderness" into space, "the final frontier." Before JFK was assassinated, he had been a youthful president who supported the arts and volunteerism with his famous line, "Ask not what the country can do for you, but what you can do for your country." In reference to the Kennedy administration, Wilder said at a State Department auditorium in Washington, D.C., in 1962, "I am filled with great pleasure that Washington is becoming the lighthouse on the hill for things which we have spent our lives," echoing John Winthrop's depiction of New England as a city upon a hill.[1] And let us not forget that Kennedy committed American troops and arms to the Vietnam War for an ostensibly noble purpose: to prevent a defenseless people from Soviet- and Chinese-sponsored revolutionaries who would seize their possessions, including the land of farmers, overthrow the established government, and eliminate freedom of speech, the press, and religion under a totalitarian regime. The U.S. had fought a similar war during the 1950s in Korea with some success, and at least one scholar has even viewed the U.S.'s Cold War strategy of containment in response to Communist expansion as an outgrowth of Puritanism.[2] Finally, the Civil Rights movement resulted in

1. Linda Simon, *Thornton Wilder, His World,* 238.
2. In "God's Chosen People: Anglican Views, 1607–1807," Pascal Covici Jr. writes,

Our nineteenth- and twentieth-century national efforts to impose either Democracy or a *Pax Americana* on the rest of the world might be misguided, but at least they made sense in the light of our own unique past. . . . Our participation in the New Colonialism meant that we were still the victims of a uniquely vicious, however well intentioned and sincerely believed, insistence that we, and we only, were God's new chosen people, picked out by Him for His own purposes, just as had been the ancient Jews of the Old Testament. (98)

the passage of landmark legislation to enforce the American values of equal-
ity and opportunity, which also inspired one of the great expressions of the
American ideal in Reverend Martin Luther King's "I Have a Dream" speech
during the march on Washington, D.C., in 1963. Given that Wilder's ancestors were abolitionists, including one who provided financial support to the
Africans who had seized the slave ship *Amistad,* it seems he would have approved of how "the times, they [were] a-changin'"—at least in part. Besides,
in reference to the youth movement, hadn't Wilder championed "the aspirations of the young (and not only the young) for a fuller, freer participation in
life" (*TP,* xiii) in *The Matchmaker?*

Wilder had won many awards by this time, with one more major honor,
the National Book Award, to come for *The Eighth Day.* At 435 pages it was his
longest work, published when he was seventy years old. And the way Wilder
chose to write this novel suggests that he was as tuned in to his Judeo-
Christian-Puritan roots as ever, for he exiled himself in the Arizona desert, à
la John the Baptist, who was, as the Gospel of Matthew says, "The voice of
one crying in the wilderness, 'Prepare ye the way of the Lord, make his paths
straight'" (3:3).[3] As discussed in Chapter Four, this was the biblical verse on
which Samuel Danforth preached in his Election Day sermon when he
coined the now famous phrase "errand into the wilderness" to describe the
Puritans' immigration to New England.

There is an aspect of Puritanism that lends itself to a cultural explanation
of why Wilder's penultimate novel would brim with affirmation and optimism: Covenant theology. A little review is in order. As a result of the appli-
cation of typology to post–New Testament history, even to then-current events,
the New England Puritans came to believe that they were, as a whole, chosen by God to be his people. As Bercovitch explains, "New Canaan was not
a metaphor for them as it was for other colonists. It was the New World reserved from eternity for God's latter day elect nation." The federal theologians, as discussed in Chapter One, formulated an ideology out of theology,
seeing themselves as being in covenant with God. Such influential New
England Puritans as William Bradford, John Winthrop, and the Mathers
(Richard, Increase, and Cotton) embraced Covenant theology as the founda-
tion of a theocratic model for governing their society in the New World.
Again, not every colonist who came to America in the seventeenth century
was a Puritan, but as Emory Elliott notes, "Even those who embraced the

---

3. Gilbert A. Harrison notes that one of the working titles for *The Eighth Day* was *Make
Straight in the Desert* (*The Enthusiast: A Life of Thornton Wilder,* 354), showing that Wilder
clearly identified the novel with the place of its writing. Richard H. Goldstone compares
Wilder's retreat to the desert to Thoreau's retreat to Walden Pond, and he compares
John Ashley, the hero of the novel, to Thoreau (*Thornton Wilder: An Intimate Portrait,* 252).

theological tenets of Methodism and Anglicanism learned to think in terms of America as a chosen New Israel and to dwell upon the need for individual self-sacrifice to the common ordained goal."[4]

Scholars studying American literature and history have cited evidence that Covenant theology underlies more secular expressions of our national destiny. For example, Howard Mumford Jones writes of turn-of-the-century American writer William Vaughn Moody's patriotic poetry, "It can be argued that these expressions do not differ radically from the language of the New England theocracy, that of a providential view of American history, or the concept of manifest destiny." Jones goes on to quote President Grover Cleveland in 1887 celebrating the centenary of the Constitution, which he called "this ark of the people's covenant." Finally, Jones quotes a speech by a historian who "did not know it but he had revived the language of the New England theocracy" when he said, "No one but He who rules the destiny of all nations in all ages could have ordained that the bright sun of Canaan should rise again in after ages with refulgent splendor over the vast continent of America, and that the pure and unselfish spirit of Moses, Joshua, and Samuel should live again in a Franklin, a Washington, and an Adams." If there is or was such a thing as American optimism, then surely it stems from the Puritans' optimism created by their faith in Covenant theology. As Perry D. Westbrook asserts, "History and evolution were deemed to be on America's side [by Whitman, Theodore Roosevelt, and other American optimists]; one need only flow along with the natural course of events and America's dominance would be assured."[5] Wilder's optimism, then, may well have been a modern manifestation of the New England Puritans' beliefs about where America fits in the grand scheme of things, as determined by God, and *The Eighth Day* may be Wilder's expression of this national faith. Thus in *The Eighth Day* we will see how Wilder, like George Antrobus in *The Skin of Our Teeth,* once more takes up the challenge not just to survive, but to continue to make progress on his and our long journey through the twentieth century.

The opening paragraph of *The Eighth Day* establishes the scenario of the novel as succinctly as possible: "In the early summer of 1902 John Barrington Ashley of Coaltown, a small mining center in southern Illinois, was tried for the murder of Breckenridge Lansing, also of Coaltown. He was found guilty and sentenced to death. Five days later, at one in the morning of Tuesday, July 22, he escaped from his guards on the train that was carrying

---

4. Bercovitch, "The Modernity of American Puritan Rhetoric," 52; Elliott, "The Puritan Roots of American Whig Rhetoric," 108.

5. Jones, *The Age of Energy: Varieties of American Experience, 1865–1915,* 36, 37, 38; Westbrook, *Free Will and Determination in American Literature,* 130.

him to his execution" (3). Wilder then sets about narrating the events that led up to the killing of Lansing and the effects on his family of Ashley's conviction and escape. Not only do we learn of the events that led up to the shooting, but also of those that led up to Breckenridge Lansing marrying his wife, Eustacia; their moving to Coaltown, Illinois; and their son George's running away on the same day as the shooting. Wilder also narrates those events that led up to John Ashley marrying his wife, Beata, and their moving to Coaltown and raising their four children: Roger, Lily, Sophie, and Constance.

Although we can see that there is a less universal and more particular plot in *The Eighth Day* than in *Our Town* and *The Skin of Our Teeth,* Wilder is once again writing in an allegorical mode. Despite George Greene's claim that "The Ashley's community is no cousin of Grover's Corners," early on Wilder has Dr. Gillies, the town sage, think to himself, "Coaltown is everywhere" (18).[6] John Ashley, the hero of the novel, is described as having "commonplace features" (121), as being "neither dark nor light, tall nor short, fat nor thin, handsome nor homely" (284); in other words, he is average, generic, allegorically any one of us, all of us. But it is all of us as Americans, for *The Eighth Day* is quite self-consciously an American novel.[7]

The Eighth Day is replete with evidence that Wilder is writing about Americans.[8] The Ashleys, like the Antrobuses, Gibbses and Webbs, and Kirbys—and the Wilders—are meant to be read as representative Americans, or, rather, idealized Americans at their best.[9] Sounding as if he were describing the Kirbys in *Happy Journey,* the narrator of *The Eighth Day* tells us, "Up to the time of the First World War—which started Americans moving about all over the country and changing their residences on a whim—every man, woman, and child believed that he or she lived in the best town in the best state in the best country in the world" (7); however, no one in the novel thinks Coaltown is the best town,[10] though the Ashleys are the best family.

6. Greene, "An Ethics for Wagon Trains: Thornton Wilder's *The Eighth Day,*" 332. Simon writes, "Coaltown was Our Town enlarged, sprawled out, untidy at the edges" (*Thornton Wilder, His World,* 243).

7. Goldstone writes, "*The Eighth Day* is essentially American, one of the most consciously *American* novels written in this century" (*Intimate Portrait,* 247).

8. W. D. Maxwell-Mahon interprets Dr. Gillies's speech in which he says "We are children of the eighth day": "The 'we' in this speech may be taken to represent the American people"; he goes on to note, "This theme appears to be the regeneration of the Ashley family; in reality it is the genesis of the spirit of Americanism" ("The Novels of Thornton Wilder," 43).

9. Rex Burbank writes about Ashley, "he and his children are the best American democracy can produce, and they are the best hope for the human race" (*Thornton Wilder,* 119).

10. Helmut Papajewski writes, "Coaltown is the diametrical opposite of the ideology of progress" (*Thornton Wilder,* 184), and the descriptions of it would seem to support that

We are told more than once that Roger Ashley excels at everything he sets his mind to: "Roger was the first student in the high school; he was the captain of the baseball team" (40); "He became the school's best student and athlete" (223). In Roger's early achievement, it was a case of "like father, like son": "He was the little lord in a small town, as his father had been before him" (40). Maxwell-Mahon comments similarly: "One of the difficulties in reading *The Eighth Day* is the shifting focus on Ashley and his son, Roger. Perhaps the shift should be seen as an attempt deliberately to blur the distinction between the two characters and make them seem a composite picture of an American."[11]

Although the Ashleys did not come from the Midwest, let alone Coaltown, they are supposed to be as American as Tom Everage, Wilder's Everyman from his journal notes on the American characteristics book he worked on during the 1950s. John Ashley, we learn, is the son of a banker from Pulley Falls, New York; Beata Kellerman is the daughter of a prosperous brewer from Hoboken, New Jersey, where she and John meet and fall in love while he attends engineering school. After graduation he takes a job in Ohio; unsatisfied with that, he then moves farther west to take a position with the coal mining company in Coaltown. The Ashleys are already modeling a migratory pattern that has become so commonplace in the latter part of the twentieth century. To ensure that we recognize them as American through and through, Wilder even has an expatriate author, perhaps modeled after T. S. Eliot, include a chapter on the Ashleys in his book: "In particular there was a chapter on them—it was called the 'Gracchi'—in a privately printed volume *America Through a Telescope* by a writer who called himself 'Atticus.' This 'Atticus' declared himself to be happy to have left America for the shores of the Thames and the Seine. From that safe distance, having taken out British citizenship, he reviewed the horrors and the absurdities of his native land" (305).[12] It should be noted that the brothers Gracchus or the Gracchi were Roman reformers and orators—like the Puritans, like the Wilders, like the Ashleys.[13] After listing the many faults Atticus claimed the Ashleys had, the narrator tells us how the expatriate writer concluded his chapter on them: "He reserved his most biting depreciation for

---

reading. Perhaps that is why, ultimately, all of the Ashleys, who are embodiments of progress, leave Coaltown.

11. Maxwell-Mahon, "Novels of Thornton Wilder," 43.

12. "Atticus" is derived from "Attica," the region surrounding Athens, and is the source of the adjective "Attic," by which we mean classical Greece. T. S. Eliot, of course, was a classicist, both as a critic and as a dramatist, though as a poet he was a modernist.

13. Goldstone sees *The Eighth Day* as Wilder's tribute to his own family (*Intimate Portrait*, 251).

the end of his chapter. The last paragraph developed the idea that the Ashleys were—indubitably (he hated to say it, but the truth must come out; they were indubitably) Americans" (306).

The Ashleys are signified as representative Americans not only through the above passages, but also by their possessing the attributes that Wilder delineated as American characteristics in his Norton lectures at Harvard. On three occasions they are described as being abstract: "Few of these genealogists and biographers observed—or, at least, attempted to describe—what we have called the Ashley 'abstraction' or 'disattachment'" (305; see also 9 and 294). The Ashley children are also future-oriented, committed to progress, and caught up in their plans and projects (see, for example, 51, 403, 268). The narrator describes John Ashley as a man of faith; these men of faith are said to have "their eyes on the future," and their faith is defined as " 'faith in life,' in the 'meaning of life,' in God, in progress, in humanity" (107). And, most specifically, the Ashleys are American by Wilder's definition because they seem to have an instinct for founding a new religion or morality or otherwise reinventing whatever they are occupied with. In the chapter devoted to John Ashley's escape from the train and his subsequent adventures in South America, he is described as looking like "a wan theological student" (116); later we are told, "He had come to resemble one of the Apostles—a John or a James" (121), and that others see him as a "pious-looking youth" (122). In the chapter on Roger's going out on his own in Chicago the narrator tells us, "We shall see later how his father 'invented' marriage and paternity" (224). Later, in the chapter on the families and courtship of John and Beata in Hoboken, New Jersey, the narrator tells us, "John Ashley wanted all things new" (300), and "His first year of marriage was like the discovery of a new continent. . . . He walked the mile to his place of work like Adam going forth to his daily task of naming the plants and animals," filling him "with the gravity of one who has founded the human race" (301), like George Antrobus in *The Skin of Our Teeth*. Ashley is, in fact, an inventor, like Antrobus, another representative American Adam.[14] Roger is clearly his father's son and the founding fathers' son: "He now drew up an explanation of the nature of things; he derived ethics from the order in the cosmos; he designed the constitution of an ideal state" (225), and when he chooses journalism as his profession, the same as Wilder's father, Roger sets about "inventing a new kind of journalism" (230). Thus it is clear that the Ashleys, like the Kirbys et al., are meant to represent Americans and America.

And the character of the America they represent is emphatically Puritan. John Ashley often sounds like an iconoclastic Puritan: "He had been a rebel

14. Goldstone points out that Ashley "combines the New England transcendentalism of an Emerson with the ingenuity of a Ford or an Edison" (*Intimate Portrait,* 247–48).

only to the extent of erecting a wall between himself and his doting parents and of rejecting their idols" (146). In the section providing historical background on John's and Beata's ancestors, Wilder is retelling the story of the Puritan migration to America in terms similar to his screen treatment *The American Melting Pot* and his Norton lectures that were briefly discussed in the Introduction:

> John Barrington Ashley's immediate ancestors were farmers and small merchants on the western banks of the Hudson River. As Ashley, Ashleigh, Coghill, Barrington, Barrow, and so on, they had left the Thames Valley in the 1660's, fleeing from religious persecution, and had crossed the Atlantic. . . . ("Brother Wilkins, will ye remove with us?") Once arrived at the shores of New England they pushed westward, felling trees and building the meetinghouse and the school; then pushed further. . . . They were steeled on the Lord's day by four-hour sermons that were largely occupied with sin. (302)

The narrator tells how the Dutch families in the Ashley genealogy came from Amsterdam (303), which is where the Pilgrims had first removed to before coming to America. Furthermore, we are told that Beata's "mother's grandmother was of a Huguenot family, weavers who had fled from religious persecution in France at the Revocation of the Edict of Nantes" (303); the Huguenots were French Calvinists.

One of the stereotypical associations with Puritans in America is wealth as a sign of God's favor, and that notion is represented in *The Eighth Day:* "The Christian religion, as delivered in Coaltown, established a bracing relation between God's favor and money. Penury was not only a social misfortune; it was a visible sign of a fall from grace" (45). The narrator then cites an example of this: "Mrs. Cavanaugh had once been proud, happy, and well-to-do. God had turned his face away from her. . . . Often such reversals are called 'judgments'" (46–47). A Chilean woman also refers to Americans as a "great people who were rich, who ate at tables, who could read and write—who had been favored by GOD and who carried magic within them" (161). Since the language in some of these quotations echoes Wilder's essays in *American Characteristics* or his relevant journal entries (including the allegory of Tom Everage), *The Eighth Day* may have been Wilder's attempt to resurrect that incomplete project in the form of a novel.

As discussed in Chapters One and Two, searching for signs, almost as if reading all of the natural world and human history as an allegory, is very much in the Puritan mode.[15] An example of the Puritan interpretation of

15. "The great task of life was disposing oneself to the divine grace that alone could work one's salvation. Inasmuch as this grace was thought to show itself in signs, both interior and exterior, the discernment of the signs of grace was a major Puritan preoccu-

events as signs can be found in Samuel Danforth's jeremiad "Errand into the Wilderness":

> How sadly hath the Lord testified against us because of our loss of our first love and our remissness and negligence in his work? Why hath the Lord smitten us with blasting and mildew now seven years together, superadding sometimes severe drought, sometimes great tempests, floods, and sweeping rains that leave no food behind them? Is it not because the Lord's house lyeth waste, temple-work in our hearts, families, churches is shamefully neglected? What should I make mention of signs in the heavens and in the earth—blazing stars, earthquakes, dreadful thunders and lightnings, fearful burnings?[16]

Some of the characters of *The Eighth Day* search for and find signs: The Deacon of the Covenant Church tells Roger, "The sign of God's way is that it is strange. . . . Can it be that your family has been marked" (430). Eustacia lives in expectation of signs: "There would be some revelation. That is what life is—an unfolding" (379). Olga Doubkov sees John Ashley as revelation: "He was chosen. He was a sign. When she called at the house now she was renewing her strength; she was warming her spirit at a flame, at a place where 'real things' had been revealed" (71), and she felt "This was indeed a house of signs" (85).

Another trace of the Puritan heritage in *The Eighth Day* is the mention of Christian denominations or descriptions of sects that resemble the fundamentalist-like Protestant faith of the Puritans. Specific denominations mentioned include Presbyterian, Lutheran, and Baptists (the most often cited), and others who resemble the Puritans in some way. For example, Ashley's grandmother "had joined one of those peculiar religious sects—rigidly ascetic, yet given to emotional camp meetings and to 'speaking in tongues'— that were particularly prevalent in northern New York State" (149)—not that the Puritans spoke in tongues. Eustacia describes Coaltown as being adverse to certain kinds of celebrating: "Lots of people in town think that dancing's wicked" (358).

Even the Indians at Herkomer's Knob resemble the Puritans; here their church building is described as stark and spare as any Puritan meeting house: "They went into the church. There were no Christmas decorations. There was a table and many benches. It resembled a schoolroom" (426). In addition, similar to Puritans' naming of their children, "Their given names were

---

pation" (Denise Lardner Carmody and John Tully Carmody, *The Republic of Many Mansions: Foundations of American Religious Thought*, 21).

16. Danforth, "A Brief Recognition of New England's Errand into the Wilderness," 73–74.

the source of much amusement. Some were taken from the Bible, but the large number were from the two works that always accompanied the earliest adventurers from Virginia into the Wilderness: *Pilgrim's Progress* and Plutarch's *Lives*. There was many a Christian and a Good Works" (422). Furthermore, "the members of the Covenant Church elected the sagacious" (422).[17] The Covenant Church is obviously a verbal echo of New England Puritans' Covenant theology. The Residents of Coaltown who are of European descent refer to the Kangaheela Indians with nicknames that mock their devotional practices: "Throughout the seventies and eighties the members of the community were much derided as 'screechers,' 'jumpers,' and 'holy rollers'" (422–23), just as the Puritans, Quakers, and Shakers had been derisively named. The Deacon of the Covenant Church sounds very much like a John Winthrop or a Cotton Mather in his view of America: "Can it be that this country is singled out for so high a destiny—this country which so greatly wronged my ancestors?" (431). The destiny the Deacon refers to is to be a messiah-bearing family as was the family of Abraham, whose story is told in the Bible (430).

Despite Wilder's ecumenical inclusion of characters who are Catholic, Orthodox, and mainstream Protestant, the descriptions of the beliefs of Christianity in *The Eighth Day* almost always sound like Puritan doctrine. In the narration of Ashley's adventures after escaping from the train, a minor character named Dr. MacKenzie, who is a duplicate of cynical Dr. Gillies of Coaltown but transported to Chile for Ashley to converse with, lectures Ashley: "Christianity is a Jewish religion. . . . You Hebrews came along and tossed us [Greek gods] off our thrones. You brought in that unhappy conscience of yours—all that damned moral anxiety. Maybe you're a Christian. Always denying yourselves any enjoyment, always punishing yourselves" (166). Roger realizes what sounds like total depravity and original sin: "*The whole world's wrong,* he saw. There's something wrong at the heart of the world and he would track it down" (224, emphasis in original). The characterization of God at times resembles the stern, distant Calvinist deity or the Old Testament God of wrath that the Puritans feared, as in what is almost certainly an allusion to and may be a quote from Jonathan Edwards's famous sermon "Sinners in the Hands of an Angry God": "Oh my beloved brothers and sisters, consider what a terrible thing to fall into the hands of an angry God!" (302); and here, too, it is fear rather than love associated with God: "Lansing had set out to found that greatest of all institutions—a God-fearing American home" (351).

17. Wilder mentions the most famous Puritan author, John Milton, twice in *The Eighth Day* (39, 313).

Another code for the New England Puritan origins of the American self that Wilder employs in *The Eighth Day* is the phrase that early American literature scholars such as Perry Miller and Sacvan Bercovitch have seen as evidence of the Puritans' protonationalist intentions. The narrator uses the phrase "lighthouse on a hill," echoing Winthrop's "city upon a hill," a couple of times (10, 164) in reference to a city as a model for the rest of humanity.[18] Wilder used this phrase over and over throughout his life, suggesting he was aware of the Puritans' belief that God meant America to be an example to the world.[19] Recounting the settlement of America, the narrator also uses the term "wilderness" on several occasions; for example, the Covenant Church is described as "one of the many communities that survived, like vestigial pockets, from the days of the Great Wilderness—moving westward from Virginia to Kentucky and Tennessee and beyond" (421).

Even Wilder's metaphor and language in *The Eighth Day* at times echo the Puritan writers. When the Deacon of the Covenant Church tells Roger about the church and how John Ashley helped them rebuild it, he shows him a tapestry that on one side makes a design but on the reverse is "a mass of knots and of frayed dangling threads" (428); he explains to Roger, "You cannot see the design" (429). Edward Taylor used the same metaphor three hundred years before Wilder in *God's Determinations*:

> His Wildred state will wane away, and hence
>   These Crooked Passages will soon appeare:
> The Curious needlework of Providence,
>   Embrodered with golden spangles Cleare.
>   Judge not this web while in the Loom, but stay
>   From judging it untill the judgment day.
> For while it's foiled up, the best Can see
>   But little of it, and that little too
> Shews weather beaten: but when it shall bee
> Hung open all at once, Oh, beautious shew!
> Though thrids run in and out, cross snarle and twin'de,
> The Web will even be enwrought you'l finde. (98)

18. Warren French writes, "The U.S.—at least Wilder's New England—was founded at least in part as an attempt to give substantial form to the City of God in this world" ("Christianity as Metaphor in *The Eighth Day*," 6). That's not quite right: "City of God" is Augustine—Catholic; "City on a hill" is Winthrop—Puritan.

19. In *The Melting Pot* screen treatment, a character named Samuel—a name that recurs in Wilder's oeuvre perhaps to be an American signifier (allusion to Uncle Sam) in the manner of George—says, "This country has been given to us by God—to *us*—to hold for *Him*."

The similarity of sensibility and language in these passages written by Taylor and Wilder is striking enough to make one wonder if Wilder had read *God's Determinations* by the time he wrote *The Eighth Day*.[20]

Lastly, as we saw primarily in Wilder's works of his twenties, the Puritan bias against Catholicism attached itself to all of these Puritan codes and structures. Olga Doubkov is said to practice "idolatry—that is, a corner of her sitting room held a number of icons with burning lamps beneath them, before which she crossed herself on entering and leaving the room" (68–69). Olga is probably Russian Orthodox, and despite similar doctrines and devotional practices to Catholicism, she reveals her own prejudice when telling Lily Ashley why she should break it off with a traveling salesman with whom she wants to run away: "Besides, I think he's a Pole and a Roman Catholic" (92). During his illness, Breckenridge Lansing rails at his wife, who is from the Caribbean, "You and your Roman Catholic mumbo-jumbo!" (360). Of course Lansing is the "villain" of the novel, and we are meant to consider the source when we read this.[21]

What distinguishes *The Eighth Day*'s references to Catholicism from references in Wilder's earlier works is that here Wilder shows Catholics having a similar aversion to Protestants. For example, the salesman with whom Lily runs off tells Mrs. Ashley, "But even if I were free I couldn't marry her. She's not Catholic" (96). While in Chile, Ashley meets a priest who looks disdainfully at Ashley's boss after his disrespectful remark about the Chilean's religious practices: "Ashley caught the expression that the priest turned toward the managing director; it contained a faint smile and seemed to say, 'Oh, sir, not as oafish as you Protestants' " (174). Later we are told, "Ashley could scarcely apprehend the extent to which he [the priest] carried an irrational repulsion from Protestants" (175). The omniscient narrator tells us directly what the Priest thinks: "He assumed that Protestants were a despised minority on the earth's surface, crawling about abashedly, aware of their abjection but too satanically proud to acknowledge their error" (176).[22]

But Wilder also expresses the more ecumenical acceptance of differing faiths that we saw in *The Happy Journey* and *Heaven's My Destination*. After she has

20. In 1960, *God's Determinations* was republished in *Poems,* ed. Donald E. Stanford (New Haven: Yale University Press, 1960).

21. As one last bit of evidence that Wilder was not consciously or actively prejudiced against Catholics, though it is extratextual: according to Harrison (*Enthusiast,* 210), Wilder served on a national committee to elect Senator John F. Kennedy, the only Catholic president in the history of the United States.

22. Dennis Loyd also sees Ashley as "puritanistic" with an "acceptance based upon God's predestinary powers" ("Thornton Wilder's Americans," 1), but then contradictorily he writes, "It is difficult to call this novel's religious influence a Christian influence, particularly if one means by that term the usual Catholic or Protestant conceptions" (3).

become a successful singer in Chicago, Lily Ashley brags to her brother Roger, "Then I had my wonderful baby in a Catholic hospital. I loved everything about it. I sang to the other girls. I sang even when I was having the baby. The doctor and sisters were laughing" (262). Felicite Lansing, whom the omniscient narrator hints Roger will marry one day, studies to be a nun (278), and the novel's tone toward her, as toward her mother, Eustacia, is respectful. In the narrative of how Eustacia and Breckenridge met and married, Wilder represents Catholic doctrine without irony: "As soon as she was able she stumbled through the snowdrifts to a church of her faith. Toward the end of the hour on her knees she assumed the yoke [of her marriage to Lansing] as punishment for her disobedience. She had made a mistake, but she trusted that the sacrament of marriage would, in some unforeseeable way, support her" (321). That the sacrament apparently did support her is a reasonable conclusion readers can draw once they have the overview of Eustacia's life with her husband.

Thus we have ample evidence in *The Eighth Day* that in writing his penultimate novel Wilder resurrected his Puritan American heritage, which he saw as defining the best elements of American culture. Even more specifically, though, we can see Wilder wrestling with the issues of Puritan theology and ideology that were examined in Chapters Two and Three: predestination, Providence, and progress.

Predestination of the elect and reprobate was the hardest of the doctrines the Puritans borrowed from Calvin, and although in *Our Century* Wilder seemed to be satirizing that kind of exclusivity in the form of a gentlemen's club, in *The Eighth Day* he presents the belief straightforwardly and without criticism. The fortune teller Maria Icaza tells John Ashley, "You are a creature whom God loves—particularly loves. You are being born" (135), and later she says, "If God plans to give you His greatest gifts, it is because you always merited them" (136). The narrator describes Roger's deeds growing up in Coaltown as if they were destined: "He had leapt at runaway horses, parted fighting dogs, and rushed into burning houses as though he had had been singled out to do so" (208). In Chicago, Roger tells one of his lovers during the promiscuous phase of his education, "We all have to be as we're made" (256). Most explicitly, the narrator says late in *The Eighth Day*, "We are as Providence made us" (381).[23]

23. Burbank's reading of *The Eighth Day* is at times quite close to my own: "The basic conflicts of the novel are waged between secular saints and sinners, the Elect and the Damned, the renate and reprobate" (*Thornton Wilder*, 119). About the renate Burbank writes, "Wilder's secular elect . . . have the Protestant virtues of responsibility, industriousness, and independence" (120)—and he means people like the Ashleys. Burbank thinks that Breckenridge Lansing is more superficially American, but inside he is corrupt: "He represents the enormous economic, social, and puritanical moral power of the establishment" (119).

George Lansing, who is labeled early in the novel as "the town's 'holy terror'" (15) and turns out to be the murderer of his father, Breckenridge Lansing, appears to qualify as *The Eighth Day*'s representative of the Reprobate.[24] Wilder even has the narrator discuss that precise Calvinist term: "The word 'reprobate' is used loosely; this was the world of reprobates. . . . They have been judged and they agree with their judges. They tell few lies. They have nothing to hide and little to gain" (127). Indeed, George seems to see "the writing on the wall" as he explains to his sister Felicite in a letter, "It's the way God made the world. He can't stop it now or change it. Some people are damned before they are born. You won't like that, but I know. God doesn't hate the damned. He needs them. They pay for the rest. Paryas hold up the floors of homes. Enough said" (384). This is literal Calvinistic predestination, presented straightforwardly, without irony, so that one wonders just how much Wilder had thrown off his father's stern Calvinism.

Traces of the Puritans' deterministic belief that all of history and even most of what happens in daily life is controlled by Providence, which Wilder treated in *The Bridge of San Luis Rey,* appear throughout *The Eighth Day.* Olga Doubkov tells George Lansing, "For every man there is one great task that God has given him to do" (340). John Ashley overhears a Chilean girl telling her mother, "If Papa didn't leave us anything, it was the will of God" (144). Later Ashley remembers his grandmother had faith in God's plot: "Her thought turned always on God's plan for the universe. She asked to be shown her part in it. She complained of His slowness in its fulfillment. She asked that God be merciful to those who in wickedness or in ignorance had interfered with His great design" (149). Ashley himself "believed that illness and accident are apportioned to those who deserve them" (284). Mrs. Wickersham, Ashley's friend and ally in Chile, chides him, "You think some special providence watches over you. There are no special providences" (196), but later the narrator counters this with "grave accidents do not befall young Ashleys" (287) in the context of describing Ashley's college experiments. (One accident does befall John Ashley shortly after the just-quoted conversation he has with Mrs. Wickersham, but the explanation may simply be that he was no longer young.) Even cynical old Dr. Gillies buys into some form of determinism: "We keep saying that we 'live our lives.' Shucks! Life lives us" (309), which he has passed on to others who are believers, such as Eustacia Lansing: "That's what destiny is. Our lives are a seamless robe. All was ordained, as the English language put it. She arrived at a position much like Dr. Gillies'. We don't live our lives. God lives us" (367). Finally, at the

24. David Castronovo writes, "George Lansing is a more fully developed, highly charged, and clearly motivated version of Henry Antrobus in *The Skin of Our Teeth*" (*Thornton Wilder,* 144).

beginning of the last chapter, the narrator says, "This is a history. But there is only one history" (395); on the last page the narrator reverts to the tapestry parable or metaphor: "History is *one* tapestry," and the last paragraph begins, "There is much talk of a design in the arras" (435, emphasis in original). That design is God's plot, the providential view of history handed down generation after generation from the Puritans to present-day Americans.

And where will that history end? Although Judgment Day itself is never explicitly mentioned in *The Eighth Day,* several oblique allusions to the eschatological worldview that was manifested in Wilder's earliest works of his and the century's twenties, as discussed in Chapter Two above.[25] Judgment Day is alluded to in the guise of other religions, as Dr. MacKenzie explains Egyptian belief concerning the afterlife to John Ashley: "Yes, that his soul . . . descended the Nile in his death boat to the hall of judgment. There . . . it was weighed on a balance" (162). Certainly there is plenty of judgment on earth in *The Eighth Day:* "In the street people put on a face so that strangers won't read their souls. A crowd is a sterner judge than a relative or a friend. The crowd is God. LaSalle Street is like hell—you're being judged all the time. . . . Suicide very logical" (213). According to the narrator, the Kangaheela Indians believe in a God they call the "All-Father," who has plans for the future similar to the God of Christianity: "There are many peoples on the earth—more men than there are leaves in the forest—but He has singled out the Kangaheelas from among them. He will return. Let them BLAZE THE TRAIL against that day. The race of men will be saved by a few" (14). The penultimate sentence parallels the Christian hope in the second coming of Christ and the New England Puritans' belief that their errand into the wilderness was blazing a trail against that day (Christ's return), which was almost upon them. An early scene of *The Eighth Day* that takes place on New Year's Eve 1899 depicts a kind of millennial fever among the citizens of Coaltown waiting for the courthouse clock to strike the new century: "There was a mood of exaltation in the crowd, as though it expected the heavens to open. The twentieth century was to be the greatest century the world had ever known" (15). Peter Bogardus, a Buddhist whom Roger Ashley meets in Chicago, accuses Christianity of impatience: "You want your supreme happiness next Tuesday. You can't wait ten billion billion years—that's Christ's fault—impatience; always announcing the end of the world, next week, next month" (220). Later, Roger meets a representative of a secret society whose motto is Isaiah 40:3, which is quoted in the Gospels as prophesying about

---

25. Roy M. Anker also thinks that Wilder's career-long theme of a providential view of history is found in this novel, and that there is "an eschatological expectation" ("The Road to the Eighth Day: Hope, Faith, and Love in Wilder's *The Eighth Day,*" 1).

John the Baptist: "Make straight in the desert a highway for our God" (242). He tells Roger they are trying "to make Chicago the greatest, the most civilized, the most humane, the most beautiful city in the world. . . . They are thinking of some Jerusalem here in the future—a free Jerusalem" (243), which suggests not only the prophecy of a New Jerusalem come down from heaven after the second coming of Christ, as in the book of Revelation, but also the Puritans' attempt to make New England be that New Jerusalem, that city on a hill.

The Deacon of the Covenant Church believes in such an appointed time: "So on the sea of human lives *one* wave in many hundreds of thousands rises, gathers together the strength—the power—of many souls to bear a Messiah. At such times the earth groans; its hour approaches" (429, emphasis in original). But he confesses that he too, like Bogardus said of the Christians, may be "guilty of the sin of impatience. . . . It may be that this family and this America are mirages of my old eyes. Of my impatience" (431). Finally, showing that he has read Revelation and all that it prophesies about the end of the world and Christ's second coming and eternity, the Deacon tells Roger, "The dead are given new names in Heaven" (425).[26] Thus the Puritans' belief in the imminence of the second coming was alive and well in Thornton Wilder fifty years after he dramatized Judgment Day in *And the Sea Shall Give Up Its Dead* and *The Trumpet Shall Sound.*

The final major Puritan tenet that Wilder resurrected in *The Eighth Day* is the faith in progress on multiple levels of existence: the macrocosmic or metaphysical, the anthropological or social, and the microcosmic or personal. We saw in Chapter Three how Wilder's 1930s works dealt extensively with the issue of time and history: whether they are evolutionary, cyclical (static), or entropic. As in *The Long Christmas Dinner* plays and *Heaven's My Destination* (as well as *Our Town* and *The Skin of Our Teeth*), in *The Eighth Day* Wilder presents all three positions and includes statements supporting each, but if one weighs the evidence it is clear that his stance in this novel, as in his earlier works, is that progress has been and will continue to be made, that God's plot is still marching forward.

Wilder raises the issue of progress, often represented as evolution, only to cast a skeptical light on whether it is continuing in ways other than the biological (the literal evolution of species). Very early on in *The Eighth Day* the narrator poses the question of progress in terms of human creativity: "Is there more and more of it, or less and less?" (10), and then he asks, "Is it possible

---

26. In Rev. 2:17 Jesus says, "To him who overcomes, I will give some of the hidden manna. I will also give him a white stone with a new name written on it, known only to him who receives it" (KJV).

that there will someday be a 'spiritualization' of the human animal?" (10). Some of the novel's characters would answer the question with an emphatic "No!" For example, Mrs. Wickersham tells Ashley, "The human race gets no better. Mankind is vicious, slothful, quarrelsome, and self-centered. . . . When I was young I used to be astonished at how little progress was made in the world. . . . From time to time everyone goes into an ecstasy about the glorious advance of civilization—the miracle of vaccination, the wonders of the railroad. But the excitement dies down and there we are again—wolves and hyenas, wolves and peacocks" (198). Yet Mrs. Wickersham cries after this speech, "ashamed of herself," and she admits, "Yes . . . everything is hopeless, but we are the slaves of hope" (198).

In some passages in *The Eighth Day* Wilder's description clearly indicates the dissolution of order and the decay of human achievement, such as this statement that is reminiscent of the clock motif in *Our Town:* "The mines were running down like a tired clock" (29); shortly thereafter the mines are described as a "vast collapsing skeleton" (30). But we must remember, as the Stage Manager subtly reminds us at the end of *Our Town* when he rewinds his watch, clocks can be wound up again; that is, decline is not necessarily irreversible, as we see in *The Eighth Day* with the mines: thanks to Ashley and his improvements, "The skeleton began to twitch and right itself" (31). A few scholars have identified Wilder with the narrator of the novel and/or the Stage Manager in *Our Town,* but they do not see the narrator as affirming progress. Warren French even says that "the narrator, like Dr. Gillies, does not believe in the doctrine of progress . . . , but sees all 'centuries' as like one another."[27] Yet clearly the omniscient voice of the narrator holds out hope for progress: "In this history there has been some discussion of hope and faith. It is too early to treat of love. The last appearing of the graces is still emerging from the primal ooze. . . . It may be that after many thousands of years we may see it 'clarify'—as is said of turbid wine" (153–54). Despite this tentative statement, just as the narrator of *The Bridge of San Luis Rey* appeared to be skeptical about the philosophical issue but proceeded to dramatize that the bridge falling was providential, so too does *The Eighth Day* assert and dramatize progress.

In some scenes we can find a representation of or allusion to the natural cycle of birth, death, and new birth, which has been a central theme of Wilder's oeuvre. For example, one day in November Roger and Lily take a streetcar ride from Chicago to a small town in order for Roger to meet Lily's mentor,

27. French, "Christianity as Metaphor in *The Eighth Day,*" 3. Maxwell-Mahon thinks Dr. Gillies is "one of Wilder's *persona*" ("Novels of Thornton Wilder," 44) in the novel. Hermann Stresau notes that the narrator "takes much the same position as the Stage Manager in *Our Town*" (*Thornton Wilder,* 106).

a classical music maestro. At one point Roger seems to register the natural cycle in a hopeful tone: "The day had begun with frost; now in the somnolent heat a scarcely perceptible steam arose from the earth—a promise of renewal as compelling as those in the early days of April" (274). However, as T. S. Eliot told us, April can be viewed as "the cruelest month" if one projects forward from the renewal of life in the spring to the inevitable decay and death of that life in the fall and winter. Thus a cyclical view of the world is not the same as making progress; in fact, a cycle implies stasis or "spinning one's wheels," not going anywhere, everything remaining the same. The maestro tells Roger as much: "Those who see *progress* in it [history] are as deluded as those who see a gradual degeneration. A few steps forward, a few steps back. Human nature is like the ocean, unchanging, unchangeable. Today's calm, tomorrow's tempest—but it's the same ocean. Man is as he is, as he was, as he always will be" (264). And this is the position that many of the commentaries on *The Eighth Day* have taken.[28]

However, as we have seen time and again, Wilder acknowledges the repetition of the fundamental aspects of human experience, but he asserts that there is progress overall and that there can be progress on the individual level. This belief is rooted in America's New England Puritan origins, but it became as essentially American as democracy and capitalism, as Westbrook explains: "Carnegie's faith in the inevitability of progress—'all is well since all grows better'—suggests another common ground shared by social Darwinism and early American Calvinism. Though Carnegie doubtless felt that the tendency for all to grow better was worldwide, he took the United States as the bellwether of progress, as indeed did many other Americans of the nineteenth century."[29] In fact, hell is defined in *The Eighth Day* as the absence of progress. Near the end of the novel the Deacon of the Covenant Church points to Coaltown and tells Roger, "They walk in despair. If we were to describe what is Hell it would be the place in which there is no hope or possibility of change: birth, feeding, excreting, propagation, and death—all on some mighty wheel of repetition" (431). Thus we will see how *The Eighth Day* is Wilder's last testament to the doctrine of progress, and it is precisely this

28. For example, Burbank writes, "The power and effects of Breckenridge Lansing and his kind are obvious enough to prevent any undue optimism and put to rest any residual belief in progress. The human race, Wilder says, doesn't change much from one period to another; civilizations rise and fall in accordance with which values they adhere to" (*Thornton Wilder*, 122).

29. Westbrook, *Free Will*, 128. Sacvan Bercovitch also sees the Puritans as the source of an American faith in progress: "Students of the Great Awakening have used this distinction [pre- versus post-millennialism] to make Edwards out to be a radically innovative historian, the first New World spokesman for an optimistic view of human progress" (*The American Jeremiad*, 94–95).

theme that resurrects the affirmative tone that was absent from his postwar works.

The broadest level of progress is the universal, for which Wilder establishes a macrocosmic setting: the narrator tells us that Roger has come to accept the belief in "the powers of light and the powers of darkness that were engaged in some mighty conflict behind the screen of appearances" (427). As part of the epic scope of *The Eighth Day,* there are references to the stars and to the millions and billions of years of evolution. John Ashley compares the solar system moving through the galaxy to a human level of progress: "It's as though we were on a great ship moving through the skies" (337). Of course, the title of the novel suggests progress on both the macrocosmic and human levels, as in this speech by Dr. Gillies: "Nature never sleeps. The process of life never stands still. The creation has not come to an end. The Bible says that God created man on the sixth day and rested, but each of those days was many millions of years long. That day of rest must have been a short one. Man is not an end but a beginning. We are at the beginning of the second week. We are children of the eighth day" (16). Dr. Gillies further comments, "In this new century we shall be able to see that mankind is entering a new stage of development—the Man of the Eighth Day" (17). However, shortly after this uplifting speech, the narrator tells us, "Dr. Gillies was lying for all he was worth. He had no doubt that the coming century would be too direful to contemplate—that is to say, like all the other centuries. . . . Dr. Gillies had no faith in progress, in the future of mankind" (17). Yet the old cynic apparently has a change of heart later on, perhaps seeing progress in the big picture though in evolutionary terms only: "Well maybe NATURE after hundreds of millions of years has begun selecting for intelligence and mind and spirit. Maybe NATURE is moving into a new era. Breed out the stupid; breed in the wise" (318). Roger even repeats part of Dr. Gillies's eighth-day speech, so that lying or not Dr. Gillies passed on the belief in progress; Roger tells Lily, "He said that evolution was going on and on. After a while—maybe millions of years—a new kind of human being will be evolved. All we see now is just a stage that humanity's going through—possession and fear and cruelty. People will outgrow it, he said" (276). When Lily asks Roger if he thinks this is true, he says, "Oh, one would have to live ten thousand years to notice any change. One must feel it inside—that is, believe it" (276). In other words, progress on the universal level is a matter of faith, whether one attributes the movement to God or to nature or to the collective efforts of the human race over time. This brings us to the next level of progress: the anthropological or social.

In the final paragraph of *The Eighth Day,* the hope for social progress is again held out: "Some are strengthened by seeing a pattern wherein the oppressed and exploited of the earth are gradually emerging from their bondage" (435). The source of this hope is based in religious belief, as the narrator says early in the novel: "Palestine, for a thousand years, like a geyser in the sand, producing genius after genius, and soon there will be no one on earth who has not been affected by them" (10). Wilder may have been alluding to the spread of Christianity, but Palestine actually takes in all three great monotheistic religions stemming from the patriarch Abraham: Judaism, Islam, and Christianity. Wilder even throws in a little Buddhist progress for good measure: "Through the merit of Gautama Buddha himself and those who have followed him all men tend to rise. Finally, when they have lived as many lives as the sands of the Ganges, they will arrive at the threshold of supreme happiness" (218). Thus Wilder wants us to realize that human beings, imperfect though they are, have the potential to enact the progress of civilization.

That was the Puritans' belief as well, in spite of their determinism with regard to individuals' souls and God's creation overall. The errand into the wilderness was about advancing Christianity across the north American continent and the world; as Bercovitch says, in this sense, "errand" means progress. Although this was a religious belief, it was manifested in the Puritans' actions. William J. Schafer explains, "The quest of Americans for the frontier is as much the theological as geographical, a pilgrimage seeking limits of the divine."[30] This is not to say that every trailblazer was on a mission from God, but that the American cultural disposition to trailblazing is, in part, owing to the Puritan settlers' sense of mission in the New World.

On the most concrete level of narrative, Wilder's characterization manifests the microcosmic level of progress; *The Eighth Day* is replete with testimonies and examples of personal progress in both major and minor characters. Beginning with the hero of the novel, John Ashley grows in understanding of himself, others, and life in general as he makes his way from Illinois to Chile. At one point he falls into a slough of despond (or despair) like George Brush in *Heaven's My Destination,* but then he recovers and the narrator tells us, "His ascent had begun, perhaps" (130). Later Ashley asks himself, "Is this what growing older is—seeing always more clearly the things we failed to see" (145). Maria Icaza tells him, "Only those who have suffered ever come to have a heart that is wise" (160); Ashley had, of course, suffered as a result of being accused and falsely convicted of the murder of George Lansing. Critics have generally agreed that Wilder created Ashley as an example of the Kierkegaardian "knight of faith," and that "the real basis of his development is faith."[31]

30. Bercovitch, *American Jeremiad,* 12; Schafer, "About the Size of God: Radical Religious Ideas from the Puritan Revolution and American Literature," 46.
31. Papajewski, *Thornton Wilder,* 181.

Created in the image of his father, Roger Ashley makes progress throughout the novel.[32] Constance asks Roger if people "change any—while they're growing up?" and he replies, "Yes! I've changed—haven't I? And Lily's changed; you remember that she didn't notice anything. Today I learned that your best friend Anne Lansing has changed" (433). If nothing else, these changes imply growing up, becoming an adult, and Roger is the novel's prime example of physical and emotional maturation. Like his father his development is also partly spiritual; as Edward E. Erickson writes, "John Ashley's soul is not the only one we watch progressing in this novel." Erickson goes on to mention Eustacia Lansing and Roger, and he notes that at the end of the novel when Roger is with the Deacon of the Covenant Church, "The seeker has found."[33] Besides Roger, the oldest Ashley daughter, Lily, also matures and becomes wiser, as she tells Roger: "That day my education took a little jump forward" (272).

It isn't only the Ashleys who make progress, though. In the background story of how Eustacia and Breckenridge met and married, the narrator tells us how her mother "watched Eustacia's progress" (315) when she was a young girl. But Eustacia's progress is ongoing, beyond merely growing up. Of Felicite and her mother, Eustacia, the narrator tells us, "Both were journeying, both were straining to understand. . . . We came into the world to learn" (331). Even as a middle-aged wife and mother, her moral progress continues: "At 'St. Kitts' she had overmastered anger. At Fort Barry she divested herself of the last pangs of envy" (338).

In the case of Eustacia's son, George Lansing, although he will ultimately commit the regressive Oedipal act of killing his father, he nevertheless makes progress in some areas. For example, he seems to be a prodigy in language study, which Olga Doubkov realizes as she tutors George in Russian: "Miss Doubkov had no experience of teaching languages, but she suspected that her pupil's progress was remarkable. . . . His progress between lessons astonished his teacher" (344). His sister Felicite is concerned about a more significant progress he needs to make, as she writes him, "You said that you were a CHILD OF THE EIGHTH DAY. . . . What frightens me now is that you may have let some mistaken fancy ROB YOU OF FOUR YEARS OF YOUR LIFE, warp you, dwarf you. You'll slip back to the SIXTH DAY, or earlier. . . . God forgives us all if we acknowledge our weakness. He sees billions of people. He knows everybody's road" (391).

Even the unlikable and unsympathetic character Breckenridge Lansing

---

32. Dalma Brunauer states that both John and Roger Ashley experience growth ("Some: An Examination of the Religious Tenets of Thornton Wilder's *The Eighth Day*," 54).

33. Erickson, "The Figure in the Tapestry: The Religious Vision of Thornton Wilder's *The Eighth Day*," 10, 12.

makes spiritual progress near the end of his life: "She [Eustacia] was trying to assist a soul to birth—to being born into self-knowledge, contrition, and hope" (354). Later she writes to George, "Your father died at the moment when his real self was beginning to find expression" (388). Here we again observe a note of tragedy in Wilder: as with Emily in *Our Town* and the Marquesa in *The Bridge of San Luis Rey,* Lansing dies before he can live out his transformation. As Maxwell-Mahon writes, "His tormenting of Eustacia eventually has a cathartic effect and he is resurrected, as it were, in the knowledge of her self-sacrifice for him. As is so often the case in Wilder's novels, this moment of revelation is followed swiftly by death, as he is shot down, supposedly by John Ashley."[34]

What redeems this aborted progress in *The Eighth Day,* as in Wilder's other works, is that life goes on. Eustacia tells Breckenridge, "Do you know what children are, Breck? They're the continuation of ourselves. They carry out what we wanted to be" (373). We aren't given much information about the Lansing children's futures except for George; he becomes a famous actor in Russia, which is probably meant to suggest his personal growth to achievement, though his life too is apparently cut short in the Bolshevik revolution, perhaps representing a providential punishment for his deadly sin of fratricide. We also know that Felicite marries Roger. As for the Ashley children, Roger becomes a famous journalist who will receive a state funeral in Washington when he dies; Lily becomes a famous opera singer; and Constance becomes a famous social reformer (396). Among the Ashleys only Sophia was arrested in her progress (i.e., in her emotional development), perhaps like Wilder's own sister Charlotte, who had to be institutionalized.

Even minor characters in *The Eighth Day* are said to have grown. For example, Ruby Morris, one of Roger's lovers during his experimental phase, is characterized by the narrator as outgrowing her parents, teachers, and others who "had hovered over her progress" (253). This is not to say that *The Eighth Day* attests to everyone making personal progress all the time. Mrs. Wickersham tells Ashley, "We go up or we go down—forward or back. I was slipping back" (203), but perhaps implying that now she will go forward again. Occasionally the omniscient narrator informs us unequivocally that not every character makes progress. Of Roger and Felicite's son we are told, "His later story was a long, lamentable self-destruction" (435). But most of the characters we encounter in *The Eighth Day* do grow up, learn, develop, advance. For the Ashleys, the representative Americans and the descendants of the Puritans, making progress seems almost destined, as the salesman tells Mrs. Ashley about the special people he calls "stars": "They're chosen. . . . They're

34. Maxwell-Mahon, "Novels of Thornton Wilder," 44.

only interested in one thing—doing their job better and better: *being perfect*" (96–97, emphasis in original). Late in *The Eighth Day* there is even an implicit echo of the Stage Manager's long speech in *Our Town* that suggests the soul continues to make progress after death: "But funerals are only in appearance the end of anything" (396).

Nevertheless, Wilder was enough of an existentialist to believe that humans have free will, which they can exercise for improvement or dissolution, so that progress on the individual level must be determined on a case-by-case basis. In fact, the way French has interpreted *The Eighth Day*'s final paragraph, which appears to stop mid-sentence, sounds very much like the Puritans' Covenant theology: "Perhaps one implication of the unfinished sentence at the end of the book is that the point has arrived at which others must take over from the original creator."[35] As discussed in Chapter One regarding the plot construction of *God's Determinations,* Covenant theology pertaining to individuals could be summed up as "God has done his part; now it is up to us to do ours."

Thus we have seen many passages from *The Eighth Day* that in some way testify to progress, whether on the universal, social, or individual level. The frequency of these references comes from the didactic purpose of writing in the Puritan narrative tradition, which also results in an overdetermination of key points, as we saw with Judgment Day in *The Trumpet Shall Sound* and progress in *Heaven's My Destination*. With a text so saturated with the codes of progress—and those quoted above were by no means all of them—one can only wonder how some critics have concluded that *The Eighth Day* denies progress and derides America.[36] As we have seen, Wilder's penultimate novel affirms America and progress with the same hard-won optimism as *The Cabala, The Long Christmas Dinner, Pullman Car Hiawatha, The Happy Journey to Trenton and Camden, Heaven's My Destination, Our Town,* and *The Skin of Our Teeth.*

Finally, *The Eighth Day* reads as if it were Wilder's "last hurrah," as if he were putting into it everything he had to say, and further, everything he had ever said. Indeed, he admitted in an interview about *Theophilus North* (1973), which turned out to be his actual last novel, "I hadn't expected to write another book and I worked on it in one year, April to April."[37]

A decade prior, Wilder referred to *The Seven Deadly Sins* and *The Seven Ages*

---

35. French, "Christianity as Metaphor," 5.

36. Goldstone thinks *The Eighth Day* shows that by the turn of the century "The American Dream had already gone sour" (*Intimate Portrait,* 247), and that the failure of America is the theme of *The Eighth Day* (248). Burbank, in *Thornton Wilder,* agrees that Wilder "belongs to what R. W. B. Lewis called the 'Party of Hope'" (122), but he goes on to assert that characters in *The Eighth Day* demonstrate resignation (129). That is certainly not the case with the Ashleys.

37. Michael Kernan, "Thornton Wilder: A Wizard, a Magus, a Waver of Wands," K3.

of Man as his artistic summing up, but subsequently he regretted making that statement. One can only speculate as to why he would regret it, but perhaps he had sensed at that point he was not through writing, that one last grand effort to communicate his vision was forthcoming. *The Eighth Day* reads as a much more comprehensive summing up of Wilder's ideas and passions in his previous works written over six decades than the two play cycles, which seem like an anomaly in the Wilder corpus, especially when compared to his last two novels. In many ways, *The Eighth Day* is Wilder's grand finale, as critics have commented.[38] But this epic novel is not just a summing up in terms of a reiteration of his major themes; *The Eighth Day* is also a summing up in the sense of reminding readers of the specific works and narrative elements within them that have developed and supported those themes.[39] That is, in his longest novel, Wilder reminds us of his earlier novels and plays with many allusions, character parallels, and verbal echoes sprinkled throughout the text. We have seen many comparisons to his earlier works already in this chapter, but Wilder included his own implicit comparisons in his true artistic summing up.

One type of intertextuality between *The Eighth Day* and the earlier works is in characters' names. For example, Ashley's rescuer, the Deacon of the Covenant Church, tells Roger his given name is Samuel (425); the narrator of *The Cabala* was nicknamed Samuele by the aristocratic Europeans he meets. While in South America John Ashley is called "Don Jaime" (130), the name of Camila's son in *The Bridge of San Luis Rey,* which is also set in South America, and he is helped by a character named Esteban (202), a name also from *The Bridge.* George Lansing shares the all-American Christian name of George Brush in *Heaven's My Destination,* George Gibbs in *Our Town,* George Antrobus in *The Skin of Our Teeth,* and George Walbeck, the ex-con in *Bernice.* Finally, the oldest Ashley daughter is named Lily, which was one of Sabina's names in *The Skin of Our Teeth* and a prostitute's name in *Heaven's My Destination.*

However, most of the allusions to Wilder's earlier works are more substantive than names. One way to demonstrate the intertextuality between this penultimate novel and the earlier works is to proceed chronologically; thus we begin with the *Angel Plays.* There is a statement in *The Eighth Day* about the ultimate fate of souls—the loss of individual identity—that is similar to that metaphysical concept in the final stage direction of *And the Sea*

38. For example, Burbank calls it Wilder's "capstone work" (*Thornton Wilder,* 116), and Erickson writes that *The Eighth Day* "seems destined to become considered Wilder's *Magnum Opus*" ("Figure in the Tapestry," 1).

39. Brunauer notes that *The Eighth Day* contains everything in it that was in all the earlier works ("Some," 2).

Shall Give Up Its Dead, quoted in Chapter One, and later in *Our Town,* quoted in Chapter Four: "But there is only one history. It began with the creation of man and will come to an end when the last human consciousness is extinguished" (*ED,* 395). Earlier in this chapter we saw that although Judgment Day is never explicitly mentioned in *The Eighth Day,* it is alluded to in a few places.

As in *The Cabala* when Samuele learns he is Hermes (the god who escorts the dead to the underworld), John Ashley is asked which of the gods he takes after: "Are you Hermes!—businessman, banker, lawyer, liar, cheat, newspaperman, god of eloquence, guide and companion to the dying? No, you're not merry enough" (165). But Roger Ashley is, as we see him help dying patients in the Chicago hospital where he works as an orderly. Wilder makes sure we make that connection when later in the chapter the Maestro shows Roger a gem that has the following carved into it: "Mercury—Hermes Psychopompos—leading the soul of a dead woman to the field of the blest" (266).

A character who is familiar with the circumstances of many people's dying explains to Ashley a theory similar to Brother Juniper's in *The Bridge of San Luis Rey:* "Bristow then went on to tell stories of deaths he had witnessed that arrived opportunely, at some right moment—deaths that beautifully crowned an enterprise or averted disgrace, or that lifted an intolerable burden. . . . Every death is a right death. We did not choose the day of our birth; we may not choose the day of leavetaking. They are chosen" (189). T. G., a journalist Roger rooms with, parallels Uncle Pio before he met Camila, in that he too is described both as an anarchist and a nihilist (234), and he had worked at many sordid "professions." This parallel character confirms the reading of Uncle Pio in Chapter Two as an allegory of Satan: the narrator of *The Eighth Day* reports that T. G. had written some plays in verse, one of which was titled *Lucifer* (235). A final connection between Wilder's second and sixth novels is the subject of Eustacia's letter to her son George; in it she raises the same philosophical issues as *The Bridge,* which also contained letters by the Marquesa as part of the novel's form: "How you used to argue—with your whole soul in your eyes and in your voice—about God and the creation of goodness and evil and justice and mercy and destiny and chance! . . . Justice rests upon understanding *all* the facts. God, who sees all, is Justice—Justice and Love. . . . Then the fatal accident took place" (387, emphasis in original). The end of the quotation could have come directly from *The Bridge.*

As with Wilder's drama and fiction of the 1930s, there are many journeys in *The Eighth Day,* some on trains, others on boats. We saw in *The Happy Journey, Pullman Car Hiawatha,* and *Heaven's My Destination* that these physical acts of progress symbolize other kinds of progress: financial, social, intellectual, and spiritual. Furthermore, temporal journeys parallel the geographical

journeys. For example, *The Eighth Day* compares two generational family stories (the Ashleys' and Lansings'), as with one family, the Bayards, in *The Long
Christmas Dinner*. Besides the paragraph quoted earlier in this chapter that reminds one of Ma Kirby in *Happy Journey* praising her family, their car, and
the state of New Jersey as the best in the world, when Roger returns to Coaltown at Christmas, Constance gives him a tour of the downtown, telling
him, "Here's Porky's store. Look, he's making it bigger" (401), reminiscent of
Caroline Kirby noticing how Beulah's street and house were bigger than
theirs, suggesting the next generation has progressed in prosperity. Readers
of *The Eighth Day* should also be reminded of *Heaven's My Destination* by one
of Sophia Ashley's early boarders: "Three days later he sent over an itinerant
preacher, Brother Jorgenson, who was making himself obnoxious by trying
to save souls in the barroom" (62). Finally, like George Brush, Breckenridge
Lansing's goal in life was "to found that greatest of all institutions—a God-
fearing American home" (351).

The Eighth Day alludes to *Our Town* in multiple ways, as previous studies
have pointed out.[40] Several lines echo the play: "People in Coaltown had
locked their doors at night from as long ago as anyone could remember"
(20), which the Gibbses comment on in Act One of *Our Town*. Like the Stage
Manager in his Act Two sermon, T. G. tells Roger, "Nature's only interested
in one thing—to cover the earth with as thick a layer of protoplasm as possible: plants, fishes, insects, and animals" (240–41). The litany of "thousands"
and "millions" in *Our Town* is repeated here, along with certain common images: "I just have the thoughts that millions of people have when they look at
the sea or stars" (361); "There was once a million people in Babylon" (396).
Occasionally, the narrator even speaks in the folksy, familiar tone of the Stage
Manager: "For these two families the first ten years went by without remarkable event: pregnancies, diapers, and croup; measles and falling out of trees;
birthday parties, dolls, stamp collections, and whooping cough.... Constance refused to speak to her best friend Anne for a week. You know all
that" (324). Or the narrator speaks as if he were a member of the community, as did the Stage Manager: "It is absurd to compare our children of the
Kangaheela Valley to the august examples of good and evil action I have referred to above" (11).

Wilder also included characters in *The Eighth Day* that parallel characters
in *The Matchmaker*. After John Ashley is convicted of murder and escapes from
the train, Mrs. Ashley apparently went through a stage similar to what Dolly
Levi had gone through after her husband died, but then, like Dolly, she

---

40. For example, Burbank compares the novel to *Our Town* for its focus on two families
close to each other (*Thornton Wilder*, 117).

rejoins the living, though not voluntarily at first: "She felt cornered, dragged back into life" (60). Mrs. Wickersham sounds a little like a matchmaker herself: "All those girls she had collected and trained and married" (182). Olga Doubkov, who is an entrepreneur of various means (e.g., seamstress, manager of a linen room, tutor in the Russian language), also seems intended to make us remember Wilder's most endearing character who carried a variety of business cards: "Mrs. Dolly Gallagher Levi, Varicose Veins Reduced" (*M,* 275), "Mrs. Dolly Gallagher Levi, Aurora Hosiery. Instruction in the guitar and mandolin" (*M,* 276).

There are several parallels between Wilder's epic novel and the allegorically epic play *The Skin of Our Teeth.* In the same way that Antrobus was simultaneously alive during the ice age and present day—was Adam, Noah, and the highest evolved mammal—so too the narrator of *The Eighth Day,* tongue as firmly in cheek as in the play, makes a character exist in two times: "It was somewhere in the Mesozoic age that Mr. Goodhue, Coaltown's banker, exchanged an outraged glance with his wife. They rose and left the room, head high, gazing straight before them. *Evolution!* Godless evolution!" (16, emphasis in original). Calling to mind the instability of the scenery in Act One of *The Skin of Our Teeth,* we read, "Ashley felt his deprivation keenly; in its place he put this absurd superstition—if he failed, *the walls of "The Elms"* [the Ashley home] *would sway, totter, and collapse*" (169, emphasis in original). Also, George Lansing, who has already been compared to Henry Antrobus, describes an experience he had as an actor that occurs in Act Three of *The Skin of Our Teeth* between the actors playing George and Henry Antrobus: "I got into a fight on the stage, right in front of an audience. The fight was written in the play" (388).

Apart from both works depicting a murderer who is a member of a small-town American family, *The Eighth Day* and *Shadow of a Doubt* both have characters awaiting divine intervention, Young Charlie in the film and Eustacia and Felicite in the novel: "They never doubted that some miracle would arrive" (331). There are allusions to Wilder's postwar works in *The Eighth Day,* but the only one worth mentioning here is that the seven deadly sins seemed to still be on his mind; avarice (148), sloth (156), and envy (338) are named, as well as the unpardonable sin—at least from a Puritan perspective—sloth, which is mentioned at least four times (52, 107, 154, and 156).[41]

Thus there is ample evidence that in writing *The Eighth Day* Wilder was thinking back over the works he had written before his longest novel, which

---

41. Mildred Kuner thinks Wilder finished the cycle plays in writing *The Eighth Day,* claiming that one can find seven ages of man and seven deadly sins in the novel (*Thornton Wilder: The Bright and the Dark,* 193).

he expected to be his last work. Indeed, *The Eighth Day* reads quite well as a culmination of his career, so Wilder may have asked himself, "What does one do for an encore to one's Swan Song?" We shall briefly look at his answer.

Coda to Chapter Six

A Puritan "Satyr Play":
Theophilus North as Epilogue to Wilder's Career and Life

We arrive at the end of Thornton Wilder's long career as a writer of plays and novels with the publication of *Theophilus North* in 1973, almost fifty years after his first novel was published. Wilder was seventy-six years old, in poor health, and, from a critical point of view, already part of the distant past of American letters. At the same time, he had won many awards, had a large reading and theater public, and his works were the subject of seven books and many articles by literary scholars. Surely, he had nothing left to prove to himself or the critics. *Theophilus North,* then, may have been for him something of a lark. If he had written *The Eighth Day* as his magnum opus and probable last work, perhaps he saw *Theophilus North* as an opportunity not for the missionary work he said he aspired to in his preface to *The Angel That Troubled the Water and Other Plays,* but to indulge himself, to have fun, to write what Graham Greene called his less serious works—an entertainment. Indeed, the most often used word in reviews of *Theophilus North* is "entertaining."

With few exceptions, critical response to *Theophilus North* has taken the position that it is not a major or serious work, that it is lighter than any other Wilder novel or play, except for, perhaps, *The Matchmaker.*[42] Critical commentary has tended to focus on how autobiographical the novel is and how it compares to Wilder's earlier work. That is, some scholars take the protagonist and narrator, Theophilus North, as Wilder's thinly disguised self-portrait, while others dismiss that interpretation. Goldstone thinks North is Wilder in his private life: "It became clear that he performed for all these people the role of a sort of guru-shaman-philosopher-priest," and he refers to Wilder's friends as his "parishioners. . . . It was this philanthropic aspect of his life that Wilder chose to celebrate in the fictional concoctions of *Theophilus North.*" In his review "The Wilder Side of Life," Malcolm Cowley also thinks North "is

---

42. As an example of the exception, Castronovo writes, "If Freud had read the new novel, he certainly would have pronounced it an advance, in its vision of the troubled human psyche, on *Heaven's My Destination*" (*Thornton Wilder,* 118).

hard to distinguish from the author." However, Simon claims North is not Wilder: "Despite superficial coincidences, Theophilus North is not Thornton Niven Wilder. . . . He is essentially another Wilder archetype, a saintly man, for all his sexual encounters. He is Samuele. He is John Ashley. He is a man of faith, of good will, and he proves, again and again, that Goodness can overcome Evil."[43]

How autobiographical is *Theophilus North*? North tells us that his parents were of New England and Scottish ancestry (5), that his father was from Maine (9) but moved to Madison, Wisconsin, to become a newspaper editor (63); and that Madison is where North was born (11). Then his father took a consular post in China (63) where North attended a missionary school (2). For his college education, North went to Yale (8) where he wrote a play titled *The Trumpet Shall Sound,* which was published in *Yale Literary Magazine* (56). During World War I he served in the Coast Guard (337). After college he spent a year in Italy and went on an archeological dig that unearthed a Roman road (373), met Sigmund Freud (4), then returned home to teach at a boys' prep school in New Jersey (1), a position from which he has just resigned at the beginning of the novel. These biographical details of North's life to that point certainly resemble quite closely the details of Wilder's life to just before he published *The Cabala* in 1926. And Theophilus North is as American as any of Wilder's protagonists: "I am a member of the middle class—in fact, of the middle of the middle classes—from the middle of the country. We are doctors, parsons, teachers, small-town newspaper editors, two-room lawyers" (334). North mentions that his older brother is a minister (17), and Thornton's older minister brother, Amos, has pointed out that "North" is an anagram for a shorter form of Wilder's first name, and that "Theophilus" was the name their parents had given to Thornton's stillborn twin brother.[44] Thus Wilder has certainly given readers who may be familiar with his background reason to see the novel as autobiography.

However, two bits of textual evidence show that the characterization of Theophilus North is not identical to the personality of Thornton Wilder. The first is that North is heterosexual whereas Wilder was, apparently, a mostly celibate homosexual, as noted in the Introduction. The second is that North claims to be an atheist: "Unfortunately I had ceased to believe in the existence of God in 1914 (my seventeenth year)" (2). If we take the position that North is Thornton, how do we account for this confession? Or was this line slipped in to trick jaded, skeptical critics into thinking that this time

43. Goldstone, *Intimate Portrait,* 262; Malcolm Cowley, "The Wilder Side of Life," 5; Simon, *Thornton Wilder, His World,* 257.
44. Amos Niven Wilder, *Wilder and His Public,* 10.

Wilder wouldn't proselytize? Or perhaps this is the best evidence of all that the novel only appears to be autobiographical in the superficial circumstances of North and Wilder's childhoods, family backgrounds, and first jobs. Despite the profession of atheism in the beginning of *Theophilus North,* North doesn't sound like an atheist throughout the rest of the novel. For example, he says to a woman who told him she would go to hell to make her husband happy, "Alice, I'm ashamed of you. . . . That *you*—who know that the heart of Jesus is as big as the whole world—you think that Jesus would send you to hell for a little sin that would make George happy or a little sin that you had to do to keep alive in a cruel city like Norfolk" (271). And other statements by North sound like the religious characters in Wilder's earlier works: "Heaven sent me an idea" (358); "*Gottes Zeit ist die allerbeste Zeit*" ("God's time is not our time," 308). Whatever Wilder's actual religious beliefs, his plays, novels, interviews, and other writings are filled with references to and comments on religious faith, some of them suggesting he was a believer and some not, though the former far outnumber the latter.

Nevertheless, when the episodes in the novel are examined, one can't help but wonder if any of it was based on actual events in the life of Thornton Wilder. In all that he does, Theophilus North appears to be imbued with supernatural powers with which he saves others from difficult and undesirable situations almost as if he were a more realistic superhero than in comic books, or literally divine, as many critics have discussed in various terms. For example, Dennis Loyd says of Theophilus, "North's omniscience casts him in the role of God." Every critic takes note that Theophilus means "one who loves God" in Greek, as we are told in chapter ten (239), but North's other name, Theodore (142), means "gift from God." In his review of *Theophilus North,* Granville Hicks writes, "It might be argued that Theophilus is what some critics would call a Jesus-figure. He heals the sick after his own fashion, and his deeds attract a large following. Members of the establishment denounce him for stirring up people. But I don't want to push this as far as it might be pushed." Hicks also compares Theophilus to a faith healer, since he does seem to heal physical and mental/emotional disorders. North even "exorcises" the haunted house of Miss Wyckoff and the Newport community of a rumor about the death of Persis's husband. Allen Lane, in his review "Angelism in New England," describes North as an angel, perhaps thinking of *The Angel That Troubled the Waters,* one of Wilder's three-minute plays. Kernan compares Theophilus to Prospero in *The Tempest:* "A Prospero figure—a controller of destinies—appears in nearly all of Wilder's works," citing Samuele, the Stage Manager, and Dolly Levi. Hicks also compares Theophilus to Dolly Levi, with good reason: he plays matchmaker in chapter ten, "Mino," and later in chapter thirteen, "Bobo and Persis."[45]

Clearly Theophilus is, as one character calls him, "a planner" (343), an advisor, and an orchestrator, much like the Stage Manager in *Pullman Car Hiawatha.* That comparison is appropriate since North is constantly performing, often literally playacting with some of his tutors or "patients," reading from plays or improvising situations and dialogue. In one scene within a scene, North tells us, "Like a stage director I whispered some suggestions to him— some business, some lines" (184). Lyall H. Powers notes how certain speeches in the novel are "reminiscent in function of the 'intrusive' remarks of the Stage Manager in *Our Town* or the 'extrusive' observations of Lily Sabina in *The Skin of Our Teeth,* both of which are calculated to emphasize the quality of the plays as works of art."[46] One such example occurs in a flashback to North's tour of duty in the Coast Guard during World War I. When his ship arrives at port, he sees a bonfire celebrating the end of the war (352–53), just as Sabina did in Act Three of *The Skin of Our Teeth.* After describing the jubilant pandemonium, North says, "Reader, it was gorgeous!" (353).

North's semidivine powers and his role as narrator of the action make the character a final example of the typological habit of mind we have observed throughout Wilder's oeuvre. It was noted in Chapter Four in the section on *The Matchmaker* that Dolly Levi may be regarded as the antitype or most concrete realization of the Stage Manager type that originated in a simile in *The Cabala* and then was incarnated in the Stage Managers of *The Happy Journey, Pullman Car Hiawatha,* and *Our Town.* Dolly may be a type character, but she has more depth and complexity than any of the Stage Managers. Theophilus North, though idealized, is even more multidimensional than Dolly, as Mary Ellen Williams notes: "The dig in Newport reveals more than the artifacts of the city: it also reveals the reality of Theophilus North. That reality is complex, a fusion of many aspirations and acts."[47] This time Wilder's arranger-

---

45. Loyd, "Thornton Wilder's Americans," 13; Hicks, "*Theophilus North,*" 56–57, 55; Kernan, "Thornton Wilder," K1. Simon points out that the episode concerning Miss Wyckoff and her allegedly haunted house with servants misbehaving while the owner is away is reminiscent of *The Trumpet Shall Sound* (*Thornton Wilder, His World,* 254). In that play Peter Magnus was a Jesus figure, though Jesus on Judgment Day. Furthermore, in this last novel Wilder reuses "Flora" (30) and "Dexter" (11), two of the names in *Trumpet.*

46. Powers, "Thornton Wilder as Literary Cubist: An Acknowledged Debt to Henry James," 38.

47. Williams, *A Vast Landscape: Time in the Novels of Thornton Wilder,* 101. Williams comes close to identifying Wilder's method as typological: "Wilder also demonstrates that the American past is a source of prototypes" (96). She cites Rip Van Winkle and Edgar Allan Poe as examples, observing that "Wilder comments upon the cyclic, repetitive use of recurring character types" (104). Another study almost describes typology. Comparing Wilder's technique to cubist painting, Powers says, "The same effect is achieved in Chap-

manager-orchestrator-teacher-minister-God-hero is truly heroic and the closest to being a literal dramatization of the antitype of all antitypes, Jesus Christ. North heals the sick, raises the dead (in a manner of speaking), instructs young and old alike with parables, reconciles husband and wife, rescues innocent victims from criminals, and, overall, purifies and blesses a community full of lost souls during a summer-long "ministry." Thus, from the alpha to the omega of Wilder's career as a novelist—simile in *The Cabala* to idealized self-portrait in *Theophilus North*—the Stage Manager type recurred, evolved, and progressed into an incarnation of divine and human nature.[48]

If North is a fictional representation of Jesus Christ, whom we haven't seen on a Wilder stage or page since *The Angel Plays,* given that those three-minute plays were written when he was in high school and college, then in writing *Theophilus North* Thornton Wilder truly ended his writing career where he began, and two short years from when, after a lifetime of progress, he would end his errand into the wilderness of life on earth.

---

ter 11 'Alice,' by the association of the lonely navy wife with Homer's Penelope. Again the association is not mere comparison: it is, rather, immediate juxtaposition that strongly implies identification, simultaneous co-existence" ("Wilder as Literary Cubist," 38–39). Yet these perceptive readings of *Theophilus North* did not identify the source of this technique as the New England Puritans.

48. Like many critics, Williams (*Vast Landscape*) points out the symmetry of Wilder's career in his first and last novels being so autobiographical. Burbank notes that *Theophilus North* is the only novel since *The Cabala* to be written in the first person (*Thornton Wilder,* 123). Cowley writes that *Theophilus North* is so much like *The Cabala* that "one might even say that the seventh novel is a sequel to the first" ("The Wilder Side of Life," 5).

Conclusion

Passing the Torch

Thornton Wilder and His Influence on American Drama

Literature has always more resembled a torch race than a furious dispute among heirs. The theatre has lagged behind the other arts in finding the "new way" to express how men and women think and feel in our time. I am not one of the new dramatists we are looking for. I wish I were. I hope I have played a part in preparing the way for them. I am not an innovator but a rediscoverer of forgotten goods and I hope a remover of obtrusive bric-a-brac.

—Thornton Wilder, *Three Plays*

In the above statement assessing his contribution to drama, Thornton Wilder claims the role of John the Baptist rather than that of the Messiah, for whom he hopes he had "prepared the way." As we have seen, some of those "forgotten goods" Wilder rediscovered—philosophical and aesthetic—are the legacy of the New England Puritans. If his voice crying in the wilderness sounded a great deal like seventeenth-century preacher, poet, and playwright Edward Taylor's, then perhaps the Puritan errand into the wilderness had not ended after all. In fact, Wilder did "pass the torch" of the Puritan narrative tradition on to at least two American playwrights who came after him: Tennessee Williams and Edward Albee. In the following discussion, we shall see how Puritanism continued its errand into the theatrical wilderness.

Wilder's Influence upon Tennessee Williams

He also recalls a violent thunderstorm that tore the awning off the porch. I re-member that thunderstorm, too. Ozzie and I raced around the house trying to make it safe against the storm. I knew Tom was deathly afraid of thunder and lightning and so, when I saw him running back and forth from the yard into the house, all the while talking to himself, I stopped for a moment and lis-tened. He was pleading, "Please, God. Wait. Just wait a minute, God, until I get all my toys in."

—Edwina Williams, *Remember Me*

Throughout his life Tennessee Williams believed that God was thunder and lightning, and he feared His wrath. Many of his plays demonstrate that his fear of God closely resembles the potential for individual fatalism in the Puritans' cosmic optimism, which we saw in Edward Taylor's *God's Determi-nations*. That is, Tennessee Williams's plays may be read within the Puritan narrative tradition as manifesting the fear of being reprobate in a Calvinistic universe.

As with Wilder, the continuity of the Puritan ethos and aesthetic in Ten-nessee Williams's oeuvre is predicated first and foremost upon transmission through the religious beliefs of his family, his cultural background, and the indirect influence of his reading of classic American literature. But it is also possible that another source of the presence of New England Puritan theol-ogy, ideology, and aesthetics in Williams's plays is the example of Thornton Wilder, whose greatest theatrical successes immediately preceded Williams's first success, *The Glass Menagerie* (1945).[1] In fact, Williams may have been at-tempting to write reprobate (or, more literally, Southern) answers to Wilder's New England optimism in *Our Town* and *The Skin of Our Teeth*. As discussed in Chapter One, the parody and satire of literary predecessors is another way in which the Puritan narrative tradition has continued within American lit-erature.[2]

1. According to Donald Spoto's biography, *The Kindness of Strangers: The Life of Tennessee Williams,* Williams saw *Our Town* performed by the Provincetown Players during the sum-mer of 1940 before he had written *The Glass Menagerie* (80). He almost certainly would have seen *The Skin of Our Teeth* as well during the period in which he was living in Manhattan and attending the theater as often as possible with the help of his agent, Audrey Wood. Spoto thinks that a one-act written and performed at this time, *The Long Good-bye,* was modeled after Wilder's *The Long Christmas Dinner* (78). Later, Spoto notes, Williams met Wilder, who praised and encouraged Williams's work, notably a reading of *The Unsatisfactory Supper* at Nantucket in 1946 (128).

2. The animosity Williams had for Wilder apparently did not begin until the rehear-sals for *A Streetcar Named Desire,* during which Wilder, sitting in on a rehearsal, found Stella's marriage to Stanley implausible (Spoto, *Kindness of Strangers,* 137).

A few Williams scholars have commented that Tom's narration in *The Glass Menagerie* may owe something to the Stage Manager in *Our Town*[3] and noted that both *Camino Real* and *The Skin of Our Teeth* were directed by Elia Kazan. *The Glass Menagerie* does contain subtle indications of Williams's conscious or unconscious imitation of Wilder's technique. Tom's pantomime of eating dinner as the stage directions in Scene One refer to an imaginary knife and fork (1:146)[4] parallels the pantomime of the Webb and Gibbs families at breakfast in *Our Town*. Reminiscent of the Stage Manager, Tom as narrator "remains standing with his cigarette by the portieres" (1:147) after exiting the scene; stage directions indicate that Tom "plays this scene as though reading from a script" (1:148), which is what the Stage Manager in *The Happy Journey* literally does.

Another theatrical echo of Wilder in Williams's drama is the projection of scene titles Williams employed in his script for *The Glass Menagerie*. Williams scholars have not considered Wilder's use of screen projections at the beginning of *The Skin of Our Teeth*, which was produced on stage only three years before *The Glass Menagerie*, as possible inspiration for this device. The function of Wilder's images were to help set the farcical tone of the play and to imitate the kind of newsreels of World War Two events movie audiences in America were watching; Williams's proposed use was also to control the play's tone.[5]

In Williams's allegorical play *Camino Real* (1953) the character Gutman announces the beginning of "blocks" (scenes or episodes), addresses the audience, and also plays stage manager or director at the end of the play: "(to the audience) The Curtain Line has been spoken! (To the wings) Bring it down!" (591). Falk compares Gutman's calling out the block divisions in *Camino Real* to the Stage Manager in *Our Town*.[6] Spoto makes the most substantive comment in all of Williams scholarship on the similarity between *Camino Real* and *The Skin of Our Teeth*:

> The play had been structured as if it were modeled on Thornton Wilder's *The Skin of Our Teeth:* the narrative stretched time and place arbitrarily; the emotional truth of the play was the truth of dream and fantasy, of memory and longing and hope—the truth of poetry, not the truth of verisimilitude. From

3. See Foster Hirsch, *A Portrait of the Artist: The Plays of Tennessee Williams,* 37; Roger Boxhill, *Tennessee Williams,* 73.

4. Unless otherwise specified, all quotations of Williams's plays are from *The Theatre of Tennessee Williams,* 8 vols.

5. See Brian Parker's excellent analysis of the use of screen projections in *Glass Menagerie* to avoid the pitfall of sentimentality ("The Composition of *The Glass Menagerie:* An Argument for Complexity").

6. Signi Falk, *Tennessee Williams,* 2d ed., 95.

the start Williams hoped that Elia Kazan would direct *Camino Real;* this hope, in fact, seems to have influenced the construction of the play, for it was with *The Skin of Our Teeth* that Kazan's directorial career had been firmly established.[7]

The degree to which critics have overlooked Thornton Wilder's role in American drama is evident in Mary Ann Corrigan's and Louis Broussard's claims that there had been nothing on Broadway like *Camino Real* for the thirty years since Elmer Rice's *The Adding Machine.*[8]

These suggestions of influence based upon structural or stylistic similarities aside, the major evidence that the Puritan narrative tradition passed through American culture and literature and Wilder's works into Williams's works lies ultimately in textual analysis. That is, if one brings an informed understanding of New England Puritanism to a study of Tennessee Williams, an inevitable conclusion is that, like Wilder, Williams was more quintessentially American than has been realized.

Generally the scholarship on Williams agrees that his is a pessimistic, defeatist outlook, though Williams sometimes countered that generalization.[9] Most studies recognize the use of Christian elements in the plays; a few even regard Williams's philosophy as essentially Christian.[10] Attempts to classify his aesthetic have acknowledged that Williams is not a realist, though several scholars maintain that his dramaturgy is a combination of realistic and non-realistic techniques.[11]

7. Spoto, *Kindness of Strangers,* 177.

8. Corrigan, "Beyond Verisimilitude: Echoes of Expressionism in Williams' Plays," 396; Broussard, *American Drama: Contemporary Allegory from Eugene O'Neill to Tennessee Williams,* 105.

9. "I think I am mostly optimistic. I believe very strongly in the existence of good. I believe that honesty, understanding, sympathy, and even sexual passion are good. So I don't think I'm a pessimist altogether" (Williams quoted in Albert J. Devlin, ed., *Conversations with Tennessee Williams,* 40).

10. On Williams's use of Christian myth, see Judith Thompson, *Tennessee Williams' Plays: Memory, Myth, and Symbol;* Nancy Baker Traubitz, "Myth as a Basis of Dramatic Structure in *Orpheus Descending*"; and Gilbert Debusscher, "Tennessee Williams' Lives of the Saints: A Playwright's Obliquity." For Williams's worldview as Christian (as well as his use of Christian or biblical motifs), see Nancy M. Tischler, *Tennessee Williams: Rebellious Puritan,* her pamphlet, *Tennessee Williams,* and "Tennessee Williams' Bohemian Revision of Christianity." See also Philip M. Armato, "Tennessee Williams' Meditations on Life and Death in *Suddenly Last Summer, The Night of the Iguana,* and *The Milk Train Doesn't Stop Here Anymore*"; John J. Fritscher, "Some Attitudes and a Posture: Religious Metaphor and Ritual in Tennessee Williams' *Query of the American God*"; and Delma Eugene Presley, "The Search for Hope in the Plays of Tennessee Williams" and "Little Acts of Grace."

11. "Poetic realism" is the term commonly used in reference to Williams; other classifications include theatricalist realism (John Gassner, *Theatre in Our Times*), expressionism

As with Wilder, the writers regarded as having influenced Williams are mostly European: D. H. Lawrence, Anton Chekhov, August Strindberg, Henrik Ibsen, and Federico García Lorca.[12] And as with Wilder, the importance of European movements, authors, and individual works is not denied here; Williams admits reading or seeing works by Lawrence, Chekhov, and Ibsen and being impressed with their subject matter or formal construction. However, as with Wilder, the philosophical and aesthetic aspects of Williams's plays that scholars think he encountered for the first time in modern European drama and literature (for example, romantic or transcendental themes, Christian symbolism, allegorical violence and sex) were present within his native literary tradition.

The term "Puritan" (with both upper- and lower-case "P") occurs even more frequently in Williams criticism than it does in Wilder criticism, but, as with Wilder, scholars usually use the term "Puritanism" to connote sexual repression, especially when discussing Williams's homosexuality.[13] "Puritan" also appears in discussions of Williams's work in binary opposition to what scholars perceive as antipuritan.[14]

(Corrigan, "Beyond Verisimilitude"; Peggy Prenshaw, "The Paradoxical Southern World of Tennessee Williams"; Stephen S. Stanton, ed., *Tennessee Williams: A Collection of Critical Essays*), symbolist (Beate Hein Bennett, "Williams and European Drama: Infernalists and Forgers of Modern Myths"), and romanticism (Esther Merle Jackson, *The Broken World of Tennessee Williams*). A few scholars have given some emphasis to the cinema as an aesthetic influence upon Williams, which may suggest why screen adaptations of his plays, even when badly adapted, sometimes have been more commercially successful than the plays themselves; see Boxhill, *Tennessee Williams*, 3, 23, and Jackson, *Broken World*, 54. For those describing Williams's aesthetic as realism combined with other aesthetics, see Presley, "Search for Hope," 42; Benjamin Nelson, *Tennessee Williams: The Man and His Work*, 180); Francis Donahue, *The Dramatic World of Tennessee Williams*, 225; Gerald Weales, *Tennessee Williams*, 35; and John Buell, "The Evil Imagery of Tennessee Williams," 182.

12. For Lawrence, see Norman J. Fedder, *The Influence of D. H. Lawrence on Tennessee Williams*. For Chekhov (thinking of Williams in a realistic tradition), see, for example, Felicia Hardison Londre, *Tennessee Williams: Life, Work, and Criticism*. For Strindberg, see Tischler, *Rebellious Puritan;* Donahue, *Dramatic World;* and Boxhill, *Tennessee Williams*. For Ibsen, see Presley, "Search for Hope." For Lorca, see Boxhill, *Tennessee Williams*.

13. For examples of the narrow use of "Puritan" by Williams scholars, see C. W. E. Bigsby, *A Critical Introduction to Twentieth-Century American Drama*, 12; Boxhill, *Tennessee Williams*, 83; and Falk, *Tennessee Williams*, 26.

14. The other pole is expressed variously as Cavalier (Tischler, *Tennessee Williams*, 1); hedonist (Thomas E. Porter, *Myth and Modern American Drama*, 158); bohemian (Jean Gould, *Modern American Playwrights*, 236); demonic (Judith Thompson, *Tennessee Williams' Plays: Memory, Myth, and Symbol*, 11); and Southern (Thomas P. Adler, *Mirror on the Stage: The Pulitzer Plays as an Approach to American Drama*, 34). A few scholars or theater critics do mean Puritan or Calvinist in the cultural and theological sense; however, they have not examined in any depth how the religious/philosophical purview in Williams's plays resembles that of the authors of the earliest American literature. For the discussion that comes the closest to the cultural criticism approach of this study, though it relies more on psychoanalytic criticism, see John J. Fritscher, "Some Attitudes and a Posture: Religious Metaphor and Ritual in Tennessee Williams' Query of the American God."

The most famous labeling of Williams as a Puritan is, of course, Nancy Tischler's early study (1961), *Tennessee Williams, Rebellious Puritan*. She, too, means Puritan in the narrow sense: "The human need for the warmth of another person and the Puritan horror of the physical are the recurrent adversaries in Williams's continued battle of angels." Tischler uses the term "Calvinist" only once in her book, referring to original sin, though her description of Williams's view of the human condition is probably what she understands as Calvinist or Puritan theology: "In a universe that rolls on its inevitable way, living in a society that we cannot change, we are powerless to influence or even understand our fate. The best we can do is face our doom with fortitude and reach out our hands in sympathy to our doomed fellow-beings." Not only is this not an accurate description of Calvinistic theology—neither Calvin nor the Puritans believed that the human race as a whole is damned or doomed—it is also not an accurate reading of the worldview expressed in Williams's plays. That is, for Williams, Everyman is not damned.[15]

The fate that befalls the Wingfields, Blanche DuBois, Alma Winemiller, Brick Pollit, Chance Wayne, and Sebastian Venable is not universal. There are the Jim O'Connors, the Stanley and Stella Kowalskis, the John Buchanons, the Maggie Pollits, the Alexandra del Lagos, and the Catharine Hollys—among others—who seem to be chosen as arbitrarily as in a Calvinistic universe to live happily, even if they must suffer for a time. Williams's and our sympathies are with the doomed characters, and we may be repulsed by the nominally elect characters (e.g., Stanley in *A Streetcar Named Desire*), but Williams seems to show that those unsympathetic characters are elected by God or selected by nature or materialistic American culture not just to survive, but to thrive. What Williams scholars rarely consider is that God may be the God of wrath or justice to some, to the reprobate, and the God of love or mercy to others, to the elect. The worst of all nightmares to a Puritan, especially to a rebellious Puritan, is the fear that he belongs to the group for which God is the harsh Judge on the Day of Doom.

More important than scholarly appraisal of his works is that Williams ascribed the term "Puritan" to himself and to his works long before any scholarly study of his plays had been written. In a 1945 interview, he said, "My grandfather was an Episcopalian minister. We were brought up in an atmosphere of Southern Puritanism. . . . It's like Northern Puritanism except that

15. Tischler, *Rebellious Puritan*, 120, 264, 300. That the doomed protagonist of a Williams play represents humanity is a fairly common misreading. See, for example, Presley, who sees him as "a dramatist of lost souls" ("Little Acts of Grace" 580), and Jackson, who says Williams writes of the anti-hero and that "all men are anti-heroic" (*Broken World*, 87). Other scholars have characterized the microcosmic setting of the typical Williams play as hell, which implies a universal condition of damnation; see Bigsby, *Critical Introduction*, 130; John L. Von Szeliski, "Tennessee Williams and the Tragedy of Sensitivity," 60; Weales, *Tennessee Williams*, 39; and Falk, *Tennessee Williams*, 92, 163.

it's more fractious. Also more old-fashioned."[16] Sometimes Williams also uses the term "Puritan" in the sense of "puritanical," but the above statement demonstrates that he was aware that Puritanism was a cultural force in America, both in the North and South. In his own analysis of his cultural heritage, Williams said, "My father, a man with the formidable name of Cornelius Coffin Williams, was a man of ancestry that came on one side, the Williams, from pioneer Tennessee stock and on the other from early settlers of Nantucket Island in New England. My mother was descended from Quakers. Roughly there was a combination of Puritan and Cavalier strains in my blood which may be accountable for the conflicting impulses I often represent in the people I write about."[17]

Williams displays a less abstract familiarity with the seventeenth-century Puritans in his short story "The Yellow Bird," which was the inspiration for the full-length play *Summer and Smoke,* about which Williams said, "You can say it is a tragedy of Puritanism. That is life in America."[18] In "The Yellow Bird" Williams is almost certainly modeling his characters' heritage after the most famous Puritan family, the Mathers, and actual records of the Salem witch trials:

> Alma's father was named Increase Tutwiler, the last of a string of Increase Tutwilers who had occupied pulpits since the reformation came to England. . . . The first American progenitor had settled in Salem, and around him and his wife, Goody Tutwiler, nee Woodson, had revolved one of the most sensational of the Salem witch-trials. . . . One of [the circle girls, a group of hysterical young ladies of Salem who were thrown into fits whenever a witch came near them] declared that Goody Tutwiler had appeared to them with a yellow bird . . . which served as interlocutor between herself and the devil to whom she was sworn. . . [Her Reverend husband also claimed to see the yellow bird. She was] condemned and hanged but this by no means was the last of the yellow bird named Bobo. It had manifested itself in one form or another, and its continual nagging had left the Puritan spirit fiercely aglow, from Salem to Hobbs, Arkansas, where the Increase Tutwiler of this story was preaching.[19]

What studies of Williams have not fully understood is how the Calvinistic doctrine of predestination informs Williams's tragic vision. My claim is that

16. Devlin, *Conversations,* 16.
17. Williams, *Where I Live,* 58. For other examples of Williams characterizing himself as a Puritan, see Devlin, *Conversations,* 51, 78, 79, 210, 228, 232.
18. Williams, *Where I Live,* 26.
19. Williams, "The Yellow Bird," *Three Players of a Summer Game,* 128–29. In *The Congregational Way: The Role of the Pilgrims and Their Heirs in Shaping America,* Marion L. Starkey's discussion of the Salem witch trials reports that Abigail Parris saw the soul of one woman in the form of "a little yellow bird" (*Congregational Way,* 250). Williams evidently had read some historical account of this episode in New England Puritan history.

Williams does not rebel against this view of the universe, but that he writes about the suffering of characters who are doomed by it. Even if Williams thought he was rebelling against that heritage, his literary production served nonetheless to give voice to the darker side of the Puritan ethos and to extend the narrative tradition. To demonstrate the validity of this point, we can briefly examine a few of Williams's plays to find some of the same vestiges of Puritanism that were present in Wilder's texts.

In *Battle of Angels* (1940), Williams's first major professional production, an oppressive fatalism hangs over the small Southern town in which the action takes places, and even the characters seem aware of it: "Both of us equally damned and for the same good reason" (1:45). But the damnation is not necessarily universal: "There's absolutely no justice in nature. I mean the way she ties some women down [with pregnancy] while others can run hog wild" (1:40). The dichotomous view of the human race in the heroine's death speech at the end of the play completes her personal version of Christ's parable of the fig tree and parallels Calvinistic doctrine: "Isn't it funny that I should just now remember what happened to the fig tree? It was struck down in a storm, the very spring that I hung those [Christmas] ornaments on it. Why? Why? for what reason? because some things are enemies of light and there is a battle between them in which some fall!" (1:116).

In a Calvinistic theology, how one sees God depends, finally, on how one sees oneself: as elect or reprobate. In his 1958 play *Suddenly Last Summer,* Williams fashions a parable from Puritan paranoia, though—as the old joke goes—"It isn't paranoia if the universe really is out to get you." As a poet/philosopher, Sebastian Venable falls within the American literary tradition as influenced by Puritan origins: "My son was looking for God. I mean for a clear image of Him" (3:357). Upon viewing the scene of the sea gulls preying upon the newly hatched turtles on the Encantadas, Mrs. Venable reports Sebastian saying, " 'Now I've seen Him!'—and he meant God" (3:357). Catherine confirms the nature of Sebastian's quest that led to his destruction: She explains that she tried to "save him" from "completing!—a sort of!—image!—he had of himself as a sort of!—sacrifice to a!—terrible sort of a—" The Doctor asks, "—God?" to which Catherine replies, "Yes, a—cruel one, Doctor! (3:397).[20] As Debusscher says, "The world of *Suddenly Last Summer* appears like a vindication of Sebastian's views: devouring is the all-pervading impulse, the prime mover of the universe."[21] Being devoured was the image of judgment and damnation used by Satan in Taylor's *God's Determinations;* in fact, as we have seen, in "Satans Rage at them in their Conversion" Satan

---

20. For my complete discussion of *Suddenly Last Summer,* see "Puritan Paranoia: Tennessee Williams's *Suddenly Last Summer* as Calvinist Nightmare."
21. Debusscher, "Lives of the Saints," 156.

twice employs an eating metaphor for the judgment and damnation of the second and third ranks: "You Rebells all, I Will you gripe and fist; / I'le make my Jaws a Mill to grin'de such grists. . . . What will you do when you shall squezed bee / Between such Monstrous Gyants Jaws as Wee?" (48, 49). The "We" is Christ and Satan; in other words, both God and the Devil are out to get the Second and Third Ranks. Williams himself has said, "Do they work together, God and the devil? I sometimes suspect that there's a sort of understanding between them, which we won't understand until Doomsday."[22] As we have seen in analyzing Wilder's texts, "Doomsday" has been a particularly New England Puritan code ever since Michael Wigglesworth's *The Day of Doom,* the first best seller on the North American continent, other than the Bible.

Predictions of Armageddon, the second coming, Judgment Day, and Christ's millennial reign are ever with us, and frequently in Williams's works. For example, like her Greek namesake, Cassandra in *Battle of Angels* warns of impending doom, striking an eschatological note: "I have it on the very best of authority that time is all used up. There's no more time. Can't you see it? Feel it? The atmosphere is pregnant with disaster! Now, I can even hear it! . . . A battle in heaven. A battle of angels above us! And thunder! And storm!" (99–100). In *Stairs to the Roof,* another pre-*Menagerie* apprentice play, numerous speeches contain apocalyptic imagery and prophecies of doom suggesting that it is "later than we think."[23] In Scene Two, entitled "No Fire Escape," a symbol Williams later uses in *The Glass Menagerie,* an executive tells his mistress on the phone, "I'm calling to give you some dreadful information. I'm way up high in a building that's caught on fire. There's no way out. There aren't any fire-escapes. . . . What am I talking about?—The state of the world we live in! It's cracking up, it's plunging toward destruction!" (15).

At the end of the play, after a godlike character named "Mr. E" has appeared on the roof of a skyscraper and sent the hero and heroine off to colonize a new star, the stage directions make it clear that Williams did in fact write an eschatological allegory of the Second Coming of Christ and the heralding of the Millennium:

22. Williams, *Where I Live,* 102.

23. A secondhand quote of Williams's found in Francis Donahue's *Dramatic World.* Donahue writes that in 1958 Williams "was quoted as believing that mankind was living in one of the most dreadful periods of human history; Armageddon was practically at hand, for it is 'later than we think'" (122). Williams was paraphrasing the lyric of a popular song that encourages us to enjoy ourselves because we may be nearer the end of our lives than we realize; that is, we could die tomorrow. However, Williams raised the line of the song to the macrocosmic level of human history and divine plan. His prophecy of doom is in the tradition of eschatological interpretations of current events begun in America by seventeenth-century Puritan writers.

There are loud cheers. The band strikes up a stirring martial air. Heavenly days! Bells are ringing all over the whole creation! Roman candles and pinwheels are filling the pale blue dusk with the most outrageous drunken jubilation! What is it? The Millennium—Possibly! Who knows! Voices in the crowd repeat, "What is it? The Millennium?" "The Millennium" grows to a repeated murmur as the crowd looks upward to where Ben has disappeared. Perhaps a banner reading THE MILLENNIUM appears from that direction. (98–99)

In an essay entitled "On a Streetcar Named Success," reprinted as "The Catastrophe of Success" as an introduction to *The Glass Menagerie* in *The Theatre of Tennessee Williams: Volume I,* Williams shows another legacy of New England Puritanism: "I have arrived at our American plan of Olympus.... Our great technology is a God-given chance for adventure and for progress which we are afraid to attempt. Our ideas and our ideals remain exactly what they were and where they were three centuries ago. No. I beg your pardon. It is no longer safe for a man to even declare them!" (136, 139). Interestingly, in this statement Williams initially affirms his faith in progress, declares that America has not made progress from its seventeenth-century origins (that is, makes a continuity statement with a negative tone—stagnation), then corrects himself in saying that we have strayed from those founding values. In this essay Williams slips into the rhetoric of the American jeremiad—an affirmation of and criticism for falling away from the "Puritan origins of the American self."

With the increasing competitiveness of the nuclear arms race between the United States and the Soviet Union, the apocalyptic mood of the world did not abate after World War Two, but increased. In *Camino Real,* Kilroy, the American Everyman, says, "Time is short, Baby—get ready to hitch on wings!" (456), and wings are the only sure way to be rescued from the Camino Real, as one character explains: "There are no flights out of here till further orders from someone higher up," though there is "a rumor of something called the Fugitivo..., one of those nonscheduled things" (500). As Presley notes, "The airplane 'Fugitivo' is the messianic symbol in *Camino Real*."[24]

Like *The Skin of Our Teeth, Camino Real* has a Gypsy who is a prophetess; she says, "Do you feel yourself to be spiritually unprepared for the age of exploding atoms?... Does further progress appear impossible to you?" (458), raising the issue of progress, one of Wilder's favorite themes. As Esther Jackson implies, the age of atoms suggests an eschatological point of view: "Williams's vision in this drama is theological, even apocalyptic," which is true of *The Skin of Our Teeth* as well. Various speeches in the play sound the jeremiad lament. Like Wilder's Esmeralda, who is called "Mrs. Jeremiah" in

24. Presley, "Search for Hope," 33.

The Skin of Our Teeth, the Gypsy decries the current generation: "There's nobody left to uphold the old traditions! You raise a girl. She watches television. Plays bebop. Reads *Screen Secrets.* Comes the Big Fiesta. The moonrise makes her a virgin—which is the neatest trick of the week! And what does she do? Chooses a Fugitive Patsy for the Chosen Hero!" (538).

In an almost literal incarnation of the rhetoric of the jeremiad, *Camino Real* laments Kilroy's fate and thus America's as well: "This was thy son, America—and now mine. . . . Think of him, now, as he was before his luck failed him, remember his time of greatness, when he was not faded, not frightened. . . . He had clear eyes and the body of a champion boxer. . . . He had the soft voice of the South and a pair of golden gloves. . . . His heart was pure gold and as big as the head of a baby" (578–80). Williams includes a straightforward call to recommit to the errand: "Be champ again! Contend in the contest! Compete in the competition!" (535). Earlier in *Camino Real,* despite his assertion that "There is a passion for declivity in this world," the English romantic poet Byron advocates, "Make voyages! Attempt them! There's nothing else" (508). Reprobate or not, in *Camino Real,* probably his most optimistic play besides *The Night of the Iguana,* Williams affirms a philosophy of life as a quest or pilgrimage for redemption, but in particular terms of American Puritanism. In fact, the Gypsy in *Camino Real* describes the human condition in a manner quite similar to the Puritans' worldview: "We're all of us guinea pigs in the laboratory of God. Humanity is just a work in progress" (543).

As I have argued elsewhere,[25] it is possible to see Thornton Wilder and Tennessee Williams as two sides of the same force in American culture. That is, Williams functions as Wilder's doppelganger with regard to the Puritan narrative tradition within American literature. Whereas Wilder affirms cosmic optimism, Williams laments individual fatalism; whereas Wilder employs allegory to represent the progressive plots of elect pilgrims, Williams adopts allegory to represent the entropic plots of reprobate wanderers; and whereas Wilder represents reality abstractly and his characters one-dimensionally in a plain prose and theatrical style to serve his overdetermined didactic intention, Williams represents reality more concretely and his characters multidimensionally in a poetic style that also serves an overdetermined didactic intention, though in part by the means of vivid symbols. More succinctly, if Wilder writes from the point of view of the elect, Williams writes from the point of view of the reprobate. Combining theatrical terminology with Puritan terminology, Taylor and Wilder dramatize God's plot as a divine

25. Lincoln Konkle, "Errand into the Theatrical Wilderness: The Puritan Narrative Tradition in the Plays of Wilder, Williams, and Albee."

comedy; Wigglesworth and Williams dramatize Man's Stories, at least for some, as a human tragedy.

The ethos and aesthetic represented by Edward Taylor's Puritan morality play *God's Determinations* lives on, then, but it becomes polarized in American drama. The elect and reprobate poles of the Puritan tradition were synthesized by the leading member of the next generation of American playwrights, Edward Albee.

Wilder's Influence upon Edward Albee

I was raised in the Episcopal Church, which I left when I was six years old. ...Why did I leave it? I was terribly upset about the idea of the crucifixion. As a child I had to be taken out, crying, from Sunday school or church during the story of the crucifixion. I was really a kid, and that upset me a lot.
  —Edward Albee, quoted in Kolin, *Conversations with Edward Albee*

Evidently whatever upset Edward Albee about the crucifixion as a child made a lasting impression upon him, for such plays as *The Zoo Story, The Death of Bessie Smith, Tiny Alice,* and *Who's Afraid of Virginia Woolf?* dramatize or otherwise signify Christ-figures who are allegorically crucified. Albee himself has admitted, "I begin to suspect that I put an awful lot more Christian symbolism in my plays than I was consciously aware of."[26]

Albee addresses many of the same theological and ideological issues as Wilder and Williams, and he dramatizes them in a manner that is part of the Puritan narrative tradition in American literature that extends back through the nineteenth and eighteenth centuries to the seventeenth century. In fact, since family and cultural continuities of Puritanism were not as great a factor in Albee's life as they were in Wilder's and Williams's, and since he has not commented as substantively upon nineteenth-century American literature and culture as Wilder or Williams, the traces of the Puritanism in Albee's plays may be more immediately accounted for in part by the direct influence of those elements within the plays of Wilder and Williams.[27]

It is widely known that Wilder suggested to Albee at the McDowell colony that he switch from poetry to drama. Albee has made occasional references to that event in interviews, but the interviewers apparently have not deemed

---

26. Albee quoted in Rutenberg, *Playwright in Protest,* 112
27. When asked about his reading of Puritan or classic American authors, Albee did not recall the former but affirmed the latter: "Thoreau, Whitman, Melville, Dickinson—yes, of course. Those four I admire greatly.... Except for one or two books, most of Melville affected me considerably" (personal interview).

Wilder's influence an important enough issue to explore.[28] Because scholars have neglected Thornton Wilder's role in the establishment of a modern American drama tradition into which Albee entered as part of a third generation of playwrights, it is worth quoting Albee at length on Wilder's influence upon him and the significance of Wilder's contribution to American drama:

> Two of the most affecting moments that I remember having in the American theater when I was formative came from Thornton's plays. That moment in *The Skin of Our Teeth* when Mrs. Antrobus finally calls her son by his correct name—she calls him Cain—a moment that even if I think about it practically brings me to tears; now that's pretty strong emotional stuff. And just about everything from *Our Town,* of course. Not this cheery play that everybody thinks it is, but one of the most existentialist plays that I've ever come across. You know, when I went back to see the revival of it last year, I said, "Oh, come on, Edward, you know this play backwards"—I sighed to have to go see it again—"Come on, you're not going to be taken in by this thing again." I tell you by the time we got to the proposal—even before that—the memories started flooding back, and I just cried hysterically in the theater in the last half of the play. And I don't know what it is about Wilder that does this to me, whether it's my background, this religious matter—I'm not quite sure what it is—but it managed to affect me enormously in ways that most drama doesn't. Moments in Wilder obviously tie into my own sources. But why everybody thinks *Our Town* is such a cute little play, I don't know.[29]

Albee described Wilder's contribution not only as a personal influence on him but also as important in the development of modern American drama:

> I remember being enormously affected by them [*Our Town* and *The Skin of Our Teeth*]; I don't know why he's the forgotten man of American drama, I don't understand that. . . . It's always nice when American drama moves away from the kitchen sink school [realism], and certainly Wilder did that early enough on. I mean he didn't make experiments like Sophie Treadwell or Elmer Rice or those people who believe in that particular kind of mechanistic drama, but he reminded us that the mind could be functioning as well as the gut at the same time in drama, and that is not an American preoccupation.[30]

28. For example, asked about his meeting W. H. Auden and Wilder and their influence upon him, Albee said, "I wasn't so much inspired by them as I was copying them; I suppose that's a certain inspiration" (Albee quoted in Philip Kolin and J. Madison Davis, eds., *Critical Essays on Edward Albee,* 197). There was no follow-up as to which of Auden's and Wilder's works Albee considered himself to be copying. Their major publications? Or, in Wilder's case, major productions?

29. Personal interview.

30. Ibid. Since Albee went to Lawrenceville in 1944 after Wilder had achieved his literary fame, he might also have been exposed to the earlier one-acts in *The Long Christmas*

Thus, for Albee, Thornton Wilder was important to American drama attaining the status of literature (an achievement usually credited to Eugene O'Neill alone), as opposed to the tradition of commercial entertainment that was a legacy of the nineteenth-century American theater for which Albee has continuously criticized theater owners, producers, and playwrights.[31]

As Williams scholars have noted a number of superficial similarities between Wilder's and Williams's drama, so too have some Albee scholars pointed out stylistic similarities in Wilder's and Albee's plays. For example, while Albee's early one-act play *The Death of Bessie Smith* (1960) owes more to the influence of Williams for its Southern theme and setting, *The American Dream* (1961) and *The Sandbox* (1960) bear a greater resemblance to Wilder's aesthetic and vision in manifesting the American jeremiad in dramatic form. The characters appearing in both plays—Mommy, Daddy, Grandma, and the Young Man/American Dream/Angel of Death—are even more abstract than Wilder's Ma, Pa, Caroline, and Arthur Kirby in *The Happy Journey;* Albee apparently means his characters to be as representative of his time as Wilder's were of his. As in *Pullman Car Hiawatha, Our Town,* and *The Skin of Our Teeth,* the characters acknowledge the artifice of the performance in *The American Dream* and *The Sandbox.* Grandma especially functions similarly to the Stage Manager in *Our Town* in her running commentary that provides the moral base from which to view the action.[32]

Though not as appreciative of Tennessee Williams's work as a whole, Albee does suggest that he admired some of the aesthetic qualities Williams shares with Wilder and some that he does not:

> I guess my only judgment as to usefulness of the drama, that which affects me, [is] it has to grab me both emotionally and intellectually at the same time; it ultimately comes from his [Williams's] sympathy, his compassion, his poetry, more than anything else. There's a lot of Tennessee's work that I've become less fond of as the years have gone. I tend to like some of his tougher plays that nobody seems to like, *Suddenly Last Summer,* for example—extraordinary play.

Dinner and Other Plays: "I don't know whether in schools they'd done some of his shorter plays or not; [if published in 1931] I could have easily seen them in school" (ibid.).

31. Albee flatly denies that it was Wilder whom he attacked as member of the commercial theater in *Fam and Yam,* an imaginary interview between a famous American playwright and a young American playwright: "No, that was a cross between Bill Inge and Tennessee Williams. . . . The descriptions were a little tricky there so no one could figure out who it was. It was more Bill Inge than anybody. I like Thornton a lot more than to do that to him. I wouldn't do that to Thornton" (personal interview).

32. Though not mentioning the Stage Manager specifically, Richard E. Amacher compares "the rather obvious air of improvisation" to Wilder's *Our Town* (*Edward Albee,* 44). Albee did use a literal narrator who addresses the audience directly in his adaptation of Carson McCuller's *The Ballad of the Sad Café* (1963).

There's an awful lot going on in *Camino Real* that I like a great deal. The more naturalistic ones I don't like all that much.[33]

Of significance to this study, the plays by Tennessee Williams that Albee respects are the paranoid fear of being reprobate in a Calvinist world (*Suddenly Last Summer*) and the allegorical apocalyptic and jeremiad play presided over by Gutman, a God of wrath to the reprobate (*Camino Real*). Both plays also have Christ figures central to the story. Because Albee is an American writer whose plays contain Christian symbolism and national themes, his literary production can and should be examined in the context of the continuity of the Puritan ethos and aesthetic in American literature.

However, as with Wilder and Williams, critics and scholars have placed Albee in a context of modern drama—that is, twentieth-century philosophical ideas and theatrical styles of European intellectuals and writers. Though Martin Esslin included Albee in his 1961 study *The Theatre of the Absurd,* critics have subsequently demonstrated the inaccuracy of classifying Albee as an absurdist, at least with regard to his worldview, since absurdism judges the universe as meaningless and human endeavor as pointless; Albee is never that nihilistic. As he told Matthew Roudane, "If I were a pessimist I wouldn't bother to write. Writing, itself, taking the trouble, communicating with your fellow human being is valuable, that's an act of optimism. There's a positive force within the struggle."[34]

From an aesthetic point of view, most scholars have associated Albee with the theatrical techniques of those dramatists most commonly labeled as making up the Theatre of the Absurd: Beckett, Pinter, Genet, and Ionesco.[35] Yet, as has been pointed out in this study, such techniques as one-dimensional characters; abstract and symbolic settings; fragmented, non-Aristotelian plots; and actors acknowledging the artifice of the play and the existence of the audience are not the discovery or modern rediscovery of those European

33. Albee, personal interview.

34. Albee quoted in Roudane, *Understanding Edward Albee,* 193. Those scholars who deny Albee is philosophically an absurdist include Rutenberg, *Playwright in Protest,* 11; C. W. E. Bigsby, ed., *Edward Albee* 19, 35, 106; Anita Marie Stenz, *Edward Albee: The Poet of Loss,* 2; Foster Hirsch, *Who's Afraid of Edward Albee?* 33; and Gerry McCarthy, *Edward Albee,* 8. Those who follow Esslin in classifying Albee as absurdist or who see him generally as nihilistic include Debusscher, *Tradition and Renewal,* 82; Amacher, *Edward Albee,* 5–6; and Anne Paolucci, *From Tension to Tonic: The Plays of Edward Albee,* 4.

35. See Ronald Hayman, *Edward Albee,* 96, for Beckett; Roudane, *Understanding,* 48, for Pinter; Debusscher, *Tradition and Renewal,* 8, for Genet; McCarthy, *Edward Albee,* 9, for Ionesco. Other European figures cited in studies of Albee as influences include Strindberg (Hirsch, *Who's Afraid of Edward Albee?* 98; McCarthy, *Edward Albee,* 26 and passim); Noel Coward (Amacher, *Edward Albee,* 24); Pirandello (Paolucci, *From Tension to Tonic,* 5); and Eliot—unless one classifies him as American (Bigsby, *Critical Introduction,* 328).

playwrights who came to the fore in the 1950s; Thornton Wilder employed them in the 1930s. As with Wilder and Williams, this is not to deny that modern European philosophers and writers made an impression upon Albee as both an intellectual and a dramatist, but once again it is too simplistic to regard the ideas and techniques associated with modern drama or the Theatre of the Absurd as uniquely modern or European. Albee himself questions the classification in his essay, "Which Theatre Is the Absurd One?"; to illustrate his point, he imagines Ionesco, Beckett, and Genet running into each other in Paris:

> IONESCO: Well, what's new in The Theatre of the Absurd?
> BECKETT: Oh, less than a lot of people think. (They all laugh.)[36]

Only the briefest of references to the influence of American playwrights such as O'Neill, Wilder, Williams, and Miller appear in studies of Albee's plays; no substantive comparative analysis has been done for intertextualities between Albee and those playwrights, nor has there been an attempt to identify attributes of an American literary tradition present in Albee's plays.[37] Albee is so self-consciously an American playwright (see *Fam and Yam*) that the influence of his native tradition needs to be taken more into account. Even Albee's own statements lend support for this position: "I'm not a regionalist. But I think I'm more American than European as a writer. . . . I must be since all of my perspectives have been formed growing up and living in this particular society and standing to one side of it." In another interview Albee said, "The myth of the American Dream, if you're an American writer, is not only your cultural background but your set of paints and brushes. The picture you create is indeed colored by your environment and what you experience, live through."[38]

In contrast to the numerous occurrences of "Puritan" in Wilder and Williams scholarship, the term rarely appears in studies of Albee; when it does, it is in the narrow sense of puritanical, even if Puritan is used with a capital

36. Albee, "Which Theatre Is the Absurd One?" 170.

37. In his introduction to *Edward Albee: Modern Critical Views,* Bloom cites Albee as part of what is now a tradition of modern American drama, and his description is one of the few that includes Thornton Wilder: "Edward Albee is the crucial American dramatist of his generation, standing as the decisive link between our principal older dramatists— Eugene O'Neill, Thornton Wilder, Tennessee Williams, Arthur Miller—and the best of the younger ones—Sam Shephard and David Mamet, among others" (1). Bloom sees (but, then, he would) an "anxiety of influence" underlying *Fam and Yam* with Williams as the precursor that haunted Albee (1).

38. Albee quoted in Philip C. Kolin, *Conversations with Edward Albee,* 12; Kolin and Davis, eds., *Critical Essays,* 196.

"P," as in Richard Schechner's scathing review of *Who's Afraid of Virginia Woolf?* Schechner writes: "Like children or never-quite-reformed Puritans who cannot forget Jonathan Edwards we enjoy thinking of ourselves as 'naughty,' and we eagerly exaggerate our naughtiness into hard vices and our vices into perversities." Albee himself employs "puritanical" or "Puritan" only twice in interviews or in his plays: "I have always been interested in the fact that theatre audiences have always been offended by hearing or seeing on stage the same behavior that they themselves indulge in privately. It is a curious double standard which is a holdover from the hypocrisy of our Puritanical beginnings. Of course there is a lot of exploitation going on because we are a Puritanical society, which means we are a great deal more obscene than we admit to be."[39] At the beginning of Act Two of *All Over,* the Daughter uses the term in a historical statement that is somewhat opaque, but clearly its reference is to a wider meaning than puritanical: "Back to that 'degradation' of mine. Imagine her!, degrading a family as famous as this, up by its own boot straps—well, the only one of it who mattered, anyway—all the responsibility to itself, the Puritan Moral soul" (Albee, *Selected Plays of Edward Albee,* 333).

Albee's plays decry the contemporary scene with the fervor and rhetoric of that Puritan Moral soul. Though he has been called the "angry young man" of the American theater, "Playwright in Protest," and a contemporary satirist of the stage, his statements on the purpose of art obviously are the products of a moralist who thinks he has a responsibility to society: "The function of art is to correct"; "If we lived in a utopian society, there would be no need for art because the function of art is to make people better." Perhaps, then, most of Albee's plays could be read as American jeremiads, in that they not only follow to varying degrees the rhetorical pattern of the New England Puritan jeremiads, but also because they make America or Americans, even if representing western civilization or the human race as a whole, the target of their criticism.[40]

Although his parents lived in a wealthy suburb of New York City rather than New England, the Albees were an old American family, having landed in Machias, Maine, "somewhere around sixteen-something."[41] Geographi-

---

39. Bigsby, *Collection of Critical Essays,* 62–63; Albee quoted in Kolin, *Conversations,* 95.

40. McCarthy, *Edward Albee,* 8; Rutenberg, *Playwright in Protest;* Lee Baxandall, "The Theatre of Edward Albee," 37; Kolin, *Conversations,* 160; Patricia De La Fuente, ed., *Planned Wilderness: Interviews, Essays, and Bibliography,* 7. There is a subtle persistence of the rhetorical structure of evoking the past to shame the present into resuming the errand into the future. For example, by allowing Grandma to step out from the wings and utter a brief epilogue at the end of *The American Dream,* Albee is "invoking the American past in order to attack the vacuity of the American present" (Bigsby, *Critical Introduction,* 263)—the rhetorical strategy of the jeremiad.

41. Albee, personal interview.

cally, and perhaps intellectually, he was closer to the former nexus of the Puritan ethos when he was sent away to boarding schools. The first school he attended, from 1940–43, was the Presbyterian-affiliated Lawrenceville near Princeton University; as mentioned in the Introduction, Wilder taught at Lawrenceville from 1921–28 when a direct descendent of Cotton Mather was headmaster. After being expelled consecutively from Lawrenceville and Valley Forge Military Academy (1943), Albee attended Choate from 1944 to 1946 in Wallingford, Connecticut, which is only fifty miles south of Westfield, Massachusetts, where Edward Taylor was a frontier minister. Wallingford's history reveals at least one instance of the phenomenon for which New England Puritans are infamous—the witch hunts and trials.[42]

In reference to having revisited Choate for a class reunion, Albee observed, "The altar is gone; it's no longer an Episcopal school, but it is imbued by this particular Puritan ethos—very interesting—so I dare say I was more influenced by them than I like to think because I was in reaction against so much of what I considered wrong about it." Furthermore, he confirmed that the presence of biblical allusions in his plays are not the product of scholars' imaginations but derive from the religious education, including Bible study, that had been part of his schooling: "I don't have it [the Bible] memorized, but I'm more or less familiar with the territory. I went to Sunday school all the time. Every school I went to had chapel—even Valley Forge military academy had chapel. Their hymns were all fairly war-like."[43]

Although the Puritan codes occur less purely in Albee than in Wilder or Williams, an analysis of selected plays demonstrates that Albee takes some of his thematic and aesthetic cues from both Wilder and Williams, as well as the Puritan legacy with American literature and culture.

As in several of Williams's plays, in *The Death of Bessie Smith,* his second one-act play, the hot climate of the South evokes hell: "The west is burning . . . fire has enveloped fully half of the continent . . . the fingers of the flame stretch upward to the stars . . . and there is a monstrous burning circumference hanging on the edge of the world" (1:94). The North, as a supposedly less racist region than the South, represents heaven to the South's hell; the Nurse advises an African American orderly, "You go north, boy . . . you go up to New York City, where nobody's any better than anybody else" (1:90). Famous African American blues singer Bessie Smith is also striving to reach the earthly equivalent of the Celestial City; the drive to New York City is an

42. Peter Prescott, a *Newsweek* editor and Choate alumnus, researched his book on the school (*A World of Our Own*) during the 1967–68 academic year. In his description of the milieu, he notes one recorded conviction of a Wallingford mother and daughter for witchcraft in 1700 (24).

43. Albee, personal interview.

attempt to resurrect her career, but metaphorically it functions analogously to Wilder's *The Happy Journey to Trenton and Camden* and *Heaven's My Destination*. Jack, Bessie's companion, prompts her, "You gotta get goin' again. . . . 'Cause it's gettin' late, honey . . . it's gettin' awful late. . . . Bessie . . . let's get up. We're goin' north again!" (1:81–82). However, Bessie's progress is aborted in the car crash, and the denial of her admission to "Mercy" hospital represents being racially reprobate in the South, where whites consider themselves the chosen race.

Albee satirizes the cultural color/race symbolism when the Nurse uses an eschatological metaphor to mock the Orderly, who has been bleaching his skin to make it lighter: "Well, boy, you are going to be one funny sight come the millennium. . . . The great black mob marching down the street, banners in the air . . . that great black mob . . . and you right there in the middle, your bleached-out, snowy-white face in the middle of the pack like that" (1:88–89). The Intern seems to represent a potential savior figure—the white knight for the Nurse, the healer for the injured Bessie—but he is unable to save either of them, as the Nurse's mocking speech suggests: "Maybe he thought you'd bring her back to life . . . great white doctor" (1:126).

Albee believes in the ideal of progress,[44] but he is not a cosmic optimist like Wilder, whose works suggested that progress had taken place and was ongoing because his view of history was, essentially, typological and thus providential. In *Who's Afraid of Virginia Woolf?* Albee reads American history not as progressive but as regressive or, in Puritan terms, as a reverse typology in which representative American characters demonstrate that we have become types rather than antitypes of the founders.

Like Wilder, who named three of his American everyman characters George, Albee is practicing a kind of national allegory in *Who's Afraid of Virginia Woolf?* His explanation of naming George and Martha after George and Martha Washington has been often quoted by critics to support readings of *Who's Afraid of Virginia Woolf?* as an American allegory of sorts: "[It is] not its most important point, but certainly contained within the play [is] an attempt to examine the success or failure of American revolutionary principles."[45]

---

44. Albee apparently believes in the progressive liberal values associated in particular with America in the nineteenth and first half of the twentieth centuries, as he can be found to assert straightforwardly on occasion: "We are nowhere near utopia anywhere on this planet but I do believe in the perfectibility of society. So I'm an optimist, I suppose" (Albee quoted in Bigsby, *Critical Introduction,* 279).

45. Albee, "Edward Albee," 338. Ruby Cohn goes as far as to invent a new term to describe Albee's aesthetic: "The Albeegory is that distinctive allegorical drama in which ideas are so skillfully blended into people that we do not know how to divorce them or how to care about one without the other" (*Edward Albee,* 44).

George is the jeremiad voice in *Who's Afraid of Virginia Woolf?*, trying to instruct the new generation to recommit themselves to the American values of individualism, liberty, and self-determination, as well as to values of community, communication, and shared morality that can then enact social progress. In Act Two, George laments, "Through all the sensible sounds of men building, attempting, comes the Dies Irae. And what is it? What does the trumpet sound? Up yours" (*Selected Plays,* 121–22). The narration ends disappointingly, a more developed expression of George's witty declension, "Good, Better, Best, Bested" (*Selected Plays,* 83), yet the disappointment depends upon an expectancy stemming from the awareness that America had been making progress at one time. That is, the trumpet is supposed to sound an affirmative note, as in Wilder's eschatological vision expressed in *And the Sea Shall Give Up Its Dead, The Trumpet Shall Sound,* and *The Cabala.*[46]

Tiny Alice, Albee's most explicit play on issues of faith, reflects Puritan doctrine more than Catholic.[47] Brother Julian seems to affirm a providential God: "May I . . . propose [a toast]. To the wonders . . . which may befall a man . . . least where he is looking, least that he would have thought; to the clear plan of that which we call chance, to what we see as accident till our humility returns to us when we are faced with the mysteries" (2:157). This theology is close to that of the Puritans, as Lawyer almost seems to be aware: "Dear Julian; we all serve, do we not? Each of us his own priesthood; publicly, some, others . . . within only; but we all do. . . . Predestination, fate, the will of God, accident . . . All swirled up in it, no matter what the name. And being man, we have invented choice, and have, indeed, gone further, and have catalogued the underpinnings of choice. But we do not know. Anything" (2:160).

The statements made by Lawyer throughout *Tiny Alice* seem to align him with Protestant devotional doctrine and against Catholicism; in fact, Lawyer

---

46. For my complete analysis of *Who's Afraid of Virginia Woolf?* as jeremiad, see "'Good, Better, Best, Bested': The Failure of American Typology in *Who's Afraid of Virginia Woolf?*"

47. As Samuel Terrien points out, Albee's making Julian and the Cardinal Roman Catholics has more to do with theatricality than anything else:

> He needed to set the problems of faith against the sham of ecclesiasticism, and however demonic the pretenses of Protestant denominations may be, one has to admit that none of these pretenses offers sufficient elements of theatricality. Protestant deviousness about money or power may be at times just as sordid as its Catholic counterpart, but it lacks brilliance, style and picturesqueness.... The Roman Curia is only a histrionic prop that Albee uses as a background. The play deals with human existence; the stage is the universe. ("Demons Also Believe," 141)

The language Julian uses to describe one of his recurring hallucinations in the asylum is also decidedly Protestant: "Oh, sometimes I would say to a nurse or one of the attendants, 'Could you tell me, did I preach last night? To the patients? A fire-and-brimstone lesson'" (2:61).

was once a member of the Catholic faith but has, as the Cardinal says, "fallen away from the Church" (2:13). Though Lawyer's animosity toward the Cardinal is due in part to their past relationship in school, his complaints are often doctrinal: "He is a man of God, however much he simplifies, however much he worships the symbol and not the substance" (2:105); earlier he explained his feelings toward the Cardinal with a credo that ought to make him and Julian allies: "I have learned . . . never to confuse the representative of a . . . thing with the thing itself" (2:39).

Albee gives us hints of Alice's nature, which are mostly suggestive of hunger. Julian's conceptualization of God and the ultimate service to his cause has been that of a deity which desires martyrs. One of Julian's martyr fantasies is being eaten alive by a lion (2:124). The manifestation of Alice at the end when Julian dies may be, in fact, a projection of that fantasy—being swallowed up in the darkness of the lion's mouth. If so, then Julian is sacrificed to an image of God-as-eater, much like Sebastian in Williams's *Suddenly Last Summer.*[48]

How might these Puritan traces buried in our cultural unconscious manifest themselves during a period in which the nuclear arms race made the prophecy of Armageddon a possibility? *The Lady from Dubuque* (1980) offers one possible answer, for when a work mingles America, dying, doomsday, and godlike figures who judge some characters and comfort others, it is almost certainly an heir of Michael Wigglesworth's *The Day of Doom,* as were Wilder's *The Trumpet Shall Sound* and Williams's *Stairs to the Roof* and *Camino Real.*

Elizabeth's description of her dream is one of several indications in the text that Albee is concerned with dying on the macrocosmic level, inviting an eschatological interpretation of the play. Near the end of *The Lady from Dubuque* Elizabeth tells Sam he does not know what death is, and then she narrates her dream of nuclear holocaust as Jo is dying upstairs in the care of Oscar. Sam says, "That was . . . that was the end of the world"; Elizabeth's response—"I thought that's what we were talking about" (159)—makes clear Albee's micro/macro perspective on death.

Although Fred is the character to introduce the idea of doomsday in *The Lady from Dubuque* when he mocks Edgar, Jo—facing her own personal doomsday—seizes upon it like a street corner prophet: "The sky might fall? And Doomsday come? (A long hollow sound) Doooooooooooooomsday!" (25). She howls again, and then she begins to play with the idea, which may be an oblique warning of the trial of all flesh: "Doomsday. It follows Thursday . . .

48. "The play raises the domineering woman figure that recurs obsessively in Albee's writing to the exalted position of rapacious, all-consuming Deity" (Hirsch, *Who's Afraid of Edward Albee?* 114); "Julian is seduced by Miss Alice so he may serve as a sacrifice to glut the maw of the implacable goddess" (C. N. Stavrou, "Albee in Wonderland," 54).

if you're lucky" (26). Thursday is named after Thor, the thunder God in Norse mythology; perhaps Albee is alluding to the image of God as thunder and lightning in Tennessee Williams's *The Night of the Iguana*. Jo's final rumination on doomsday brings Sam, the representation of America, into the equation, which might be read as a nonsensical version of Puritan millennialism: "We all like Sam, and that should make it Samsday. Samsday precedeth Doomsday: Samsday, Thurmsday, Doomsday. Isn't that how it goes, Fred?" (27). Having introduced the idea of doomsday into a play in which one character is dying and two mysterious characters appear just past midnight to comfort her and judge the others, Albee is almost certainly drawing upon Christian prophecies of the apocalypse to warn us about the present danger of nuclear or social apocalypse.

The question of Sam's allegorical identity may be answered with a reading particularly Calvinistic, at least, in relation to his wife: Sam may be reprobate, Jo elect.[49] As other scholars have noted, *The Lady from Dubuque* follows *All Over* in portraying a dying character who is more alive than the physically healthy characters.[50] Clearly, the couples in this play are lost souls, displaying cruelty toward their friends and spouses or lovers and indifference or ignorance toward their own condition. Sam, who represents "more than one person" (10), says near the end of the play, "I'm dying" (157), which, of course, is not a reference to his physical condition. Albee commented upon ways of dying in an interview about *Tiny Alice* that has relevance here: "So, next, we come to the question of the soul—is it immortal? I believe the soul dies far too often while people are alive. Christianity is also keeping the soul alive while you're alive."[51] Sam's soul, his spiritual self, his humanity that should be manifest in his treatment of his friends and especially of his dying wife, has died. In using dialogue as authorial comment when read double, Oscar says of his revival of Sam, "We woke him and how did he repay us: he shrieked to raise the very dead." Elizabeth's follow-up has wider implications: "The very dead; who hear nothing; who remember nothing; who are nothing." The very next line of dialogue—"Was that Sam?" (138)—is purposely ambiguous in the antecedent of "that." That is, it works

---

49. This is not to suggest that Albee is consciously allegorizing the Calvinistic doctrine of God's predestination of humanity as elect and reprobate; rather, the dichotomous structure of characters literally as elect and reprobate in Puritan narrative works such as Taylor's *Gods Determinations* or Wigglesworth's *Day of Doom* has been passed down to us as a cultural code that manifests itself in different terms. When those terms occur in a context of literal or allegorical religious concerns, especially within a Protestant worldview, it is reasonable to conclude that this is a trace element of the cultural continuity of Puritan thought we have been unearthing in this study.

50. For example, see Roudane, *Understanding Edward Albee*, 155.

51. Paul Gardner, "Tiny Alice Mystifies Albee, Too."

literally and metaphorically, referring both to Oscar's cliché as a description of Sam's yelling and to Elizabeth's amplifying the cliché into a metaphysical statement. In other words, Sam is the "very dead."

Applying the Puritans' Calvinistic doctrine, Jo may be nominally elect by default in that she is dying and not one of the very dead, the living dead, but there are also a few indications in the text that she is the positive character type in Albee's universe. Jo is the active, truth-telling character in the group; it may be that her dying is the stimulus for this behavior, which the others frown upon, but for whatever reason she does tell it like it is to all of them. Jo also is also marked as elect by what is said about her in *The Lady from Dubuque*. Though statements such as Elizabeth's "Oh, Jo! You are a good girl!" (130) would be throwaway lines in realistic drama, coming from Elizabeth in a play so concerned with identity—not in a literal sense—invite us to treat them as significant and authoritative. This line, as with many in the second act, is an echo of a first-act line spoken by Jo to Carol: "I'm a good girl. Who are you?" (54).

If Sam and Jo, as the major couple in this Judgment Day play, fulfill the roles of, respectively, the reprobate and the elect, the separation of the goats from the sheep, or—at least—the very dead from the dying, then it is logical to ask who plays the role of the judge—Christ? Elizabeth and Oscar are non-realistic characters who have come at the hour of Jo's need.[52] There is no way to make literal sense out of their coming, which is precisely the mistake Sam persists in making all through the second act. Although there is no obvious Christ-figure symbolism as there was in Wilder's *The Trumpet Shall Sound* or Williams's *Suddenly Last Summer* and *Camino Real*, Elizabeth and Oscar appear after Jo, who is feeling the highest level of pain we have witnessed in the play thus far, cries out to Sam, "Sweet Jesus [screams] God! God! God! Try to lift me!" (72). She utters this particular expletive only one other time, at the end when Oscar, substituting for Sam as comforter, is carrying her upstairs to die.[53]

If action defines identity in *The Lady from Dubuque* as scholars have argued,[54] then it should be noted that a great deal of Elizabeth's and Oscar's

---

52. Previous readings of *The Lady from Dubuque* have described the mysterious couple as angels or messengers of death similar to the character in *The Sandbox* (Adler, "Pirandello in Albee," 139), as "otherworldly Romance guides [who] provide a pathway to a displaced world beyond or, at least, to a different state of being" (Roudane, *Understanding Edward Albee*, 175), and as "Godot" (June Schlueter, "Is It All Over for Edward Albee?" 114).

53. Although Adler ("The Pirandello in Albee") states that there is "no religious context" (136) in the play, he also admits that Sam's "'Dear, great God, Woman' might be more than expletive" (139).

54. For example, McCarthy comments, "Identity is the fruit of action" (*Edward Albee*, 158).

speeches are direct and indirect judgments upon Sam and the other characters. One of the possible identities Oscar mockingly offers Sam as alternatives to who they say they are is "House inspectors," and almost immediately
upon their arrival they do inspect the house, though with implications of a
wider frame of reference, as when Elizabeth says, "Do you always leave your
lights on? Glasses about? I straightened up for you a bit. If you have a fire
going, do you . . . abandon it, and hope for the best? Civilizations have gone
down that way, you know" (75).

But though they judge Sam, Elizabeth and Oscar's major task is to comfort Jo as she dies. Her fear intensifies in proportion to her pain, and Elizabeth transforms it into a childhood sensibility that can be dealt with by the
motherly compassion she offers: "Protect you from the dark and from the
thunder?" (118).[55] By the end, Jo has accepted dying, pleading with Sam as
Oscar carries her upstairs, "Just let me die . . . please?" (156). Thus, as with
Williams, God or representations of divinity are dramatized by Albee in the
Calvinist tradition as a God of Wrath to the reprobate or God of Mercy to
the elect.[56]

As with Thornton Wilder's and Tennessee Williams's works, Edward Albee's plays may be placed in the vein of the American literary tradition flowing from the seventeenth century precisely because he deals with many of
the same theological, epistemological, and ideological issues the Puritans
did, and because he casts his inquiries in aesthetic forms similar to those employed by writers trying to express the Puritan worldview, like Edward Taylor in *God's Determinations.*

Thus, we have seen that Wilder's unconventional dramaturgy and his treatment of America as subject had immediate impact on two of the major
American playwrights of the twentieth century. Even Arthur Miller, in such
plays as *All My Sons, The Crucible, After the Fall,* and *The Creation of the World and
Other Business,* would be aptly described as an allegorical writer in which the
belief in a metaphysical dimension to life is acknowledged, though his more
immediate focus is upon the social present (the obvious example of an entire
play for which this is true is *Death of a Salesman*). In this respect, Miller could
also be classified as an American Jeremiah, except that the sense of a national religious mission is missing from his plays. Even *The Crucible* (1953),
which is in itself an argument, in a sense, that a continuity of Puritanism exists in American culture, since Miller employed a dramatization of the Salem
witch trials as an allegory of McCarthyism in the 1950s, does not concern

55. In *The Sandbox,* Grandma's death was also signified by the offstage rumblings of
thunder, adding—along with the Angel of Death—a metaphysical dimension to that play.
56. For my complete discussion of *The Lady from Dubuque,* see "American Jeremiah:
Edward Albee as Judgment Day Prophet in *The Lady from Dubuque.*"

itself so much with matters of theology or faith but with cultural hysteria and personal integrity.

As another indication of Wilder's influence on modern American drama, in a 1950s poll of then contemporary American playwrights including Elmer Rice, Maxwell Anderson, Moss Hart, Lillian Hellman, Clifford Odets, William Inge, Tennessee Williams, Arthur Miller, Robert Anderson, and Arthur Laurents, Wilder was listed as "favorite playwright" four times, tied with Irish playwright Sean O'Casey for the lead. Furthermore, Barnard Dukore speculated that if it were up to theatergoers and readers, Wilder might be chosen "the most quintessentially American dramatist of the period 1918–45."[57] The point is, his peers, theater critics of his time, and audiences and readers regarded Wilder highly for his work in American theater. To further assess Wilder's contribution to American drama, we should turn to the next generation of dramatists who were getting their start in the sixties, seventies, and eighties to see how lasting an impact he has had.

Wilder's Influence upon the Current Generation of American Dramatists

When Wilder said of himself as playwright that he removed "obtrusive bric-a-brac" (*TP*, xiv), he was referring to the feature of his dramatic works that he is most remembered for, the elimination of most of the theatrical elements, such as scenery and props, that create an illusion of reality, as in *Our Town, The Happy Journey,* and *Pullman Car Hiawatha.* As mentioned in Chapter Five with regard to *Our Century,* a few scholars have briefly noted that Wilder deserves some credit for having paved the way for the Theatre of the Absurd, but none have cared to pursue this issue in any depth. Those who see Wilder as foreshadowing the Theatre of the Absurd have cited *The Skin of Our Teeth* for its breaking of the fourth wall, its cartoon-like characters, and the slapstick action and farcical dialogue. However, as discussed above, Wilder's little-known one-act play *Our Century* demonstrates even better than *The Skin of Our Teeth* that the Puritan aesthetic was flexible enough to have evolved into a Christian Theatre of the Absurd (speaking in terms of dramaturgy and production style, not, obviously, in terms of philosophy). But the Theatre of the Absurd was primarily a European movement that had its own influence upon contemporary American dramatists. What influence did Wilder have upon them?

In his assessment of Wilder's impact, Donald Haberman writes, "In the

57. Henry Hewes, *American Playwrights Self-Appraised;* Dukore, *American Dramatists,* 121.

great outpouring of American plays since the 1960s, many of the writers have shown themselves to a greater or lesser degree as Wilder's heirs. Even if some of these writers could be totally unaware of Wilder, their plays have a family resemblance to his. Actually, it is unimaginable that an American playwright after World War II could be ignorant of Wilder's plays." He cites Williams, Albee, A. R. Gurney, David Rabe, Israel Horovitz, Ed Bullins, and others as having written plays that owe something to Wilder. He could have added John Guare, Nickey Silver, and Paula Vogel, all of whom acknowledge Wilder's influence.[58]

With the several centennial celebrations of Wilder's birth and career in the late 1990s, a number of playwrights, directors, theater critics, and academic literary scholars commented on Wilder's importance, not only as dramatist but as novelist as well. Most of these comments have not been recorded and widely distributed for access by the public and the academic community; however, one comment by American playwright Donald Margulies is too apropos to Wilder's influence not to relay. When Margulies attended the 1988 Lincoln Center revival of *Our Town*, he

> was struck again by how uncannily modern Wilder's approach to playwriting was. . . . The use of time in Wilder was revolutionary. We have to remember the context in which *Our Town* was first seen. Faulkner was writing then, Dos Passos was writing then; but nobody was doing this on the stage. The fact that you could take an event and dissect it that way and basically shatter it and use the shards of it and rearrange it in a dramatic way is very thrilling.[59]

Most comments on Wilder's legacy speak to his experiment with theatrical style and dramatic form, but he may have passed on some of the ideas associated with Puritan theology, ideology, and aesthetics as well. For example, could Puritan cosmic optimism lie behind the affirmative vision of America in plays such as Lanford Wilson's *Fifth of July* and Beth Henley's *The Miss Firecracker Contest? A Chorus Line*'s producer-director, who is only known as a disembodied voice from the darkened auditorium for much of the play, evokes a God of wrath on the day of doom when he puts the dancers on the line and commands them to tell their life stories. Obviously, such readings would have to be based upon in-depth analyses of the text, but the potential to widen the scope of this study of American drama should be apparent.

58. Haberman, "'Preparing the Way for Them': Wilder and the Next Generations," 134, 143–45. For Guare, Vogel, and Nicky Silver, see Silver's article "A Loony Landmark that Inspired a Seventh Grader." John Guare cited Wilder's influence on him at the Wilder Centennial Symposium in 1997 at Yale; Paula Vogel did as well at the Thornton Wilder Tribute in 2004 at the 92d Street Y in Manhattan.

59. Margulies quoted in Joel A. Smith, ed., *Wilder Rediscovered,* 34.

In fact, it may not be going too far to suggest that any time an American writer composes a work primarily and explicitly about America—its history, ideology, and religious character—then Puritan paradigms, structures, and codes reappear, and that when the writer is working within drama, he or she has probably inherited some of those signs, in the semiotic sense of the word, from Wilder. A recent example is Tony Kushner's *Angels in America: Millennium Approaches,* subtitled "A Gay Fantasia on National Themes." Kushner's play shows the influence not only of Thornton Wilder (cf., *The Skin of Our Teeth*), but of the Puritan vein of American culture as well.[60] Kushner's epic play is set during the 1980s at the height of Ronald Reagan's presidency, which was itself something of a renaissance of Puritanism. Reagan countered Jimmy Carter's pronouncement of a "national malaise" with a national, if not cosmic, optimism ("It's morning in America"). He demonized the Soviet Union as the "evil empire," and he returned the national economy to laissez-faire capitalism with deregulation, tax breaks, and other practices that came to be known as "Reagonomics." He also occasionally referred to his belief that we are living in the last days, the period prior to the prophesied Armageddon and second coming of Christ. Reagan even used the phrase "city on a hill" in some of his speeches, which he never failed to end with "God bless you, and God bless America." As Sacvan Bercovitch writes regarding the continuity of Puritan rhetoric, "The legacy of this ritual mode may be traced through virtually every major event in the culture, from the Great Awakening through the Revolution and the westward movement to the Civil War, and from that Armageddon of the Republic to the Cold War and the Star Wars of our latter days."[61]

Angels in America shows the social panorama of the eighties, from corrupt lawyers making a killing in markets and other financial enterprises (Roy Cohn) to people suffering from AIDS. And the Puritan perspective is what Kushner was representing, though obviously in reaction to it. By making one of the major characters, Joe Pitt, a Mormon ("Latter Day Saints"), which is the only truly American "home-brewed religion," and making the subtitle "Millennium Approaches," he gave an epic sense of significance, urgency, and destiny to the American characters and their actions. Like Wilder, Kushner employed a mostly bare stage, constructed an episodic plot, and dramatized the supernatural, as the play came to a powerful conclusion with the descent of the American angel "Moroni" calling the dying Prior to be a prophet. Other fantasy elements were the main character Prior Walter's dreams that

60. I owe the *Angels in America/The Skin of Our Teeth* comparison to Norma Jenckes, editor of the journal *American Drama*. Since then Fisher has published his article comparing *The Skin of Our Teeth* and *Angels in America*.

61. Bercovitch, "The Modernity of American Puritan Rhetoric," 58.

included his ancestors, one of whom is from the seventeenth century, and Hannah Pitt's drug-induced hallucinations. Roy Cohn made a delightfully Satanic antagonist, as much a pretender to omniscience as Uncle Pio and as cynical as Uncle Charlie. The idea of America as a promised land is theatrically created by the scene in Utah in which a real estate agent shows Joe Pitt's mother a vast panorama of mountains and valleys bathed in sunlight from heavenly clouds and calls it paradise. In *Angels in America* Kushner rejects gays' status in America as the de facto reprobate; in fact, he even seems to suggest that gays are a sign of the approaching millennium.

An even more recent play influenced by Wilder is Moisés Kaufman and the members of the Tectonic Theater Project's play *The Laramie Project,* which has even been called "An *Our Town* for the new millennium."[62] No other American play that I know of has so successfully emulated Wilder's radical dramaturgy as this deeply moving investigation of the contemporary small-town American psyche. In his *New York Times* review, Ben Brantley notes,

> What Mr Kaufman and his team are after is less a portrait of any person than one of the ethos of a place. In the deliberate, simple formality of its staging, in which eight radiantly clean-scrubbed performers embody 60 different people against Robert Brill's bare-bones set, *Laramie* often brings to mind *Our Town,* the beloved Thornton Wilder study of life, love and death in parochial New Hampshire. To some degree, *Laramie* is indeed presented as a latter day Grover's Corners, a cozy place where everyone appears to know everyone else's business and actually finds comfort in this. But if *The Laramie Project* nods conspicuously to Wilder, this play is *Our Town* with a question mark, as in "Could this be our town?"[63]

Thus, any future attempt to analyze American drama as a product of American culture and as a modern tradition of playwrights writing in succession should take into consideration the achievements of Thornton Wilder. The preceding analysis of the literary production of this playwright, novelist, essayist, and screenwriter demonstrates the similarity of his and the Puritans' worldview and aesthetics. Though scholars assert that Wilder adapted European ideas and corresponding aesthetics to American subjects, and that these characteristics are particularly modern, they rarely consider the possibility that the themes and styles were part of Wilder's American cultural heritage. Again, this is not to deny that European thinkers and writers had an effect upon Wilder, but that does not necessarily mean, as studies of

62. Review excerpts in front matter of Moisés Kaufman, *The Laramie Project* (New York: Random House, 2001).
63. Brantley, "A Brutal Act Alters a Town."

Wilder so often assert, that he imported the philosophy and aesthetics from Europe and adapted them to American characters and actions and settings. Wilder was American through and through; like American culture as a whole, he assimilated external influences into an aesthetic sensibility strongly influenced by the beliefs and values and lifestyles of Americans from the seventeenth century to the twentieth.

One of the most succinct and precise comments made in the centennial year of Wilder's birth was not by a theater critic or artist, nor was it by an academic scholar at a conference; Mary S. Elcano, Postal Service Senior Vice President and General Counsel, said in dedicating a U.S. Postal stamp honoring Wilder, "Is there a high school in the nation that hasn't presented *Our Town* as the class play sometime in the last 30 years? And while those small-town values are something we keep in our collective memories, Thornton Wilder has also sprinkled this play with forecasts and reminders of death that make us mindful of the value of life, and how little it is appreciated while being lived." Yes, *Our Town* has become part of our shared cultural heritage. And, as Leon Edel said in his eulogy of Wilder, "If there is such a thing as 'the great American play,' *Our Town* may very well be that ideal creation of which young writers like to dream."[64]

But it isn't just *Our Town* that we should remember. *The Bridge of San Luis Rey* was an international bestseller because in it Wilder addressed questions about the meaning of life that are part of every culture in the past, the present, and the future. That it has remained in print for over seventy years attests to its timelessness, as does its selection by the Modern Library as number thirty-seven in a ranking of the hundred best novels of the twentieth century—ahead of such novels as *The Sun Also Rises, Women in Love, Light in August, The Age of Innocence, Heart of Darkness, Main Street,* and, somewhat ironically, *Finnegans Wake.*[65] Such attempts to rank great works of literature are highly subjective, of course, but the Modern Library's list affirms Wilder's achievement in the novel as well as drama.

Therefore, the following question should be asked: Has Wilder had any influence upon the American novel in the twentieth century? Since my expertise is in drama, I can't make an authoritative assessment, but I will offer the following observation: To my knowledge, no American novel written before Wilder's *The Bridge of San Luis Rey* was published in 1927 used a nonlinear structure in which the same period of time and the events that took place within it are gone over again and again. Faulkner's famous novels make use

64. "Thornton Wilder Stamp Dedication Scene of Carol Channing 'Hello Dolly' Reprise"; Lyall H. Powers, "Thornton Wilder as Literary Cubist: An Acknowledged Debt to Henry James," 34.

65. Paul Lewis, "*Ulysses* at Top as Panel Picks 100 Best Novels," 4.

of that technique, but *The Sound and the Fury, As I Lay Dying,* and *Absalom, Absalom,* were published in 1929, 1930, and 1936, respectively. Since completing the first draft of this book, an article has been published that does suggest Wilder, along with fellow Wisconsin native Glenway Wescott, did help break the modernist novel away from chronological narrative:

> Although the two early works of fiction of each author are not generally tied into the history of the novel, they deserve to be integrated into the story of the development of American modernism. The plots of Fitzgerald's *The Great Gatsby* and Hemingway's *The Sun Also Rises* are far more linear than those of the early Wilder and Wescott novels, and yet the former are used to define American modernist fiction to a much larger extent. Both Wilder and Wescott developed a form much closer to *Nightwood* in its use of a non-linear plot with character sketches. Djuna Barnes's celebrated novel of the 1930s continues in the narrative pattern laid down by these earlier works.[66]

Christensen also notes the similarity between *The Sound and the Fury*'s construction and Wilder's and Wescott's novels.

Finally, Marilynne Robinson's fiction and essays published since the late 1980s demonstrate that Puritanism—or the knowledge of it in people other than Puritan scholars—is not dead, but she seems to lament that it is dead for all intents and purposes. That is, she welcomes that we have left behind the response to natural or manmade catastrophe (e.g., crop failures) as a sign of God's displeasure with our wicked ways, but she thinks the lack of a moral base we hold in common is leading us to even greater catastrophe: "We are approaching the end of the day."[67] This statement comes right out of Puritan eschatology; in fact, her collection of essays can be seen as a jeremiad, though not with the optimistic call for a return to a golden age as Bercovitch describes in *The American Jeremiad* (though it is, perhaps, implicit). With her second novel *Gilead* having just won the Pulitzer Prize for fiction, it would seem that the Puritan narrative tradition is still being recognized as something essentially American.

Given the influences he has had on other American dramatists, the initial popularity of his novels, and the continuing popularity of his three major plays, it seems reasonable to predict that Thornton Wilder—or his spirit, at least—will continue to make progress in the minds of his audiences and readers well into the new millennium.

---

66. Peter G. Christensen, "Human Relatedness and Narrative Technique in the Early Novels of Thornton Wilder and Glenway Wescott," 203.

67. Robinson, *The Death of Adam: Essays in Modern Thought,* 151, 245.

Appendix

Edward Taylor's God's Determinations Touching His Elect *(segment titles)*[1]

1. The Preface
2. Prologue
3. The Effects of Mans Apostacy
4. A Dialogue between Justice and Mercy
5. Mans Perplexity When Call'd to an Account
6. Gods Selecting Love in the Decree
7. The Frowardness of the Elect in the Work of Conversion
8. Satans Rage at them in their Conversion
9. The Souls Address to Christ against these Assaults
10. Christs Reply
11. The Effect of this Reply with a fresh Assault from Satan
12. First Satans Assault against those that first Came up to Mercys terms
13. The Accusation of the Inward Man
14. The Outward Man accused
15. The Soul accused in Serving God
16. The Souls Groan to Christ for Succour
17. Christs Reply
18. An Extasy of Joy let in by this Reply returned in Admiration
19. The Second Ranke Accused
20. The Third Rank accused

1. Based on Edward Taylor, *The Poetical Works of Edward Taylor,* ed. Thomas H. Johnson. All spelling and punctuation are as they appear in the table of contents of this edition.

Bibliography

Adler, Thomas P. *Mirror on the Stage: The Pulitzer Plays as an Approach to American Drama.* West Lafayette, Ind.: Purdue University Press, 1987.

——. "The Pirandello in Albee: *The Lady from Dubuque.*" In *Edward Albee: Modern Critical Views,* ed. Harold Bloom, 131–40. New Haven, Conn.: Chelsea House, 1987.

Albee, Edward. "Edward Albee." In *Writers at Work: The Paris Review Interviews,* ed. George Plimpton, 321–46. 3d series. New York: Viking, 1967. Reprint from *Paris Review* 10 (1966): 93–121.

——. *The Lady from Dubuque.* New York: Atheneum, 1980.

——. Personal interview. May 24, 1990.

——. *Selected Plays of Edward Albee.* Garden City, N.Y.: Nelson Doubleday, Inc., 1987.

——. *Who's Afraid of Virginia Woolf?* New York: Penguin Books, Inc., 1983.

Alder, Henry. "Thornton Wilder's Theatre." *Horizon* 12 (1945): 89–99.

Alter, Maria P. "The Reception of Nestroy in America as Exemplified in Thornton Wilder's Play *The Matchmaker.*" *Modern Austrian Literature* 20, nos. 3–4 (1987): 32–42.

Amacher, Richard E. *Edward Albee.* Rev. ed. Boston: Twayne, 1982.

Anker, Roy M. "The Road to the Eighth Day: Hope, Faith, and Love in Wilder's *The Eighth Day.*" In *Literature and Religion: Thornton Wilder's "The Eighth Day": Papers Collected for MLA Seminar 4,* comp. Paul Schleuter. Evansville: University of Evansville, 1970.

Armato, Philip M. "Tennessee Williams' Meditations on Life and Death in *Suddenly Last Summer, The Night of the Iguana,* and *The Milk Train Doesn't Stop Here Anymore.*" In *Tennessee Williams: A Tribute,* ed. Jac Tharpe, 558–70. Jackson: University Press of Mississippi, 1977.

Atkinson, Brooks. *Broadway Scrapbook.* New York: Theatre Arts Inc., 1947.

Ballet, Arthur H. "In Our Living and in Our Dying." *English Journal* 45 (May 1956): 243–49.

Baltzell, E. Digby. *Puritan Boston and Quaker Philadelphia: Two Protestant Ethics and the Spirit of Class Authority and Leadership.* Boston: Beacon Press, 1979.

Barbour, Douglas. "*Gods Determinations* and the Hexameral Tradition." *Early American Literature* 16 (1981–82): 214–25.

Baxandall, Lee. "The Theatre of Edward Albee." *Tulane Drama Review* 9 (1965): 19–40.

Bennett, Beate Hein. "Williams and European Drama: Infernalists and Forgers of Modern Myths." In *Tennessee Williams: A Tribute,* ed. Jac Tharpe, 429–62. Jackson: University Press of Mississippi, 1977.

Bensick, Carol M. "Preaching to the Choir: Some Achievements and Short-comings of Taylor's *God's Determinations.*" *Early American Literature* 28, no. 2 (1993): 133–47.

Bercovitch, Sacvan. *The American Jeremiad.* Madison: University of Wisconsin Press, 1978.

——. "The Ends of American Puritan Rhetoric." In *The Ends of Rhetoric: History, Theory, Practice,* ed. John Bender and David E. Wellbery, 171–90. Stanford, Calif.: Stanford University Press, 1990.

——. "The Modernity of American Puritan Rhetoric." In *American Letters and the Historical Consciousness. Essays in Honor of Lewis P. Simpson,* ed. J. Gerald Kennedy and Daniel Mark Fogel, 42–66. Baton Rouge: Louisiana State University Press, 1987.

——. *The Puritan Origins of the American Self.* New Haven: Yale University Press, 1975.

——, ed. *The American Puritan Imagination: Essays in Revaluation.* New York: Cambridge University Press, 1974.

——, ed. *Typology and Early American Literature.* Amherst: University of Massachusetts Press, 1972.

Berryman, Charles. *From Wilderness to Wasteland: The Trial of the Puritan God in the American Imagination.* Port Washington: Kennikat Press, National University Publications, 1979.

Bevington, David M. *From Mankind to Marlow: The Growth of Structure in the Popular Drama of Tudor England.* Cambridge: Harvard University Press, 1962.

Bigsby, C. W. E. *A Critical Introduction to Twentieth-Century American Drama.* 3 vols. Cambridge: Cambridge University Press, 1984.

——, ed. *Edward Albee: A Collection of Critical Essays.* Twentieth Century Views Series. Englewood Cliffs, N.J.: Prentice-Hall, 1975.

Blank, Martin. "Broadway Production History." *Theatre History Studies* 5 (1985): 57–71.

——. "Introduction." In *Critical Essays on Thornton Wilder,* ed. Martin Blank, 1–24. New York: G. K. Hall & Co., 1996.

——. "*Shadow of a Doubt:* A Study of Authorship, Twinship, and the Nature of Evil." *Thornton Wilder: A Centennial Symposium,* September 18, 1997, Whitney Humanities Center, Yale University, New Haven, Conn.

——. "Thornton Wilder and Film." In *Wilder Rediscovered,* ed. Joel A. Smith, 37–38. Louisville: Actors Theatre of Louisville, 1997.

——. "Thornton Wilder's Early Work in the Theatre." *Journal of American Drama and Theatre* 8 (Winter 1996): 18–37.

——. "Wilder, Hitchcock, and *Shadow of a Doubt.*" In *Thornton Wilder: New Essays,* ed. Martin Blank, Dalma Hunyadi Brunauer, and David Garrett Izzo, 409–16. West Cornwall, Conn.: Locust Hill Press, 1999.

——, ed. *Critical Essays on Thornton Wilder.* New York: G. K. Hall & Co., 1996.

Blank, Martin, Dalma Hunyadi Brunauer, and David Garrett Izzo, eds. *Thornton Wilder: New Essays.* West Cornwall, Conn.: Locust Hill Press, 1999.

Bloom, Harold, ed. *Edward Albee: Modern Critical Views.* New Haven, Conn.: Chelsea House, 1987.

Bogard, Travis. "The Comedy of Thornton Wilder." In *Modern Drama,* ed. Travis Bogard and W. Oliver, 355–73. New York: Oxford University Press, 1965. Reprint from "Introduction" to *Three Plays by Thornton Wilder.* New York: Harper, 1962.

Book of the Month Club Editorial Board, comp. *The Well-Stocked Bookcase: Sixty Enduring Novels Published by Americans between 1926–1986.* Book of the Month Club, 1986.

Boxhill, Roger. *Tennessee Williams.* New York: St. Martin's Press (Modern Dramatists), 1987.

Brantley, Ben. "A Brutal Act Alters a Town." *New York Times,* May 19, 2000, late ed., E1.

Brockett, Oscar G., and Robert R. Findlay. *Century of Innovation: A History of European and American Theatre and Drama since 1870.* Englewood Cliffs, N.J.: Prentice-Hall, 1973.

Broussard, Louis. *American Drama: Contemporary Allegory from Eugene O'Neill to Tennessee Williams.* Norman: University of Oklahoma Press, 1962.

Brown, Edward K. "A Christian Humanist: Thornton Wilder." *University of Toronto Quarterly* 4 (1935): 356–70.

Brunauer, Dalma. "Some: An Examination of the Religious Tenets of Thornton Wilder's *The Eighth Day*." In *Literature and Religion: Thornton Wilder's "The Eighth Day": Papers Collected for MLA Seminar 4,* comp. Paul Schleuter. Evansville: University of Evansville, 1970. Reprinted as "Creative Faith in Wilder's *The Eighth Day*." *Renascence* 25 (Autumn 1972): 46–56.

Bryer, Jackson R. "Thornton Wilder at 100: Wilder's Literary Legacy." In *Wilder Rediscovered,* ed. Joel A. Smith. Louisville: Actors Theatre of Louisville, 1997.

———, ed. *Conversations with Thornton Wilder.* Jackson and London: University Mississippi Press, 1992.

Buckham, John Wright. *Progressive Religious Thought in America: A Survey of the Enlarging Pilgrim Faith.* Boston: Houghton Mifflin Co., 1919.

Buell, John. "The Evil Imagery of Tennessee Williams." *Thought* 38 (1963): 167–89.

Burbank, Rex. *Thornton Wilder.* Rev. ed. New York: Twayne, 1978.

Burns, Edward, and Ulla E. Dydo, with William Rice, eds. *The Letters of Gertrude Stein and Thornton Wilder.* New Haven: Yale University Press, 1996.

Bush, Sargent, Jr. *The Writings of Thomas Hooker: Spiritual Adventure in Two Worlds.* Madison: University of Wisconsin Press, 1980.

Butman, Harry R. *The Lord's Free People.* Wauwatosa: Swannet Press, 1968.

Carmody, Denise Lardner, and John Tully Carmody. *The Republic of Many Mansions: Foundations of American Religious Thought.* New York: Paragon House, 1990.

Castronovo, David. "Strange Discipline: Wilder's One-Act Experiments." In *Critical Essays on Thornton Wilder,* ed. Martin Blank, 99–115. New York: G. K. Hall & Co., 1996.

———. *Thornton Wilder.* New York: F. Ungar, 1986.

———. "Thornton Wilder and the One Deadly Sin." In *Thornton Wilder: New Essays,* ed. Martin Blank, Dalma Hunyadi Brunauer, and David Garrett Izzo, 443–53. West Cornwall, Conn.: Locust Hill Press, 1999.

The Century, 1847–1946. New York: The Century Association, 1947.

Chase, Richard. *The American Novel and Its Traditions.* Garden City, N.J.: Doubleday & Co., Inc., 1957.

Christensen, Peter G. "Human Relatedness and Narrative Technique in the Early Novels of Thornton Wilder and Glenway Wescott." In *Thornton Wilder: New Essays,* ed. Martin Blank, Dalma Hunyadi Brunauer, and David Garrett Izzo, 185–206. West Cornwall, Conn.: Locust Hill Press, 1999.

CineBooks' Motion Picture Guide. *Microsoft Cinemania '95*. Microsoft Corp., 1995.

Clark, Michael. "The Honeyed Knot of Puritan Aesthetics. In *Puritan Poets and Poetics: Seventeenth Century American Poetry in Theory and Practice,* ed. Peter White, 67–83. University Park: Pennsylvania State University Press, 1985.

Colacurcio, Michael J. "*Gods Determinations* Touching Half-Way Membership: Occasion and Audience in Edward Taylor." *American Literature* 39 (1967): 298–314.

Conner, Frederick William. *Cosmic Optimism: A Study of the Interpretation of Evolution by American Poets from Emerson to Robinson.* Gainesville: University of Florida Press, 1949.

Corrigan, Mary Ann. "Beyond Verisimilitude: Echoes of Expressionism in Williams' Plays." In *Tennessee Williams: A Tribute,* ed. Jac Tharpe, 375–412. Jackson: University Press of Mississippi, 1977.

Corrigan, Robert W. "Thornton Wilder and the Tragic Sense of Life." *Educational Theatre Journal* 13 (1961): 167–73.

Costello, William T. *The Scholastic Curriculum at Early Seventeenth-Century Cambridge.* Cambridge: Harvard University Press, 1958.

Covici, Pascal, Jr. "God's Chosen People: Anglican Views, 1607–1807." *Studies in Puritan American Spirituality* 1 (December 1990): 97–128.

Cowley, Malcolm. "Introduction." *A Thornton Wilder Trio.* New York: Criterion Books, 1956. Reprint from "The Man Who Abolished Time." *Saturday Review,* October 6, 1956, 13–14, 50–52.

———. Letter to Thornton Wilder. October 21, 1975. Thornton Wilder Papers. Beinecke Rare Books and Manuscripts Library, Yale University.

———. Letter to Thornton Wilder. November 4, 1975. Thornton Wilder Papers. Beinecke Rare Books and Manuscripts Library, Yale University.

———. "The Wilder Side of Life." *Book World,* October 21, 1973, 5.

Cunnar, Eugene R. "Milton, *The Shepherd* of Hermas, and the Writing of a Puritan Masque." In *Milton Studies XXIII,* ed. James D. Simmonds, 33–52. Pittsburgh: University of Pittsburg Press, 1988.

Damrosch, Leopold Jr. *God's Plot and Man's Stories: Studies in the Fictional Imagination from Milton to Fielding.* Chicago: University of Chicago Press, 1985.

Danforth, Samuel. "A Brief Recognition of New England's Errand into the Wilderness." In *The Wall and the Garden: Selected Massachusetts Election Sermons 1670–1775,* ed. A. W. Plumstead, 53–77. Minneapolis: University of Minnesota Press, 1968.

Davies, Horton. *Worship and Theology in England: From Cranmer to Hooker, 1534–1603.* Princeton: Princeton University Press, 1970.

Davis, Richard Beale. *Intellectual Life in the Colonial South, 1585–1763.* 3 vols. Knoxville: University of Tennessee Press, 1978.

Davis, Thomas M. *A Reading of Edward Taylor.* Newark: University of Delaware Press, 1992.

Debusscher, Gilbert. *Edward Albee: Tradition and Renewal.* Trans. Anne D. Williams. Brussels: American Studies Center, 1967.

———. "Tennessee Williams' Lives of the Saints: A Playwright's Obliquity." In *Tennessee Williams: A Collection of Critical Essays,* ed. Stephen S. Stanton, 149–57. Englewood Cliffs, N.J.: Prentice-Hall, 1977.

———. "Tennessee Williams' Unicorn Broken Again." In *Tennessee Williams' The Glass Managerie,* ed. Harold Bloom, 47–57. Reprint from *Revue Belge de Philologie et d'Histoire* 49, no. 3 (1971): 875–85.

De La Fuente, Patricia, ed. *Planned Wilderness: Interviews, Essays, and Bibliography.* Living Author Series, no. 3. Edinburg, Tex.: Pan American University, 1980.

Devlin, Albert J., ed. *Conversations with Tennessee Williams.* Jackson: University Press of Mississippi, 1986.

Dexter, Frank N. *A Hundred Years of Congregational History in Wisconsin.* N.p.: The Wisconsin Congregational Conference, 1933.

Diamond, Liz. "Thornton Wilder's Theatre of Consequence." In *Wilder Rediscovered,* ed. Joel A. Smith, 49–51. Louisville: Actors Theatre of Louisville, 1997.

Ditsky, John. *The Onstage Christ: Studies in the Persistence of a Theme.* Totowa, N.J.: Barnes & Noble, 1980.

Donahue, Francis. *The Dramatic World of Tennessee Williams.* New York: Frederick Ungar, 1964.

Drukman, Steven. "Wilder Times." In *Public Access: The Program of the Public Theater/New York Shakespeare Festival at the Delacorte Theatre,* June/July 1998, 11–13.

Dukore, Bernard F. *American Dramatists, 1918–1945.* New York: Grove Press, 1984.

Elliott, Emory. "From Father to Son: The Evolution of Typology in Puritan New England." In *Literary Uses of Typology from the Late Middle Ages to the Present,* ed. Earl Miner, 204–27. Princeton: Princeton University Press, 1977.

———. "New England Puritan Literature." In *The Cambridge History of American Literature Volume 1: 1590–1820,* ed. Sacvan Bercovitch, 169–306. Cambridge: Cambridge University Press, 1994.

———. "The Puritan Roots of American Whig Rhetoric." In *Puritan Influences in American Literature,* ed. Emory Elliott, 107–27. Illinois Studies in Language and Literature 65. Urbana: University of Illinois Press, 1979.

——, ed. *Puritan Influences in American Literature*. Illinois Studies in Language and Literature 65. Urbana: University of Illinois Press, 1979.

Ellison, Jerome. *God on Broadway*. Richmond, Va.: John Knox Press, 1971.

Erickson, Edward E. "The Figure in the Tapestry: The Religious Vision of Thornton Wilder's *The Eighth Day*." In *Literature and Religion: Thornton Wilder's "The Eighth Day": Papers Collected for MLA Seminar 4*, comp. Paul Schlueter, 1–19. Evansville: University of Evansville, 1970.

Esslin, Martin. *The Theatre of the Absurd*. Rev. ed. Garden City: Anchor, 1969.

Falk, Signi. *Tennessee Williams*. 2d ed. Boston: G. K. Hall, 1978.

Fedder, Norman J. *The Influence of D. H. Lawrence on Tennessee Williams*. London: Mouton, 1966.

Feinsod, Arthur. *The Simple Stage: Its Origins in the Modern American Theater*. New York: Greenwood Press, 1992.

Fergusson, Francis. *The Human Image in Dramatic Literature*. New York: Doubleday & Co., Inc., 1957.

——. "Three Allegorists: Brecht, Wilder, and Eliot." *Sewanee Review* 64 (1956): 544–73.

Finkle, David. "Hello, Thornton!" In *Wilder Rediscovered*, ed. Joel A. Smith, 38–40. Louisville: Actors Theatre of Louisville, 1997.

——. "'San Luis Rey' is back, on tape and . . . unabridged." *Trenton Times*, February 22, 1998, CC4.

Firebaugh, Joseph J. "Farce and the Heavenly Destination." *Four Quarters* 16 (1967): 10–17.

——. "The Humanism of Thornton Wilder." *Pacific Spectator* 4 (1950): 426–38.

Fischer, David Hackett. *Albion's Seed: Four British Folkways in America*. New York: Oxford University Press, 1989.

Fisher, James. "'Troubling the Waters': Visions of Apocalypse in Wilder's *The Skin of Our Teeth* and Kushner's *Angels in America*." In *Thornton Wilder: New Essays*, ed. Martin Blank, Dalma Hunyadi Brunauer, and David Garrett Izzo, 391–407. West Cornwall, Conn.: Locust Hill Press, 1999.

Fitzgerald, F. Scott. *This Side of Paradise*. New York: Scribners, 1920. Reprint, New York: Scribners, 1970.

French, Warren. "Christianity as Metaphor in *The Eighth Day*." In *Literature and Religion: Thornton Wilder's "The Eighth Day": Papers Collected for MLA Seminar 4*, comp. Paul Schlueter. Evansville: University of Evansville, 1970.

Fritscher, John J. "Some Attitudes and a Posture: Religious Metaphor and Ritual in Tennessee Williams' *Query of the American God*." *Modern Drama* 13 (1970): 201–15.

Fuller, Edmund. "Thornton Wilder: The Notation of the Heart." *American Scholar* 28 (1959): 210–17.

Fulton, A. R. "Expressionism—Twenty Years After." *Sewanee Review* 52, no. 1 (1944): 398–413.

Gallup, Donald. "Five Thousand Letters to Alexander Woollcott." *Harvard Library Bulletin* 32, no. 4 (Fall 1984): 401–7.

———. "Introductory Note." In *The Collected Short Plays of Thornton Wilder Volume I,* ed. Donald Gallup and A. Tappan Wilder, 105–112. New York: Theatre Communications Group, 1997.

———. Letter to the author. January 28, 1998.

———. *Pigeons on the Granite: Memoirs of a Yale Librarian.* New Haven: Yale University Press, 1988.

———, ed. *The Flowers of Friendship: Letters Written to Gertrude Stein.* New York: Alfred A. Knopf, 1953.

Gardner, Paul. "Tiny Alice Mystifies Albee, Too." *New York Times,* January 21, 1965, 22.

Gassner, John. *Form and Idea in Modern Theatre.* New York: Dryden Press, 1956.

———. *The Theatre in Our Times: A Survey of the Men, Materials and Movements in the Modern Theatre.* New York: Crown Publishers, Inc., 1954.

———. "The Two Worlds of Thornton Wilder." In *The Collected Short Plays of Thornton Wilder Volume I,* ed. Donald Gallup and A. Tappan Wilder, 311–20. New York: The Theatre Communications Group, 1997. Reprint from *The Long Christmas Dinner and Other Plays in One Act.* New York: Harper & Row Publishers, 1963, vii–xx.

Gatta, John, Jr. "The Comic Design of *Gods Determinations touching his Elect.*" *Early American Literature* 10 (1975): 121–43.

———. *Gracious Laughter: The Meditative Wit of Edward Taylor.* Columbia: University of Missouri Press, 1989.

Gay, Peter. *A Loss of Mastery: Puritan Historians in Colonial America.* Berkeley: University of California Press, 1966.

Gilmore, Michael T. *The Middle Way: Puritanism and Ideology in American Romantic Fiction.* New Brunswick: Rutgers University Press, 1977.

Gold, Michael. "Wilder: Prophet of the Genteel Christ." *New Republic* (October 22, 1930); 266–67.

Goldstein, Malcolm. *The Art of Thornton Wilder.* Lincoln: University of Nebraska Press, 1965.

Goldstone, Richard H. "The Art of Fiction XVI: Thornton Wilder." In *Writers at Work: The Paris Review Interviews,* ed. Malcolm Cowley, 101–18. New York: Viking Press, 1958.

———. *Thornton Wilder: An Intimate Portrait.* New York: Dutton, 1975.

Goldstone, Richard H., and Gary Anderson. *Thornton Wilder: An Annotated Bibliography of Works by and about Thornton Wilder.* New York: AMS Press, Inc., 1982.

Gottfried, Martin. *Jed Harris: The Curse of Genius.* Boston: Little, Brown, and Co., 1984.

Gould, Jean. *Modern American Playwrights.* New York: Dodd, Mead & Co., 1966.

Grabo, Norman. *Edward Taylor.* New York: Twayne, 1961.

——. "The Veiled Vision: The Role of Aesthetics in Early American Intellectual History." In *The American Puritan Imagination,* ed. Sacvan Bercovitch, 19–33. New York: Cambridge University Press, 1974.

Grebanier, Bernard. *Thornton Wilder.* Minneapolis: University of Minnesota Press, 1964.

Greene, George. "An Ethics for Wagon Trains: Thornton Wilder's *The Eighth Day.*" *Queen's Quarterly* 88, no. 2 (Summer 1981): 325–35.

——. "The World of Thornton Wilder." *Thought* 37 (Winter 1962): 563–84.

Guare, John. "Introduction." In *The Collected Short Plays of Thornton Wilder Volume I,* ed. Donald Gallup and A. Tappan Wilder, xv–xxvii. New York: The Theatre Communications Group, 1997.

Gussow, Mel. "Theater View: The Darker Shores of Thornton Wilder." *New York Times,* December 11, 1988, H7, H37.

——. "A Theatrical Vision Endures." *New York Times,* December 20, 1987, sec. 2, p. 36.

Haberman, Donald. "The Americanization of Thornton Wilder." *Four Quarters* 16 (1967): 18–27.

——. *Our Town: An American Play.* Twayne's Masterwork Studies No. 28. Boston: Twayne, 1989.

——. *The Plays of Thornton Wilder.* Middletown, Conn.: Wesleyan University Press, 1967.

——. "'Preparing the Way for Them': Wilder and the Next Generations." In *Critical Essays on Thornton Wilder,* ed. Martin Blank, 129–40. New York: G. K. Hall & Co., 1996.

Haims, Lynn M. "Puritan Iconography: The Art of Edward Taylor's *Gods Determinations.*" In *Puritan Poets and Poetics: Seventeenth Century American Poetry in Theory and Practice,* ed. Peter White, 84–98. University Park: Pennsylvania State University Press, 1985.

Hayman, Ronald. *Edward Albee.* New York: Ungar, 1971.

Harrison, Gilbert A. *The Enthusiast: A Life of Thornton Wilder.* New Haven: Ticknor and Fields, 1983.

Herron, Ima Honaker. *The Small Town in American Drama.* Dallas, Tex.: Southern Methodist University Press, 1969.

Hewes, Henry. *American Playwrights Self-Appraised.* New York: Saturday Review Associates, 1955.

Hewitt, Bernard. "Thornton Wilder Says 'Yes.'" *Tulane Drama Review* 4 (1959): 110–20.

Hicks, Granville. "*Theophilus North.*" In *Critical Essays on Thornton Wilder,* ed. Martin Blank, 54–57. New York: G. K. Hall & Co., 1996.

Hirsch, Foster. *A Portrait of the Artist: The Plays of Tennessee Williams.* Port Washington, N.Y.: Kennikat Press, 1979.

———. *Who's Afraid of Edward Albee?* Berkeley, Calif.: Creative Arts Book, 1978.

Howard, Alan. "Art and History in Bradford's 'Of Plymouth Plantation.'" *William & Mary Quarterly,* 3d series, 28 (1971): 237–66.

Jackson, Esther Merle. *The Broken World of Tennessee Williams.* Madison: University of Wisconsin Press, 1965.

Jameson, J. Franklin. "Introduction." In *Wonder-Working Providence of Sions Savior, 1628–1651,* by Edward Johnson. New York: C. Scribner's Sons, 1910.

Johannesen, Richard L. "The Jeremiad and Jenkin Lloyd Jones." *Communication Monographs* 52 (June 1985): 156–72.

Johnson, Edward. *Wonder-Working Providence of Sions Savior, 1628–1651.* New York: C. Scribner's Sons, 1910.

Jones, Howard Mumford. *The Age of Energy: Varieties of American Experience, 1865–1915.* New York: Viking Press, 1971.

Joseph, Keith A. "Grover's Corners Reinterpreted." In *Transformations: From Literature to Film—Proceedings of the Fifth International Conference on Film of Kent State University,* ed. Douglas Radcliff-Umstead, 70–74. Kent, Ohio: Romance Languages Department, Kent State University, 1987.

Keller, Karl. "Alephs, Zahirs, and the Triumph of Ambiguity: Typology in Nineteenth-Century American Literature." In *Literary Uses of Typology from the Late Middle Ages to the Present,* ed. Earl Miner, 274–302. Princeton: Princeton University Press, 1977.

———. *The Example of Edward Taylor.* Amherst: University of Massachusetts Press, 1975.

———. *The Only Kangaroo among the Beauty: Emily Dickinson and America.* Baltimore: Johns Hopkins University Press, 1979.

———. "'The World Slickt Up in Types': Edward Taylor as a Version of Emerson." In *Typology and Early American Literature,* ed. Sacvan Bercovitch, 175–90. Amherst: University of Massachusetts Press, 1972.

Kernan, Michael. "Thornton Wilder: A Wizard, a Magus, a Waver of Wands." *Washington Post,* November 18, 1973, K1, K3

Kerr, Walter. "Thornton Wilder's Small Gem." In *Critical Essays on Thornton Wilder,* ed. Martin Blank, 84–85. New York: G. K. Hall & Co., 1996.

King, John O., III. *The Iron of Melancholy: Structures of Spiritual Conversion in*

America from the Puritan Conscience to Victorian Neurosis. Middletown, Conn.: Wesleyan University Press, 1983.

Kolin, Philip C. *Conversations with Edward Albee.* Jackson and London: University Press of Mississippi, 1988.

Kolin, Philip, and J. Madison Davis, eds. *Critical Essays on Edward Albee.* Boston: G. K. Hall, 1986.

Konkle, Lincoln. "American Jeremiah: Edward Albee as Judgment Day Prophet in *The Lady from Dubuque.*" *American Drama* 7.1 (Fall 1997): 30–49.

——. "Errand into the Theatrical Wilderness: The Puritan Narrative Tradition in the Plays of Wilder, Williams, and Albee." Ph.D. diss, University of Wisconsin-Madison, 1991. Ann Arbor: UMI, 1991. 3391495.

——. " 'Good Better, Best, Bested': The Failure of American Typology in *Who's Afraid of Virginia Woolf?*" In *Edward Albee: A Casebook,* ed. Bruce Mann, 44–62. New York and London: Routledge, 2003.

——. "Puritan Epic Theatre: A Brechtian Reading of Edward Taylor's *Gods Determinations.*" *Communications from the International Brecht Society* 19, no. 2 (1990): 58–71.

——. "Puritan Paranoia: Tennessee Williams's *Suddenly Last Summer* as Calvanist Nightmare." *American Drama* 7, no. 2 (Spring 1998): 51–72.

Korshin, Paul J. "The Development of Abstracted Typology in England, 1650–1820." In *Literary Uses of Typology from the Late Middle Ages to the Present,* ed. Earl Miner, 147–203. Princeton: Princeton University Press, 1977.

Koster, Katie de, ed. *Readings on Thornton Wilder.* The Greenhaven Literary Companion to American Authors Series. San Diego: Greenhaven Press, 1998.

Krutch, Joseph Wood. *The American Drama since 1918: An Informal History.* New York: George Braziller, Inc., 1957.

Kuner, Mildred. *Thornton Wilder: The Bright and the Dark.* New York: Crowell, 1972.

Landow, George P. "Elegant Jeremiahs: The Genre of the Victorian Sage." *Victorian Perspectives* (1989): 21–41.

Lane, Allen. "Angelism in New England." *Times Literary Supplement,* July 12, 1974, 741.

Leverenz, David. *The Language of Puritan Feeling.* New Brunswick: Rutgers University Press, 1980.

Levy, Babette M. "Early Puritanism in the Southern Island Colonies." *American Antiquarian Society, Proceedings* 70 (1960): 60–348.

Lewalski, Barbara. *Protestant Poetics and the Seventeenth-Century Religious Lyric.* Princeton: Princeton University Press, 1979.

Lewis, Allan. "Thornton Wilder and William Saroyan—The Comic Vein and

'Courage for Survival.'" In *American Plays and Playwrights of the Contemporary Theatre*, ed. Allan Lewis, 66–80. New York: Crown, 1965.

——. "Wilder's Use of Staging." In *Readings on Thornton Wilder*, ed. Katie de Koster, 83–91. The Greenhaven Literary Companion to American Authors Series. San Diego: Greenhaven Press, 1998.

Lewis, Paul. "*Ulysses* at Top as Panel Picks 100 Best Novels." *New York Times*, July 20, 1998, E1, E4.

Lifton, Paul. "Symbolist Dimensions of Thornton Wilder's Dramaturgy." In *Critical Essays on Thornton Wilder*, ed. Martin Blank, 116–28. New York: G. K. Hall & Co., 1996.

——. *Vast Encyclopedia: The Theatre of Thornton Wilder*. Westport, Conn.: Greenwood Press, 1995.

Lindholt, Paul. "Arts and Letters: Iconoclasm as a Puritan Art." *Sewanee Review* 96, no. 3 (Summer 1988): 464–68.

Londre, Felicia Hardison. *Tennessee Williams: Life, Work, and Criticism.* Fredericton, N.B., Canada: York Press, 1989.

Lowance, Mason I., Jr. *The Language of Canaan: Metaphor and Symbol in New England from the Puritans to the Transcendentalists.* Cambridge: Harvard University Press, 1980.

——. "Sacvan Bercovitch and Jonathan Edwards." In *Sacvan Bercovitch and the Puritan American Imagination*, ed. Michael Schuldiner, 53–68. Lewiston: Edwin Mellon Press, 1992.

Loyd, Dennis. "Thornton Wilder's Americans." In *Literature and Religion: Thornton Wilder's "The Eighth Day": Papers Collected for MLA Seminar 4*, comp. Paul Schlueter. Evansville: University of Evansville, 1970.

Luxon, Thomas H. *Literal Figures: Puritan Allegory and the Reformation Crisis in Representation.* Chicago: University of Chicago Press, 1995.

Lynen, John F. *The Design of the Present: Essays on Time and Form in American Literature.* New Haven: Yale University Press, 1969.

MacGregor, Alan. "Edward Taylor and the Impertinent Metaphor." *American Literature* 60, no. 3 (1988): 337–58.

Maxwell-Mahon, W. D. "The Novels of Thornton Wilder." *UNISA ENGLISH STUDIES Journal of the Department of English* 16, no. 1 (May 1978): 35–44.

McBride, Mary. "Misanthropic Diabolism—Antagonist to Man: A Study of Evil in Thornton Wilder's *The Skin of Our Teeth*." In *Literature and Religion: Thornton Wilder's "The Eighth Day": Papers Collected for MLA Seminar 4*, comp. Paul Schlueter. Evansville: University of Evansville, 1970.

McCarthy, Gerry. *Edward Albee.* New York: St. Martin's Press, 1987.

McCarthy, Mary. *Sights and Spectacles, 1937–56.* New York: Farrar, Straus and Cudahy, 1956.

McClatchy, J. D. "Wilder and the Marvels of the Heart." *New York Times,* April 13, 1997, 35. Reprint in *Readings on Thornton Wilder,* ed. Katie de Koster, 54–58. The Greenhaven Literary Companion to American Authors Series. San Diego: Greenhaven Press, 1998.

McLaughlin, James. "All in the Family: Alfred Hitchcock's *Shadow of a Doubt.*" In *A Hitchcock Reader,* ed. Marshall Deutelbaum and Leland Poague, 141–52. Ames: Iowa State University Press, 1986.

Miller, Jordan Y., ed. *Twentieth-Century Interpretations of "A Streetcar Named Desire."* Englewood Cliffs, N.J.: Prentice-Hall, 1971.

Miller, Perry. *Errand into the Wilderness.* Cambridge: Harvard University Press, 1956. Reprint, New York: Harper, 1964.

——. *The New England Mind: From Colony to Province.* Cambridge: Harvard University Press, 1953.

——. *The New England Mind: The Seventeenth Century.* New York: Macmillan, 1939. Reprint, Cambridge: Harvard University Press, 1954.

——. *Orthodoxy in Massachusetts, 1630–1650: A Genetic Study.* Cambridge: Harvard University Press, 1933.

Miner, Earl, ed. *Literary Uses of Typology from the Late Middle Ages to the Present.* Princeton: Princeton University Press, 1977.

Mitchell, Henry. "Life Viewed as a Totality versus Gobblydegarble." *Washington Post,* July 6, 1975, H1, H2.

Mordden, Ethan. *The American Theatre.* New York: Oxford University Press, 1981.

Morgan, H. Wayne. "The Early Thornton Wilder." *Southwest Review* 43 (Summer 1958): 245–53.

Morgan, Joseph. *The History of the Kingdom of Basaruah and Three Unpublished Letters,* ed. Richard Schlatter. Cambridge: Harvard University Press, 1946.

Murdock, Kenneth B. "Clio in the Wilderness: History and Biography in Puritan New England." *Early American Literature* 6 (1972): 201–19. Reprint from *Church History* 24 (1955): 221–38.

——. "The Colonial and Revolutionary Period." In *The Literature of the American People, an Historical and Critical Survey,* ed. Arthur Hobson Quinn, 3–174. New York: Appleton-Century-Crofts, Inc., 1951.

——. "Introduction." In Michael Wigglesworth, *The Day of Doom, Or A Poetical Description of the Great and Last Judgment, with other Poems,* iii–xi. New York: Russell & Russell, 1966.

——. *Literature and Theology in Colonial New England.* Cambridge: Harvard University Press, 1949.

Nash, Charles Sumner. *Congregational Administration.* Boston: Pilgrim Press, 1909.

Nelson, Benjamin. *Tennessee Williams: The Man and His Work*. New York: Ivan Obolensky, 1961.

"New American Play Is Quite Fantastic." *New York Times,* December 11, 1926, 15.

"1943 Pulitzer Prizes." *Saturday Review,* May 8, 1943, 12.

Niven, Penelope. "Signposts, Footprints, Clues: Thornton Wilder in His Work." In *Wilder Rediscovered,* ed. Joel A. Smith, 8–21. Louisville: Actors Theatre of Louisville, 1997.

"An Obliging Man." *Time,* January 12, 1953, 44–49.

Otten, Ted. "McCarter Opens Season with *Matchmaker.*" *Trenton Times,* September 27, 1994.

Paolucci, Anne. *From Tension to Tonic: The Plays of Edward Albee*. Carbondale: Southern Illinois University Press, 1972.

Papajewski, Helmut. *Thornton Wilder.* Trans. John Conway. New York: F. Ungar, 1968.

Parker, Brian. "The Composition of *The Glass Menagerie:* An Argument for Complexity." In *Essays on the Modern American Drama: Williams, Miller, Albee, and Shephard,* ed. Dorothy Parker, 12–26. Toronto: University of Toronto Press, 1987.

Patterson, Daniel. *Edward Taylor's God's Determination and Preparatory Meditations: A Critical Edition*. Kent, Ohio: Kent State University Press, 2003.

Pearce, Roy Harvey. *The Continuity of American Poetry*. Princeton: Princeton University Press, 1961.

Phillips, Gene D. *Alfred Hitchcock*. Boston: Twayne Publishers, Inc., 1984.

Plumstead, A. W. *The Wall and the Garden: Selected Massachusetts Election Sermons, 1670–1775*. Minneapolis: University of Minnesota Press, 1968.

Popper, Hermione. "The Universe of Thornton Wilder." *Harper's* 230 (1965): 72–81.

Porter, Thomas E. *Myth and Modern American Drama*. Detroit: Wayne State University Press, 1969.

Powers, Lyall H. "Thornton Wilder as Literary Cubist: An Acknowledged Debt to Henry James." *Henry James Review* 7, no. 1 (Fall 1985): 34–44.

Pradhan, N. S. *Modern American Drama: A Study in Myth and Tradition*. New Delhi: Arnold-Heinemann, 1978.

Prenshaw, Peggy. "The Paradoxical Southern World of Tennessee Williams." In *Tennessee Williams: A Tribute,* ed. Jac Tharpe, 5–29. Jackson: University Press of Mississippi, 1977.

Prescott, Peter S. *A World of Our Own: Notes on Life and Learning at a Boys' Preparatory School*. New York: Coward-McCann, 1970.

Presley, Delma Eugene. "Little Acts of Grace." In *Tennessee Williams: A Tribute,* ed. Jac Tharpe, 571–80. Jackson: University Press of Mississippi, 1977.

——. "The Search for Hope in the Plays of Tennessee Williams." *Mississippi Quarterly* 25, no. 1 (1971–72): 31–43.

"Puritan spoon." *Random House Dictionary of the English Language,* 2d ed. New York: Random House, Inc., 1987.

Quilligan, Maureen. *The Language of Allegory: Defining the Genre.* Ithaca: Cornell University Press, 1979.

Raleigh, John Henry. "The American Quixote: George Brush." Introduction to *Heaven's My Destination,* by Thornton Wilder, 1–16. Garden City: Doubleday, 1960.

——. *Eugene O'Neill.* Carbondale: Southern Illinois University Press, 1965.

Robinson, Douglas. *American Apocalypses: The Image of the End of the World in American Literature.* Baltimore: Johns Hopkins University Press, 1985.

Robinson, Marilynne. *The Death of Adam: Essays in Modern Thought.* Boston: Houghton Mifflin Co., 1998.

Rohmer, Eric. *Hitchcock: The First Forty-Four Films.* New York: Frederick Unger Publishing Co., 1979.

Roosevelt, Eleanor. "My Day." *New York World-Telegram,* March 2, 1938, 21.

Rothman, William. *Hitchcock–The Murderous Gaze.* Cambridge: Harvard University Press, 1982.

Roudane, Matthew C. *Understanding Edward Albee.* Columbia: University of South Carolina Press, 1987.

Rowe, Karen E. "Prophetic Visions: Typology and Colonial American Poetry." In *Puritan Poets and Poetics: Seventeenth Century American Poetry in Theory and Practice,* ed. Peter White, 47–66. University Park: Pennsylvania State University Press, 1985.

——. *Saint and Singer: Edward Taylor's Typology and the Poetics of Meditation.* Cambridge: Cambridge University Press, 1986.

Rutenberg, Michael E. *Edward Albee: Playwright in Protest.* New York: Avon, 1969.

Rutman, Darrett B. *John Winthrop's Decision for America: 1629.* Philadelphia: J. B. Lippincott Co., 1975.

Schafer, William J. "About the Size of God: Radical Religious Ideas from the Puritan Revolution and American Literature." *Durham University Journal* 53, no. 1 (January 1992): 43–50.

Scheick, William J. "The Jawbones Schema of Edward Taylor's *Gods Determinations.*" In *Puritan Influences in American Literature,* ed. Emory Elliott, 38–54. Illinois Studies in Language and Literature 65. Urbana: University of Illinois Press, 1979.

Schlueter, June. "Is It All Over for Edward Albee? *The Lady from Dubuque.*" In *Planned Wilderness: Interviews, Essays, and Bibliography,* ed, Patricia De La Fuente, 112–19. Living Author series, no. 3. Edinburg, Tex.: Pan American University, 1980.

Schlueter, Paul, ed. *Literature and Religion: Thornton Wilder's "The Eighth Day":* *Papers Collected for MLA Seminar 4.* Evansville: University of Evansville, 1970.

Schroeder, Patricia R. *The Presence of the Past in Modern American Drama.* Rutherford: Fairleigh Dickinson University Press, 1989.

Schuldiner, Michael, ed. *Sacvan Bercovitch and the Puritan American Imagination.* Lewiston: Edwin Mellon Press, 1992.

Scott, Winfield Townley. "*Our Town* and the Golden Veil." *Virginia Quarterly Review* 29 (1953): 103–17.

"*Shadow of a Doubt.*" "CineBooks' Motion Picture Guide Review," on *Microsoft Cinemania '95.* Microsoft Corp., 1995.

Shunami, Gideon. "Between the Epic and the Absurd: Brecht, Wilder, Durrenmatt, and Ionesco." *Genre* 8 (1975): 42–59.

Silver, Nicky. "A Loony Landmark that Inspired a Seventh-Grader." *New York Times,* June 28, 1998. "Arts and Leisure Desk," 5, 12.

Simon, Linda. *Thornton Wilder, His World.* Garden City: Doubleday, 1979.

Simpson, Lewis P. *The Dispossessed Garden: Pastoral and History in Southern Literature.* Athens: University of Georgia Press.

Slocum, Bill. "The Legacy of Thornton Wilder." *New York Times,* September 14, 1997, 1, 4.

Smith, David E. *John Bunyan in America.* Bloomington: Indiana University Press, 1966.

Smith, Joel A., ed. *Wilder Rediscovered.* Louisville: Actors Theatre of Louisville, 1997.

Smith, Susan Harris. "Generic Hegemony: American Drama and the Canon." *American Quarterly* 41, no. 1 (1989): 112–22.

Solberg, Winton U. *Redeem the Time: The Puritan Sabbath in Early America.* Cambridge: Harvard University Press, 1977.

Spoto, Donald. *The Art of Alfred Hitchcock: Fifty Years of His Motion Pictures.* New York: Hopkinson and Blake, Publishers, 1976.

——. *The Darkside of Genius: Life of Alfred Hitchcock.* Boston: Little, Brown and Co., 1983.

——. *The Kindness of Strangers: The Life of Tennessee Williams.* Boston: Little, Brown, 1985.

Stanton, Stephen S., ed. *Tennessee Williams: A Collection of Critical Essays.* Englewood Cliffs, N.J.: Prentice-Hall, 1977.

Starkey, Marion L. *The Congregational Way: The Role of the Pilgrims and Their Heirs in Shaping America.* Garden City: Doubleday & Co., Inc., 1966.

Stavrou, C. N. "Albee in Wonderland." *Southwest Review* 60 (1975): 46–61.

Stenz, Anita Marie. *Edward Albee: The Poet of Loss.* The Hague: Mouton, 1978.

Stephens, George D. "*Our Town*—Great American Tragedy?" *Modern Drama* 1 (1959): 258–64.

Stewart, Randall. *American Literature and Christian Doctrine*. Baton Rouge: Louisiana State University Press, 1958.

Stresau, Hermann. *Thornton Wilder*. Trans. Frieda Schutze. New York: F. Ungar, 1971.

Sweet, William Warren. *Religion on the American Frontier, 1783–1850*. Vol. 3 of *The Congregationalists*. New York: Cooper Square Publishers, Inc., 1964.

Szondi, Peter. *Theory of the Modern Drama: A Critical Edition*. Minneapolis: University of Minnesota Press, 1987.

Taylor, Edward. *Poems*. Ed. Donald E. Stanford. New Haven: Yale University Press, 1960.

——. *The Poetical Works of Edward Taylor*. Ed. Thomas H. Johnson. Princeton: Princeton University Press, 1971.

Taylor, John Russell. *Hitchcock: The Life and Times of Alfred Hitchcock*. New York: Pantheon, 1978.

Terrien, Samuel. "Demons Also Believe." *Christian Century* 87 (1970): 1481–86.

Tharpe, Jac, ed. *Tennessee Williams: A Tribute*. Jackson: University Press of Mississippi, 1977.

Thompson, Bard. *Liturgies of the Western Church*. Cleveland and New York: Williams Collins Publishers, 1962.

Thompson, Judith. *Tennessee Williams' Plays: Memory, Myth, and Symbol*. University of Kansas Humanistic Studies, vol. 54. New York: Peter Lang, 1987.

Thompson, Tazewell. "In Search of Wilder." In *Wilder Rediscovered*, ed. Joel A. Smith, 55–59. Louisville: Actors Theatre of Louisville, 1997.

"Thornton Wilder and American Playwrights." Panel discussion with Liz Diamond, John Guare, A. R. Gurney, and Donald Margulies. *Thornton Wilder: A Centennial Symposium*, September 18, 1997, Whitney Humanities Center, Yale University, New Haven, Conn.

"Thornton Wilder Stamp Dedication Scene of Carol Channing 'Hello Dolly' Reprise." *Postal News*. United States Postal Service. April 17, 1997. Stamp News Release Number 97-34. http://www.usps.gov/news/stamps/97/97034stp.htm accessed September 19, 1997.

Tichi, Cecelia. *New World, New Earth: Environmental Reformation in American Literature from the Puritans through Whitman*. New Haven: Yale University Press, 1979.

Tischler, Nancy M. *Tennessee Williams*. Southern Writers Series, no. 5. Austin, Tex.: Steck-Vaughan, 1969.

——. *Tennessee Williams: Rebellious Puritan*. New York: Citadel Press, 1961.

——. "Tennessee Williams' Bohemian Revision of Christianity." *Susquehanna University Studies* 7, no. 2 (1963): 103–8.

Traubitz, Nancy Baker. "Myth as a Basis of Dramatic Structure in *Orpheus Descending*." *Modern Drama* 19 (1976): 57–66.

Truffaut, François. *Hitchcock*. New York: Simon & Schuster, 1967.

Valenti, Peter. "Thornton Wilder, Sol Lesser, and the Demands of Hollywood Narrativity in *Our Town*." *Thornton Wilder: A Centennial Symposium*, September 18, 1997, Whitney Humanities Center, Yale University, New Haven, Conn.

Vivion, Michael. "Thornton Wilder and the Farmer's Daughter." *Thalia: Studies in Literary Humor* 3 (Spring–Summer 1980): 41–45.

Von Szeliski, John L. "Tennessee Williams and the Tragedy of Sensitivity." In *Twentieth-Century Interpretations of "A Streetcar Named Desire,"* ed. Jordan Y. Miller, 65–72. Englewood Cliffs, N.J.: Prentice-Hall, 1971. Reprint from *Western Humanities Review* 20 (1966): 203–11.

Waggoner, Hyatt H. *American Poets from the Puritans to the Present*. Rev. ed. Baton Rouge: Louisiana State Press, 1984.

Walker, Williston. *The Creeds and Platforms of Congregationalism*. Boston: Pilgrim Press, 1960.

Walzer, Michael. *The Revolution of the Saints: A Study of the Origins of Radical Politics*. Cambridge: Harvard University Press, 1965.

Way, Brian. "Albee and the Absurd: *The American Dream* and *The Zoo Story*." in C. W. E. Bigsby, ed., *Edward Albee*, 26–44. Edinburgh: Oliver & Boyd, 1969.

Weales, Gerald. *The Jumping-Off Place: American Drama in the 1960s*. London: Macmillan Co., 1969.

——. *Tennessee Williams*. Minneapolis: University of Minnesota Press, 1965.

——. "Unfashionable Optimist." *Commonwealth* 67 (1958): 486–88.

Webster's Seventh New Collegiate Dictionary. Springfield, Mass.: G & C Merriam Company, 1969.

Weeks, Edward. "The Peripatetic Reviewer." *Atlantic Monthly* 232 (November 1973): 122–28.

Westbrook, Perry D. *Free Will and Determination in American Literature*. Cranbury, N.J.: Associated University Press, Inc., 1979.

Wheatley, Christopher J. "Acts of Faith: Thornton Wilder and His Critics." *Thornton Wilder: A Centennial Symposium*, September 18, 1997, Whitney Humanities Center, Yale University, New Haven, Conn.

——. "Thornton Wilder." In *American Playwrights 1880–1945*, ed. William W. Demastes, 437–52. Westport: Greenwood Press, 1995.

——. "Thornton Wilder, the Real, and Theatrical Realism." In *Realism and the American Dramatic Tradition,* ed. William W. Demastes, 139–55. Tuscaloosa and London: University of Alabama Press.

White, Peter, ed. *Puritan Poets and Poetics: Seventeenth-Century American Poetry in Theory and Practice.* University Park: Pennsylvania State University Press, 1985.

Wigglesworth, Michael. *The Poems of Michael Wigglesworth.* Ed. Ronald A. Bosco. Lanham: University Press of America, 1989.

Wilder, Amos Niven. *Thornton Wilder and His Public.* Philadelphia: Fortress Press, 1980.

Wilder, Thornton. *The Alcestiad or A Life in the Sun: A Play in Three Acts with a Satyr Play, The Drunken Sisters.* New York: Harper & Row, 1977.

——. *American Characteristics and Other Essays.* Ed. Donald Gallup. New York: Harper & Row, 1979.

——. *And the Sea Shall Give Up Its Dead.* In *The Collected Short Plays of Thornton Wilder Volume II,* ed. Donald Gallup and A. Tappan Wilder, 49–52. New York: The Theatre Communications Group, 1997.

——. *The Angel That Troubled the Waters and Other Plays.* New York: Coward-McCann, 1928.

——. *The Bridge of San Luis Rey.* New York: A. & C. Boni, 1927. Reprint, New York: Perennial Library, Harper & Row Publishers, 1986.

——. *The Cabala.* New York: A. & C. Boni, 1926. Reprint, New York: Carroll & Graf Publishers, Inc., 1987.

——. *The Collected Short Plays of Thornton Wilder Volume I.* Ed. Donald Gallup and A. Tappan Wilder. New York: The Theatre Communications Group, 1997.

——. *The Eighth Day.* New York: Harper & Row, 1967.

——. *The Happy Journey,* a play in one act. Rev. ed. New York: Samuel French, 1934.

——. *The Happy Journey to Trenton and Camden.* In *The Collected Short Plays of Thornton Wilder Volume II,* ed. Donald Gallup and A. Tappan Wilder, 84–102. New York: The Theatre Communications Group, 1997.

——. *Heaven's My Destination.* New York: Harper & Brothers, 1935.

——. *The Ides of March.* New York: Harper & Brothers Publishers, 1948.

——. *The Journals of Thornton Wilder, 1939–1961.* Ed. Donald Gallup. New Haven: Yale University Press, 1985.

——. *The Long Christmas Dinner,* a play in one act. New York: Samuel French, 1933. Rev. ed. 1934.

——. *The Long Christmas Dinner.* In *The Collected Short Plays of Thornton Wilder Volume I,* ed. Donald Gallup and A. Tappan Wilder, 3–25. New York: The Theatre Communications Group, 1997.

——. *The Melting Pot.* Film Treatment. Thornton Wilder Papers. Beinecke Rare Book and Manuscript Library, Yale University.

——. "Novelist into Playwright, an Interview with Thornton Wilder," by Ross Parmenter. *Saturday Review of Literature* June 11, 1938, 10–11.

——. *Our Century, a Play in Three Scenes.* New York: Century Association, 1947.

——. *Our Town.* New York: Samuel French, Inc., 1938, 1965.

——. *Proserpina and the Devil.* In *The Collected Short Plays of Thornton Wilder Volume II,* ed. Donald Gallup and A. Tappan Wilder, 13–15. New York: The Theatre Communications Group, 1997.

——. *Pullman Car Hiawatha.* New York: Samuel French, Inc., 1931.

——. *Pullman Car Hiawatha.* In *The Collected Short Plays of Thornton Wilder Volume I,* ed. Donald Gallup and A. Tappan Wilder, 41–59. New York: The Theatre Communications Group, 1997.

——. *Shadow of a Doubt.* Film Treatment. Thornton Wilder Papers. Beinecke Rare Book and Manuscript Library, Yale University.

——, writ. *Shadow of a Doubt.* Videocassette. Dir. Alfred Hitchcock. MCA Home Video (Universal, 1942).

——. *Theophilus North.* New York: Harper & Row, Publishers, 1973. Reprint, *Mr. North.* Carroll & Graf Publishers, Inc., 1973.

——. "Thornton Wilder." In *Writers at Work I,* 99–118. New York: Viking, 1958. Reprint from *Paris Review* 16 (1957): 37–57.

——. *Three Plays: Our Town, The Skin of Our Teeth, The Matchmaker.* New York: Harper Perennial & Row, 1998.

——. *The Trumpet Shall Sound. Yale Literary Magazine* 85 (October, November, December 1919; January 1920): 9–26, 78–92, 128–46, 192–207.

——. *The Woman of Andros.* New York: Albert & Charles Boni, 1930.

Williams, Mary Ellen. *A Vast Landscape: Time in the Novels of Thornton Wilder.* Pocatello: University of Idaho Press, 1979.

Williams, Michael V. "Errors in Thornton Wilder's *The Eighth Day.*" *English Language Notes* 27, no. 3 (March 1990): 69–72.

Williams, Tennessee. *The Theatre of Tennessee Williams.* 7 vols. New York: New Directions, 1971–76.

——. *Where I Live: Selected Essays.* New York: New Directions, 1978.

——. "The Yellow Bird." In *Three Players of a Summer Game,* 128–37. London: Secker and Warburg, 1960.

Willson, Lawrence. "The Puritan Tradition in American Literature." *Arizona Quarterly* 13 (1957): 33–40.

Wilson, Edmund. "Mr. Wilder in the Middle West." *New Republic.* January 16, 1935, 282.

Wixson, Douglas C., Jr. "The Dramatic Techniques of Thornton Wilder and Bertolt Brecht: A Study in Comparison." *Modern Drama* 15 (1972): 112–24.

——. "Thornton Wilder and Max Reinhardt: Artists in Collaboration." *Studies in the Humanities* 9, no. 2 (September 1982): 3–14.

——. "Thornton Wilder and the Theater of the Weimar Republic." In *Thornton Wilder: New Essays,* ed. Martin Blank, Dalma Hunyadi Brunauer, and David Garrett Izzo, 297–320. West Cornwall, Conn.: Locust Hill Press, 1999.

Woolcott, Alexander. "Mr. Wilder Urges Us On." *Atlantic Monthly* 171 (March 1943): 121, 123. Reprint in *Long, Long Ago.* New York: Viking Press, 1944, 244–47.

Wright, Nathalia. "The Morality Tradition in the Poetry of Edward Taylor." *American Literature* 18 (1946): 1–18.

Ziff, Larzer. "The Literary Consequences of Puritanism." In *The American Puritan Imagination,* ed. Sacvan Bercovitch, 34–44. New York: Cambridge University Press, 1974.

——. *Puritanism in America: New Culture in a New World.* New York: The Viking Press, 1973.

Index

Abbess, in *The Bridge of San Luis Rey*, 83, 85, 88–89

Abbott, Mather, 17

Adler, Thomas S., 142n32, 256n53; on *The Skin of Our Teeth*, 157n63, 161n74

Affirmative vision, Wilder's, 99, 165, 253, 259; criticism of, 4–5; in other plays, 155, 173, 224; in *Our Town*, 141–45. *See also* Optimism

Albee, Edward, 182n14; *The Lady from Dubuque*, 254–57; Puritan influence on, 234, 248–51, 253–54, 257; *Tiny Alice*, 253–54; *Who's Afraid of Virginia Woolf?* 252–53; Wilder and, 136n18, 247n31; Wilder's influence on, 245–58; worldview of, 248, 252–53

Alcestiad, The (A Life in the Sun), 155, 164n79, 175, 177

Alchemist, The (Jonson), 67

Allegory, 20n37; Albee's use of, 247, 252; in *The Cabala*, 80; divine perspective through, 52, 160n69; in *The Eighth Day*, 206; in *God's Determinations*, 38–39, 42–43, 52–53; *The Happy Journey* as, 105; in *Heaven's My Destination*, 122–23, 124; in jeremiads, 170; Miller's use of, 257–58; in *Our Century*, 184; in *Our Town*, 136, 138–39, 140n26; in *Pullman Car Hiawatha*, 109, 113; in Puritan narrative tradition, 37n23, 45–47, 55, 122–23, 209–10; of Satan, 73, 77–78, 80–81, 86–88, 117, 151, 171; in *Shadow of a Doubt*, 169; in *The Skin of Our Teeth*, 155, 160; in *Stairs to the Roof*, 242–43; in *The Trumpet Shall Sound*, 67–71, 73; typology vs., 34; Wilder's use of, 21–22, 86–87, 121n53, 244; Williams's use of, 244

All Over (Albee), 250

Alter, Maria P., 150

Amacher, Richard E., 247n31

America, 114, 224; allegory of, 122, 170, 252; in *Angels in America*, 260–61; egocentrism of, 107–8, 204–5; mood of, 18, 188, 202–4; progress of, 106–7; Puritan idea of Last Days, 57–58, 80; Puritan legacy in, 79, 240; Puritan protonationalism and, 212, 221; wilderness theme of, 174, 221. *See also* Puritanism: English vs. American

American, The (James), 78

American Characteristics and Other Essays, 4, 19n35, 133

American Dream, The (Albee), 247

Americanism, 122; of Albee, 249; of faith in progress, 219; of melancholy, 178–79; of sermons, 128–29; of Williams, 237

Americanism, Wilder's, 261–62; down-